Black Writing, Culture, and the State in Latin America

■

EDITED BY *Jerome Branche*

D1560332

Vanderbilt University Press

NASHVILLE, TENNESSEE

© 2015 by Vanderbilt University Press
Nashville, Tennessee 37235
All rights reserved
First printing 2015

This book is printed on acid-free paper.
Manufactured in the United States of America

Library of Congress Cataloging-in-Publication Data on file
LC control number 2014044808
LC classification number PQ7081.7.B55B58 2015
Dewey class number 860.9'89608—dc23

ISBN 978-0-8265-2062-3 (cloth)
ISBN 978-0-8265-2063-0 (paperback)
ISBN 978-0-8265-2064-7 (ebook)

Black Writing, Culture, and the State in Latin America

Contents

Acknowledgments   **vii**

Introduction   **1**

1   The Altar, the Oath, and the Body of Christ:
Ritual Poetics and Cuban Racial Politics of 1844   **9**
by Matthew Pettway

2   Seeking Acceptance from Society and the State:
Poems from Cuba's Black Press, 1882–1889   **33**
by Marveta Ryan

3   Imagining the "New Black Subject":
*Ethical Transformations and Raciality in the
Post-Revolutionary Cuban Nation*   **61**
by Odette Casamayor-Cisneros

4   Realism in Contemporary Afro-Hispanic Drama   **83**
by Elisa Rizo

5   Bojayá in Colombian Theater:
Kilele: *A Drama of Memory and Resistance*   **103**
by María Mercedes Jaramillo

6   Uprising Textualities of the Americas:
*Slavery, Migration, and the Nation in Contemporary
Afro-Hispanic Women's Narrative*   **127**
by Lesley Feracho

7   Disrobing Narcissus: Race, Difference, and Dominance
(Mayra Santos Febres's Nuestra Señora de la noche
Revisits the Puerto Rican National Allegory)   **149**
by Jerome Branche

8 Bilingualism, Blackness, and Belonging:
*The Racial and Generational Politics
of Linguistic Transnationalism in Panama*   **171**
by Ifeoma Kiddoe Nwankwo

9 Racial Consciousness, Place, and Identity
in Selected Afro-Mexican Oral Poems   **193**
by Paulette A. Ramsay

10 Afro-Uruguayan Culture and Legitimation:
Candombe *and Poetry*   **213**
by Melva M. Persico

11 Quilombismo and the Afro-Brazilian Quest for Citizenship   **237**
by Niyi Afolabi

12 (W)riting Collective Memory (De)Spite State:
Decolonial Practices of Existence in Ecuador   **253**
by Catherine Walsh with Juan García Salazar

Contributors   **267**

Index   **269**

Acknowledgments

I would like to thank, first and foremost, my esteemed colleagues who contributed with their time and their labor toward the realization of this project, and for their patience as it came together over the many months. My thanks also to ASWAD, the Association for the Study of the Worldwide African Diaspora, for affording us a space on the program of the 2011 meeting to air and discuss early versions of many of the papers presented herein. Last but not least, I would like to thank the editorial team at Vanderbilt University Press for their invaluable assistance in helping to bring the varying styles of writing of disparate authors toward its present final shape, and the Center for Latin American Studies at the University of Pittsburgh for assistance in indexing.

Introduction

This book has two primary objectives: (a) to add a needed contribution to the analysis of Afro-Hispanic literary culture, a field of inquiry which, although no longer new, still has significant lacunae that require scholarly attention, and (b) to expand the scope of the current research efforts beyond the standard genres of the lettered tradition. It therefore includes, alongside narrative and lyrical poetry, analyses of film and popular theatre, material from the oral tradition, and in one case, the speech act of the oath. By orienting the attention of the chapters toward the racialized rule of the colonial and postcolonial Latin American state, and the critical consequences this held for the formerly enslaved and currently marginalized community, the book presents a fuller and more representative reflection of the lifeworld of Afro-descendants in contemporary Latin America and the means by which their concerns have been expressed and continue to be expressed. The authors featured in *Black Writing* examine the state less in terms of everyday politics and the bureaucratic structures of governance and more in terms of the strictures to the ideological and aesthetic content of literary practice that might directly or indirectly be brought to bear from its center/s of power, and the possible limitations as to who among the imagined community that makes up the national conglomerate might exercise the arts of expression. This is what explains the book's focus on apprehending and appreciating the voices of those (enslaved) subjects who were ab initio not held to be part of the colonial cluster of *vecinos* or *colonos*, or of the two "republics" of Spaniards and Indians, following an early colonial paradigm. In this latter regard, it can hardly be stated enough that sale and enslavement for the captive Africans and their descendants in colonial Latin America implied a multilateral suffocation of their subjectivity. It would take fully five hundred years after the Columbus landing, with the new constitutions of the post-dictatorial period in the 1990s, for some Latin American states to recognize the retrograde slave-era content of the term *negro* that designated these subjects, to attempt to detach them from the social debasement and the stigma of forced labor, or to recognize their essential citizenship. This context also determines the degree to which a definition of "writing," in the canonical sense, is amplified in order to allow for the range of expression reflected herein, so that varying registers of orality (or "oraliterature"), of literacy, and of artistic technique and convention of the kind that guides critics and anthologizers might be encompassed.

Recent social theory has stressed the close relationship between the formation of modern states and their racial fashioning. It sees the process of racial differentiation and the ensuing state-supported racial exclusion and exploitation of those identified racially as "others" as a key factor in the establishment of either the "modern state" or the "racial state" (Goldberg 2002). This premise is particularly relevant for Latin

1

Americanists, given the early establishment of Spain as a modern state, produced precisely around the expulsion of the Moors and the Jews, beginning at the end of the fifteenth century. Given the presence of sub-Saharan Africans in that scenario at the moment, Spain's nationalist quest for homogeneity around the identifier of Christianity and *limpieza de sangre* (blood purity), might be seen more in terms of the ethno-cultural determinant, though it would have to be pointed out that the blacks, as a mainly enslaved minority, would also be symbolically "expelled" or disassociated from the national body, as we note from studying Spain's Renaissance and Baroque literature. In the context of colonial expansion and conquest, the radical difference of the indigenous Americans and of enslaved Africans would produce a caste society in Latin America in which the qualifier of blood purity would move from its putative location "inside" the body to its exterior, and epidermic whiteness would grow to signify not only religious orthodoxy, but also political, social, and economic power as waves of royal edicts poured out of Spain to limit or exclude the so-called *castas* from positions of power in the colonial bureaucracy, in the church, in the trades, and so on (Branche 2006).

Amongst the dizzying array of racial labels invented to identify the dozens of mestizo types produced in the New World mixtures of African, indigenous, and European peoples, existed numerous labels for the *castas* that were associated with zoology. These provide the strongest evidence of the binary construction of whiteness as *human* in Latin America, and everyone else as somehow subhuman. To the more familiar term *mulato* (derived from mules), we might add the less familiar *lobo* (wolf), *cabro* (goat), *cuatralbo* (reminiscent of a dark horse with four white feet), and *albarazado* (again reminiscent of a dark animal with white spots) (Branche 2006). If whitening or *blanqueamiento* became an existential objective of black, Indian, or mestizo families in colonial Latin America, it was no less so for the countries themselves at the time they got their independence in the nineteenth century. In the latter decades of the nineteenth and the first decades of the twentieth centuries, millions of white Europeans were imported into Brazil, Cuba, Argentina, and other countries, ostensibly to counterbalance the presence of the so-called inferior races on the premise that racial whiteness was the only way toward industrialization and development. While Enlightenment philosophers Hobbes, Jefferson, Locke, Rousseau, Hegel, Kant, Hume, and Edwards were theorizing race and trying to fix racial characteristics as natural, permanent, and unchanging in order to reify the supremacy of whiteness and erect a racial wall against racial otherness, Spain had already put the notion of supremacy into practice in its own way. One recalls that the key arguments of sixteenth-century humanist Juan Ginés de Sepúlveda in the great Valladolid debate (1550–1551) sought to establish that the Amerindians were "natural slaves," per Aristotelian thought, and that Spain was authorized, on account of their idolatry, sodomy, and cannibalism, to subject them to a "just war." His famous opponent, Bartolomé de las Casas, after witnessing the devastation wrought by the sword of colonialism, would favor an emphasis on peaceful conversion and the way of the cross instead. As Aimé Césaire pointedly reminds us in his *Discourse on Colonialism* (14), the twentieth-century racist states of Nazi Germany and South African apartheid drew on colonial antecedents established by Spain and by England in its turn. In the final analysis, as Theo Goldberg argues, the difference between the racial state and the properly racist state is only a matter of degree. According to Goldberg:

> We might usefully bear in mind here the distinction Etienne Balibar insists upon between "(*official*) *state Racism*" and "*racism within the State . . .*" A state may license racist expression within the jurisdiction simply by turning a blind eye, by doing nothing or little to prevent or contest it, by having no restrictive rules or codes or "failing" to enforce those on the books. In contrast, a state like Nazi Germany, apartheid South Africa, or Jim Crow Louisiana may assume racism as a state project, definitive of state formation, articulation, in a word (national) state identity . . . so while *racist* states seem exceptional, their very possibility is underpinned by the normalcy of the *racial* state. (114)

Black writers and intellectuals, as do other minority groups in different areas of modern life, have carved out in Latin America what is easily recognized as a "subaltern counterpublic," to borrow a phrase from Nancy Fraser. Their purpose is to organize and to critique not only the dominant norms and values of the state, but also those of oppositional positions articulated by the too-often Eurocentric and masculinist bourgeois caucus within civil society. The black counterpublic that emerged in twentieth-century Latin American countries like Colombia and Brazil was heterogeneous and concerned itself with varying spheres of cultural production such as folklore, popular dance, creative writing, and, more recently, with more overt forms of political activism and mobilization. This multipronged activity is exemplified in the art and activism of Brazil's Abdias Nascimento, with his famous Black Experimental Theatre that started in 1945, or that of Colombia's Manuel Zapata Olivella, through his roles as writer, folklorist, and anthropologist, and of his sister, Delia, a renowned promoter of Afro-Colombian traditional dance forms both locally and internationally. The heterogeneous nature of the black counterpublic has expressed itself in political terms also, and it is noteworthy that ostensible "race defenders" can be found occupying different positions on the political spectrum.

Colombia's new constitution of 1991, in what is ultimately a deployment of force and persuasion by the racial state, has shown a marked flexibility on the racial question, though its contours are beyond our objectives to fully develop here. Several racially proactive developments mark this movement, however. They include the recognition for the first time since emancipation in 1851 of Afro-Colombians as legal subjects (Catherine Walsh in this volume will make a similar point regarding Afro-Ecuadorans when she refers to that country's 1998 constitution); a census by the National Department of Statistics that produced an estimate of 10.5 percent in 2005[1]; the recognition, through Law 70 of 1993, of collective legal title to lands traditionally occupied by Afro-descendants since slavery; an affirmative action program for disadvantaged racial minorities; and even a process of ethnic categorization for blacks under the auspices of the Colombian Institute of Anthropology and History, which parceled the Afro-Colombian population into varying groups such as *raizales*, *palenqueros*, and *afrodesendientes*. In 2001 a Día Nacional de la Afrocolombianidad was introduced, and eventually in 2010 a massive eighteen-volume black literary collection, the *Biblioteca de Literatura Afrocolombiana*, was published. Two permanent positions for black representatives in the Chamber of Representatives of the Congress were also created. There is a sense, then, in which blacks in Colombia are "no longer invisible," as the title of a recent publication suggests. But the firmly entrenched traditions of state-centered clientelism and paternalism have undermined the ideals behind these democratic intentions and greatly frustrated the hopes of racial minorities who had hoped for betterment in their day-to-day existence (Oslender; Wade).

As an example of the above reference to orality and literature as a "continuum," I suggest that "literary" culture for blacks, dehumanized and commoditized under the two-tiered—local and metropolitan—hegemony of the colonial state, has an important paradigm in Cuba's Juan Francisco Manzano (1797–1854). This individual, who claimed to have taught himself to write and from whom we have the only extant slave autobiography in Latin American literature, represents not only the rawness of untutored linguistic expression, as evinced in the many editorial intrusions that tamed and regularized the grammar and orthography of his original manuscript, but also the (colonial) mimicry of the metropolitan models of literary expression that he sought to emulate, along with a corresponding desire to be accorded recognition and the cultural capital of the literati. Perhaps just as importantly, Manzano represents the yearning that one day it might be his fortune to write the novel that spoke of and to the nation as he knew it. As it turned out, his famous *Autobiografía* served as ur-text for what came to be known as the Cuban antislavery novel, generating corresponding and disproportionate critical recognition for the (white) writers who based their works on his life story. In spanning the discursive spectrum from Afro-Creole orality to the Petrarchan sonnet, Manzano hints at an Afro-Latino episteme and lifeworld that, at the very least, claims our attention for its particularity even as it expands the horizon of what an eventual definition of "Latin" American literature must incorporate. An important analogue to Manzano would be Colombia's Candelario Obeso (1849–1884), not least because this other poet, novelist, and playwright (who was also a teacher, diplomat, and linguist) embraced the black vernacular in spite of his erudition, as seen in his *Cantos populares de mi tierra* (1877), while dominating the vocabulary and syntax of the *Real Academia de la Lengua Española*. Manzano's Cuban successors at the end of the century, as we see in Marveta Ryan's chapter in this volume, endorsed middle-class decency and assimilation, as did the poet himself, while uttering a muted critique of raciality and repression. A similar stance of accommodation and sometimes covert critique would characterize the black arts of socialist Cuba almost a century and a half later, as discussed in Odette Casamayor's essay.

If Manzano, as putative playwright (*Zafira*, 1842), chose not to write directly of the oppression around him but to locate its scenarios in an exotic North African setting, this is to be seen as the result of two registers of "state-originated" censorship. On the one hand, the direct repression by the Spanish capital of any discourse that invoked freedom, as applied even to the rich white landowner and literato Domingo Del Monte who sponsored him; on the other, the equally powerful pressure he faced as a "mulatto among *negros*" (his term) to disavow the culture of the newly arrived forced African migrants on account of the dominant dictates of race. However, with this work, and its involuntary exoticism, he offers another noteworthy counterpoint to the realism invoked in *Kilele*, the contemporary, "unschooled," and collectively-written drama documenting the genocidal attack in the Colombian Chocó, which is addressed in María Mercedes Jaramillo's chapter below. Similarly, the immanence of his protest, suffocated by slavery, should be valued just as we appreciate the overt oppositionality in the writing of today's poets like Nancy Morejón, also Cuban, or of Puerto Rico's Mayra Santos-Febres, discussed in the chapters by Lesley Feracho and Jerome Branche, respectively. The degree to which these works, over a century and a half apart and spanning both the colonial and republican eras, reflect the conditions under which Afro-descendants have lived in Latin America is a graphic reminder of the *longue dureé* of their oppression. Manzano's importance as a foundational and symbolic figure in black and subaltern Latin American writing and in the broader canon is therefore beyond dispute. His (white) Venezuelan contemporary Andrés Bello, of neoclassical orientation, might have brought attention to the natural landscape of independence-era Latin America, anticipating by decades the famous *novela de la tierra* or "novel of the land." Through his belated introduction of Romanticism, Argentine writer Esteban Echeverría cemented regional writers' organized pursuit of the form and function of the European aesthetic, culminating in Ruben Darío's famous *modernismo* toward century's end. Manzano, however—language and genre aside, and as putative bridge between "high" and "low" culture in Latin America— offers an important glimpse into the interiority of the oppressed and is therefore an important touchstone for the discursivity that this volume seeks to explore, although none of the essays herein directly addresses his work.

Over the past few decades, the field of Afro-Hispanic literature may be described as having gone through three phases in its development. In the first phase in the 1970s, attention was paid to the historical presence of Africans and Afro-descendants in the Hispanic world—that is, the Iberian Peninsula and Latin America in a broad sense— and to their corresponding literary representation in the context of colonialism and the development of race in the modern period. Some of the important works in this phase are by Wilfred Cartey, Richard Jackson, Lemuel Johnson, and Miriam DeCosta Willis. A subsequent period focused on country studies and on Afro-descendant writers therefrom (for example, Peru, Argentina, Colombia, etc.). This produced an important mapping of black novelists and poets and their efforts to enter into and participate in the Lettered City (Angel Rama's term) within their respective nations. Some of the compulsory references in this phase are to Marvin Lewis, Laurence Prescott, Michael Handelsman, Ian Smart, and William Luis. Current scholars of Afro-Hispanic literary criticism seek to build on this foundation and expand its parameters. They include the graduates of the Afro-Romance Institute of the University of Missouri, Columbia, founded by Marvin Lewis, and the many contributors to the two primary journals in the field, the *Afro-Hispanic Review*, edited by William Luis, and the *Publication of the Afro/Latin American Research Association*, edited by Laurence Prescott and Antonio Tillis. In addition, Tillis was the 2012 editor of *Critical Perspectives on Afro-Latin American Literature*. Similarly, in 2012 Conrad James edited *Writing the Afro-Hispanic: Essays on Africa and Africans in the Spanish*

Caribbean. These latter are the only two books to attempt to address the field from a "collective" standpoint since *Blacks in Hispanic Literature: Critical Essays* (1977) by Miriam DeCosta Willis.

As indicated, one of the primary achievements of the above body of work has been to locate Afro-descendant writers in the lettered tradition in their respective countries and to advocate for their recognition at the national and, just as importantly, the academic and curricular levels. *Black Writing and the State in Latin America* supports and contributes to the canonizing thrust of the work mentioned above but also wishes to bring attention to the importance of other areas of cultural production, particularly to the extent that they complement the traditional belles-letristic genres. Of its twelve chapters, therefore, six deal with poetry and narrative (including one on folk couplets or *coplas*), one with film, two with popular theatre, one with rap and hip hop, and another with the oath as a declarative political statement. The book closes with a double-authored chapter that seeks to capture the heterogeneous voices that express the Afro-Ecuadoran folk vision. The chapters are united thematically in their counter positioning vis-à-vis centralized power embodied in the state and its associates or derivatives, and their investment in documenting the Afro-Latin American lifeworld and asserting Afro-descendant humanity in the face of often dehumanizing social and political forces. The book also maps the less palpable demographic presence, in that not only are the countries with a high percentage of Afro-descendants represented, such as Cuba, Brazil, Colombia, and Panama, but so are those with a lower population density, such as Uruguay, Ecuador, and Mexico.

The intersecting thematic strands that emerge provide us with a useful picture of the varying positions of these populations vis-à-vis the states in which history and the processes of diaspora have deposited them and open a window on both their commonalities and differences. For example, the first three chapters (by Pettway, Ryan, and Casamayor-Cisneros, respectively) offer revealing insights into nineteenth- and twentieth-century Cuba from the standpoint of insurgent slaves (Chapter 1), a lettered black middle class anxious about assimilation and propriety (Chapter 2), and critical, if cautious, black film makers under the ethics of socialism's New Man (Chapter 3). The two chapters that follow, by Rizo and Jaramillo, look at contemporary Afro-Hispanic theatre across the landscapes of Costa Rica, Uruguay, Colombia, and even across the Atlantic in Equatorial Guinea. While Uruguay, also discussed by Melva Persico in Chapter 10, and Costa Rica speak to the question of marginalization and the struggle over recognition and inclusion in the urban space and in national culture (Chapter 4), the Colombian case is much more dramatic. Coming in the wake of recent statist recognition of a history of black writing in the country, which took the form of an eighteen-volume collection of black writers, Jaramillo's chapter on popular drama in Colombia's rural Chocó region (Chapter 5) records for us without fanfare the agonized response of the survivors of a near-genocidal onslaught by the agents of capital who dislodged these communities in order to appropriate their ancestrally-held lands. Specifically women's writing occupies the next two chapters. Feracho's work on memory and the challenges faced by black women in Cuba, Ecuador, and Puerto Rico aims to highlight what she calls an "oppositional consciousness" in the poetry and novels of these writers (Chapter 6). In Branche's paper on Puerto Rico (Chapter 7), the "gendered" nationalism that Feracho speaks of combines with a forceful critique of the racist marginalization of black presence as author and poet Mayra Santos Febres reminds Puerto Rico of its population's diverse origins.

If extensive racial mixture and its ideological corollary in *mestizaje* make an invisible presence of blacks in Mexico, Paulette Ramsay's analysis of popular poetry in Mexico's *Costa Chica* region of Guerrero (Chapter 9) leaves no doubt as to the sense of racial awareness and pride of origins in this population, in spite of an array of overwhelmingly negative images inherited from the colonial past. A similar attitude of respect for inherited community values, referred to as *casa adentro*, is revealed in the Afro-Ecuadoran collective that Catherine Walsh and Juan García Salazar seek to document (Chapter 12). Their efforts contest the statist manipulation of its own versions of "blackness" and the drive to appropriate the natural resources of yet another area of the Black Pacific. Niyi Afolabi, writing on Brazil, shares with us the nation's myth of inclusion and racial "democracy" through a sample of the work of five poets of African descent and discloses opinions that are as personal in their depth and sincerity as they are representative of the larger ethos of what it means to be black in Brazil (Chapter 11). With Ifeoma Kiddoe Nwankwo (Chapter 8), we go beyond national parameters to appreciate a dynamic and translocal sense of blackness among Panamanians whose language marks them as legatees of older movements of people engaged in the ongoing confrontation with modernity and their place in the world. It is the hope of its contributors that this volume addresses in some modest measure, through its attention to genre, gender, and place, a gap in a field that is still full of possibilities.

Note

1. Academics and the black leadership refute this figure. They propose a significantly higher percentage of between 20 and 25 percent. See María Inés Martínez and Peter Wade.

Works Cited

Blanco, José Antonio Carbonell, et al., eds. *Biblioteca de literatura afrocolombiana*. 18 vols. Bogotá, Colombia: Ministerio de cultura, 2010.

Branche, Jerome C. *Colonialism and Race in Luso-Hispanic Literature*. Columbia: University of Missouri Press, 2006.

Césaire, Aimé. *Discourse on Colonialism*. New York: Monthly Review Press, 1972.

Goldberg, David Theo. *The Racial State*. Malden, MA: Blackwell Publishers Inc. 2002.

Fraser, Nancy. "Rethinking the Public Sphere: A Contribution to the Critique of Actually Existing Democracy." *Social Text*, 25–26 (1990): 56–80.

Martínez, María Inés, ed. Prefacio. *El despertar de las comunidades afrocolombianas*. San Juan, PR: Centro de Investigaciones Sociales, 2012. 36–38.

Minority Rights Group, ed. *No Longer Invisible: Afro-Latin Americans Today*. London: Minority Rights Publications, 1995.

Oslender, Ulrich. "The Quest for a Counter-Space in the Colombian Pacific Coast Region: Toward Alternative Black Territorialities or Co-optation by Dominant Power?" *Black Social Movements in Latin America: From Monocultural Mestizaje to Multiculturalism*. Ed. Jean Muteba Rahier. New York: Palgrave Macmillan, 2012. 95–112.

Wade, Peter. "Afro-Colombian Social Movements." *Comparative Perspectives on Afro-Latin America*. Eds. Kwame Dixon and John Burdick. Gainesville: University Press of Florida, 2012. 135–55.

The Altar, the Oath, and the Body of Christ

Ritual Poetics and Cuban Racial Politics of 1844

Matthew Pettway

In the shadow of the Haitian Revolution (1791–1804), free and enslaved persons of African descent organized a series of insurrections designed to abolish slavery, depose the Spanish military government, and boldly institute a new republic of blacks and mulattoes on the island of Cuba. Government interrogations confirmed that the chief conspirators had initiated their plans in 1841 (Paquette 263–65) and subsequently concealed the plot by compelling would-be rebels to swear unconditional allegiance to give up their lives before revealing anything to their white enemies. To this end, loyalty oaths were a pervasive means to effectively organize anti-slavery revolts, maintain secrecy, and assure unity among insurgents.[1] The 1844 Movement particularly alarmed colonial authorities because it enjoyed widespread appeal among blacks, effectively recruited both enslaved and free persons, and was composed of multiple nuclei that traversed the urban/rural divide (Paquette 263–65).[2]

The historical record confirms that loyalty oaths had both a political and spiritual component (Finch 171). Members of the chief junta inducted Cuban and African-born persons alike through ritual initiations wherein would-be rebels pledged abiding allegiance to the cause. On occasion, loyalty oaths involved the transgressive appropriation of Catholic rituals in an apparent attempt to confer religious significance on the uprisings and to invoke divine power in hope of speeding its success. In this essay, I analyze the oaths administered by mulatto sacristan José Amores, a constituent of the 1844 Movement. I argue that Amores knowingly appropriated, refashioned, and resignified Catholic rituals in accordance with an African-based religio-cultural paradigm so that the tools of normative religious discourse became instruments of insurgent activity. African-born captives and their Cuban descendants appropriated Christian religious figures and images in order to dissemble African-derived sacred practices (Sandoval 41, 53). The appropriation of Catholic practices speaks to a transcultural historical moment wherein Africans and their descendants amalgamated the rites, rituals, and symbols of the dominant religious order with the cultural values of African divine spirits. Insurgency rituals—such as the oath performed by José Amores—reworked the sacraments through the lens of an African-based spiritual worldview, thus transculturating the Blessed Sacrament and the sacred speech act.

The seditious engagement of José Amores with Christian ritual and his reliance on hallowed speech acts warrant careful study. My archival research at Harvard University's Houghton Library revealed that the sacristan's clandestine activities involved taking hold of the Eucharist to administer scared loyalty oaths. Amores's initiations adopted what are among the holiest symbols of Catholicism: the altar, the oath of fidelity, and the Body of Christ. My cultural-studies reading of historical text explores how the oaths transgressed church dogma and assigned a new system of meaning to otherwise normative rites. In this way, José Amores's activities were not only politically subversive but also endangered Hispano-Catholic notions of the colonial order.

Not much research has been conducted concerning the loyalty oath as a component of the counter-hegemonic thinking that informed the 1844 Movement. To my knowledge, no literary scholars in either Cuba or the United States have seriously engaged the topic. Nevertheless, I am familiar with historians who have touched upon the matter: Aisha Finch, Jane Landers, and Robert Paquette. In her ground-breaking dissertation, "Insurgency at the Crossroads: Cuban Slaves and the Conspiracy of La Escalera, 1841–1844," Finch effectively excavates the narrative of African-descendant political struggle and demonstrates that rural Africans helped to organize and lead the 1844 Movement.[3] Finch acknowledges the sacred character of the loyalty oath and characterizes chief conspirator Gabriel de la Concepción Valdés as one responsible for administering such oaths to would-be rebels (171). Jane Landers offers a far more abridged discussion of the loyalty oath, mentioning Plácido's 1840 poem "El Juramento" ("The Oath") without any analysis of its religio-political significance to the 1844 Movement (204, 227). As part of a broader discussion about the use of African ritual powers as insurgent tools, Robert Paquette mentions the curious account of a mulatto sacristan by the name of José Amores, who was convicted of perverting that which is holy to recruit an enslaved person to rebellion (243). While these studies contribute to our knowledge of the oath as a tool of insurgency in nineteenth-century colonial Cuba, research remains to be done that examines the transcultural sacrality of such a speech act.

The *Sentencia pronunciada por la Seccion de la Comisión militar establecida en la ciudad de Matanzas para conocer la causa de la conspiración de la gente de color* (Sentence pronounced by the Section of the Military Commission established in the city of Matanzas to uncover the motives of the conspiracy of the colored people), an eight-page Spanish-government document dating from 1844, is located at Harvard University's Houghton Library.[4] The *Sentencia* is an authoritative and condemnatory text, legitimated by Queen Isabel II but executed under the auspices of Captain General Leopoldo O'Donnell, who was charged with performing the will of the monarch. The Military Commission's account had three stated functions: to name those accused of conspiratorial activities, to frame the uprisings in terms of an indefensible race war, and to graphically detail the executions of persons condemned to death. The Commissioners characterized the oath that José Amores issued to an enslaved rebel as a particularly abominable act because it dishonored the Blessed Sacrament—the holiest of Christian relics—in a religio-political struggle to deconstruct the colonial order.

I analyze the aforementioned text as a conspiracy narrative whose espousal of conflicting worldviews is grounded in a Christian as well as an African belief in the inherent power of the spoken word. From the hegemonic viewpoint, the Afro-Cuban exploitation of Catholic rituals for conspiratorial ends was a terrifying prospect. Such symbolic inversions of the religio-political order threatened to Africanize Cuba and transform the island into another Haiti (Paquette 211). Nevertheless, if we read the government account from the rebels' vantage point, the loyalty oath emerges as a sacred pact among brethren whose ritual poetics equipped them for revolutionary exploits. This essay examines how peripheral discourses appropriated the tools of dominant society in an effort to gain discursive presence. My research has presented a series of questions that require our attention because they have yet to be explored. What is the religio-political function of the loyalty oaths that José Amores professed and administered to others? How might scholars make an Afro-Cuban subject position legible in a government narrative that sought to efface it? I contend that the oath is a transgressive representation of Catholicism and a sacred speech act that usurps and resignifies the normative authority of religious discourse, thus transforming the dark body into a sacred vessel consecrated for uprising.

Government accounts of uprising tend to portray events in a way that highlights the legitimacy of the power of the colonial state. Such narratives deliberately create silences, speak in coded language, and otherwise dissemble the truth. Self-dissembling further complicates an already difficult task since the critic must make the text readable in order to do a suitable analysis. In order to make the *Sentencia* legible to a broader readership, I have adopted an interdisciplinary historicist method that draws upon religious ethnography, literary theory, and theories of transculturation. Colonial-era documents tend to obscure, misrepresent, and/or omit African and Afro-Cuban points of view because they were written for a white bureaucratic readership. The Military Commission's racialized account requires that we read between the lines, observing silences and speaking where the text does not. Drawing upon multiple disciplinary practices, my aim is to identify, disinter, and effectively reconstruct African descendant subject positions.

The loyalty oath was a spoken utterance, not a written text; thus, it evaded the power of an austere censorship regime. Documents from the colonial era illustrate the role censorship played as a technology of power intricately designed to maintain the imperial order.[5] Censorship is an example of what Michel Foucault has termed the rarefaction of discourse: determining what can be said, choosing among subjects to speak, and avoiding *chance appearances* of speech that does not belong "within the true" (216).[6] My research at Harvard University's Houghton Library yielded an original 1835 decree from Captain General Miguel Tacón published in *Diario de la Habana,* concerning the censorship of religious writings.[7] Spanish censorship was an observable system of control for African and European descendant writers whose true power was less visible to the reading public. Colonial censors were chosen by and directly responsible to the Captain General, the chief military officer appointed by the crown. For my purposes, there are three themes that require attention: prohibitions on religious writings that contradict the holy faith, slanderous statements about the monarchy, as well as any reference to liberty or progress.[8]

I employ a theoretical framework that privileges the inherent power of the spoken word, the oath, body politics, and religious transculturation. Giorgio Agamben's *The Sacrament of Language* situates the oath in the intersection between religion and politics (Prodi qtd. in Agamben 1) so that the utterance performs a sacred and secular function. The oath represents a pact, a socio-political commitment between diverse interlocutors within a given polity. Political crises arise when the sworn oath has been disregarded or even dishonored by one or all of the actors in question. Agamben's philosophical archaeology of the oath also explores how Christian monotheism establishes a precise correlation between words and reality. According to such a formulation, the words of God are oaths since he alone swears truly. As a consequence, human beings can know nothing of God that his *word* does not reveal because his *word* "testifies with absolute certainty for itself." The oaths administered and received by humans represent an attempt to conform human language to the divine model in order to enhance its credibility (Philo qtd. in Agamben 21).

Inherently, the oath is a religio-political utterance, so it cannot be said that religion preexisted the oath. On the contrary, as Agamben says, the oath is "[the] originary performative experience of the word." Therefore, it is the oath that gives explanation to jurisprudence and religious faith (65). The oath-event is both a speech act intended to swear faithfulness and a "consecration of the living human being through the word to the word" (Agamben 66). J. L. Austin says that the speech act considers the entirety of the situation in which speech occurs in order to establish a parallel between statements and performative utterances (52). Austin envisions the issuing of a performative utterance as the realization of a deed, which is given life through language, so that "the utterance is the performing of an action" (6–7). According to this rendering, "I do"—the most important declarative statement of the matrimonial ceremony—seals a contractual pact and weds two individuals in sacred ritual (5, 7). For the purpose of this project, I define ritual poetics as verbal practices performing language as sacred discourse inscribed upon the body. Ritual poetics derives its power from the speech act's capacity to manifest language in quotidian circumstance, having been forged through the intractable conflict and asymmetrical dialogue between disparate spiritual traditions in the Cuban colonial context.[9] Though I acknowledge the top-down relationship between the sacristan and his African recruit, I also recognize that such a hierarchical affiliation was the result of church power, not African-descended political organization. As transculturator, the African recruit is active in the process of meaning making, thus transforming the clergy/laity relationship into a sacred pact among brethren.

All of this is relevant to my analysis of the government's portrayal of insurgent loyalty oaths. José Amores professed and administered oaths that broke faith with the authority of the colonial regime and delegitimized the official religion of the colony, which he was sworn to uphold and defend. By focusing on the oath as a religio-political contract breached by an officer of the church, I seek to determine the way in which Afro-Cuban interlocutors selectively appropriated and resignified Christian speech acts in order to create conditions for a new covenant among what might have been an emerging racial community.

Pronouncing Judgment and Condemning Bodies: The *Sentencia pronunciada por la Comisión militar establecida en Matanzas*

The Spanish government's account of the conspiracies and uprisings of 1844 is a violent story of intrigue and chaos, designed to manipulate entrenched white suspicions of African descendants' ambitions for political power.[10] The *Sentencia* is a racialized religious narrative legitimated within normative ideas about whiteness and Catholicism in an attempt to construct Cuba within the Hispanic imaginary. Colonial society is written in Hispano-Catholic terms as a divinely sanctioned social structure besieged by vicious persons who would pervert its holy mission and natural hierarchy. I analyze the *Sentencia* as the official government narrative of the events of 1844 that makes explicit claims to veracity in order to justify the imprisonment, torture, executions, and coercive expatriations of enslaved and free persons of African descent thought to be involved in the plot. Sanctioned by Queen Isabel II de Borbón, the *Sentencia* reads as an acerbic refutation of conspiracy and revolt. I seek to illustrate how the *Sentencia* unwittingly portrays Africans and their descendants as religio-cultural subjects who appropriated and refashioned normative rites in order to administer ritual oaths of spiritual adherence and insurrectionary commitment.

The government's story portrayed people of African descent in a way that spoke to their socio-economic standing in the colonial order. Ifeoma Kiddoe Nwankwo's close reading of the judgment against the political leaders of the 1844 Movement sheds light on the process of racialization. Her analysis foregrounds the judgment made against Gabriel de la Concepción Valdés (also known as Plácido), who was convicted of being the president, mastermind, and recruiter of an island-wide plot to abolish slavery and exterminate the white population.[11] The conspiracies and uprisings were carried out by *pardos libres*, *morenos libres*, *negros esclavos*, and *las negradas* (free people of mixed race, free blacks, black slaves, and the black masses). The government supposed that free people of mixed race who wished to improve their social condition had organized the conspiracy and that free blacks had joined under the assumption that it might benefit them as well. However, it did not explain the motivation of enslaved blacks, who were cited only for their superior strength (35–36). Nwankwo's study reveals the inherent contradictions of Cuban racial discourse, which professed to be a multipartite racial order while in reality it functioned like a black/white dichotomy with insignificant shades of gray.[12]

In the 1844 judgment against the town of Bainoa, which I am analyzing here, the conspiracy is described in two distinct but related ways: "el proyectado levantamiento y conspiracion contra la raza blanca de esta Isla" (the projected uprising and conspiracy against the white race of this island) and "el plan de sublevación fraguado por la jente de color . . . para esterminar la raza blanca y privar á la madre patria de esta Antilla (sic)" (the plan of rebellion conceived by the people of color . . . to exterminate the white race and deprive the mother country of this Antilles). By depicting the plot in terms of racial extermination, the white population becomes the plausible victim of ethnic cleansing and, at the same time, African-descendant aspirations for abolition and racial egalitarianism are silenced. This rhetorical omission establishes the discursive strategy of the text: repossess the island as a bastion of white Hispanic values under siege by what was repeatedly, although erroneously, characterized as the impending destruction of African barbarism.

Haiti was the second nation to gain independence from a European colonial power and the first black republic ever to exist; the Haitian Revolution was the shot heard around the world.[13] At once, Haiti became a potent symbol of black nationalism and a terror to slave-owning white elites throughout Latin America and the Caribbean (Trouillot 37). Haiti represented a veritable threat to the political and cultural dominance of the emerging landed gentry that hoped to generate wealth through the exploitation of captive African labor. Demographic shifts in the racial and cultural composition of the island were reminiscent of the numeric predominance of blacks in Saint-Domingue prior to the Haitian Revolution.[14] In the late eighteenth century and during the Latin American wars for independence (1810–1825), opponents of Cuban independence manipulated the white public with the racialized nightmare of a Haitian-style revolution on Cuban soil. They argued that the notion of Cuban independence was counter to and indeed threatened the white Hispano-Catholic ideal. In both racial and religio-cultural terms, Haiti came to signify blackness in the white imaginary.

Rapid growth of the enslaved black and free mulatto populations on the island was but one factor that terrified white Cuban planters. Accounts from Saint-Domingue also warned of the efficacious use of African ritual powers in warfare against the French. Haitian soldiers who had fought in the Revolution were largely African-born, and there was evidence to suggest that their religio-cultural frame of reference in the form of incantations and oaths of secrecy had guided them in combat (Thornton 71–72). Historians note that prior to launching a full-blown revolt in Bois Caïman on the Choiseul plantation, Boukman and other rebels sacrificed a black pig, drank his blood, and carried swatches of his hair as protective elements in warfare. Boukman—who had been enslaved as a driver/coachman—was the most visible leader during the first days of the Haitian Revolution (Dubois 99–100). Following this collective ritual act, conspirators swore a sacred oath before inaugurating their revolutionary activities (Landers 61). Largely outnumbering white colonists, several thousand enslaved persons set plantation houses ablaze, burned sugarcane fields, and destroyed refining equipment and other tools of colonial oppression. The revolutionaries succeeded in destroying more than one thousand plantations in the north of Saint-Domingue (Landers 61). African ritual practices provided the spiritual groundwork for Haitian revolutionary activity, and the sacred oath functioned as an initiatory speech act, consecrating dark bodies for what would become the only successful revolution ever conceived and executed by persons who had been enslaved. The 1812 Aponte Rebellion is yet another important antecedent to the 1844 Movement because it also relied on the Haitian Revolution as both political and religio-cultural frame of reference. Historian Matt Childs revises Cuban historiography by demonstrating that the first declaration of independence on the island did not come at the hands of white Creoles but rather was engineered by free and enslaved insurgents of African lineage who endured racialized oppression (77, 179).

Undoubtedly, there was a religious component to the Military Commission's racialized fantasies. Spain's endeavor to avert the Africanization of Cuba not only meant the perpetuation of military power over ever-increasing urban and rural black populations, but it also implied preventing the systematic implementation of African ritual powers as tools of insurgent combat. In Cuba, African-derived religion stirred anxiety in the white public, and it was anathema to Catholic doctrine. Instead of punishing unorthodox ritual practice, colonial authorities were more worried that non-Catholic beliefs might translate into anti-colonial fervor and insurrectionary activity since slave revolts were regularly attributed to the influence of African-based religion and to the authority of "African-style—spiritual leaders" (Palmié 228). The *Sentencia* decreed against the conspirators of Bainoa reveals that sacred oaths of loyalty played an analogous role in the inauguration of the Cuban plantation uprisings of 1844. The activities of free and enslaved conspirators in Cuba bore resemblance to Boukman's revolt, so Haitian ritual was the spiritual antecedent to Afro-Cuban revolutionary activity. Even though there is no mention of the *cabildos* in the *Sentencia* that I am analyzing here, loyalty oaths taken by alleged conspirators are a very present and recurring theme in the text and merit careful consideration. For that reason, it is necessary to inquire about the religious meanings that would-be rebels constructed with regards to the ritual oath-event.

The government's representation of the events of 1844 relies on contemporary stereotypes about African-descended persons as uninhibited agents of violence pining for a race war that would put an end to a Christian sense of social propriety and tranquility.

> Se afectaba una tranquilidad aparente en la raza de color tanto libre como esclava; pero no habia uno solo que no hubiera penetrado la ponzoñosa intriga de los crueles asesinos de aquellos pacíficos moradores. En todas las fincas habian arreglado y combinado su bárbaro y destructor plan; estaban elejidos los principales caudillos para el dia en que debia rasgarse el sangriento velo de la anaraquia y el asesinato: no hay una sola declarcion que no revele el inhumano objeto de la jente de color, cuya tendencia era la de acabar con todos los hombres blancos, dejando entregado el débil sécso á los horrores que eran consiguientes (sic).[15]

> There was an apparent tranquility among the colored people both freemen and slaves; but there wasn't one of them that hadn't entered into the venomous plot to cruelly murder those peaceful inhabitants. On all the farms they had gotten together and collaborated their barbarous and destructive plan; the chief *caudillos* had been designated for the day in which they would tear back the bloody veil of anarchy and assassination: there isn't one testimony that doesn't reveal the inhuman intentions of the colored people, whose proclivity was to do away with all white men, subjecting the weaker sex to the corresponding horrors.[16]

The aforementioned passage portrays the enslaved and free populations of African descent as a violent monolith, lying in wait to carry out venomous machinations that would result in the murder of the "peaceful inhabitants," that is, peaceable white settlers. Acting in unison with a sole purpose in mind, free mixed-race people, free blacks, and enslaved blacks are subsumed into a single racial category: the colored people whose destructive plan was pervasive throughout the region and implicated activity on all plantations. In this gendered story of violence, the annihilation of all white male persons precipitates unspeakable horrors to be inflicted upon the white female body.[17] Anarchy and assassination are coupled with the defilement of the white female so that white readers of the *Sentencia* (a largely male audience to be sure) would be filled with an abiding sense of dread and revulsion. In line with the government's rhetorical strategy, white slaveholders are depicted as peaceful settlers, Afro-Cuban aspirations for freedom and equality go unmentioned, and the violence of racial slavery is silenced.

The gender politics of the government's narrative is coupled with racist stereotypes of the African-descendant male as sexual menace. Free persons of color are presented as the intellectual agents of conspiracy, purportedly scheming to seduce a passive black plantation population. The previously mentioned racial binary reappears in the text. According to the government, urban sophisticates assured enslaved males that by killing their masters, they would gain freedom, become owners of the land, and be permitted to marry white women. Such promises speak to entrenched white fears that the uprising of 1844 might implement an absolute inversion of the socio-cultural and economic order of colonial Cuba. Things that assured the political power of the white male minority—the enslavement of Africans and their descendants, the husbandry of the land, and considerable power over the white female body—would come to a sudden end with the triumph of a Haitian-style revolution on Cuban soil.

I want to point out that the agency assigned to *libertos* is crafted in the religio-moral idiom of Catholicism. To paraphrase the government scribe, the conspirators left nothing to chance:

En las fincas, en los caminos y hasta en los mismos bohíos penetraban los libertos, esparciendo por todas partes sus maléficas ideas: no se ocupaba de otra cosa hacia algun tiempo; la semilla habia penetrado en todas direcciones, y solo faltaba la señal para dar principio a tan horrendo sacrificio (sic).[18]

The freedmen penetrated the farms, the country roads, and even the *bohíos* themselves, disseminating their maleficent ideas: they haven't concerned themselves with anything else for some time now; the seed had penetrated in all directions, and they only needed a sign to set in motion such a horrifying sacrifice.

Once more, the Military Commission casts free persons of color as active agents of sedition. Penetration is the chosen metaphor to characterize the grave extent of the freedman's power and influence over rural plantation populations. Alluding to the sexual act, penetration implies a sort of symbolic violence and impropriety, an uninvited infiltration so to speak, since the urban and rural areas of colonial society (representing free and enslaved persons, respectively) were thought to be separate social and cultural spheres. In this way, freedmen—the dominant actors in the government's *Sentencia*—violate the most intimate spaces of plantation life to indoctrinate would-be rebels. The scribe's choice of words is not inconsequential. This is best demonstrated by the reiteration of the word *penetrate*. Not only do the interlopers force their way into plantation dwellings, but they also disperse the seed of their maleficent ideas in every direction imaginable, making revolution difficult to contain. For Hispanic Catholics, the freedmen's sins are many: sedition, inducing others to violent revolt, and the scattering of conspiratorial ideas that would result in the horrendous sacrifice of white bodies.

The *Sentencia* is a fundamentally Christian narrative deeply rooted in the biblical language of sin and punishment. The dichotomous nature of ecclesiastical discourse structures the text so that any spiritual practice departing from church dogma is deemed unholy, pernicious to the faith and, by extension, to the political and economic interests of the colonial state. The passage that follows draws attention to the Military Tribunal's preoccupation with loyalty oaths:

> El Jueves Santo prócismo pasado era el señalado para dar principio á tan monstruoso proyecto. Los libertos eran los colaboradores tenían sus juntas, y en ellas se distribuian los empleos, siendo los principales directores el mulato José María Ramos, que se halla adjudicado al cuaderno á cargo del fiscal D. Ramon Gonzalez . . . tenian sus correos, y por ellos se comunicaban con el mulato Plácido de Matanzas, y demas individuos que componian la junta directiva. Los juramentos de morir antes que revclai algo a los blancos han sido el método político y medio de que se han valido para conservar el secreto por tanto tiempo (sic).[19]

> The previous Good Thursday was the day slated to set in motion such a monstrous scheme. The freedmen were collaborators; they had meetings in which they assigned tasks; the mulatto José María Ramos, being among the chief directors, is cited in the records of Prosecutor Don Ramón González . . . they maintained correspondence, employing it to communicate with Plácido, a mulatto from Matanzas, and the other individuals that made up the chief junta. The oath to die before revealing anything to the whites was the political method and means that they relied on in order to maintain this secret for so long.

According to the government's account, conspirators from the countryside and the city designated Good Thursday as the day to mount what is described as a "monstrous scheme." Once again, free persons of color were said to be the natural leaders of the conspiracy and were deemed responsible for the organizational framework and for assigning insidious tasks. The account names Plácido among the chief conspirators and accuses the poet of being intimately familiar with the surreptitious network that channeled communications between the city and the Cuban countryside.[20] On this particular point, the government account appears to be accurate. Although the facts have been fiercely debated for nearly two centuries by Cuban and US scholars alike, more recent studies have corroborated that the popular poet was indeed involved in the 1844 Movement and played a leading role.[21]

Plácido transformed his extraordinary lyrical talent into an instrument of conspiracy, conveying messages back and forth to his collaborators. The poet is represented as a leader of the original junta who proselytized free blacks and mulattoes and compelled them to swear oaths of white extermination, revealing nothing to their enemies lest they be assassinated. In the judgment against Plácido, the oath also functions as an avowal of political and racial allegiance that creates space wherein free mulattoes and blacks conspired to subvert the socio-cultural order, devising an "iniquitous project" at the home of Marcos Ruiz and Manuel Quiñones. Plácido's 1840 poem entitled "El Juramento," which augured the swearing of sacred oaths, heightened the Military Commission's sense of political urgency.[22] In strictly racialized terms, loyalty oaths are portrayed as the *political method* of choice designed to conceal the pervasive nature of anti-colonial activity from white colonists. Persons of African descent appear as an indivisible political monolith disposed to sacrifice life and limb to avoid revealing the plot. The narrative's reference to successive plantation uprisings to commence on Holy Thursday not only speaks to the government's need to defend the holiness of religious festivals commemorating the passion and resurrection of the Christ, but also points to the symbolic inversion of a Christian holiday by African-descendant conspirators. As historian Manuel Barcia says, festival holidays were well placed for the launching of rebellious activities (111) since they allowed for the movement of enslaved rural populations to urban centers to celebrate festivities with African and Afro-Cuban confraternities (Sandoval 53). In this way, African-descended conspirators—like the sacristan José Amores—employed the loyalty oath in order to actively subvert religio-political norms.

Seditious Sacristy: The Altar, the Oath, and the Body of Christ

The government's account of the activities of José Amores provides the most remarkable portrayal of oath taking in the entire text. In his groundbreaking book *Sugar is Made with Blood*, historian Robert Paquette mentions the case of José Amores as part of a broader discussion of the use of African ritual powers in the Ladder Conspiracy (243). I have since found no other mention of the alleged conspirator, so what we know about José Amores is entirely derived from this particular government document. Since Spanish legal tradition required scribes to record the full name, national origin, and place of residence (among other things) about each witness, I am able to provide some general ideas about the subject in question.[23] José Amores was a free person of color, referred to as *mulato* or *pardo* in the government account, who was originally from the small town of Caraballo in western Cuba, north of Bainoa and west of Matanzas. In his function as sacristan for the parishioners at San Pablo de Bainoa, Amores was entrusted with purifying the sacred vessels containing the Holy Eucharist and delivering the first homily. Although the sacristan was responsible for assisting the priest in his holy duties, the priest alone was permitted to lay hands on the Host, considered by the Catholic Church to be the transubstantiated body of Jesus Christ (Estepa Llaurens 295). José Amores's function as a custodian of sacred vessels and erstwhile guardian of normative religious rites provides context for the oaths he is said to have administered.

In 1844, thirty-six different witnesses accused José Amores of conspiratorial activities, twenty-four claimed that he had seduced and initiated them into the rebellion. The most damning denunciation, however, came from the mouth of an enslaved African by the name of Fermin Gangá.[24] I have chosen to cite extensively from the *Sentencia* in order to provide the precise context in which Amores administered such an oath:

> Entre los infinitos ardides que han empleado para seducir y alucinar las esclavitudes los hay atroces é inauditos; tal es el que aparece puesto en ejecucion por uno de los principales corifeos, pues no contento con aumentar sus prosèlitos por medio de los juramentos ordinarios, y las amenazas de muerte, holló lo mas sagrado y respetado de todo ser cristiano: tuvo valor para sacar del santo sagrario de la iglesia del pueblo de San Pablo de Bainoa, la custodia de Santísimo Sacramento, y haciéndola besar á un esclavo, le hizo jurar su adhesion al partido esterminador, prometiendo sijilo y ofreciendo morir antes que revelar nada á los blancos; asi lo declara Fermin gangá de D. Antonio García Flores á fojas 937 que hizo tan grave juramento. Este mulato audaz y sacrìlego ejercía las funciones de sacristan, se titulaba padre de la Iglesia, y consta era el que debia decir la primera misa en el pueblo de Caraballo, en accion de gracias al Todopoderoso después de haber consumado su atroz plan. (sic)
>
> El segundo, José Amores, se halla acusado por treinta y seis testigos marcándole veinte y cuatro como seductor; con la horrenda y ecsecrable circunstancia ya referida de haber tomado juramento á un esclavo con el Santísimo Sacramento que se hallaba depositado en la iglesia de San Pablo de Bainoa; tiene además cinco de complicidad, igual nùmero de indicios, y dos como cabecilla jeneral. (sic)[25]

Among the infinite schemes that they have employed to seduce and astonish the slave masses are atrocious and unmentionable [acts]; such is the plan executed by one of the chief spokesmen, not content with increasing his proselytes through ordinary oaths, and death threats, he trampled on the most sacred and respected item of all Christians: he had the audacity to remove the ciborium of the Holiest Sacrament from the tabernacle, and obliging a slave to kiss it, he made him swear his support to the exterminator party, promising stealth and offering to die before revealing anything to the whites; so testifies Fermin Gangá of Don Antonio García Flores on record sheet 937 who swore such a severe oath. This audacious and sacrilegious mulatto exercised the function of the sacristan; he called himself Father of the Church, and was supposed to give the first mass in the town of Caraballo, giving thanks to the Almighty after having consummated such an atrocious plan.

The second individual, José Amores, finds himself accused by thirty-six witnesses of which twenty-four identify him as a seducer; with the aforementioned abominable circumstance of having administered an oath to a slave with the Holiest Sacrament that is found in the Church of St. Paul Bainoa; furthermore, five other witnesses accused him of complicity, the same number [of witnesses] of circumstantial evidence, and two [identified him] as the leading conspirator.

Under questioning, Fermin Gangá not only claimed that José Amores had urged him to take an oath but also that the sacristan had presented him with the consecrated vessels and obliged him to seal his vow by kissing the ciborium. The scene is narrated with indignation, depicting the misdeed of José Amores as an extraordinary crime that superseded the white imagination. Amores is rendered an audacious and sacrilegious mulatto who trampled on the holiest and most highly revered article of the Christian faith. From a Hispano-Catholic point of view, the nature of the offense is exacerbated by the fact that José Amores was himself an officer of the church, entrusted with the custodianship of sacred objects and texts. As the narrative progresses, the implication is that Amores literally laid hands on the Host to embark on a seditious plot of white annihilation.

Once again, the government's representation of race is an unapologetic gendered vindication of whiteness that is fraught with contradictions. The text locates José Amores and Fermin Gangá in a single racial category since both *black* bodies came into contact with the Eucharist and thus defiled it. Even so, Amores is a mulatto, and as such, occupies the leadership role as someone who allegedly seduced the *slave*.[26] The government portrayal of José Amores as a mulatto situates him both culturally and religiously above enslaved blacks while also implying that he sought to usurp the social power reserved for white men. In this way, Amores is likened to the *pardo* racial stereotype. This is critical, in view of the fact that *los pardos*, mixed-race people, were thought to be the closest to white persons in physical appearance and cultural attainment. As Ifeoma Nwankwo has shown, colonial racial stereotypes maintained that *pardos* exhibited a certain polarity: either they would do anything to mimic white people or they vehemently hated and resented them (38). As an officer of the church, Amores could be read as a fully assimilated mulatto whose conversion to Christianity did not involve amalgamation with African practices or beliefs. As I read it, the sacristan's social and religious position qualified him to preach a white Christian gospel. The scribe uses the words *seduce* and *seducer* on multiple occasions in the judgment decreed against the town of Bainoa. Seduction is part and parcel of the government's narrative thread, suggesting a psychosexual undertone to an African ritual pact.[27]

The disproportionate number of priests to parishioners in colonial Cuba may explain why a sacristan was required to perform Sunday mass. Despite its designated function in colonial law as the official religion of the empire, the Catholic Church's sphere of influence in early nineteenth-century Cuba was considerably muted. Whereas in the eighteenth century the priesthood was large enough to minister to the needs of practicing Catholics, by the beginning of the 1800s it had diminished even as the enslaved and free population of color increased. The priesthood became increasingly Spanish because Cubans were unwilling to join the sacred orders (Sandoval 21–23). Consequently, the Catholic Church managed to have only limited influence on the growing enslaved population.

I submit that there is an implicit theological perspective embedded in José Amores's determination to issue this particular loyalty oath to Fermin Gangá. Amores's quasi-priestly role with the congregations at St. Paul Bainoa and in Caraballo leaves little doubt that he was a literate person who was intimately familiar with biblical texts, the sacraments, and church doctrine. In addition to discharging his duties as a sacristan, José Amores was charged with delivering the first Sunday mass in his hometown of Caraballo. The sacristan enhanced the limited, but by no means insignificant, authority granted him by claiming the esteemed title of "Father of the Church."[28] The appropriation of a title reserved for the likes of St. Thomas Aquinas and the Pope himself bears witness to the edifice of religious authority that Amores constructed for himself within communities of African descent. Such an edifice of priestly authority in the hands of a free man must have bolstered the spiritual (and political) legitimacy of his conspiratorial activities among enslaved persons.

The altar, the Holy Sacrament, and the oath are at the center of what I am calling a transgressive representation of Catholicism. In the Catholic Church, the altar is a consecrated space at the head of the sanctuary adorned with the ciborium that contains the transubstantiated Body of Christ. Catholic theologian M. Shawn Copeland proposes an alternative reading of the Body of Christ, wherein the Eucharist is inexorably linked to the violent destruction of the collective black body, and the cross on which Jesus Christ was crucified is analogous to the lynching tree (122). Copeland remarks, "Eucharist, then, is countersign to the devaluation and violence directed toward the exploited, despised black body." The celebration of Holy Communion, then, does not seek to "directly expose a tortured body," but it does make known the presence of a body displaying the scars of violence (127).[29] From this theological standpoint, José Amores's determination to dislodge the host from the ciborium can be read as a way to associate the Body of Christ with the ravaged bodies of enslaved Africans and free persons of color.

Sworn to discharge the duties of a sacristan, José Amores deconstructed the authority of the Catholic Church in what amounted to a symbolic inversion of religious normativity and a brazen act of sedition. His intimate knowledge of catechism implies a theological choice on his part to administer the Eucharist as something more than a countersign emblematic of suffering bodies. The Eucharist was not only countersign for the devaluation of dark bodies in the sacred oath that José Amores administered to Fermin Gangá, but also a ritual initiation that resignified the Body of Christ and transformed it into a *black* body.

In the government narrative, the Host is defiled, having been dislodged from the tabernacle, removed from the altar, and made to touch the lips of Fermin Gangá, described as Amores's proselyte. However, the narrative reaches a moment of crisis when it proves unable to assure the integrity of the holy faith and, by extension, the tranquility and whiteness of the island. In this scene from the *Sentencia*, the oath administered by the sacristan belies the integrity of the holy faith and despoils its claims to purity. As I read it, the oath administered by José Amores is not only an appropriation of Catholic rites but also a subversive resignification that divested such acts of their ecclesiastical meaning by endowing them with an African-based power, both symbolic and metaphysical.

The government contended in additional documents detailing the sentences of alleged conspirators that plantation masses had been *seduced* by the widespread use of "witchcraft" (Paquette 242). Such a claim supports my reading of the oath administered not only as a transgressive representation of Catholicism but also as an African-based speech act. In this instance, the oath is an act of ritual initiation, a sacred vow taken with the Sacrament so that the Body of Christ is complicit in black revolution against the colonial state. It is not the silencing of an elaborate plot against Spain that matters here, but the confession of the mouth, since the spoken word legitimates and actualizes life. The oath administered by José Amores is a transculturated ritual speech act, dislocating the Christ from his rightful place in order to consecrate the African body for revolution. In this way, the acculturative aim of proselytization—intended to forge docile and submissive Christians out of African captives—is rendered woefully ineffective.

In many respects, there were remarkable cultural disparities between the sacristan and his alleged recruit, Fermin Gangá. Amores was a lettered mulatto, well versed in ecclesiastical doctrine and charged with proselytizing those yet to be baptized. From the Catholic standpoint, Fermin Gangá was a religious neophyte at best and, at worst, a savage idolater in need of salvation and Hispanic cultural refinement. Notwithstanding Christian notions of superiority, anthropologists have shown that as an African, Fermin Gangá's knowledge of ritual, familiarity with the power of the spoken word, and acquaintance with human/spirit interaction would not have been effaced by the catechism taught to *africanos de nación*.[30] Thus, my reading defines Fermin Gangá as an active accomplice in ritual practice, a coreligionist of sorts, whose knowledge of sacrality was not absent from the oath event.

I reject the racist fallacy of African intellectual inadequacy and the notion of the enslaved person as a passive convert of the *liberto* (free person of color). Historian Aisha Finch attests that the role of African leadership in the 1844 resistance movement was analogous to its function in the Haitian Revolution ("Insurgency at the Crossroads" 2). Fermin Gangá's cultural positionality as an African-born person provides clues to the conspirator's ideas about the scared and symbolic world.[31]

In an effort to reconstruct Fermin Gangá's religious subject position, I will briefly discuss some of the scholarship regarding African captives imported to Cuba under the name *gangá*. My intentions are not historiographical. Rather, I aim to do an innovative cultural-studies reading of an implicit African subjectivity that the government narrative might otherwise have expunged from the official record. African captives known as *gangá* in colonial Cuba did not constitute a uniform ethnic or religious grouping. Cuban scholar Alessandra Basso Ortiz's research on the *gangá* represents a rare foray into this lesser-studied yet historically significant group. Basso Ortiz explains that the *gangá* are not analogous to the *lucumí* and *arará*, which consisted of myriad ethnolinguistic groups that shared a common culture and claimed descent from the same. Instead, persons self-designated as *gangá* in Cuba had no common basis for cultural unity, which late nineteenth-century colonial archival data demonstrates (Basso Ortiz, "Los gangá longobá" 197).

Cuban scholar Jesús Guanche's pioneering study *Africanía y etnicidad en Cuba* names ten different designations for Africans brought to Cuba during the Transatlantic Slave Trade that were assigned some variant of the meta-ethnic designation *gangá*. According to Guanche's examination of the available scholarship, African bondsmen and women referred to in Cuba as *gangá* were imported from an extensive stretch of the upper Guinea coast including the modern African nations of Guinea, Sierra Leone, Liberia, and the coastal regions of Ivory Coast. Such captives represented multiple ethnic groups and spoke myriad non-Bantu languages (66, 71–76). Basso Ortiz concurs with Guanche that Sierra Leone and Liberia represent the geographic region where the so-called *gangá* originated, but her analysis excludes Guinea and Ivory Coast. Moreover, she recognizes only seven *gangá* groups for whom there is explicit evidence in the archival record. Basso Ortiz concludes that the *gangá* should not be associated with the Mandingo or exclusively classified as speakers of western Atlantic African languages (*Los gangá en Cuba* 63–65).

According to historian Manuel Barcia, Africans known in Cuba as *gangá* were involved in every form of anti-slavery resistance in the eighteenth and nineteenth centuries: they were often conspiratorial leaders and participants in antislavery revolts, sabotage, and marronage. In fact, the plantation was their primary sphere of resistance activities (22). Notwithstanding ethnic incongruities, historians agree that persons known as *gangá* were frequently involved in antislavery resistance and played a role in the 1844 Movement to abolish slavery and establish a republic of blacks and mulattoes on the island. Histories of the Ladder Conspiracy mention persons carrying the ethnonym *gangá* who accessed ritual powers as tools of insurgency against their white oppressors. The historical record names *gangás* who acted as ritual priests, harnessed sacred powers to dominate the spirits of others, and acquired natural elements to fight against white persons (Finch 311–12, 465, 431; Hall 58). In fact, the judgment against the town of Bainoa mentions eleven different individuals using the ethnic designation *gangá* that were convicted of conspiratorial activities.[32]

Fermin Gangá's involvement in the antislavery conspiracy bears resemblance to the historical pattern. The Military Commission's racialized account requires that we read against the grain, observing silences and speaking where the text does not. By definition, sacred initiation implies more than acquiescence on the part of the person swearing the oath. Sociologist of Cuban religions Jualynne Dodson says that "ritual processes of initiation" take place within sacred spaces, making use of collective rites to incorporate new adherents into ritual families. The ritual ceremonies impart explicit "socialization instructions" for the new community members (73–74). Fermin Gangá's resolve to swear an oath administered by José Amores should be read as a covenant between two interlocutors who shared disparate subject positions. Notwithstanding the disparity in social status and the apparent differences in religious practice, both persons were cognizant of the intrinsic life force embedded in the spoken word to actualize revolution. In light of this, I maintain that Fermin Gangá coalesced the Africa-derived sacred knowledge of his *nación* with José Amores's already transculturated understandings of the divine to forge a third ritual space.

The oath is a sacred speech act representing a correlation between what is uttered and what is performed (Agamben 21) in which dialogue is a fundamental component between interlocutors that collectively construct new meanings. I concur with Mary L. Pratt that although subordinated groups do not control what emanates from the dominant culture, they do actively determine what they absorb into their own cultures and how they choose to use it (6). In the case I am analyzing here, the power dynamic appears to have been somewhat more fluid between the sacristan and his recruit. Both men conspired against the Spanish crown and actively subverted and resignified Catholic ritual. As previously argued, José Amores's decision to seal the oath by obliging Fermin Gangá to kiss the Blessed Sacrament transforms the Body of Christ into a black body complicit in uprising.

Although the designation *gangá* obfuscates the precise region in Africa where Fermin Gangá might have been born, it is conceivable that African-derived knowledge of ritual informed his interpretation of and interaction with the Blessed Sacrament. Basso Ortiz's research on the cabildo *gangá longobá* in Perico, Matanzas—the only remaining *gangá* religious community in Cuba—characterizes the tradition as a belief system that is grounded in an African-based conception of the spirit world. In the absence of far-reaching anthropological studies, I will draw upon Basso Ortiz's work to perform a theoretical reconstruction of Fermín Gangá's religious subjectivity. Although marked by some liturgical disparities, the tradition of the *gangá longobá* is consistent with other Afro-Cuban religions given its emphasis on reverence for divine entities, ancestors, and the spirits of the recently deceased. Moreover, the *gangá longobá* ritual structure privileges communication with the spirit realm, promotes the creation of sacred spaces, and performs various purification rites with herbal medicines. Also part and parcel of their worship ceremonies is spirit possession of bodies, animal sacrifices, and the use of consecrated drums (Basso Ortiz, "Los gangá longobá" 199).[33] Among the array of divine spirits in the *gangá* pantheon is La Vieja (The Aged Woman), an entity represented by the color white, known for her exceptional purity, and recognized as the *dueña de las cabezas* (owner of the heads). Although the *gangá* pantheon is comprised of far fewer divine spirits than the Yoruba assemblage, it is analogous to Yoruba-based Cuban religion in some important ways. For example, La Vieja is equivalent to Obatalá in Regla de Ocha and the Virgin of Mercy in Catholicism (Basso Ortiz, "Los gangá longobá" 200). Since the *gangá* and Yoruba traditions concur with regard to the common characteristics of this particular divine spirit, I will largely rely on Yoruba religious studies, which are readily available, to analyze Fermín Gangá's third ritual space.

African divine spirits manifest themselves in myriad ways so as to communicate with practitioners through different paths. La Vieja of the *gangá longobá* is the sacred equivalent of the Obanlá (Orichanlá or Ochanlá) path to Obatalá in Regla de Ocha. Accordingly, La Vieja is a grandmotherly figure and manifests the same characteristics as Obanlá, a trembling, blind, aged woman draped with a blanket (Bolívar 80). Considering that La Vieja was transculturated with Las Mercedes and Santa Ana in Catholicism, she cannot be equated with the Holiest Sacrament, which Africans (and their religious descendants) have associated with *Odudúa* (Bolívar 74, 77). *Odudúa* (Oduduwa) is one of the paths of Obatalá that has been identified and transculturated with the Blessed Sacrament, also known as the consecrated Body of Christ (Lachatañeré 100–101). Obatalá is the *oricha* of creation and the chief of the orishas, that is, the divine supernatural beings that govern natural phenomena. More than any other divine spirit, Obatalá is especially influential in his dealings with the Supreme Being, known as Olodumare. In Yoruba-derived cosmology, Obatalá is known as *dueña de las cabezas* (the owner of heads), and the head stands for holiness, saintliness, and divinity. At the closing of the initiation ceremony, the newly initiated person's guardian orisha is placed on his head, granting him the privilege or power of being possessed by that particular divine entity (Sandoval 188–189).[34]

In my estimation, José Amores's transformation of the Holiest Sacrament into a black Christ should not be read as defilement but instead analyzed from the vantage point of the righteousness of the rebel cause. Although the *gangá longobá* did not amalgamate La Vieja with Oduduwa, such a religious prism does associate her with the Supreme Being so that the reader is at liberty to relate her maternal saintliness with that of Olodumare's son. In fact, I submit that from Fermín Gangá's vantage point, the sacristan that evoked the power of Obatalá/La Vieja to administer loyalty oaths in effect performed the function of a babalawo, a ritual priest. As Natalia Bolívar has clarified, Oduduwa is a divine spirit upon whose power babalawos, not ordinary practitioners, rely (75). Therefore, I contend that Fermin Gangá transculturated the Blessed Sacrament with Oduduwa, thus relating the sanctity and purity of Obatalá with that of Jesus Christ. In Cuba, Oduduwa embodies immaculate essence, justice, truth, intelligence, and righteousness and is often represented by lithographs of Jesus Christ (Sandoval 196–197). Fermin Gangá emerges in the text as a spiritually adept interlocutor and a prospective agent of change who swore a conspiratorial oath on the Blessed Sacrament. If Oduduwa personifies justice, then black revolution to depose a racialized colonial slave society is both righteous and true. Contrary to the government account, I do not believe that he was unknowingly seduced, hoodwinked, or deceived into the desecration of Catholic sacraments as a way of acquiescing to a revolutionary cause. Rather, Fermin Gangá constructs his subjectivity in relation to that of José Amores in hopes of achieving an agency that both were denied. From Fermin Gangá's perspective, I argue that the willing pact between both conspirators is not an abomination, as alleged by the government scribe, but a spiritual and political covenant among brethren of African descent unified in a resistance movement with revolutionary potential.

Resistance practices and warfare are consistent with Afro-Cuban conceptions of Obatalá manifested in the path of Oduduwa. In some Cuban houses of worship (*casas de santo*) Oduduwa is conceived as a warrior spirit on horseback wielding a machete. He is omnipotent, omnipresent, and omniscient, possessing the same characteristics that belong to the Supreme Being (Sandoval 196). When Fermin Gangá takes the Body and Blood of Christ, he is partaking in a body that has been darkened, if you will, by the ritual poetics of the oath administered him. In the religio-political logic of the José Amores/Fermin Gangá ritual, Jesus Christ of Nazareth is black. But in the case of Fermin Gangá, the black Body of Christ is again transfigured, this time being rendered as Obatalá. I maintain that Fermin Gangá's transculturation of the Blessed Sacrament amounts to a second theological moment. The omniscient warrior spirit will lead the sacristan and the formerly enslaved recruit in battle as they strive to abolish racial slavery and enshrine a new social order. Moreover, the oath event embodies and performs the power of the spoken word so that it is "a consecration of the living human being through the word to the word" (Agamben 66).

The oath that José Amores administered and Fermin Gangá professed signified disloyalty and rebellion to the racialized plantation order established and legitimated by the absolute power of the Spanish crown. Even so, Fermin Gangá's confession to the Military Commission breaks faith with the sacred covenant among African-descended brethren that he swore with José Amores. After all, the passages I have been analyzing are a government reconstruction of Fermin Gangá's confessions. The *Sentencia* reads, "he [José Amores] made him swear his support to the exterminator party promising stealth and offering to die before revealing anything to the whites; so testifies Fermin *gangá* of Don Antonio García Flores."[35] Fermin Gangá's detailed confession of José Amores's plot and the ritual they constructed in unison around the loyalty oath appears to have been part of an eleventh-hour strategy to save himself by denying culpability. It is not unreasonable to suppose that he was subjected to torture. Paquette has established (and my research confirms) that the testimony from the Ladder Conspiracy was highly problematic given that torture was used to extract confessions (234). By making José Amores the culprit, Fermin Gangá reinforced the racialized and gendered dimensions of the government's story: he is rendered as an African victim, intellectually incapable of devising such a comprehensive and well-ordered scheme, so that the officer of the church is the likely perpetrator.

There are, of course, questions that remain unanswered, some pertaining to government silences and others that reflect a need to conduct further research about this particular case. What was the nature of José Amores's relationship with Fermin Gangá? Was Fermin Gangá a parishioner, a recent *convert* to Catholicism, or someone else? Furthermore, did the promise of leniency motivate Fermin Gangá to confess? While we may be unable to satisfactorily answer the historical questions, I have tried to show that the government account does provide an opportunity for a counter-reading of conspiracy that reconstructs events, reads between the lines, and speaks when the text is silent.

Conclusion

Threatened by political actors whose conspiracy was grounded in transculturated African-based speech acts, the Military Commission not only ordered the execution of José Amores, but also insisted on the disfigurement of the body. José Amores was made to kneel as authorities read the sentence: he was to be executed by gunfire being shot in the back; his head would be severed from his body, mutilated, and displayed in the most public places of his hometown, Caraballo. The government's condemnation of Amores is most severe given that his crime had been deemed both blasphemous and conspiratorial. The Military Commission's overwhelming reaction to what was considered a deliberate perversion of the most holy article of Christian faith was to confine, execute, mutilate, and dismember the body that professed and administered such an oath.[36] Unlike printed materials, which could be censored with a modicum of success, the oath was a verbal speech act rooted in oral traditions and, therefore, elusive to the reach of the censor's pen. It is through the destruction of the body, however, that Spanish monarch Isabel II hoped to forever silence the illicit oath event.

The apocalyptic government narrative depicted the calamitous destruction and defilement of white bodies: the widespread massacre of white Christian males would ensure the pillaging of their land and the rape of white women. In effect, the black male—whether enslaved or free, African or *criollo*—would subvert the power structure by taking possession of what were the rightful chattels of the white male. Such a salacious account sought to rationalize the destruction and dismemberment of the collective dark body, thus rendering the confession of ritual oaths impossible. The devastating effects of the racial purge on African descendants are without dispute. The full scope of the repression was breathtaking, and colonial authorities did not forfeit the opportunity to prosecute four thousand persons by military tribunal, ninety-eight of whom were condemned to die, six hundred that were imprisoned, and more than four hundred that were deported (Hall 58).[37] In effect, the colonial government wasted no time and left no stone unturned to determine the causes behind the conspiracy of the colored people. The government ventured that the destruction of the collective *black* body would ensure the perpetual safety of white colonists and make certain the tranquility and prosperity of the island.

The ritual initiations that José Amores conducted established an explicit correlation between the empowerment of the black male body and what Copeland has termed the lynching of the Christ. In theoretical terms, the initiatory rituals of José Amores and Fermin Gangá rescued bodies of African descent from the social periphery, were countersigns to the violence of objectification, and strengthened African-descendant religio-cultural notions of personhood. Effectively, sacred oaths cannot be administered without the presence of dark bodies, since it is the mouth that professes and the transcendental power embedded in the utterance that transforms wounded flesh. José Amores's initiation rite not only implies but also relies on the ritual sacrifice of the Christ figure. Speaking when the text is silent, my reconstruction of the counter-hegemonic theology of José Amores and Fermin Gangá renders the Eucharist black, transculturating Christ into Obatalá. Thus, the crucified Christ or Obatalá in the path of Oduduwa is identified with and joins in the uprising with other racialized bodies. Just as Christ surrenders his body to redeem a sinful humanity, so the collective black body (read *pardo* and mulatto as well) must be sacrificed so that redemption is achieved through revolution.

I read African and African-descendant bodies as palimpsests that bore multiple scars of colonial racial domination. The speech act's consecration of black bodies conveyed powers upon them, thus transforming them into repositories of sacred knowledge. The oath of fidelity, the Holy Eucharist, and the altar are the recurring symbols of religious normativity that at once evoke and negate the power of the church. Given the church's position as the monopolistic system of religious belief on the island, the appearance of Catholic rites and holy spaces was in no way an anomaly among African persons and their Cuban offspring. The transformative moment in the *Sentencia* is inextricably linked to the act of enunciation. For the African-descendant subject, the oath of retribution also pledges spiritual allegiance to a new ritual family within sacred space. Thus, the oath is a transculturated speech act, subverting and resignifying the ever-pervasive dogma of dominant society, to consecrate the dark body for revolution.

Notes

1. José Augusto Escoto Cuban History and Literature Collection (MS Span 52). Houghton Library, Harvard University.
2. A special thanks to Professors Sue Houchins and Baltasar Fra-Molinero for the myriad comments, suggestions, and insightful conversations with regards to an earlier draft of this chapter. I would also like to give much thanks to the Humanities Rock Stars Peer Writing Group at Bates College for reading my draft and helping me to rethink the presentations of my ideas.
3. Finch has reworked her dissertation into a book, *Rethinking Slave Rebellion in Cuba: La Escalera and the Insurgencies of 1841–1844*, to be published as part of the University of North Carolina Press's Envisioning Cuba series in the summer of 2015.
4. MS Span 52 (717), folder 2, Houghton Library, Harvard University. In the process of researching this project as well as prospective ones, I consulted manuscripts and archival materials at Harvard University and at the National Cuban Archive in Havana.
5. The following is an 1835 decree from Capitan General Miguel Tacón published in *Diario de la Habana*, concerning the censorship of all written references to religion or

the authority of the Spanish crown: Art. 16. En el inesperado caso de que cualquiera censor aprobare alguna obra que contenga contrarias á nuestra santa fé, buenas costumbres y las regalias de la corona, ó algun libelo infamatorio, calumnias o injurias contra algun cuerpo ó individuo ademas de perder su empleo sufrirá las penas impuestas por las leyes contra los fautores de esos delitos (sic).

Art. 16. In the unforeseen case that any censor approves any work that contains views contrary to our holy faith, good customs, and the royal regalia, or some defamatory statements, slander, or injury against a body or an individual, besides being dismissed from employment, shall also suffer the penalties imposed by law against those who committed these crimes.

6. In the appendix to the *Archaeology of Knowledge*, Michel Foucault writes: "In every society the production of discourse is at once controlled, selected, organized, and redistributed according to a certain number of procedures, whose value is to avert its powers and its dangers, to cope with chance events, to evade its ponderous awesome materiality" (216).

7. José Augusto Escoto Cuban History and Literature Collection (MS Span 52). Houghton Library, Harvard University.

8. Newspaper clippings of a Plácido biography written by his contemporary Sebastián Alfredo Morales can also be found in the José Augusto Escoto Collection at Houghton Library. In this biography, simply entitled *Plácido: El poeta*, Morales explains that the rigidity of colonial censorship made it a crime for the words *libertad* and *progreso* to appear in print. Ms Span 52 (552–60), Houghton Library, Harvard University.

9. For more on the concept of ritual poetics in diasporan contexts, please see Harrison, Walker II, and Edwards, eds., *Black Theatre: Ritual Performance in the African Diaspora*.

10. Historians and literary scholars alike have debated whether the 1844 Movement was a veridical event or merely a concoction of the colonial regime meant to justify wide-scale terrorism against the free population of color. Historian Robert Paquette examined this ongoing dispute among Cuban and North American scholars. After assessing voluminous testimony from the Military Commission, correspondence between involved parties, and a close study of the historiography concerning *La Conspiración de la Escalera* (The Ladder Conspiracy), as well as other forms of evidence, Paquette concluded that the conspiracy of *La Escalera* did indeed exist. His book states that this string of conspiracies was organized from 1841 to 1844 and was comprised of many autonomous yet related centers of seditious activity. The conspiracies and subsequent uprisings were led and executed by two distinct councils; one made up of white Cubans and another of both enslaved and free people of color. Additional support was provided (and later revoked) by certain elements of the British government (Paquette 263–64).

11. On June 23, 1844, the Spanish military government executed Gabriel de la Concepción Valdés (a.k.a. Plácido), Cuba's most prolific nineteenth-century poet, as the ringleader of a series of anti-colonial conspiracies and insurrections dispersed throughout the island. Among the most contentious figures in the history of early nineteenth-century Cuba, Plácido was born in 1809 to a Spanish mother and a quadroon father; his racial ancestry and widespread celebrity made him a convenient target for the pro-slavery colonial regime. Although he did not publish until 1836—more than ten years after Juan Francisco Manzano—he became the most prolific poet and renowned improvisator throughout the island (Horrego Estuch 71). No other Cuban poet, black or white, published more than Plácido in the nineteenth century.

Nwankwo consulted *La Sentencia pronunciada por la Sección de la Comision militar establecida en la ciudad de Matanzas para conocer la causa de conspiración de la gente de color* (sic) in the Archivo Nacional de Cuba: Asuntos Políticos, Legajo 42, No. 15 (Nwankwo 221).

12. For a cultural and literary history of blackness in the Luso-Hispanic world spanning the fifteenth to twenty-first century, please see Jerome Branche's groundbreaking book *Colonialism and Race in Luso-Hispanic Literature* (2006).

13. I have appropriated language used about the first battles of the American Revolution at Lexington and Concord for what I consider to be a far more suitable context. The thirteen colonies gained their independence from Great Britain in 1776, becoming the first nation in the western hemisphere to do so.

14. In Saint-Domingue enslaved persons and free people of color made up the overwhelming majority of the population, numbering 480,000, which dwarfed the colony's 40,000 white inhabitants. Naturally, this system of radical social inequality and brazen economic exploitation engendered a colonial environment where racial tensions ran high (Dubois 61).

15. José Augusto Escoto Cuban History and Literature Collection (MS Span 52). Houghton Library, Harvard University.

16. All translations are mine.

17. The white female character was elevated as the ideal feminine beauty and as an object of moral and aesthetic purity in Hispanic Renaissance poetry (Young 4).

18. José Augusto Escoto Cuban History and Literature Collection (MS Span 52). Houghton Library, Harvard University.

19. José Augusto Escoto Cuban History and Literature Collection (MS Span 52). Houghton Library, Harvard University.

20. In 1844, colonial authorities charged, prosecuted, and eventually executed Plácido for treason as the ringleader of a series of plantation uprisings that came to be known as *La Conspiración de la Escalera* (The Ladder Conspiracy). After he was put to death, Plácido came to be regarded as a paragon of anti-colonial fervor among people of color and as a traitor among whites who feared the power of black revolution on Cuban soil. Even in death, the colonial government's dread of Plácido lingered, so that it was forbidden to recite his poetry, consecrate his memory, or even speak his name (Paquette 265).

21. For more on Plácido's role in the 1844 Movement, please see Daisy Cué Fernández's *Plácido: El poeta conspirador* (2007) and Aisha Finch's *Rethinking Slave Rebellion in Cuba: La Escalera and the Insurgencies of 1841–1844* (2015).

22. Jorge Castellano's *Plácido, poeta social y político* (1984) and Daisy Cué Fernández's *Plácido: El poeta conspirador* (2007) examine the correlation between Plácido's lyrical voice and conspiratorial activity.

23. According to Spanish legal tradition, scribes were to record the full name, national origin, place of residence, age, occupation, marital status, and religious background of each witness, along with his or her sworn oath to tell the truth (Finch, "Insurgency at the Crossroads" 471).

24. The sentence against the town of Bainoa does not state explicitly that Fermin Gangá was African born. Indeed, in colonial Cuba some free persons of African descent used hispanicized African ethnonyms as identity markers. However, since the vast majority of enslaved persons on plantations were African born, the likelihood is high that Fermin Gangá was himself born on the African continent. Please see historian Manuel Moreno

Fraginals, "Africa in Cuba: A Quantitative Analysis of the African Population of Cuba" (1977).

25. José Augusto Escoto Cuban History and Literature Collection (MS Span 52). Houghton Library, Harvard University.

26. I generally use "enslaved person" to emphasize that the legal status of captive Africans and their descendants did not speak to the fullness of their collective or individual identities. The term "enslaved person" draws attention to the multiple acts of violence committed against the individual and the collective dark body that were physical, psychological, and juridical in nature. In this instance, I use "slave" in reference to colonial jurisprudence as portrayed in the *Sentencia*.

27. The judgment against Plácido reads that the mixed-race people (*pardos*) and free blacks (*morenos*) were said to have seduced one another to join the conspiracy. *Sentencia pronunciada por la Seccion de la Comison militar establecida en la ciudad de Matanzas para conocer de la causa de conspiracion de la gente de color* (sic). Colección Plácido, Oficina del Historiador de la Ciudad de la Habana. Courtesy of Eusebio Leal.

28. *Sentencia pronunciada por la Seccion de la Comison militar establecida en la ciudad de Matanzas para conocer de la causa de conspiracion de la gente de color* (sic). Colección Plácido, Oficina del Historiador de la Ciudad de la Habana. Courtesy of Eusebio Leal.

29. In the second sentence, Copeland cites page 142 from the work of Andrea Bieler and Luise Schottroff, *The Eucharist: Bodies, Bread and Resurrection*.

30. Please see the Catholic Church's catechism for enslaved Africans, entitled *Explicación de la doctrina cristiana acomodada a la capacidad de los negros bozales* (in Duque de Estrada).

31. In *Seeds of Insurrection: Domination and Resistance on Western Cuban Plantations, 1808–1848*, Manuel Barcia says that there is no evidence proving that the *gangá* belonged to a single African ethnic group or subgroup. There is more than one hypothesis pointing to the possible African cultural background of the *gangás*. Some scholars associate the group with the Gbangba River close to the border between Sierra Leone and Liberia, while others believe the denomination might derive from *Gangara*, an Arab word used to refer to the Mande (21).

32. José Augusto Escoto Cuban History and Literature Collection (MS Span 52). Houghton Library, Harvard University.

33. In *El Monte*, Lydia Cabrera says that in the 1880s in Marianao, *gangá* religiosity involved the playing of consecrated drums, the feeding of divine entities, and appropriate sacrifice to river spirits. Cabrera characterizes African-based spiritual practice in Marianao as religiously inclusive so that Yoruba, Congo, and *gangá* practitioners shared common ritual patterns and revered some of the same spirits (25).

34. Sandoval says that in the liturgical dance, Oduduwa does not possess the new initiate since he is far too powerful to reside in the human vessel (197).

35. José Augusto Escoto Cuban History and Literature Collection (MS Span 52). Houghton Library, Harvard University.

36. After charging Afro-Colombian General José Padilla with pretensions of provoking a race war, Simón Bolívar ordered his execution and decapitation in 1828. His head was displayed in public places, as a warning to other would-be rebels of African descent. Padilla was stripped of his military rank and sentenced to an inglorious death for a conspiracy he did not plan and murder he did not commit (Helg 462).

37. Africans and their descendants overwhelmingly suffered the brunt of colonial retribution. More people died from starvation, cruel beatings, and other tortuous forms of punishment than were executed, having a destructive effect on the overall size of free

and enslaved populations. The devastation was such that between 1841 and 1846 the number of enslaved persons sharply declined by nearly 100,000 persons from 436,495 to 326,759, while the free populace lost almost four thousand (Hall 59–60).

Works Cited

Agamben, Giorgio. *The Sacrament of Language*. Cambridge, UK: Polity, 2010.

Austin, J. L. *How to Do Things with Words*. 1962. New York: Oxford UP, 2009.

Barcia, Manuel. *Seeds of Insurrection: Domination and Resistance on Western Cuban Plantations, 1808–1848*. Baton Rouge: Louisiana State UP, 2008.

Basso Ortiz, Alessandra. *Los gangás en Cuba: La comunidad de Matanzas*. Havana: Fundación Fernando Ortiz, 2005.

———. "Los gangá longobá: El nacimiento de los dioses." *Boletín Antropológico* (2001): 195–208.

Bolívar, Natalia Aróstegui. *Los orishas en Cuba*. La Habana: Ediciones Unión, 1990.

Branche, Jerome. *Colonialism and Race in Luso-Hispanic Literature*. Columbia: U of Missouri P, 2006.

Cabrera, Lydia. *El Monte: Igbo finda ewe orisha vitti nfinda*. 1954. novena reedición ed. Miami: Ediciones Universal, 2006.

Castellanos, Jorge. *Plácido, poeta social y político*. Miami, FL: Ediciones Universal, 1984.

Childs, Matt D. *The 1812 Aponte Rebellion in Cuba and the Struggle Against Atlantic Slavery*. Chapel Hill: U of North Carolina P, 2006.

Colección Plácido, Oficina del Historiador de la Ciudad de la Habana. Courtesy of Eusebio Leal.

Copeland, M. Shawn. *Enfleshing Freedom: Body, Race and Being*. Nashville: Fortress, 2010.

Cué Fernández, Daisy A. *Plácido: El poeta conspirador*. Santiago de Cuba: Editorial Oriente, 2007.

Dodson, Jualynne. *Sacred Spaces and Religious Traditions in Oriente Cuba*. Albuquerque: U of New Mexico P, 2008.

Dubois, Laurent. *Avenger of the New World: The Story of the Haitian Revolution*. Cambridge: Belknap-Harvard UP, 2004.

Duque de Estrada, Nicolás. *Explicación de la doctrina cristiana acomodada a la capacidad de los negros bozales*. La Habana: Biblioteca Nacional José Martí, 2006.

Estepa Llaurens, José Manuel. *Catecismo de la iglesia católica*. New York: William H. Sadlier, 1992.

Finch, Aisha. "Insurgency at the Crossroads: Cuban Slaves and the Conspiracy of 1844." Diss. New York: NYU, 2007.

———. *Rethinking Slave Rebellion in Cuba: La Escalera and the Insurgencies of 1841–1844*. Chapel Hill: University of North Carolina Press, 2015.

Foucault, Michel. *The Archeology of Knowledge*. New York: Pantheon, 1972.

Fraginals, Manuel Moreno. "Africa in Cuba: A Quantitative Analysis of the African Population of Cuba." *Annals of the New York Academy of Sciences* (1977): 292.

Guanche, Jesús. *Africanía y etnicidad en Cuba: (Los components étnicos africanos y sus multiples denominaciones)*. Havana: Ed. Ciencias Sociales, 2009.

Hall, Gwendolyn Midlo. *Social Control in Slave Plantation Societies: A Comparison of St. Domingue and Cuba*. Baltimore: John Hopkins, 1971.

Harrison, Paul Carter, Victor Leo Walker II, and Gus Edwards, eds. *Black Theatre: Ritual Performance in the African Diaspora*. Philadelphia: Temple UP, 2002.

Helg, Aline. "Simón Bolívar and the Spectre Of 'Pardocracia': José Padilla in Post-Independence Cartagena." *Journal of Latin American Studies* 35.3 (2003): 447–71.

Horrego Estuch, Leopoldo. *Plácido: El poeta infortunado.* La Habana: Talleres Tipográficos de Editorial Lex. Amargura, 1960.

José Augusto Escoto Cuban History and Literature Collection (MS Span 52). Houghton Library, Harvard University.

Lachatañeré, Rómulo. *El sistema religioso de los afrocubanos.* La Habana: Editorial de Ciencias Sociales, 2001.

Landers, Jane. *Atlantic Creoles in the Age of Revolutions.* Cambridge: Harvard UP, 2010.

Palmié, Stephan. *Wizards and Scientists: Explorations in Afro-Cuban Modernity and Tradition.* Durham: Duke UP, 2002.

Paquette, Robert. *Sugar Is Made with Blood: The Conspiracy of La Escalera and the Conflict between Empires over Slavery in Cuba.* Middletown: Wesleyan UP, 1988.

Pratt, Mary Louise. *Imperial Eyes: Travel Writing and Transculturation.* London: Routledge, 1992.

Sandoval, Mercedes Cros. *Worldview, the Orichas, and Santería: Africa to Cuba and Beyond.* Gainesville: UP of Florida, 2006.

Thornton, John. "African Soldiers in the Haitian Revolution." *Journal of Caribbean History* 25.1 and 2 (1991): 58–79.

Trouillot, Michel-Rolph. *Silencing the Past: Power and the Production of History.* Boston: Beacon, 1995.

Young, Ann Venture. *The Image of Black Women in Twentieth Century South American Poetry.* Washington, DC: Three Continents, 1987.

2

Seeking Acceptance from the Society and the State

Poems from Cuba's Black Press, 1882-1889

Marveta Ryan

Throughout the colonial period, Cubans of African descent struggled to end slavery and to claim their human and civil rights. Besides engaging in various forms of resistance, they sometimes took up arms. There were numerous local slave rebellions throughout the first half of the nineteenth century. Also, slaves on multiple plantations collaborated with free people of color and with sympathetic whites to carry out three major uprisings, in 1811 in Puerto Príncipe and Oriente (led by José Aponte), and in 1825 and 1843 in Matanzas. During the Ten Years' War of 1868 to 1878, enslaved and free blacks and mulatos led, served, and fought alongside white Creoles for the independence of Cuba and the abolition of slavery. This war ended with the Pact of Zanjón, which granted freedom only to slaves who had officially served in the insurgent Cuban army. This incomplete emancipation prompted even heavier participation of blacks and mulatos in the Little War, that is, the insurrection of 1879 to 1880. These wars and other political and economic factors weakened the institution of slavery such that a series of laws gradually abolished it by 1886. Yet, the community of color continued to experience severe discrimination. Furthermore, some whites falsely accused Afro-Cubans of wanting to start a war against whites in Cuba reminiscent of the Haitian Revolution (Ferrer 112).

In response to these indignities, the community of color organized itself and struggled against discrimination and for full integration into Cuban society, this time more with the pen than with the sword. The 1880s and the early 1890s saw remarkable activity among Afro-Cubans: they vigorously established new mutual aid societies, recreation centers, and schools. 1887 brought the founding of an Afro-

33

Cuban umbrella organization called the Directorio Central de Sociedades de la Raza de Color, which coordinated legal efforts against discriminatory laws and practices. Furthermore, thanks to an 1886 law that allowed for more freedom of the press and expression of pro-independence ideas, Afro-Cubans began to publish newsletters, newspapers, and magazines. Many of these publications were affiliated with organizations and societies throughout the island, but there were also influential black newspapers based in Havana like *La Fraternidad* and *La Igualdad*. Historian Ada Ferrer points out that the increase in Afro-Cuban periodicals was part of a "minor publishing boom" in Havana after the 1886 law (113). She also notes that articles from major black publications "were sometimes reprinted or summarized" in more mainstream periodicals and vice versa so that black writing was "not isolated from the national or colonial press" (129). Afro-Cuban journalists appropriated print culture to contest the marginalizing power of the "lettered city" and to envision a Cuba that included them (Chasteen xi, Rama 53). In the decade before the final war for independence (1895–1898), Afro-Cubans employed organization, litigation, and publication to seek equality and acceptance as full citizens.

In serial publications led by journalists and activists of color in the 1880s, we find writings by blacks and mulatos and by whites sympathetic to their cause. These writings conveyed a rather consistent message about the aims and values of the leaders of the Afro-Cuban community. In their publications, they constantly emphasized the need for people of color to get an education, while the organizations and the Directorio Central worked to establish schools and to pressure the government to provide access to public schools for Afro-Cuban children. The black publications also exhorted people of color to be hardworking and respectable, to marry by law, and to lay aside African cultural practices—namely music, dance, and religion— which were often condemned and persecuted under Spanish rule. These literate leaders generally believed that Afro-Cubans needed to adopt the customs and mores of the dominant whites in order to prove that people of color deserved equal rights (Helg 31–33). While the black press tended to express rather uniform political, social, and cultural ideas, these writings also reveal a textured discourse about the relationships of people of color to each other, to white people, to the law, and to the colonial state, both on the island and in Spain.

This present study focuses on the ways that poetry served as a vehicle for public discourse about race, culture, politics, and nation in Cuba in the 1880s. One of the starting points for this essay is the fact that, over the last twenty years, many scholars have addressed the role of prose works (particularly novels and short stories) in the nineteenth-century formation of Latin American nations. Many of these scholars have begun with Benedict Anderson's premise in *Imagined Communities* that the novel and the newspaper were the media that "provided the technical means for 're-presenting' the kind of imagined community that is the nation" (25). Yet, relatively few critics have examined the role of poetry in the nation-constructing process in Hispanic America. One of my aims here is to consider questions left open by Anderson: How did poetry grow into the age of print-capitalism and nationalism? Were there ways in which poetry encouraged people to imagine themselves as part of a community?

The newspapers of the Afro-Cuban press in the 1880s provide a perfect source for examining how people of African descent and their allies constructed an image of their own racially-bounded community, described their community's interactions with the state and with the society at large, and envisioned a desired nation. This study consists of a close and contextualized reading of seven poems published in Cuba in the 1880s, all but one of them in well-known Afro-Cuban serials.[1] I note how the poems are themselves performances of the Eurocentric Hispanic culture to which the Afro-Cuban elite aspired. I also identify a web of themes and strategies that appear in many of the poems and in the black press in general. These themes and strategies, I argue, speak both to whites and Cubans of color, exposing the hypocrisy of racists and creating a positive image of people of color; these poems also try to convince Afro-Cubans themselves to adopt certain values, attitudes, and opinions, all with the purpose of facilitating social integration.

The poem "A la raza de color (en la apertura del círculo de recreo Cervantes)" ("To the colored race [upon the opening of the Cervantes Recreational Center]") was penned by Antonio Rosales and appeared in a book of his poetry published in 1882, shortly after the Little War and before slavery had been fully abolished. The poem celebrates the opening of a center of recreation and instruction for people of color, and thus it testifies to a trend in the years after the first two wars: the establishment of new organizations that published newspapers about their aims and provided mutual aid and education for Afro-Cubans regardless of their African ethnic heritage.

The backstory of the poem is not altogether clear. I have not yet found evidence that the poem appeared in any Afro-Cuban serial; therefore, the poem stands on the margins of the black press. Information about the author raises some intriguing questions. According to the *Diccionario de la literatura cubana*, Antonio Rosales Morera was born in 1844 in the town of Santa Clara, and he died there in 1902 (927). (Santa Clara is located in the province east of Havana and Matanzas that in 1878 was also called Santa Clara but is now called Villa Clara.) Rosales Morera worked as an artisan but also excelled in literature. By 1870 some of his poems had gained recognition, and he contributed to newspapers in his province. Between 1872 and 1883, he published four books of poetry and prose and a comedy (928). The poem under study here is from his third book, *Páginas literarias: Escritas en prosa y verso* (Literary Pages: Written in Prose and Verse), published in 1882 in the town of Sagua la Grande and in Villa Clara province. Although I have not been able to conclusively identify the center described in the poem, given the poet's close connection with that region, the Círculo de Recreo Cervantes of Rosales's poem could be the Afro-Cuban society called Gran Cervantes, founded in 1879 and listed under Villa Clara in Carmen Montejo Arrechea's book on Afro-Cuban societies (*Sociedades* 124).

Just as intriguing is that none of the sources consulted identified Antonio Rosales Morera as being a person of color. In fact, judging by a photograph of him that appears on an Internet blog about Sagua la Grande, one might conclude that he was white ("Antonio Rosales Morera"). Still the *Diccionario de la literatura cubana* notes that Rosales Morera was very much involved in the revolutionary cause. He fought for or at least supported independence in the Ten Years' War. Apparently Rosales Morera was exiled to Spain for more than two years. In Madrid in 1874 he published a book titled *Los mambises* (The Revolutionaries). It would be interesting to learn how involved he was with Afro-Cuban organizations in his region and to what extent the members of those groups supported independence.

Rosales Morera's poem "A la raza de color (en la apertura del círculo de recreo Cervantes)" seems to have been written for a specific occasion, yet the poem addresses all blacks in a very optimistic and encouraging tone:

Raza viril que del común concierto	Virile race that for long years
alejada te tuvo luengos años,	an abominable fate had you,
con mengua del derecho, suerte infanda;	with a poverty of rights,
á la voz del Progreso, que condena	distanced from the common accord;
la ociosidad, destroza tu cadena,	to the voice of Progress, which condemns idleness,
y levántate y anda.	break your chain into pieces,
	and stand up and walk.
En tu nublado cielo	In your clouded sky,
iris de dicha osténtase brillante	a rainbow of joy brilliantly manifests itself
y puedes ya en palabras	and now you can translate into words
traducir tus hermosos pensamientos,	your beautiful thoughts,
conceptos emitir de la conciencia	and emit concepts of conscience
y aspirar á los lauros de la ciencia	and aspire to the laurels of science
y del arte y los útiles inventos.	and of art and of useful inventions.
De verte exenta de fatal desgracia	Seeing you exempt from that fatal disgrace,
el mundo aplaude ufano	the world applauds proud and content;
y gozosa, con estro soberano,	with unrivaled inspiration,
canta á tu redención la Democracia.	Democracy sings to your redemption.
Cuando la dulce libertad redime	When sweet liberty redeems the human name
de oprobioso baldón el nombre humano,	from shameful reproach,
para ensalzarla dá Naturaleza,	to praise her, Nature, radiant with beauty,
radiante de belleza,	gives talent to the bird,
génio al ave, a la planta, al Océano. (1–22)	to the plant, to the Ocean. (Rosales Morera 20–21)

The poem links enslavement with a lack of education and intellectual development, and links a new access to education with an end to enslavement and its effects. In the first stanza, the *suerte infanda* is associated with long years and with a dearth of rights, which seems to refer to the legal status of being enslaved and marginalized ("del común concierto alejada"). The third stanza refers to redemption from slavery into freedom, using the terms *redención* and *libertad*, which are often associated in this era with personal emancipation and with the abolition of slavery. Phrases like "exempt from that fatal disgrace" and "redeems . . . from shameful reproach" suggest that the race is no longer in a position of disfavor, misfortune, and shame.

Sandwiched between these references to slavery and freedom we find the end of the first stanza and the whole of the second stanza. The "abominable fate" of slavery did hold the race for many years, but now the speaker urges the race to break its own chains, to stand up and walk. These three actions would allow the race of color to destroy the immobilizing effects of enslavement, effects that can be interpreted as imposed by the institution and/or developed as internal attitudes. The second stanza begins with an image of a new and happy situation, and the words "puedes ya" (now you can) indicate that a state of intellectual disability has ended. Now the race can—is capable and/or free to—express its thoughts and aspire to greater knowledge and creativity. In a sense, then, these three stanzas seem to place intellectual freedom and ability alongside social and legal freedom; in other words, the poem suggests that the race is free or can be free from enslavement and its effects because the race can now grow intellectually.

The preterit verb "tuvo" (it had) in the first stanza suggests that the bondage and the marginalization of the colored race had, in fact, come to an end. This seems to be an overly optimistic characterization of the status of most Cubans of color at that time. If the poem was written before 1880, the Moret Law of 1870 was still in effect. That law was supposed to have freed the children born to slave mothers, slaves over the age of 60, those who had served or fought for Spain during the Ten Years' War, and slaves not listed on the 1871 slave census, as well as those confiscated from rebels and those found on captured slave ships (Howard 119–120; Scott 63–73). Historian Rebecca Scott points out, however, that many persons in these categories were granted nominal emancipation but faced obstacles in obtaining real freedom; in reality, the law "reduced the total number of slaves but freed relatively few slaves of working age" (73). The situation was not much better in 1882 when this poem was published. A law of January 1880 had established the *patronato*, "an intermediate status between slave and free" (127). The law made slave owners into *patronos* and converted slaves into *patrocinados* who were still obliged to work for their masters, albeit with a legal right to receive from the *patrono* a small monthly stipend and certain other benefits. The law did provide for a gradual emancipation of all *patrocinados* over a period of eight years. In suggesting that slavery and marginalization had ended, this poem (presumably written between 1879 and 1882) seems to be calling things that are not as if they already were. This is one way that the poem disregards or transcends the actual situation in Cuba at the time.

The fourth stanza twice assures the race that *Tienes nombre*, which could be read as "You have worth or potential or reputation." The stanza makes clear the link between the social and intellectual situation of the race: that slavery left on the intellect of the enslaved a roughness that can only be polished away through instruction.

Tienes nombre: mas llevan todavía	You have worth: but still
tu ingenio y tu criterio	your creative ability and your judgment
la corteza del rudo cautiverio	carry the coarseness of the rude captivity
que tu vida de mártir oprimía.	that oppressed your martyr's life.
Tienes nombre: mas te hallas en la infancia	You have potential: but you find yourself
de tu nuevo existir. Sólo el estudio,	in the infancy of your new existence.
gérmen de fama y perdurable gloria,	Only study, the seed of fame and lasting glory,
confunde la ignorancia	confounds ignorance
y hace á los hombres dignos de la Historia.	and makes men worthy of History.
Así como el diamante á la influencia	Just as the diamond, by the influence
de duro pulimento	of hard polishing
multiplica su bella trasparencia,	multiplies its beautiful transparency,
y semejan sus claras superficies	and its clear surfaces become
ondas de luz ó ráfagas del día;	like waves of light or flashes of day;
así al gran pulimento provechoso	so through the great beneficial polishing
de la noble enseñanza,	of noble teaching,
la inteligencia aumenta su valía	intelligence increases its value
y los laureles del saber alcanza. (23–40)	and achieves the laurels of knowledge.

(Rosales Morera 21)

The next stanza notes that the race will have to make great efforts to overcome the overwhelming cognitive effects of slavery. Echoing the first stanza's mention of a laziness condemned by Progress, the next stanza exhorts the race to let go of cognitive sluggishness and inactivity, which could be interpreted as an anti-intellectual attitude or simply as mental slowness from lack of education.

Depon la torpe inercia que tu inmortal espíritu avasalla, y con heróico aliento, porque el mundo te deba beneficios, contra la triste oscuridad batalla en que perdido está tu entendimiento.	Set aside the awkward inertia that subjugates your immortal spirit, and with heroic courage, so that the world may owe you benefits, battle against the sad darkness in which your understanding is lost.
Haz porque surjan de tu seno, ¡oh Raza! seres que ilustren sabias academias, tribunas y ateneos, y así como han brotado de tus entrañas ínclitos artistas y vates inmortales que coronan y aclaman los liceos, que broten Galileos y Spinosas y Krauses y Pascales. (41–55)	Make it so that from your bosom, Oh Race!, surge beings that enlighten learned academies, rostrums and cultural associations, and just as have already sprouted from your bowels renowned artists and immortal bards that the literary societies crown and acclaim, may there emerge Galileos and Spinozas and Krauses and Pascales. (Rosales Morera 21–22)

The speaker in the poem sets high expectations for the race. One line suggests that the world will owe the race benefits or favors once they have gained education, as if knowledge were a condition for certain unnamed social perquisites. The poem likely refers here to Blaise Pascal (1623–1662), a French physicist, mathematician, and philosopher; to the Jewish Dutch philosopher Baruch de Spinoza (1632–1677); and to the German philosopher Karl Christian Friedrich Krause (1781–1832). While it is not surprising that great European intellectuals are held up as models, it is worth noting that the poem acknowledges famous artists and poets of African descent, but now expects the race to produce other kinds of thinkers, those who work more with science and philosophy.

The poem proceeds to emphasize the need for moral behavior, which the speaker says is just as important as education and will elevate the race in the eyes of society. The Cato mentioned here is likely the *Distichs of Cato*, a book of morality proverbs written in Latin in the third or fourth century A.D. It was employed as a textbook for teaching Latin language and ethical behavior all over the Western world. (Benjamin Franklin printed a translation of it.)

A par de la instrucción que civiliza atiende á la moral. En tus costumbres de Catón los ejemplos entroniza. . . . (sic) el fruto de tal norma bendecido, será verte elevada desde el oscuro abismo de la nada, á la cumbre del nombre esclarecido. (56–62)	Equal with instruction which civilizes attend to morality. In your customs enthrone the examples of Cato. . . . the fruit of such a blessed norm will be to see you elevated from the obscure abyss of nothingness, to the summit of noble reputation. (Rosales Morera 22)

The mention of a "blessed norm" gives way to another religiously inflected metaphor, this time having to do with women:

Tus cándidas mujeres
de la fecunda educación reciban
la gracia del bautismo;
y en sus almas humanas
anidarán virtudes que recuerden
las matronas romanas.
¡Ah! cuando yace la mujer perdida
para el honor y su beldad exhibe
por agradar tan solo, envilecida
está la sociedad en que ella vive.
¡Que nunca á condición tan deshonrosa
sometan á tus bellas las pasiones!
¡Que trillen senda hermosa!
¡Que forme la moral sus corazones!
Sea este Centro de Unión y de Recreo,
que tu entusiasmo por la luz revela,
para la infancia educadora escuela,
para la juventud culto ateneo. (63–80)

May your innocent women receive
The grace of baptism
Into fertile education;
and in their humane souls
will reside virtues reminiscent
of the Roman matrons.
Ah! When the woman lies lost
to honor and exhibits her beauty
solely to please, the society
in which she lives is itself debased.
May passions never submit your beautiful ones
to such a shameful condition!
May they tread a lovely path!
May morality form their hearts!
May this Center of Union and Recreation,
that your enthusiasm for enlightenment reveals,
be for the children an educational school,
and for the youth a cultured athenaeum.
(Rosales Morera 22)

While the poem mentions the education of women, the speaker dwells more on protecting the honor and cultivating the morality of women of color for the good of society.

The next stanza exhorts the race to leave behind certain pleasurable activities that the speaker associates with slavery.

Si ayer en torpe y enervante holganza
permaneció tu espíritu, encantado
al armonioso ritmos de la danza
ó á frívolo deliquio encadenado;
Hoy que no llevas en tu frente impreso
signo afrentoso ni punzante espino,
te llama á otro camino
el estentóreo acento del Progreso. (81–88)

If yesterday in unchaste and enervating
diversion
your spirit remained enchanted
by the harmonious rhythms of dance
or chained to frivolous ecstasy;
today, now that you no longer carry
impressed on your forehead an ignominious
sign
nor a sharp thorn, the stentorian accent of
Progress calls you to another path. (Rosales
Morera 23)

Though the speaker does not specify the "rhythms of dance" as being specifically African, there is that implication. Some of the words in this stanza have various connotations, many of which are negative. *Holganza* can be translated as "idleness" or "repose" or "amusement," "diversion," or "entertainment." *Torpe* can connote "clumsy," "dim-witted," "awkward," "dull," "stupid," or even "unchaste," "lascivious," or "obscene." *Enervante* can mean "physically draining" or "debilitating" or "exasperating." *Deliquio* is defined as "swoon," "fainting fit," or "ecstasy." With this word choice, the stanza seems to suggest that participation in the dances that people

of color engaged in during slavery was a waste of energy at best, or lewd and immoral at worst. The poem suggests that the dances had too much power over the
minds of the dancers, that the dance enchanted, bewitched, and chained their practitioners and caused them to fall into fits of fainting or ecstasy. Could it be that the
poet here is alluding to certain ecstatic aspects of African religious practice? And
what of the "ignominious sign" and "sharp thorn," which at once signify the shame
of slavery and allude to the mocking of Christ at the crucifixion? Could this choice
of words be a way of claiming the race for a Christian paradigm, rhetorically rescu-
ing the race from African religion?

The final stanzas reiterate the idea that the world expects great things from the
colored race. Again, great minds of Western culture are proposed as examples of what
the race can achieve. Fidias may be Phidias (Pheidias) (ca. 480–430 B.C.), ancient
Greek sculptor and architect. Franklin is likely the American thinker, scientist, and
leader Benjamin Franklin (1706–1790). Reference is also made to French mathematician and philosopher René Descartes (1596–1650). It is not clear who or what Urbino
might be.[2]

Pendiente está de tu actitud el mundo
y acaricia la mágica esperanza
de que obtengan de tí las bellas artes
y las ciencias, el brillo peregrino
que obtuvieron de Fidias y de Urbino,
de Franklin y Descartes.

¡El siglo te comtempla! Fervorosa
consagra tu misión, y haz porque sea
este Centro de Unión y de Recreo,
que tu entusiasmo por la luz revela,
para la infancia educadora escuela,
para la juventud culto ateneo. (89–100)

The world is watching your attitude,
and it caresses the magical hope
that the fine arts and the sciences may
obtain from you the extraordinary brilliance
they obtained from Phidias and Urbino,
from Franklin and Descartes.

The century looks upon you! Fervently
consecrate your mission, and make of this
Center of Union and Recreation,
revealed by your enthusiasm for
enlightenment,
an educating school for the children,
for the youths a cultured athenaeum. (Rosales
Morera 23)

This poem takes the opening of one recreational and educational center in Cuba and,
with an almost hyperbolic tone, raises the event far above its own historical and geographical circumstances. Rather than addressing the members of the Afro-Cuban community in the area where the center opened, the poem directs itself to the whole race
of color. There is no mention of Cuba in the poem at all; the speaker puts the race on
a world stage. Although a slow process of abolition had begun in Cuba in 1870, full
emancipation did not occur until 1886, four years after the publication of this poem.
Yet, the poem not only speaks of abolition as a fait accompli, but it also suggests that
the race had achieved equal and adequate access to civil rights and to educational opportunity, another condition that was very long coming. It is as if the poem is directed
not only at Afro-Cubans of that time and place, but also at a whole race of enslaved and
formerly enslaved people in the Americas during what critic Monique-Adelle Callahan
calls the "abolition eras" (4). The disconnection between the language of the poem and

the social reality of Cuba at the time of writing can be read as a performance of profound hope or expectation that the "race of color" would indeed achieve complete freedom, mainly through its own action. The poem also expresses a faith that "the world" observing the race already celebrates the race's newfound freedom and will duly reward the race's achievements.

"A la raza de color" leaves out any mention of the Cuban whites who were holding people of color in bondage, nor does it note that racial discrimination and governmental neglect were primary reasons for the emergence of schools for people of color, like the one praised in the poem. Slave owners generally did not educate their slaves, and the laws in effect in Cuba until 1878 did not allow even free people of color to be educated beyond the elementary level (Montejo Arrechea, "Minerva" 39). In 1878, the government responded to some of the demands of the Afro-Cuban community by decreeing that children of color should be given free education and that youths of color were to be admitted to secondary and professional schools and to the university (Hevia Lanier 8, Helg 36). The following year, Cuba's governor issued a circular urging municipalities to provide education for colored children. However, these governmental wishes were of little effect. In 1878 the island only had 712 schools, 418 of which were public and the rest private, and the government contributed only about 20 percent of the money needed to maintain both types of schools (Howard 140).

In 1880, the Spanish government instituted the Ley Escolar y Plan de Estudios, which gave local governments in Cuba the responsibility of administrating their own education system. The law required or authorized each municipality to build a separate public primary school for Afro-Cuban children (Howard 141, Helg 37). The law also charged the civil and religious leaders with trying to convince *patronos* to give their *patrocinados* the religious instruction required by the 1880 law of *patronato*. Though the number of public schools did increase (to about 904 in 1895), many municipalities still did not have a school at all; and many public schools refused to admit Afro-Cuban children or demanded that they pay a special fee (Helg 37). In response, many Afro-Cuban *cabildos* and societies began after the Ten Years' War to open small elementary schools for their members. When the Directorio Central was founded in 1887, one of its main priorities was to gain for Afro-Cubans equal access to education. A census from that year showed that only 12 percent of people of color could read or write, compared to about 35 percent of Cuban whites (Ferrer 116). Only in 1893 did the Governor General rule, in response to pressure from some black residents of Havana, that all elementary schools should be desegregated. Still, some local school administrators refused to comply. By providing schools for their people, Afro-Cuban societies exhibited the self-reliance implied in the poem. By calling on the state to provide access to education, these organizations displayed a civic engagement not described in the poem.

The poem may be silent about the social conditions of the time, but some of its points became prominent issues of discussion in Afro-Cuban publications. For one, the black press constantly urged Afro-Cuban people to seek instruction. The poem's admonition to educate women was put into action by some of the Afro-Cuban societies. Philip Howard describes the society Las Hijas del Progreso, founded in Cienfuegos in 1884; it was directed mainly by women and offered girls vocational training. The education of women was repeatedly promoted in *Minerva* (1888–1889), a periodical dedicated to women of color (Montejo Arrechea, "Minerva" 37–38).

The admonition to forsake dance, particularly African dance and other African practices in favor of more European-oriented activities, was also treated at various times in the black press. In 1893 two readers of the Afro-Cuban newspaper *La Igualdad* lamented that during the carnival many people of color had dressed up as poor and enslaved blacks (Helg 31). The prominent *mulato* journalist Martín Morúa Delgado wrote that the use of certain musical instruments in holiday celebrations should be eliminated because they made people of color seem uncivilized and unworthy of respect. Morúa Delgado also called on Afro-Cubans to live morally and to avoid vices, including gambling, stating that "An immoral people, a perverted people can never be free" (Howard 167, his translation). Oilda Hevia Lanier points out that many of these publications were penned by well-educated persons of color who adopted white cultural and moral norms; she suggests that this elite group may have written so much about this cultural issue precisely because many of the people of color were less interested in abandoning familiar African-derived customs (33). These repeated exhortations to the colored community in the Afro-Cuban press were an effort to redefine the group, to ascribe to it cultural and ethical characteristics acceptable to white society. At the end of the nineteenth century and for some years hence, this rhetorical effort seems to have failed to convince all Afro-Cubans to adopt exclusively white culture in order to persuade racist whites to grant them full equality. Helg writes:

> Full participation was, in fact, impossible. However much Afro-Cubans assumed the religious beliefs, history, literature, music, dress, public behavior, and recreational forms of Spaniards and Spanish Cubans, they still faced discrimination in many ways. In addition, Afro-Cuban loyalty toward white society was constantly questioned. Thus, those seeking assimilation or claiming full participation had to deny their African heritage. . . . As a result, numerous Afro-Cubans opted for partial integration: they conducted most of their public life in mainstream, partly segregated society, and their private life in an Afro-Cuban subculture permitting unlimited participation. (33)

In 1879 renowned mulato journalist, educator, and activist Juan Gualberto Gómez founded the newspaper *La Fraternidad* in Havana. Its original motto was "Paz, justicia, fraternidad" (Peace, justice, and brotherhood), but after the 1886 law allowed for more freedom of political expression, the newspaper described itself as "Periódico político independiente. Consagrado a la defensa de los intereses generales de la raza de color" (An independent political newspaper. Dedicated to the general interests of the race of color) (Deschamps 54–56). *La Fraternidad* regularly published information about the activities of the Directorio Central (Hevia Lanier 23). The following poem by H. V. Peña appeared in its pages on August 21, 1888, just two years after slavery had been abolished in Cuba. Unfortunately, I have not yet found any information about the poem's author.

A la raza negra	To the Black Race

A la raza negra
   Ellos, los que levantan su protesta
contra la explotadora tiranía,
se erigen en soberbia oligarquía
con altivo desdén y frente enhiesta.
   Son los amos de ayer, y les molesta
que el negro, con la voz severa y fría
de la razón, les hable de armonía,
dándole la callada por respuesta.

   Lo dicen ellos: el dominio acaba
y todo privilegio al fin agota
cuando del pueblo la verdad se graba.
   Ellos os han trazado la derrota:
redima la instrucción la mente esclava
y cumplid los deberes del patriota. (1–14)

To the Black Race
   They, the ones that raise their protest
against exploitative tyranny,
set themselves up in arrogant oligarchy
with haughty disdain and an erect forehead.
   They're yesterday's masters, and it bothers them
that the black man, with the cold and severe
voice of reason, speaks to them of harmony,
giving him silence in response.

   They say it themselves: dominion
ends and all privilege finally runs out
when the truth of the people is recorded.
   They have traced for you the course and defeat:
let instruction redeem the enslaved mind,
and you, fulfill the duties of the patriot. (Peña 4)

The poem's title is interesting; Aline Helg notes that in Cuba the term *raza de color* did not differentiate mulatos from blacks, and the term *negros* has often referred to both *pardos* (*mulatos*) and blacks (*morenos*) (3). As a sonnet, the poem demonstrates a mastery of a traditional European form. Yet, its simple, direct language and its political theme distinguish it from the more lyrical nature of the most famous sonnets. As we shall see, even with such everyday language, the poem efficiently generates multiple meanings.

   Like the newspaper, Peña's poem fully engages in a current public discourse about race, culture, and nation. This poem repeatedly points to *ellos*, a certain group of white Cubans. The first and second stanzas outline the layers of power: white Cubans who were formerly *amos* (slave owners) protest the oppression of Spanish rule over them, while they continue to exercise their oligarchic power to marginalize and discriminate against the island's now emancipated blacks. The text might very well refer to either the Liberal or Autonomist Party or to the Constitutional Union party. The Autonomist Party was one of the first parties organized after the war in 1878, and it attracted island whites from various social groups, from peninsular Spaniards to a few former insurrectionists. The Autonomists advocated Cubans having political equality with citizens of Spain, unlimited immigration of Europeans, and no immigration of non-white peoples. They favored a gradual end to slavery and constraints on the labor of free people of color. After 1886, this party still thought of Afro-Cubans as inferior and endeavored to keep them from participating in politics (Howard 128, 175). The conservative, pro-Spanish Constitutional Union Party was made up of wealthy peninsular planters, businessmen, and government officials. This party controlled political power on the island. Unionists held equally racist views toward Cubans of color, while they sought for themselves equality with Spanish citizens (Howard 128, 175; Helg 43). The poem contrasts the proud and dismissive attitude of the whites with the "cold and severe voice of reason" with which the black person speaks to the whites of "harmony." The contrast underscores the hypocrisy of whites who want Spaniards to hear and engage with them but who refuse to enter into dialogue with people of color.

The third and fourth stanzas suggest more than explain, thus inviting the reader to interpret the text and act accordingly. The third stanza points out what seems to be a maxim that "they" apparently use to tout the undeniable justice and imminent victory of their cause. In other words, some Cuban whites designate themselves as "the people" and expect their "truth" to be able to end Spanish rule over them. The poem may prompt the reader to ask, Can the race of color also represent "the people," and is its cause not also the "truth" that can end the whites' discrimination against them? The third stanza subtly implies that the Cuban blacks can use the whites' tools of protest against them. The next line, "Ellos os han trazado la derrota," is perhaps the most poetic of the text, as *la derrota* has two definitions: it can mean "defeat," and it can signify "route," particularly the route of a ship. With this double entendre, the line encapsulates other messages insinuated in previous lines: that Cuban whites have plans to overwhelm Afro-Cubans and keep them in a subordinate position, while at the same time, whites are seen as a model for blacks, culturally, politically, and economically. In that sense, whites have "traced a route" for blacks to follow in order to achieve equality.

The next line indicates that one aspect of that route is education. The line "Let instruction redeem the enslaved mind" echoes the exhortation in Rosales Morera's poem that Afro-Cubans study and thereby eradicate the ignorance and dullness that slavery had forced upon them. However, the term *mente esclava* (enslaved mind) here might also connote an attitude of inferiority, servility, and dependence with respect to whites in positions of authority. The final exhortation to "fulfill the duties of the patriot" is wide open in terms of what kinds of action constitute those duties, but the key word is "patriot"—any and all action must be taken out of love for the fatherland and for the good of the nation. In a newspaper that promoted Cuban independence, this poem pithily sums up the political situation, identifies racist whites as an obstacle to Afro-Cuban interests, and appropriates the whites' political strategy of continuing to make the people's truth heard. The poem also redefines the people of color, transforming them from slaves into the builders of a nation based on racial harmony.

The following month, in the September 10, 1888, issue, *La Fraternidad* printed another poem directed at readers of color: "A algunos de mis hermanos de raza" ("To Some of My Brothers by Race") by Vicente Silveira Arjona.

According to a 1921 biography, Silveira Arjona was born in 1841 in Guanajay, in the westernmost province of Pinar del Rio. Silveira Arjona began to write at an early age. He published a book of poems and comic drama, edited and founded two periodicals, and wrote regularly for *La Fraternidad* and other publications of the black press (Guerra 15–17). One of Silveira Arjona's contemporaries described him as being a respectful black man who, although resigned to the inferior social position imposed on him, still struggled for justice and improvement for himself and his race (18). In this poem, Silveira Arjona demonstrates a mastery of form and employs various rhetorical strategies to convince his readers to adopt a certain attitude toward racist whites:

A algunos de mis hermanos de raza	To Some of My Brothers by Race

Recuerdo que leí cuant [illegible word]
Que á su Maestro un Príncipe pagando
Con ódios cruel e insano
Recompensaba el paternal cariño.
Pero el sábio Maestro le decía:
—Te amo, Príncipe, gozo en enseñarte
Y, a fuerzas de yo amarte,
Has de amarme también, por vida mía.—
(1–8)

I remember that I read . . .
That a Prince was repaying
His Teacher's fatherly affection with
Hatred, cruel and unbalanced.
But the wise Teacher was saying to him:
"I love you, Prince, I enjoy teaching you
And, since I love you,
You have to love me, too, for my life's sake."
(Silveira Arjona 3)

These first few stanzas allegorically cast the whites as the prince, cruelly wielding power, and the people of color as the teacher, whose superior knowledge, wisdom, and moral authority counter the prince's higher social status.

Contra el odio el amor! Es el sistema
Que, en el período histórico en que estamos,
Conviene que sigamos.
Llenos de fé y abnegación suprema.

Si cuando, humildes y en silencio mudo,
Soportamos el látigo infamante,
Se nos miró, no obstante,
Con desconfianza y desamor sañudo,
¿Podremos mejorar nuestros destinos
Al exhumar sucesos de dolores,
Llamando a sus autores
Injustos, sanguinarios y asesinos?
¡Imposible! La cólera al despecho
Se unirá, no más, de esa manera
Sin obtener, siquiera,
Para el reinado de la paz provecho.
Contra el odio el amor, y no la impía
Dura ley del Falcón. Somos hermanos,
Aunque algunos, insanos,
Admitirnos resistan todavía. (9–28)

Against hatred, love! This is the system
That, in the historical time that we are in,
It most behooves us to follow,
Full of faith and supreme self-denial.

If, when we, humble and in mute silence
Endured the degrading lash,
We were nevertheless looked upon
With mistrust and vicious enmity,
Can we improve our destiny
By exhuming painful events,
calling their authors
Unjust, bloodthirsty killers?
Impossible! Rage will only join
Bitterness that way,
Without even obtaining any advantage
For the reign of peace.
Against hate, love, and not the godless
Hard law of the Falcon. We are brothers,
Although some, unbalanced ones,
May still resist admitting us. (Silveira Arjona 3)

The speaker of the poem lays out an argument to convince some people of color to treat racist whites with brotherly love. He portrays enslaved people as long-suffering and humble, even to the point of not displaying anger in reaction to violence. Left unmentioned are all forms of protest and resistance during bondage. While acknowledging the pain that slavery inflicted and identifying the guilty parties, the poem rhetorically limits how people did and should respond to that pain. This is a kind of normative construction of the character of people of color, a construction shaped by an awareness of how negatively whites viewed Afro-Cubans, in the past and in the present. The poem here nearly performs a kind of paralipsis, that is, the rhetorical figure of calling attention to something by claiming to be passing over it, or of making a statement by saying that you are not going to make it. The text reveals how many people of color must have felt, while at the same time it urges them to feel otherwise, to have faith in the power of love and in the concept of human brotherhood.

The poem continues, echoing messages from Rosales Morera's poem:

Si de la odiosa corrupción que impera
En el cuerpo social, alguno traza culpar
á nuestra raza,
Dele un mentís nuestra conducta austera.
    Cuba lo sabe: de su gente esclava,
Salida á penas del estado abyecto,
El proceder correcto
El Mundo entero, con asombro alaba.
    (29–36)

If from the odious corruption that prevails
In the social body, someone schemes
To blame our race,
May our austere conduct refute him.
    Cuba knows it: The whole world,
With surprised amazement, praises
The correct behavior of her enslaved people
Barely departed from their abject state.
    (Silveira Arjona 3)

Here again is the idea that the world is watching the Afro-Cuban community and celebrating its worthy actions; therefore, it is crucial that the community live in a way that is beyond reproach. It is curious here that the speaker refers to the Afro-Cuban community as "gente esclava" (enslaved people) although slavery had been abolished by that time. While the phrase was probably chosen because it fit the rhyme and rhythm, it also seems to fit with the idea expressed more than once in this poem that Afro-Cubans are as able now to curb hateful responses as they were during slavery.

The poem goes on to model, in an imagined monologue, what people of color should say to racist whites:

Al que de hermanos el lugar nos niega,
No debemos decir:—¡Te detestamos!—
Sí, sólo: <<Deploramos
La funesta pasión que así te ciega!

    Cuba es de todos el hogar materno:
Nos hizo hermanos Dios. ¿Por qué locura
Tu vanidad procura
Romper los lazos que formó El Eterno?
    ¡Sé lógico, por Dios! ¿A qué idea
De negar al de origen africano
Su nombre de cubano?
Pues tu raza también, ¿no es europea?
    Oriundos del antiguo Continente
Somos todos los hijos de esta Antilla,
Y en nada te mancilla
Tu compatriota de morena frente.>> (37–52)

To the one who denies us our place as
    brothers,
We must not say, "We detest you!"
Yes, only this: "We deplore
The lamentable passion that so blinds you!
    Cuba is the maternal home of all:
God made us brothers. By what madness
Does your vanity attempt
To break the ties that the Eternal formed?
    Be logical, for God's sake! Why the idea
Of denying to the one of African origin
His name as a Cuban?
Since your race, too, is it not European?
    Natives of the old Continent
We are all the sons of this Antille,
And your compatriot of swarthy hue
In no way sullies you." (Silveira Arjona 3)

Implying that racism is an emotionally motivated attitude that warps one's thinking, the speaker calls on whites to be logical. As in Peña's poem, it is the black man who speaks with reason. The logic here is constructed around Christian beliefs in the brotherhood of all people, as ordained by God the creator. In effect, the poem may be responding to the accusation that Afro-Cubans were not Christian enough because many practiced African-derived religions. In effect, the poem communicates thoroughly Christian views and principles, and it subtly suggests that it is the racist whites whose Christian practice is flawed. Besides this religious argument, the speaker adds a political and cultural one: that citizenship should be based not on ancestral origin but on patriotic affection.

The final stanzas reiterate an appeal to the reader of color:

En la medida prosa que os dedico,
Mis queridos hermanos, os imploro
Que, salvando el decoro,
No desdeñéis el proceder que indico.

Si soportamos, con prudencia estoica
Cuatro siglos de bárbaras cadenas,
A ménos (sic) graves penas
¿Nos faltará resignación heróica?

Y no pretendo que mi raza duerma
En mortal inacción; busque el progreso,
Para aliviar con eso
A esta cubana sociedad enferma.

¿No veis que á los impulsos naturales
De su pecho, patriotas distinguidos
Ya nos [dan]*, conmovidos,
Besos de paz y abrazos fraternales?

Amemos, pues, al obcecado y duro
Que, en virtud, del amor que le mostramos,
Sin duda, lograremos
Que nos ame[n]* también, yo os lo aseguro.
   (53–72)
(*Illegible)

In the measured prose that I dedicate to you,
My beloved brothers, I implore you,
To not despise the behavior that I indicate,
Saving decorum or dignity.

If, with stoic prudence, we put up with
Four centuries of barbarous chains,
Faced with much less grave troubles,
Will we be lacking in heroic resignation?

And I do not claim that my race should sleep
In mortal inaction; seek progress,
In order to alleviate with it
This sick Cuban society.

Do you not see that from the natural impulses
Of their heart, distinguished patriots,
Moved with feeling, already give us
Kisses of peace and fraternal embraces?

Let's love, then, the stubborn and hardened one
Whom, by virtue and by the love we show him
Without a doubt we will cause to love us, too,
I assure you of it. (Silveira Arjona 3)

To conclude the argument, the speaker in the poem suggests that the actions and attitudes of the community of color have the power to cause the healing of society. Therefore, Afro-Cubans have the responsibility to be heroic, to exercise the kind of resignation and stoicism they learned from being enslaved, and to love racists into loving them back. The poem expresses a profound faith in love and brotherhood, as well as in the ability of both angry blacks and racist whites to change their attitudes.

Apparently, however, there was a limit to the optimism and faith that we find in these poems to the race of color by Rosales Morera, Peña, and Silveira Arjona. A poem of a very different tone appeared in the December 20, 1888, issue of *La Fraternidad*. These *décimas* with a *pie forzado* (a final line dictated by the gloss of another poem) by Santiago Ruiz express a personal disappointment in the government.

Glosa—	Gloss—
Hojas de un árbol caídas	Leaves fallen from a tree
Juguetes del viento son.	Are the toys of the wind.
Las ilusiones perdidas	Lost illusions
Son hojas ¡ay! desprendidas	Are leaves, ah!, plucked
Del árbol del corazón. (un autor)	From the tree of the heart.
	(By an author)
Cuando un pueblo inteligente	When an intelligent people
Tranquilo se ha levantado,	Has stood up, calm,
Aunque bastante indignado	Although quite indignant,
Y á su gobierno clemente	And respectfully requests of its
Pide respetuosamente	Merciful government
Las libertades queridas	The desired liberties
Que les fueron ofrecidas,	That were offered to them,
Se le presta, sí, atención	The government, yes, pays attention
Pues sus palabras no son	For the people's words are not
Hojas de un árbol caídas.	Leaves fallen from a tree.
Pero una raza sufrida	But a long-suffering race
Que trabajó muchos años	That worked many years and was the
Víctima de engaños:	Victim of deception:
Es un delito que pida.	It is a crime for that race to even ask.
Aunque mostrara la herida	Although it may show the wound
Que lleva en el corazón,	That it carries in its heart,
No se le presta atención:	No one pays any attention to this people.
¿Qué importa si rebentaran (sic)	What does it matter if they burst
Si las leyes que le amparan	If the laws that aid the people
Juguetes del viento son? (1–25)	Are toys of the wind? (Ruiz 4)

The poem draws a contrast between how the government responds to the requests of an "intelligent" and "tranquil" people, and how the government fails to respond to the claims of a formerly enslaved people. It is not clear whether the first two *décimas* are referring to specific incidents or to a trend in how the state responded to certain demands. The mention of "desired liberties that were offered to them" and to "laws that aid them" may lead one to interpret the poem as criticizing a lack of enforcement of laws that should protect certain freedoms. Might the "respectful" petitions of an indignant people be in the form of lawsuits? One would need additional information to ascertain whether the poem was in fact inspired by certain events of that time. Unfortunately, I have not yet encountered information about the author.

However, it is certainly possible that in the second *décima*, the speaker is alluding to the ongoing struggle of Afro-Cubans to end discrimination in access to schools and public places. As described above, the laws from Spain and circulars from Cuba's governor general required that schools admit children of color, but these laws were not effectively enforced. With regard to access to public places, various suits and incidents in the years just before this poem appeared in 1888 may have engendered the bitterness expressed in the poem. Historian Aline Helg notes that in 1882–1883, "Afro-Cubans were granted entrance to public parks and squares, but white communities rapidly restricted their access to certain sections" (38). In 1885, at least a year before the Directorio Central had been formed, a man of color named José Beltrán had been discriminated against in a café in Pinar del Río; he took his complaint to the governor general, who ruled in Beltrán's favor. In a circular sent to provincial governors and civil authorities, the governor general declared that persons of color should not be prohibited from entering public places and private establishments, and that authorities should "resolve immediately any acts of discrimination with justice, equity, and convenience" (qtd. in Howard 187). In 1887, Afro-Cubans protested an increase of a railroad fare that prohibited them from riding in first class, and the Consejo de Administración, a Havana governmental body that heard such cases, ruled that railroads could not in any way deny people of color the right to travel in first class (Scott 275; Howard 186). Yet, cases of discrimination continued. In February 1888 *La Fraternidad* reported on black children being barred from school, and in July, it reported that "guardians of order" had attacked men of color in Havana (Scott 275).

Perhaps a perceived last straw for the author of the poem came from the case of Emilio Leopoldo Moreno. In 1888 Moreno filed a suit in civil court in Santiago de Cuba against a café owner who refused to seat Moreno at a table because he was black, and the court sided with the café owner, as did the *audiencia* of Santiago. As if in response to these rulings, the poem appeared in December. Moreno appealed to the Supreme Court in Madrid, and the verdict came in October of the following year, overturning the decisions of the Cuban courts (Howard 186). Moreno's case leaves one with the impression that local judicial bodies in Cuba did not feel obligated to carry out the spirit of previous anti-segregation laws and rulings. Several years later, in 1894, the Directorio Central was still pressuring the governor general to impose fines for such offenses, and municipal courts even blocked Afro-Cuban complaints from being heard (Helg 38).

The third and fourth stanzas of the poem describe how racist slights affect one's mind and body and one's perceived relationship to the country.

¿Qué sacrificio no hiciera	What sacrifice would I not make
Yo por mi buen existir	For the sake of my good existence
Y no extrangero vivir	So as not to live like a stranger
En el suelo en que naciera?	On the soil on which I was born?
Sangre de mis venas diera,	I would give the blood from my veins
Tan sólo para que oídas	So that the complaints that I sustain
Fueran, y bien atendidas	Might only be heard and well attended;
[Las]* quejas que sostengo;	But I for my country have
Pero yo a mi país tengo	*Lost all illusions.*
Las ilusiones perdidas.	
Ya rebozado mi pecho	Now my bosom is overflowing
De un amargo sentimiento,	With a bitter feeling,
No hallo calma ni un momento	I do not find calm, not even for a moment,
Ni sobre mi propio lecho.	Nor upon my own bed.
Veo pisotear mi derecho,	I see my rights trampled
Por almas envilecidas,	By debased and contemptible souls,
Cuan águilas atrevidas	Who like daring eagles
Nos roban en dulce calma.	In sweet calm rob us.
Estas de libro del alma	These [persons] are leaves, ah!, plucked
Son hojas ¡ay! desprendidas. (26–45)	*From the book of the soul.* (Ruiz 4)
(*Illegible)	

It is interesting that the third stanza mentions blood sacrifice, which is usually associated with going to war, yet the language here might also remind one of Christ's passion. In other words, the sacrifice could be one of aggression or of passivity; indeed, the poem reads more like a desperate lament than an angry call to arms. The poem allows for an expression of pessimism and disillusion toward the government but in terms that carefully avoid anything that can be interpreted as a potentially violent rage. The speaker makes clear that he wants to be treated like a citizen and that certain immoral individuals in the government are preventing the state from responding as it should to a citizen's complaints.

The final stanza might just hold a dim hope that racial justice will prevail:

Con desmedida avaricia,	With unmeasured greed
Aún nos siguen explicando	They are still explaining to us,
A cada instante vejando	At each instant harassing,
Y no hay quien le haga justicia	And there is no one to do justice.
¡Con qué inefable delicia	With what ineffable delight
Hacen propio galardón	They boast of their highly vaunted
De su llevada instrucción!	learning!
Pero ya su acento es ronco	But their accent is already hoarse
Pues tiene dañado el tronco	Since the trunk of the tree
Del árbol del corazón. (46–55)	*Of their heart is damaged.* (Ruiz 4)

This stanza is a bit difficult to translate, in part because some of the words were illegible in the original text from which I copied, and because the syntax and vocabulary here seem more poetic than straightforward. For example, it was not completely clear to me what "llevada instrucción" might mean. The sense of the stanza seems to be that racist whites continue their discriminatory practices, and no one seems able to do justice, perhaps because power and authority are in the hands of those who discriminate. The last few lines were printed clearly, though, and they suggest that the corruption and immorality cannot go on forever. The hoarseness and damage connote a weakness that just might lead to a downfall of the racist system. Overall, this poem boldly expresses personal dismay with the government's treatment of people of color, while it also registers a desire to be a part of the nation and to have one's civil rights respected.

The first three poems studied here speak directly to the race of color; the final three to be analyzed primarily treat the themes of slavery and abolition. One, titled "La esclavitud" ("Slavery") appeared in *La Fraternidad* on November 20, 1888, under the author's initials A. C. In two stanzas of fourteen lines each, the poem personifies and speaks directly to the institution of slavery, outlining its crimes against humanity:

¡Oh cruel suplicio al hombre negro distes!
Y sin conciencia alguna en su estado
Del alma de su patria has arrancado
Y de un polo al otro polo la esparcistes.
Ni la inmensa distancia medistes,
Ni del temor, el [illegible], ni el delito
Contrariar pudieron [illegible] apetito,
Salvaje y cruel que consumar quisistes,
Y surcando los mares le arrojastes
En pos de humanos, carne que en mercado
En las calles y plazas profanastes
Tornando a un noble ser, en desgraciado
Por el vil metal que acumulastes,
Y el veneno que en África [has dejado]*

Oh cruel torture you gave to the black man!
And without any consciousness of his state
You have snatched him out the soul of his
    country
And scattered his country from pole to pole.
You did not measure the immense distance,
Nor could the fear, the [illegible], nor the crime
Thwart your [illegible] appetite,
Savage and cruel that you tried to satisfy,
And ploughing the seas you launched out to him
In pursuit of humans, flesh that in the market
In the streets and the plazas you desecrated,
Turning a noble being into a disgraced one
In exchange for the vile metal you accumulated,
And the venom that in Africa [you left behind].

¿Dónde has nacido, esclavitud maldita?
Decidme pues, ¿quiénes formar pudieron
Tu odioso nombre, infame que se agita
Y en el estenso mundo lo escribieron?
¿No fueron fieras? los que llevar quisieron
Supuesta ley, fúnebre y tan fuerte,
Que entre muros al nombre le pusieron
A luchar con vigor y con la muerte[.]
¿Cómo consentir el gran poder Eterno
La inquisidora idea, la alevosía
Sin castigar tu furia, proceder inferno,
Sin llamar á tus puertas solo un día
En que rugiendo las llamas del infierno
Ardiera[n] allí por siempre tu osadía. (1–28)
(*Illegible.)

Where have you been born, accursed slavery?
Tell me then, who was able to form
Your hateful name, despicable as it agitates itself
And in the wide world they wrote it?
Were they not wild animals? Those who tried to
Carry out such a lamentable and powerful law,
That inside the walls they put to the name
To fight with vigor and with death.
How could the great Eternal power consent to
The inquiring idea, the treachery
Without punishing your fury, infernal
    procedure,
Without calling at your doors on a single day
So that roaring, the flames of hell
Might burn there forever your audacity. (A. C. 4)

Significantly, the closest this poem comes to condemning the persons who enslaved blacks is a question, "¿No fueron fieras?" ("Were they not wild animals?") The poem also ends with a question about how God could have allowed slavery without also finally condemning it. Even two years after abolition, the poet is hesitant to reveal his or her identity in connection to a poem that harshly criticizes bondage, as if it were taboo to express unequivocal blame and anger against slave traders and owners. This strategy seems to be in line with Silveira Arjona's advice to hate racism but love the racist; the tactic allows the writer to acknowledge a painful past without making it personal and without the risk of alienating racist whites who might want to change their ways.

The next two poems were published in 1889 in *Minerva: Revista quincenal dedicada a la mujer de color*. This magazine for Afro-Cuban women had its first incarnation from 1888 to 1889, when it ceased publication due to financial problems. A second phase of the serial began in 1910. The early *Minerva* regularly featured articles, editorial essays, speeches, poems, and society news from across the island. While political issues were rarely if ever addressed in the initial period of *Minerva*, social issues were constantly treated. The overall aim of the magazine was to uplift women of color; therefore, many of the articles urged readers to get an education, educate their children, and marry legally so as to gain respectability. Some articles dealt with discrimination on the basis of color and/or gender. A few texts memorialized slavery and celebrated abolition. Among them were the poem "Redención" ("Redemption") by Cristina Ayala and "La abolición de la esclavitud" ("The Abolition of Slavery") by José Alcalá Galiano.

The latter poem appeared in *Minerva*'s issue dated May 30, 1889. Under its title is this preface: "Poesía recitada con éxito extraordinario, en la noche del 20 de Marzo (sic), por la señorita Adriana [name illegible] en la fiesta en honor a la abolición de la esclavitud celebrada por la Sociedad 'Nueva Aurora' de Puerto Príncipe" (Poetry recited with extraordinary success, on the night of the 20th of March, by Miss Adriana [name illegible] at the party in honor of the abolition of slavery, celebrated by the "New Dawn" Society in Puerto Príncipe). The society named in the preface might be the Afro-Cuban organization named "La Nueva Aurora" (The New Dawn) that Montejo Arrechea lists as having been established in Puerto Príncipe in 1888 (*Sociedades* 125), but this is not definite. While it gives some detail about the context in which the poem was recited, the note does not say when the poem was originally composed, nor whether it was recited in March of 1887 (several months after the abolition law of October 7, 1886) or in March of 1888 or 1889. The tenses in the poem itself lead one to believe that slavery may have been very recently abolished or that it would soon be abolished. In fact, the poem does not mention Cuba, so one might think that perhaps the piece refers to the end of slavery not only in Cuba but also on a global scale.

The poem begins by taunting the personified institution about its loss of power:

Odiosa esclavitud, pronto en la tierra 　　Serás tan solo un nombre: La libertad te declaró la guerra, 　　y te maldijo el hombre.	Odious slavery, soon on the earth 　　You will be only a name: Freedom declared war on you, 　　And man cursed you.
Desterrado del mundo y maldecida 　　En un rincón te ocultas Desde allí soberbia aunque vencida 　　Á la justicia insultas. Hoy el látigo iremos á quitarte 　　De las inicuas manos Y tus presas iremos a arrancarte 　　Pues son nuestros hermanos. (1–12)	Exiled from the world and detested 　　In a corner you hide yourself From there, arrogant though defeated 　　You insult justice. Today we are going to take the whip 　　From your wicked hands And your prey we will snatch from you 　　Since they are our brothers. (Alcalá Galiano 7)

The poem then explains why the formerly enslaved are "our brothers":

Hermanos, sí, pues llevan en la frente 　　La humana inteligencia. Hermanos, sí, porque su pecho siente 　　La voz de la conciencia.	Brothers, yes, since they carry in their forehead 　　Human intelligence. Brothers, yes, because their breast feels 　　The voice of conscience.
Hermanos, sí, que aunque su tez oscura 　　Fue por el sol quemada No pudo el sol quitarles la blancura 　　Del alma inmaculada.	Brothers, yes, who although their dark skin 　　Was burned by the sun, The sun could not remove the whiteness 　　From their immaculate soul.
Hermanos son, pues aman 　　Y padecen, y suspiran y lloran, Y á racionales leyes obedecen, 　　Y tienen fe y adoran. (13–24)	Brothers they are, since they love and suffer, 　　And sigh and cry, And obey rational laws, 　　And have faith and worship. (Alcalá Galiano 7)

The extensiveness of these explanations makes it seem that the author felt the need to convince his audience, or to at least reaffirm and give rationales to what they already believed about formerly enslaved Afro-Cubans. The reference to "rational laws" may be read as another condemnation of slavery as irrational and/or as an encouragement to the government to establish laws that would be just toward people of color. The line may also be read as a way of justifying the Afro-Cubans' acts of resistance to slavery and discrimination. The last line alludes to religious zeal, presumably for Christianity.

The next two stanzas of the poem take a surprising turn in their description of formerly enslaved persons whose humanity had been so carefully and insistently established in the lines above:

Si hoy retuercen con furia sus cadenas 　　Y sacuden sus hierros Es porque los cazaron como á hienas 　　Y [ataron]* como á perros.	If today they twist their chains with fury 　　And shake their irons It is because they hunted them as if they were hyenas 　　And [tied]* them as if they were dogs.
Si á un rebaño de brutos se parece 　　La esclava muchedumbre Es porque nada humilla ni embrutece 　　Como la servidumbre. (25–32) (*Ilegible.)	If the crowd of slaves seems 　　Like a flock of brutes It is because nothing humiliates nor stupefies 　　Like servitude. (Alcalá Galiano 7)

It is interesting that the voice here compares the enslaved or formerly enslaved to animals just at the mention of their anger and rebellion against being abused. As in Rosales Morera's poem "A la raza de color," there is the idea that slavery handicaps the mind. While Rosales Morera encourages the race to overcome those effects, the comparison here to an undifferentiated flock of animals has the effect of negating the earlier statement about human intelligence.

The next segment of the poem lauds the abolitionists, speaking as if their work continues:

Vosotros, del esclavo redentores,
    Que con amor profundo
Proclamáis, generosos luchadores,
    La libertad del mundo.
	You, the redeemers of the slave,
	    That with profound love
	As generous fighters, proclaim
	    the freedom of the world.

No consintáis que indignos mercaderes
    Con avaricia insana
Acrezcan su fortuna y sus placeres
    Vendiendo carne humana.
	Do not allow unworthy merchants
	    With insane greed
	To grow their fortunes and their pleasures
	    By selling human flesh.

Que no maneille mas la humana honra
    [two illegible words]
Aleve, que es el horror, escándalo y deshonra
    Del siglo diez y nueve. (33–44)
	May it not further stain human honor
	    [two illegible words] treacherous,
	That it is the horror, scandal, and dishonor
	    Of the nineteenth century. (Alcalá Galiano
	    7–8)

The next part of the poem again compares the enslaved blacks to animals, this time in trying to emphasize how much blacks love freedom and explain why they should not be held in captivity:

¿No se deja al león magestuoso
    Señor de su desierto?
¿Y no se deja en libertad al oso
    Allá en el polo yerto?
	Does one not leave the majestic lion
	    To be the lord of the wild?
	And does one not leave in liberty the bear
	    There in his frozen pole?

Pues si el negro infeliz de ser humano
    Ha merecido el nombre
¿Quién pretende arrancarle de la mamo
    Sus libertades de hombre?
	Well, if the unhappy black man has merited
	    The name of human being
	Who pretends to rip from his hand
	    His freedoms as a man?

Si de salvaje fuesen sus instintos
    Sus reinos naturales
Son del bosque los verdes laberintos,
    Los yermos arenales.
	If his instincts were of the savage,
	    His natural realms
	Are the green labyrinths of the forest,
	    The sandy wastelands.

Dejadle allí vivir a la inclemencia
    En la abrasada zona.
Mas (sic) quiere allí su sana
Independencia
    Que la mejor corona.
	Let him live in the harshness
	    Of the burning zone.
	There he wants his wholesome
	Independence more
	    Than the best crown.

Mas quiere ser salvaje en los desiertos
    Que siervo en las ciudades.
Allí los horizontes dan abiertos,
    Inmensas soledades.
	He wants to be a savage in the deserts more
	    Than a servant in the cities.
	There the open horizons provide
	    Immense lonely places.

No le exprimen allí con sus sudores
    La vida gota a gota,
Enriqueciendo con bárbaras labores
    Al mismo que le azota. (45–69)
	There they do not squeeze his life out of him
	    Drop by drop with his sweat,
	With barbarous labor
	    Enriching the one who flogs him. (Alcalá
	    Galiano 8)

It is not altogether clear here whether the poem is arguing for Africans to be left in Africa or for freed blacks to be allowed to live in their own isolated communities in Cuba. Perhaps the poem is not arguing either of these points but merely pointing out that, if they could choose, blacks would opt for freedom over enslavement. Still, the poem draws a dichotomy between wilderness and city, or between a space where nature prevails and a space where society prevails. The speaker of the poem says that the black man is human but with savage instincts; therefore, the most appropriate place for him, as for the lion and bear, is in the wild. Society, on the other hand, presents the black man with the danger of enslavement as long as white racists continue in their mindset.

The final stanzas speak directly to white would-be slave owners, first with an exhortation and ultimately with a moral upbraiding:

Blancos, ¿queréis el negro [illegible] bruto
   [mas]* redimido al cabo?
Llevadle del saber el santo fruto,
   Mas no le hagáis esclavo.

Blancos, si al negro de inferior linaje
   Envilecerle os plugo,
Menos deshonra es ser negro y salvaje
   Que ser blanco y verdugo. (70–77)
(*Illegible)

Whites, do you want the black man [illegible]
   brutish but redeemed in the end?
Bring to him the sacred fruit of knowledge,
   But do not make him a slave.

Whites, if it pleased you to humiliate
   The black man of inferior lineage,
There is less dishonor in being black and a
   savage
Than being white and a tyrant. (Alcalá
   Galiano 8)

This poem is fraught with tensions, one of which is between slavery and abolition, which is presented as a process still being worked through while slavery has yet to be overcome. The law is never mentioned. Abolition seems to be more a matter of getting slave traders and slave owners to change their view of people of African descent. While the poem insists on the human value of the enslaved person, the text does not succeed in portraying the enslaved person as one ready to live as a free citizen within society, because he has the "instincts of a savage" and has been degraded to the point of becoming comparable to an animal. In contrast to the poems written to the race, which emphasize self-reliance and a process of becoming a part of society, this poem suggests that whites should be responsible for educating rather than enslaving people of color.

Upon first reading, it is difficult to imagine why this poem was published in *Minerva* in 1889, since its portrayal of blacks as savages by nature, brutes by force, and slaves still in chains seems contrary to the message and mission of the magazine and of much of the black press. It is almost as difficult to understand why a performance of the poem would have been well-received in an Afro-Cuban society once slavery had already been abolished, if indeed it was recited then and there. However, certain aspects of the poem might understandably resonate with Afro-Cubans both before and after abolition, especially if they did not examine the rhetoric too closely. An audience or reader of color might agree that slavery and its aftereffects still needed to be rooted out. They might see the struggle against discrimination as an extension of the struggle against slavery. They might agree with the message that people of color should be considered as brothers of all humans. They might applaud the poem's charge to whites to educate the formerly enslaved, since for years the Afro-Cuban community urged the government to provide access to instruction. They might even cheer at the poem's audacious way of pointing out the hypocrisy of racist whites. Though an Afro-Cuban reader in 1889 may have found some reasons to applaud the poem "La abolición de la esclavitud," one hopes that such a reader would also have been astute enough to recognize the work's failure to paint an uplifting portrait of formerly enslaved people of color.

By contrast, we find a celebration of abolition and a pious image of emancipated blacks in the poem "Redención," which appeared in the February 15, 1889, edition of *Minerva*, a few months before "La abolición de la esclavitud." The author of "Redención" was Cristina Ayala, the pen name of María Cristina Fragas (1856–1936), one of the founding editors and regular contributors of the magazine. Ayala had been born free to an enslaved mother in Güines, about thirty miles southeast of Havana in the province of Mayabeque. Formally educated, she established herself as a writer during the last quarter of the nineteenth century and the first quarter of the twentieth, contributing to over twenty Cuban newspapers and journals (DeCosta-Willis 31). She compiled her abundant literary production into a 240-page volume titled *Ofrendas mayabequinas*, published in her hometown in 1926.

In spite of (or perhaps because of) Ayala's being one of the first-known Afro-Cuban women poets, her work has not received much critical attention inside or outside of Cuba. Critics Miriam DeCosta-Willis and Monique-Adelle Callahan have introduced Ayala to more readers in their recent books, so Ayala is better known now than any of the other poets featured in the present study. In fact, Callahan provides an extensive reading of "Redención" in *Between the Lines: Literary Transnationalism and African American Poetics*. Callahan reads this poem alongside the poem "Deliverance" by Frances Harper (1825–1911), an African-American woman poet from the United States, showing how both poems appropriate biblical narratives to reinterpret the history and status of blacks in the post-abolition era of their respective countries.

In "Redención" Callahan sees the formerly enslaved cast as Christ-like martyrs whose willing sacrifice as slaves and whose prayer of intercession for post-abolition Cuba redeem the imagined nation and show it the meaning of freedom (69–72). However, read in the light of other poems from Cuba's black press, a different interpretation emerges.

"Redención" opens with three stanzas that contrast the experience of bondage with the experience of abolition:

Cual trás (sic) negra tormenta un claro día	As after a black storm a clear day
Lucir suele con bellos esplendores,	Tends to shine with beautiful splendors,
Y cual brilla en un rostro la alegría	And as happiness beams on a face
Trás un cúmulo inmenso de dolores,	After an immense cloud of pains,
Así mi pobre raza que llevaba	So my poor race that led
Una vida de mísera agonía,	A life of miserable agony,
Y bajo el férreo yugo que la ahogaba	And under the iron yoke that choked it
En dura esclavitud triste gemía,	In hard slavery, moaned with sadness,
Hoy se encuentra feliz, pues con sus alas	Today finds itself joyful, since with its wings
La hermosa libertad augusta y santa	Beautiful liberty, august and holy,
La cubre, y adornada de esas galas,	Covers it, and adorned with those fineries,
Bate las palmas y sus glorias canta. (1–12)	[My race] claps its hands and sings its delight. (Ayala 7)

This poem treats abolition as a fait accompli, not as an incomplete process, as in "La abolición de la esclavitud." The emphasis here is on the celebration of a new state of freedom. While slavery is described in terms of its real physical and emotional effects, liberty is pictured figuratively as a protective and beautifying presence. The formerly enslaved race is overjoyed to be emancipated.

The next stanza shifts from third person to second person, as the voice addresses the race:

¡Raza humilde, sencilla y laboriosa,	Humble race, harmless and hardworking,
Modelo fiel de abnegación constante,	Faithful model of constant self-denial,
Que vertiste tu sangre generosa	That poured your generous blood
Al impulso del látigo infamante!	At the urge of the degrading whip!
¡Canta tu gloria, sí! pues no es posible	Yes, sing your delight! For it is not possible
Que al cesar tu baldón y tu tortura	That when your dishonor and your torture
Una plegaria mística y sensible	ceases
No se exhale de tu alma con ternura.	A mystic and sensitive prayer
Has (sic) que hasta el trono del Eterno	Not be exhaled with tenderness from your soul.
suba	Let your tone ascend to the throne of the
Tu acento, y dí con voz que tierna vibre;	Eternal
¡Perdón[,] Señor[,] te imploro para Cuba!	And say with a voice that vibrates tenderly;
¡Ya su crimen borró, ya el negro es libre!	Pardon, Lord, I beg you for Cuba!
(13–24)	It finally erased its crime, now the black man
	is free! (Ayala 7)

With the use of the words *humilde* (humble), *abnegación* (self-denial), and *látigo infamante* (degrading whip), this description of the race echoes lines from Silveira Arjona's poem; both poems suggest that the patient endurance of slavery has shaped the character of the race. In Ayala's poem, the line "que vertiste tu sangre generosa" (that poured your generous blood) does suggest a willing submission to the violence of slavery. In fact, *generosa* may also be translated as "noble" and "abundant." This line may allude to the Christ-like martyrdom that Callahan emphasizes, as do the lines from Rosales Morera's poem, "Hoy que no llevas en tu frente impreso / signo afrentoso ni punzante espino" (Today, now that you no longer carry / impressed on your forehead an ignominious sign). However, in "Redención" the race is described as "sencilla y laboriosa," too. *Sencilla* can have the connotation of "guileless" or "harmless," not just "simple" and "uncomplicated." Consequently, this stanza can be read as a kind of idealizing and normative characterization of the race, like that in Silveira Arjona's poem. Both poems leave in silence the fact that Afro-Cubans did at times resist slavery and fight against it. As such, the descriptions function to counteract the defaming notion that people of color wanted to start a race war, avenge themselves on slaveholders, and take over Cuba. These descriptions present Afro-Cubans as willing and able to set aside past hurts.

The two stanzas that follow reinforce this image of a formerly enslaved race that has made peace with Cuba, but these stanzas subtly reveal the possibility of hard feelings against Cuba. Notice that the voice commands the race: "Yes, sing your delight!" The third stanza has already established that the race does express bliss for having been emancipated. The command here makes it seem that the race might not want to keep singing about the freedom gained through abolition. Historically, the discrimination faced after abolition made freedom seem less complete than suggested in the first stanzas of the poem. The poem continues saying that it is "not possible" for the race to not issue a prayer at the end of its "dishonor and torture," which is another foreclosure on alternative feelings about enslavement and emancipation. The speaker emphasizes with repetition that the prayer should be said "with tenderness" and with a "tender voice." Silveira Arjona's poem acknowledges that some Afro-Cubans want to proclaim what they suffered in bondage and condemn those who abused them. Ayala's poem hints at this possible sentiment by negating its existence and insisting that the race only feel happiness and forgiveness.

The command to ask God to pardon a Cuba that has "erased its crime" highlights another trait that the race should have: a reliance on a divine being to rectify the situation in Cuba. These lines perform Christian faith and values, showing, like Silveira Arjona's poem, that Cubans of color share the religion of white Cubans, and they are therefore worthy of being accepted into the Cuban nation. The final stanza begins with another command to seek the aid of Providence:

Pide al hado feliz que tu derecho	Request of happy fate that your rights
Respetado en el mundo siempre veas	You will always see respected in the world
Y exclama desde el fondo de tu pecho:	And exclaim from the bottom of your heart:
¡Oh santa libertad, bendita seas! (25–28)	Oh sacred liberty, may you be blessed! (Ayala 7)

The poem here makes it seem that the race's right to not be held in captivity was already being respected. Thus, the line can be interpreted as a desire to never return to slavery. Yet the mention of this one right leads the reader to think of all of the other rights that were being denied to Cubans of color after abolition. The poem does not seem to address the issue of discrimination directly, as if doing so would ruin the tone of celebration over emancipation. Still, the speaker in the poem calls on the race of color to rely on a higher power rather than their own efforts to maintain this right and obtain other rights. Again, the poem seems to present Afro-Cubans as non-threatening because they are to pray instead of act.

The closing lines of "Redención" suggest that the race should always celebrate, value, and even worship freedom. These final lines are almost as vague as the last line of Peña's poem, "y cumplid los deberes del patriota" (And you, fulfill the duties of the patriot). It is left to the reader to determine how a love of freedom can or should be applied. Is the poem suggesting that Afro-Cubans uphold the sanctity of liberty in civil rights for themselves and for all? Or is it implying only that they should consider as sacred their human right not to be enslaved? Callahan reads the mention of rights and freedom as a suggestion that "black Cubans should . . . support a united front against Spain in the name of national unity" (70). While that interpretation goes well beyond the language of the poem itself, the emphasis on liberty at the end of the poem indeed may have been a nod toward the principle of national freedom that *independentistas* espoused. By calling on Afro-Cubans to "bless" the concept of liberty, the poem may again be showing that this formerly enslaved people were worthy of acceptance in society because they dearly held a value that many of their white compatriots championed.

Callahan concludes that "Ayala and Harper posit a reconciled relationship of African descendants with the racist nation-state. This reconciliation opens the door for active participation in the ideological and symbolic reimagining of the nation" (73).

Clearly, the poem "Redención" is a gesture of good will to the Cuban nation. The poem imagines a community of formerly enslaved people who can fit neatly into the imagined community of Cuba (colonized or independent). This image of Afro-Cubans as pious, forgiving, hardworking, and harmless counters the racists' image of uncivilized, vengeful ex-slaves who cannot be trusted to participate fully in society or politics. The poem "Redención" performs a desire for Cuba to embrace Afro-Cubans at the same time that it expresses their desire for a Cuba that offers them freedom and respect.

In the seven poems analyzed here, we have seen the same strategies at work. The poems direct themselves primarily at Cubans of color, but they also carry messages that are meant for both black and white Cubans. Some of these poems avoid placing direct blame for racial abuse. Even when the poems express pain over enslavement or dissatisfaction with discrimination, they do so in a way that presents Afro-Cubans as able to channel their feelings toward bettering Cuba. Finally, the poems construct an image of the community of color that is culturally, morally, religiously, and politically compatible with that of white Cuban society. In some of the texts, we can see the author attempting to persuade an audience of differing feelings to conform to that one image. This poetic construction of the Afro-Cuban community in the 1880s was followed in the 1890s by a similar narrative construction of the black insurgent, and along with it a recasting of the Ten Year's War as the site in which black and white patriots became brothers and equals, eliminating the possibility of a race war (Ferrer 112–138).

Was the pen of the black Cuban press of the 1880s and 1890s mightier than racist discourse? Helg finds that Afro-Cubans from the 1880s to 1912 were not able to maneuver out of a discursive straight jacket imposed by the dominant ideology: "Cuba's combination of a myth of racial equality with a two-tier racial system confronted Afro-Cubans with an unsolvable dilemma. If they denied the veracity of the myth, they exposed themselves to accusations of being racist and unpatriotic. If they subscribed to the myth, they also had to conform to negative views of blacks. Indeed, the myth made it blasphemous for Afro-Cubans to proclaim both their blackness and their patriotism" (7).

The congressional ban on the Partido Independiente de Color and the 1912 massacre of its leaders and supporters demonstrate the effectiveness of the sword in defending a racist state. On the other hand, Ferrer notes that the "fraternity in war" rhetoric fomented in the 1890s before the war of 1895–1898 did have a lasting effect: "Patriotic claims about racial integration . . . were . . . a powerful, if incomplete, attack on the ideological foundations of colonial rule"; those same concepts of racial integration "later became the republic's foundational story, the dominant nationalist narrative of Cuba's twentieth century" (138).

Notes

1. I include the poems here in their entirety because they are not easily accessible; all translations of the poems are my own.
2. The text could be making reference to the city of Urbino, Italy, which was a cultural center during the fifteenth century. Another possibility is that Urbino refers to Lorenzo di Piero de'Medici, Duke of Urbino (1492–1519), who ruled Florence and to whom Machiavelli dedicated *The Prince*. These interpretations are not completely satisfying because they depart from the pattern of naming renowned intellectuals.

Works Cited

A. C. "La esclavitud." *La Fraternidad* 20 Nov. 1888: 4.

Alcalá Galiana, José. "La abolición de la esclavitud." *Minerva: Revista quincenal dedicada a la mujer de color* 30 May 1889: 7–8.

Anderson, Benedict. *Imagined Communities: Reflections on the Origin and Spread of Nationalism.* Rev. ed. London: Verso, 1996.

"Antonio Rosales Morera." *Sagua la Grande, La villa del Undoso.* April 1, 2012. Web. April 20, 2012. *sagualagrande.blogspot.com/2012/04/antonio-rosales-morera.html.*

Ayala, Cristina. "Redención." *Minerva: Revista quincenal dedicada a la mujer de color* 15 Feb. 1889: 7.

Callahan, Monique-Adelle. *Between the Lines: Literary Transnationalism and African American Poetics.* New York: Oxford UP, 2011.

Chasteen, John Charles. Introduction. *The Lettered City.* By Angel Rama. Trans. Chasteen. Durham: Duke UP, 1996. vii–xiv.

DeCosta-Willis, Miriam. *Daughters of the Diaspora: Afra-Hispanic Writers.* Kingston, Jamaica: Ian Randle, 2003.

Deschamps Chapeaux, Pedro. *El negro en el periodismo cubano en el siglo XIX: Ensayo bibliográfico.* La Habana: Ediciones Revolución, 1963.

Diccionario de la literatura cubana. La Habana: Editorial Letras Cubanas, 1980.

Ferrer, Ada. *Insurgent Cuba: Race, Nation, and Revolution, 1868–1898.* Chapel Hill: U of North Carolina P, 1999.

Guerra, Armando. *Vicente Silveira y Arjona: "El patriarca de los poetas de Occidente." Ensayo biográfico.* Pinar del Río, Cuba: Revista Ilustrada de Artemisa, 1921.

Helg, Aline. *Our Rightful Share: The Afro-Cuban Struggle for Equality (1886–1912).* Chapel Hill: U of North Carolina P, 1995.

Hevia Lanier, Oilda. *El Directorio Central de las Sociedades Negras de Cuba (1886–1894).* La Habana: Editorial de Ciencias Sociales, 1996.

Howard, Philip A. *Changing History: Afro-Cuban Cabildos and Societies of Color in the Nineteenth Century.* Baton Rouge: Louisiana State UP, 1998.

Montejo Arrechea, Carmen [Victoria]. "Minerva: A Magazine for Women (and Men) of Color." *Between Race and Empire: African Americans and Cubans Before the Cuban Revolution.* Eds. Lisa Brock and Digna Castañeda Fuertes. Philadelphia: Temple UP, 1998. 33–48.

———. *Sociedades de instrucción y recreo de pardos y morenos que existiera en Cuba colonial: Período 1878–1898.* Veracruz, México: Gobierno del Estado de Veracruz, Instituto Veracruzana de Cultura, 1993.

Peña, H. V. "A la raza negra." *La Fraternidad* 21 Aug. 1888: 4.

Rama, Angel. *The Lettered City.* Trans. John Charles Chasteen. Durham: Duke UP, 1996.

Rosales Morera, Antonio. "A la raza de color (en la apertura del círculo de recreo Cervantes)." *Páginas literarias, escritas en prosa y en verso.* Sagua la Grande, Cuba: Imprenta El Comercio, 1882. 20–23.

Ruiz, Santiago. "Hojas de un árbol caídas." *La Fraternidad* 20 Dec. 1888. 4.

Scott, Rebecca J. *Slave Emancipation in Cuba: The Transition to Free Labor, 1860–1899.* Princeton: Princeton UP, 1985.

Silveira Arjona, Vicente. "A algunos de mis hermanos de raza." *La Fraternidad* 10 Sept. 1888: 3.

3

Imagining the "New Black Subject"

Ethical Transformations and Raciality in the Post-Revolutionary Cuban Nation

Odette Casamayor-Cisneros
Translated by Hannah Burdette

The New Man and the Cosmology of the Cuban Revolution

In the pamphlet "Socialism and Man in Cuba" (1965), Ernesto Guevara established the prototype of the New Man: a nascent subject whose formation would contribute to the development of a socialist society following the triumph of the Castro revolution in 1959. The principal characteristics of this hypothetical citizen are synergetic with what I have called the "cosmology of the Cuban Revolution"—that is, the ideas conditioned by the revolutionary experience that lend coherence to post-revolutionary Cuba and sustain its existence in emotional and rational terms (Casamayor, *Utopía* 32–35). Drawing on an epic conception of existence molded by the idea of heroic sacrifice, resistance, and permanent confrontation with internal and external enemies, the cosmology of the revolution has bolstered the relevance of the dominant political-ideological project on the island and has catalyzed the construction of national identity.

This cosmology takes shape during the 1960s and 1970s, in the context of the Bay of Pigs Invasion in 1961, the Missile Crisis one year later, and repeated counter-revolutionary attacks. For Tzvi Medin, the resulting existential framework "implies, first of all, complete identification with the guerrilla epic and with Fidel Castro, but it also implies establishing the omnipresence of a constant situation of extremity that imposes self-definition, compromise, militancy, social cohesion cemented by the indispensable national consensus, and mobilization" (29). This need to establish a national consensus is crucial to understanding the race and gender politics implemented through the Cuban Revolution; the government interpreted the struggle against racial discrimination as imperative for maintaining national unity and consequentially strengthening Cuba in the face of counterrevolutionary aggressions. Fidel Castro expressed the endeavor in these terms in March of 1959: "We are a small nation of people who rely on one another; we rely on the efforts of everyone together, yet we are going to divide ourselves now in blacks and whites? . . . What purpose does that serve but to weaken the nation, to weaken Cuba?" (Fernández Robaina 185).[1]

Blacks and the Cosmology of the Cuban Revolution

What role do blacks play in the cosmology of the Cuban Revolution? Having adopted the model of the nation laid out by José Martí—ideologue of Cuban Independence, apostle of the nation during the republic (1902–1958), and later national hero following the revolutionary triumph of 1959—the Cuban Revolution assumes that in every citizen national identification prevails over any other form of identity, as has been thoroughly studied by Ada Ferrer, Alejandro de la Fuente, Lillian Guerra, and other scholars. There is a certain underlying mysticism in the conception of Cubanness inspired by Martí, in which the nation itself takes on a sacred quality. Patriotism, which he perceives as the motor of national progress, takes precedence over racial, gendered, sexual, and cultural conditioning. Only national affiliation proves valid; in fact, in Martí's vision for his country, nationality is the key space in which contradictions between Cubans will dissolve, paving the way for absolute harmony. White racism thus supposedly disappears in the heat of the independence struggle, yet blacks only gain a place in Martí's cosmos when they become part of the revolution and set aside any sense of individuality in the name of the Cuban nationalist project. They must embrace the flag like a mother ("el cubano negro estará abrazado a la bandera, como a una madre") ("El plato de lentejas" 27). Martí recognizes, moreover, that the revolution consists of a project initially promoted by the white patriciate, the white slave-holding class cast as the sole purveyors of abolition. Significantly, this move diminishes the importance of the liberating agency of the black subject: "Cubans rose in battle, broke open the shackles of their servitude on the very first day of freedom, and converted Spanish indignity into a nation of free men at the cost of their own lives" ("El plato de lentejas" 26).[2] By calling slave-owners who participated in the revolution simply "Cubans," Martí appears to exclude black slaves from this category: they are no more than slaves. Nonetheless, within the framework of Martí's thought, these circumstances dissipate in favor of utopic national harmony.

Likewise, his well-known phrase "Man is more than white, more than mulatto, more than black" ("Mi raza" 298) dominates revolutionary ideology and structures all official reflections on racial issues that have emerged from 1959 to the present.[3] The revolutionary subject, especially the utopic construct of the New Man, lacks racial identification. He is without ethnic or cultural determinations. His color might be the same "Cuban color" that Guillén envisioned in the 1930s. His culture would be that which supposedly emerges in a new society, free from the "original sin" of not being "authentically revolutionary" that Ernesto Guevara attributed to intellectuals born before the triumph of the revolution (380). In short, the revolutionary belongs to only one kind of family, the one comprised of the Cuban people; and life for the New Man is not possible outside the bounds of the revolution.[4]

When racial segregation officially ends in 1959, ethnic heterogeneity apparently ceases to be a source of conflict, since difference is diluted in the Cuban masses faced with a common enemy and a shared tradition, immersed together in a single, well-defined future: the construction of tropical socialism. Mestizaje itself seems to materialize only with revolutionary triumph. It is not until 1959 that white Mirta and black Calixto, characters in the novel *La consagración de la primavera* (The Rite of Spring) by Alejo Carpentier (1978) can make their relationship public and get married. A similar situation plays out with the black protagonist Julián in the novel *Adire y el tiempo roto* (Adire and Broken Time), published in 1967 by Manuel Granados.[5] This character maneuvers the difficult transition from black subject in a capitalist society to a socialist society and denounces the persistence of racial prejudices within the revolutionary experience. This circumstance attracts the reproving glance of some critics who contend that the author's deep focus on the question of race results in a deviation from the parameters of the revolutionary novel.[6] Julián's protagonism in this novel is significant, given that black characters have typically been relegated to secondary roles within Cuban cultural production. This novel certainly confronts Maniquean sensibilities and monolithic postures (Uxó 184); however, I consider that *Adire y el tiempo roto* ultimately projects the redemption and awakening of the new Cuban as a necessary outcome of the revolution. Much like in Carpentier's novel, the triumph of the revolution sees Julián marrying a white woman, Cira, who is expecting his child. "I broke the placenta and was born, and I shouted: Shit, what is this?! I was standing on two columns of reinforced concrete. My feet were on the ground" (Granados 290),[7] Julián euphorically exclaims at the triumph of the revolution, though he would later perish in a counterrevolutionary attack.

His death may symbolize the elimination of the remnants of the past that the revolution required of its followers. Julián had not been able to completely free himself from an ancestral distrust toward his white compatriots or from the racial complexes that had determined his behavior throughout his life. His mestizo son, on the other hand, represents the open future on its way to becoming a reality. In this case *blanqueamiento*, or racial whitening, is less important than the promise of a New Man that the child represents. And he will be that much more "new" given that he will erase the racial differences of his parents and the effects of marginality and discrimination that endured after 1959 and that still smoldered in those inaugural years of the revolution. This unborn mestizo child symbolizes the new nation, free of that "original sin" demonized by Ernesto Guevara. He will be a new "colorless" child, without racial complexes.

These novels by Carpentier and Granados thus illustrate the interpretation that Nadine Fernández has developed regarding the ideological connotation of interracial couples during the early years of the Cuban Revolution. In her opinion, while interracial relations in the nineteenth century incorporated an overt policy of national whitening, there was no attempt in the new times to change the racial composition of the Cuban population. Instead, the revolutionary project sought to render race irrelevant: "Revolutionary identity, now conflated with national identity, was to remove race as a significant variable from the social panorama. The interracial couples under the revolution did not produce *mestizos*, but rather socialist revolutionaries. Color would not *disappear* through intermarriage and racial integration; rather, it would become *irrelevant*." (70).

The New Black?

If indeed Guevara's theories applied to the situation of the black Cuban population, then the revolution should have entailed the cultivation of a New Black—or a New Mulatto. However, this idea was never explicitly formulated as such in revolutionary society; from the end of the 1960s until well into the 1980s, any discussion concerning the question of race faced rigid barriers erected by authorities who claimed the right to legitimate defense of the revolution. There would be no more black Cubans or white Cubans, only revolutionary Cubans destined to become New Men.

Central to this utopian project of absolute synthesis is the official endeavor to recuperate history as a unitary whole around which all citizens, black and white alike, could meet in complete harmony. Moreover, certain isolated polemics emerged in opposition to the prevailing uncritical acceptance of Cuban history. Black intellectual Walterio Carbonell, for example, strove to elicit crucial revisions of Cuban historical and identitary discourse by drawing attention to the racist attitudes of some of its key figures. Carbonell indicated that many of the fundamental reflections in Cuban history and thought came from the pens of racist Cuban patricians, such as José A. Saco, Francisco Arango y Parreño, or José de la Luz y Caballero. For Carbonell, the idea of reconstructing a new society predicated on racial equality yet built on the foundations of the preexistent Eurocentric and hegemonic ideology constituted a departure from Marxist doctrine. In *Como surgió la cultura nacional* (How National Culture Emerged, 1961), Carbonell, an active communist militant during the 1950s, presents a Marxist perspective on national history, placing the racial question at the center of class struggle. His position, nonetheless, was refuted and silenced by the cultural authorities of the time, his entire work censored.

It is worth noting here, as Ana Serra has argued, that the New Man's "different appearances proposed radical changes while they also revealed assumptions regarding race, gender, class, history, culture, and nation that had prevailed in previous eras" (3). Diverse racial stereotypes and Eurocentric conceptions prevailed in the Guevarian treatise, conditioning the attitude of the revolutionary model toward the aspects of Cuban culture and society that in one way or another diverged from the portrait of the New Man. Since the New Man served as a prototype for the rest of society, he could not embody someone perceived in the social imaginary as "primitive" or "ignorant." As a necessarily virile subject (even if the New "Man" were a woman), he should also be heroic and brave. Moreover, as a communist, he should be an atheist, a Marxist-Leninist figure who believes exclusively in his political doctrine. Cuban religions of African origin, which were considered uncivilized, as well other cultural elements that might reduce the willingness of the individual to commit fully to the revolutionary project, consequentially did not factor into the values attributed to the New Man, a creature of the future responsible for leading revolutionary society toward progress.

The black, then, must improve himself if he is to become the New Black. Corresponding to this implicit requirement in the cosmology of the Cuban Revolution, two types of blacks abound in the cultural production of the period: the black alienated until 1959, exploited and marked by the evils of capitalism, and the New Black emerging from the revolution. Both character types represent stereotyped identities offered to blacks as possible protagonists in the young revolutionary society. The protagonists of the novel *Cuando la sangre se parece al fuego* (When Blood Resembles Fire, 1975) by Miguel Cofiño, as well as the Haitian character Pedro Limón in the short story "La tierra y el cielo" ("The Earth and the Sky," 1968) by Antonio Benítez Rojo, are prime examples of this pattern. Like the "servile" slave, the *mulata de rumbo* (voluptuous mulatta), the black popular musician, the *negrito catedrático* (professorial negro), and other caricatures that populate the *costumbrista* literature of the nineteenth century, these new stock characters do not exist as isolated constructs. Together, the "oppressed" and "barbarian" black prior to 1959 and the black "saved" by the new regime symbolize a greater construction: the revolution. As stereotypes, they do not represent the true Black Cuban. Instead, they are mere actors performing their designated roles in a work of fiction not of their own making.

Thus, toward the end of *Adire y el tiempo roto* it would be reasonable to posit that a certain New Black is possible, conceivably in the mestizo child of Cira and Julián, yet to reach these final pages the reader must first navigate the sea of doubts and contradictions that Julián's life represents. It is clear that, from its very inception, the New Black is far from a simple character. Even within a cosmology of the revolution that presupposes the possibility of this human transformation, the clear-cut stereotype dissipates in a novel such as *Adire y el tiempo roto*. This is not a question of an isolated vision; other creators shared with Granados the need to show the complexity of the ontological impact produced by revolutionary transformations on black Cubans accustomed to segregation and discrimination.

In order to examine these processes, particularly in marginal communities where black and mestizo Cubans are the majority, I analyze the cinematic production of Sara Gómez (Havana, 1943–1974) and Nicolás Guillén Landrián (Havana, 1938–Miami, 2003) in the pages that follow. These two black filmmakers further many of Granados's own inquiries through an audiovisual rather than novelistic medium. Like *Adire y el tiempo roto*, these films appeared in the 1960s and 1970s and faced varying degrees of skepticism and veiled or explicit censorship. They demanded critical reflection on the persistence of marginality and racism in revolutionary Cuba, even if the socialist government had undertaken significant legislative, economic, and pedagogic efforts to eradicate them.

The Unsettling Vision of Sara Gómez

Sara Gómez is the most important filmmaker in Cuban cinema. Sixteen vitally relevant documentaries and the only feature film directed by a woman attest to this fact, as well as the originality, high quality of cinematographic technique, and poetic subtlety that distinguish her work. Her family was part of a black and mulatto petty bourgeoisie in Havana largely consisting of public schoolteachers, musicians, modest businessmen, and resourceful housewives who generally sympathized with the revolutionary movement or leftist parties. However, after 1959 a young Sara Gómez devoted herself to the intellectual fervor of the early years of the revolution (Álvarez, "Sara Gómez" 38). She unexpectedly became a journalist and collaborated regularly with university and communist publications (e.g. *Revista Mella* and *Hoy Domingo*, respectively). In 1960 Gómez enrolled in the Seminary of the Institute of Ethnology and Folklore, where she studied popular culture, religion, and marginal populations. One year later she began to work as a director's assistant in the Film Institute (ICAIC), under the tutelage of important filmmakers such as Tomás Gutiérrez Alea, Santiago Álvarez, and Agnès Varda of France during her stay in Cuba. The *Enciclopedia popular cubana*, a didactic series of documentaries supervised by Álvarez, includes some of the pioneering works by Gómez, who was to become the first woman filmmaker in Cuba. The trajectory of her career is coherent: from the very beginning, in pieces such as *Plaza vieja* (The Old Plaza, 1962), *Solar habanero* (Havana Tenement, 1962), *Historia de la piratería* (The History of Piracy, 1963), and *Iré a Santiago* (I Will Go to Santiago, 1964), she presents a penetrating socio-ethnographic perspective and demonstrates a persevering interest in the daily lives of Cubans. She was a "born sociologist," as writer Tomás González once noted in a laudatory description of his collaborator (113).

In all of Gómez's work, marginalized individuals take center stage. Particularly indicative of this inclination is her documentary trilogy—*En la otra isla* (On the Other Island, 1968), *Una isla para Miguel* (An Island for Miguel, 1968), and *Isla del Tesoro* (Treasure Island, 1969) focused on youth rehabilitation on Isla de Pinos, renamed *Isla de la Juventud*, or the "Isle of Youth," by the authorities who established youth reeducation centers there. Despite Gómez's determination to show the true face of the revolution, her presentation of the subject matter avoids imposing a grandiloquent and triumphalist tone, thus nothing in her films is conclusive, as they strive to incite critical reflection and discussion regarding the formation of a new revolutionary subject. The stories of the youth on the Isla de la Juventud make it clear that the creation of the New Man remained a concrete task for socialist society.

In this regard, her works resonate with those of Guevara, who recognized in "Socialism and Man in Cuba" that "in order to build communism it is necessary to build a new man alongside the new material foundations" (372).[8] Yet, unlike the perspective of Gómez, which strives to expose the social, moral, cultural, and psychological particularities of each individual—positive and negative alike—, Guevara's extended description of the New Man leaves little space to admit its diversity. He wrote "Socialism and Man in Cuba" with the intent of refuting the criticisms that accused the socialist state of negating individual subjectivity. Even so, from the very first lines of the essay, the masses constitute an essential persona in the construction of the New Man. In an effort to expose the ways in which a new type of individual is constructed in this society by presenting his own interpretation of the history of the revolution, Guevara identifies guerrilla warfare, popular mobilization, and certain crucial events as the primary driving forces in the formation of the New Man, always as a part of the collective. The essay effectively objectifies both the individual and the masses; though both prove indispensable for carrying out social transformations, they are only able to coalesce through the catalyzing push of the vanguard (the guerrilla, Fidel Castro). Yet even within the homogenizing perspective of Guevara, the creation of the New Man is complicated: not only is society responsible for the "direct and indirect education" of the revolutionary subject, but it also must be capable of submitting itself to "a conscious process of self-education" (371).[9]

Sara Gómez recognizes that process, but she also calls attention to the fact that it does not take place in a linear fashion, unchangeable and immersed in a space filled only by socialist ideology. Beyond the economic conditions—to which Marxism accords exclusive relevance—multiple other factors determine this process, including race, culture, gender, and sexual orientation. Whereas for Guevara, youth consisted of a "malleable clay with which the new man can be constructed with none of the old defects [*taras*]" (380),[10] Gómez contests this assertion through her depiction of adolescents in the process of reeducation on the Isla de la Juventud. In order to do so, she explicitly avoids obviating or minimizing the minors' pasts. It is not certain that what the Argentine guerrilla refers to as "taras"—and which Gómez sees instead as the personal characteristics of these youths, consequences of their familial and social environs—will automatically disappear. Reeducation is far from a perfectly mechanical process involving an expert potter and malleable clay.

Thus, by introducing the complex condition of race in revolutionary Cuba, Gómez highlights the existential complexity of black individuals, unexpectedly producing a disquieting and trenchant provocation of the viewer. This kind of critical inquiry serves as a consistent strategy throughout her films, though the director always eludes any definitive and conclusive response. The questions raised by the characters and narrators of her works are rarely answered. They are left hanging before the audience, the Cuban people, to whom they are undoubtedly directed. *En la otra isla*, for example, interviews various youths on scholarship on the Isla de la Juventud. Particularly disquieting is the story of Rafael, who denounces the racial prejudices still present in socialist society that he endured while living in Havana. Rafael is a tenor trained at the National Art Schools who joined a lyric art company in 1964, where he performed in various operas and zarzuelas. However, he began to feel a certain "apathy" among his white female coworkers, who felt uncomfortable performing romantic scenes with a black tenor. Rafael's unease is palpable in this interview. The young black has trouble articulating his problem and rarely looks at the camera. He seems ashamed at being an object of racial discrimination. Sara Gómez manages to transmit this sense of discomfort to the viewer, thanks to an original technique in filming the interview: she positions herself almost behind Rafael, in the background, so that he must turn his head toward her, and away from the camera, in order to respond. He thus sustains a rather halting conversation with the director and avoids looking directly at the camera. The viewer who witnesses his story sees only his profile, while he slowly yet directly expresses himself to Sara Gómez, his interlocutor. The director thus achieves a degree of intimacy between interviewer and interviewee: the dialogue appears almost secret, just between the two of them and not open to the spectator, who instead has the impression of stumbling in—as a kind of voyeur—on an intimate conversation between two black individuals. Rafael's words are not directed to the audience; they are not public.

In another sequence, where Rafael directly faces the camera, he expresses hope that in the future, racial prejudices will disappear from Cuban society thanks to the revolution and the existence of reeducation projects like the one documented in this film. However, Gómez insists that the revolution alone cannot eliminate racial problems; this will also require the action of young men like Rafael. It is conceivable to think that her incitement to provoke change is directed not only to the interviewee but also to the spectator, to all of Cuba. She is demanding political and racial consciousness on all sides. By her revelation of the shame experienced by Rafael, the filmmaker seems to push him to shake off the fear of exposing his own suffering provoked by racial discrimination in present-day Cuba, and to thereby make him capable of naming it and to be unafraid of fighting it. Gómez opposes the silence that masks racial problems in post-revolutionary Cuba. Toward the end of the interview, Rafael asks the director if she believes that one day he will be able to perform in Verdi's *La Traviata*. There are no answers; the film ends in silence, expressing the inconclusive reflection promoted by Sara Gómez in this film as well as others.

Gómez demonstrates a similar perspective in the documentary *Guanabacoa: Crónica de mi familia* (Guanabacoa: Chronicle of My Family, 1966), which exposes the socio-economic complexity of black Cubans through their own family histories. In an effort to limit her appeal to textuality as an authoritarian form of knowledge—in other words, by avoiding subtitles and explanatory messages about history and society—, Gómez begins her presentation of the cultural and religious diversity of Havana life in Guanabacoa through visual and musical references: from the presence of the US author Ernest Hemingway and the imposing ceremonial practices of the secret fraternity of Abakuá, to views of the neighborhood Jewish cemetery and recurring scenes of a classical music performance in a public park. In the filming of this concert, the camera lingers on the proud and intent faces of some of the members of Sara Gómez's family (mostly men in the orchestra and women in the audience). The documentary opens with the appearance of their names in stylized cursive subtitles—possibly alluding to a "classical" lineage. The voice of the filmmaker herself reinforces this impression of pride and familial distinction. The recollections strung together by Madrina, her eighty-year-old great aunt, reveal the value that Gómez perceives in memory.

It is essential to note, however, that the film does not in any way represent a general historical memory of black Cubans as a whole, but rather portrays a single family, with its own internal contradictions and its similarities and differences with other blacks. Individuality—in opposition to the homogenization of the masses, once again takes on a central role in Gómez's work. In this case, the singularity brought to the viewer's attention transpires in the exposition of a rigorous morality practiced by the majority of the members of her family, who also belonged to select Societies of Color with names as significant as *El Progreso* (Progress) and *El Porvenir* (The Future). "These were societies for blacks—for *certain* blacks," emphasizes Sara Gómez's voice from off-screen, signaling the ways in which these institutions structured social divisions within the black community. The family characters shown in this first part of the documentary are exponents of the black and mulatto petty bourgeoisie who generally held instruction and education in high esteem as a means of escape from the state of poverty and discrimination suffered by blacks on the island.

After the presentation of the "distinction" and "decency" proper to this black middle class through Madrina's recollections, the images of la Tía Berta appear. Even within the same family, this character appears different: silently, the film shows her daily household chores and the humble conditions of her room. Gómez's aunt pertains to another social class, and her morality also differs from that of Madrina. While the latter emphasizes the Catholic rigor of the family in her own tale, la Tía Berta appears worshiping her altar dedicated to gods of the *Regla de Orisha* or *Santería* (a Cuban religion of Yoruba origin). Her presence is silent yet imposing. Sara Gómez confesses that Berta is her favorite aunt, because "she for one doesn't have any hang-ups."[11]

At the beginning of the documentary, the director announces that she has dedicated it to "Ms. Luisa María López y Galaimena, whom her sister's grandchildren call la Madrina."[12] Until this point, her voice had been sweet and respectful, yet she then suddenly adds: "but this is not enough,"[13] in a bitter tone. "What is not enough?" viewers might ask without receiving an answer. As an answer they will receive only the multitude of facts and experiences transmitted in the film. Any conclusion will be produced only by the viewers. Nonetheless, it is evident that Sara Gómez's new thinking plays off la Madrina and la Tía Berta, distanced yet inherited from both. Fulleda León has described the documentary as "A cinematographic poem that pulls its cards of authenticity out of the family chest, where black families have tried to hide our false aspirations, our mediocre existences, and small human miseries, like a heinous and unspeakable crime" (44).[14] The filmmaker seems to ask herself here what to do with these two branches of her family, each with its own contradictions inherited from the history of the nation and the family, in the midst of a radical, revolutionary transformation of society. Even though *Guanabacoa: Crónica de mi familia* begins with a dedication to the austere Madrina, it is with the images of la Tía Berta leaving her humble room in a tenement apartment that the film comes to a close. With these sequences Sara Gómez leaves viewers with yet another powerful question: "Must we fight the need to be a different, better black? Must we come to Guanabacoa accepting an integral history, an integral Guanabacoa, and say so?"[15] This sentence expresses the difficulty in determining to what extent black Cubans can and should change according to the standards of the new society, improving themselves and abandoning their beliefs and popular culture, and whether or not they should recognize their history as marginalized subjects. The question also prefigures the great sociological concerns that would dominate the entire cinematic production of Sara Gómez: the search for the authentic expression of being, often hidden behind body language, daily experiences, or a simple look.

Guanabacoa: Crónica de mi familia offers a healthy counterimage to the utopian, nationalistic project of complete Cuban synthesis. In this sense the film resembles Walterio Carbonell's critical posture regarding national history. Without going into the theoretical problematization put forward by Carbonell, simply by exposing the social and historical diversity of one segment of the Cuban population through the presentation of her own family, in her documentary, Sara Gómez demonstrates the impossibility of a monolithic understanding of national history produced from the limited perspective of the traditionally hegemonic white, heterosexual Cuban man.

Furthermore, by exploring history through its diverse and contradictory manifestations, Sara Gómez tended to incorporate a cultural analysis of Cuban society. The didactic documentary *Iré a Santiago* is a perfect example. In a suggestive filming technique, this work combines a narrative voice that exposes certain stereotyped conceptions of Cubans and of Santiagueros in particular—as if they were taken straight out of a tourist guide book—, with images of anonymous characters in their trajectory through the streets of the city. Gómez presents two of these inhabitants, whom the camera follows with particular interest, as "La santiaguera" and "El santiaguero." By introducing them as individuals, the narrator provides specific details rather than of-fering a uniform, general portrait of the Santiago population. Through Gómez's filmic perspective, these characters respond to personal identifications and inhabit concrete bodies that move with the rhythm intrinsic to the city. She therefore shrewdly decon-structs the myths and stereotypes that her candid yet subtly ironic voice had men-tioned earlier in the film.

There is no single, unified mass; it is impossible for Sara Gómez to portray the Cuban people as a homogeneous whole. Here, race acquires primordial connotation. She recognizes in *Iré a Santiago* that "There is no doubt regarding our Caribbean condition. But all of this is almost a Cuban legend built in a dream. Santiago is there and, in that sense, it's true: Cuba is an island in the Caribbean. And the mulatto? Mulatto is a state of being."[16] And how else is she to recreate that "state of being" but by examining the daily actions of Cuban men and women? This is precisely the focus of *Iré a Santiago*. The documentary genre, which privileges the pursuit of the truest possible representation of reality, overflows the bounds of traditional techniques in Sara Gómez's creation. *Iré a Santiago* extends beyond the simple use of the interview and compilation of historical facts in favor of a more dynamic form of expression, though the director does not forestall history in the process. In this sense, she turns to the distinctive Haitian presence in the country's east—a result of the revolution in the former French colony in 1791—as a means of exploring the ethnic, cultural, and racial particularities of the population of Santiago. Under the heading "Santiago and the French," Gómez proceeds to demonstrate the influence of Haitian immigrants and their descendants, who maintain the cultural legacy of their ancestors: "Because Santi-ago has blacks that call themselves French and dance a ballroom dance to the rhythm of the Tumba, which they call the French Tumba [or the *Tumba Francesa*],"[17] the voice of the director reminds us. Gómez points to the fact that, just as Cuban society cannot be forced into a singular, homogenized mold, its racial and ethnic groups cannot be understood without taking into account the internal singularities occasioned by the nation's diverse cultural, political, and economic dynamics. Nonetheless, a certain irony surfaces in Gómez's words when she informs us that "a century and a half later, there are no Frenchmen . . . or French coffee plantations left in Santiago."[18] Only traditions such as the *Tumba Francesa* survive, which, as Sara Gómez's voice acknowl-edges with particular emphasis, "they call it French." Cultural traditions persist, and the new society cannot simply make a clean slate of them.

The most recurrent ethical-aesthetic elements in Sara Gómez's work reappear in her most famous film, *De cierta manera* (One Way or Another, 1974), which is also her last production and the first feature film to be directed by a woman in Cuba. Considered by the critic García Borrero as "the most intense film to venture into the image of the so-called marginal zones of our society" ("Sara Gómez" [2]),[19] this film's perspective is coherent with the rest of Gómez's work: it denies any broad and easy solution and demands an understanding of the individuals and their particular issues. For the director, truth was not easily discernible. But her aesthetic procedures, which mixed fiction with documentary and analytic interrogation, allowed her to approach the question of civic subjectivity. Most remarkable is Gómez's adept juxtaposition in *De cierta manera* between documentary scenes, which express broad social changes, and fiction, which focuses on internal transformations in the individual.

Set in the 1970s, *De cierta manera* recreates the relationship between Mario and Yolanda. Mario, a mulatto, lives in Las Yaguas, a poor neighborhood in Havana whose residents would be relocated to Miraflores, a new community built by its own residents and workers. He hesitates at the possibility of joining the secret society Abakuá, which is of African origin and restricted to men only. Yolanda is a white teacher from a middle-class background who does not understand the minority enclave-mentality of her school, which is located in Mario's neighborhood. Before being sent to Las Yaguas, she thought that world "no longer existed." The couple's misunderstandings are determined by machismo, racism, and cultural stereotypes. Additionally, a voice-over and the commentaries presented through captions offer an official point of view on different situations associated with marginality. From an institutional point of view, religions of African origin are evidence of underdevelopment, elements in the life of these marginal sectors that should be eliminated. The voice-over informs the viewer that the society Abakuá, or *ñañiguismo*, is "an expression of masculine chauvinism" opposed to progress and the assimilation of "the values of modern life . . . It generates marginality and promotes parallel social relations that are the antithesis of racial integration."[20] However, in contrast with these clinical and haughty assessments, the images of a Santería celebration that Yolanda attends with Mario do not elicit a sense of disparagement or disapproval. The effective combination of fiction and documentary on the one hand, and of on-screen personalities, voice-overs, and captions on the other, provokes once again a personal reflection on the part of the spectator.

Prejudices also emanate from the characters that surround the couple, from individuals who pertain to Mario's social circle as well as Yolanda's. Some of Mario's friends, for example, perceive Yolanda as a different kind of person who would threaten Mario's masculinity and integrity. Mario himself violently blames Yolanda for the internal transformations that eventually lead him to expose a lie propagated by a coworker to the rest of group, an attitude perceived in his community as improper for a "real man." The concept of manliness, in fact, is a point of debate throughout the film, as it constitutes an essential moral element for these marginal sectors of the population. Meanwhile, prejudices also issue from Yolanda's "world." She has a mulatta friend who looks down on Mario and declares that in spite of the revolution and its transformations, "we are not all equal." Through this character, who in turn suffers the patronizing treatment of her (white) male companion, in addition to other women in the film, Sara Gómez examines the cycles of perpetuation of gender deprecation and inequality.

Meanwhile, the couple is also surrounded by the neighborhood and its process of improvement. The film constantly shows demolition projects of old houses, revealing in the process the destruction of the old and construction of the new. But it is not as easy to pulverize the past of the men and women who have lived inside those walls. It is not enough to deliver blows to the stone walls of these meager dwellings; occasionally marginality is presented as an issue of "mentality." Though the protagonists themselves use this word, no conclusive solution ever emerges. A glimmer of real hope surfaces, however, in the history of a black boxer who has reinvented himself as a vocalist. He suggests it is fear that impedes some individuals from abandoning their marginal lives. He feels that to do so requires courage, since it is difficult for those who have always lived in the confined space of the ghetto to adapt to existence outside of it, exposed to the whole of society. But this is a necessary step, he proclaims.

In general, Yolanda and Mario encounter substantial difficulties in understanding one other. She defends her independence as a woman, and he is tied to a sense of manliness that conflicts with Yolanda's behavior. Each hails from a very different sociocultural background, which the revolution has suddenly brought into contact. The fact that they come to share the same space within society does not guarantee that they will fully understand each other. The contradictions that conflict this couple, comprised of a white woman and a mulatto man in times of undeniable revolutionary exuberance, are certainly not out of the ordinary. In her study on interracial relationships in Cuba, Nadine Fernández underscores similar kinds of incongruities. While such couples integrated into a society that had supposedly overcome racial differences, these issues continued to exert a constant presence in their lives:

> The interracial couples that embodied the socialist dream of building an egalitarian revolutionary Cuba were caught in this ideological crossfire. Cubans continued to live in both a racialized social world and, in many instances, a raceless socialist society. The revolution's dreams of racelessness were sown on a terrain historically stratified by race, class, and gender inequalities. Race may have become a classic non-topic for the government, but as the interracial couples realized, race was far from being a non-topic in daily life. (79)

The last images of the film show the protagonists Yolanda and Mario walking heatedly down the streets of the neighborhood in transformation. There is a new material world surrounding them—the brand new buildings—, but they have not yet caught up to its pace. They are not yet the "New" Cubans promised by Che Guevara.

Epiphany of the Face through the Lens of Guillén Landrián

Similar processes to those utilized by Sara Gómez to recreate the existence of marginalized individuals in revolutionary Cuba are also present in the works of Nicolás Guillén Landrián (Camagüey, 1938).[21] Like Gómez, Guillén Landrián was one of the most eminent filmmakers in the country; as assistant director of ICAIC since its inception, he produced an extensive and relevant documentary oeuvre. Between 1962 and 1971, the time he spent at this institution, he directed eighteen documentaries whose themes varied from the life of peasants in eastern Cuba to the labor of the working class in different sectors of the population. Despite its impressive and suggestive poetic refinement, the majority of his work was received with suspicion by the revolutionary institutions, possibly because of his complicated existential recreation of the Cuban subject immersed in the revolutionary epic.

Emblematic in this regard is his most famous piece, *Coffea Arabiga* (1968), which ICAIC commissioned to him as a documentation of the Cordón de La Habana, an intensive coffee campaign developed around the capital toward the end of the 1960s. Particularly notable in this film is the disruptive, unsettling editing, which consistently provokes questions regarding the pertinence of agricultural tasks promoted by the government in an arbitrary manner. A vertiginous, fragmented reality transpires in the apparently incoherent interaction among history and urban or rural daily life, popular culture, traditional and modern coffee-growing techniques, the benefits of the revolution, and the anachronism of both US presence in republican-era Cuba and Soviet presence in the socialist era. There is, for example, a hurriedly done street interview of a Bulgarian woman on the question of certain technical elements of coffee cultivation that had earlier been broadcast on the radio. Paradoxically, the film accompanied the radio report with overhead shots of pre-1959 buildings in the Vedado neighborhood, when it would have undoubtedly made more sense to present rural images of coffee cultivation. The Bulgarian woman, besides, responds in her own language, incomprehensible to most viewers, though the interview did have a few words that were distinguishable on account of having been aired in radio broadcasts. The tropical sun, revolutionary mobilization, some reminiscent images of a bourgeois past in Cuban life, the arrival of new "brothers" from Eastern Europe—all of these elements comprise the contradictory, whirlwind reality artfully conveyed in the film.

Coffea Arabiga opens with several lines of poetry in praise of the victorious nation, written by his renowned uncle Nicolás Guillén Batista. From the beginning Guillén Landrián focuses on the people themselves more than the product that had instigated ICAIC's commission of the film. The first few minutes of the documentary feature images of the old coffee plantations created by French Haitian immigrants from eastern Cuba following the Haitian Revolution. Yet the caption—"black people as workforce in the coffee fields. / the blacks. / what? / the blacks?! / yes / the blacks"[22]—guides the viewer's attention toward the real producers of the coffee: the plantation slaves. These verses appear on the screen amidst photographs of chains and shackles, the sound of the *Tumba Francesa*, and images of blacks dancing to this rhythm of French origin. The presentation of the black individuals in this sequence is an affirmation, in spite of the doubts and negations surrounding the heavy weight of their existence in Cuba. Also suggestive are the still shots that for close to a minute show a black woman putting rollers in her hair while romantic verses play over the waves of Radio Baracoa. After these images emerges a series of revolutionary propaganda posters encouraging the incorporation of women in agriculture, faces of female workers also wearing rollers, and scenes of coffee harvesting—all to the rhythm of the imposing *Marcha del Guerrillero* (Guerilla March). These images all seem completely unconnected. Nonetheless, a disquieting thread emerges among the sugarcoated radio broadcast depicting romantic fantasies, the dreamy expression of the black woman changing her hairstyle, the revolutionary propaganda's peremptory call to mass mobilization, and the allusion to the guerilla and his driving, incontestable force: dream and reality, fantasy and action—all constitutive elements of the revolutionary present. During a period in which authorities exhort national cohesion, this montage is dangerously unsettling.

Who, then, are the Cuban producers—and consumers—of coffee? In *Coffea Arabiga* the people cease to be an indistinct mass, and the anonymous subject acquires a face, especially through the extended gaze of the viewer. Similar to Sara Gómez, Guillén Landrián inquires as to the individual, always within the revolution. He also understands that he cannot achieve intimacy though preconceived discourses—hence his constant appeal to showing the daily and intimate life of Cubans in their moments of solitude apart from the totalizing movement of the masses. Both filmmakers seem suspicious of generalizations and obsessed with the search for the reality underlying the intricate text fabricated through the gestures, thought, expression, and creativity of popular culture.

At the end of *Coffea Arabiga* popular cheers to revolutionary leaders mingle with the drums of the *Tumba Francesa*, and the images of blacks dancing this rhythm presented at the beginning of the film make a reappearance. The frenzy derives as much from the beating of the drums as from the multitude shouting its approval of Fidel Castro. Another caption appears at this point: "in [C]uba, all blacks and all whites and we all drink coffee."[23] This assertion paraphrases the chorus of a famous song by Eliseo Grenet titled "Mamá Inés" yet introduces a slight change from the original lyric: "Ay, Mamá Inés, all of us blacks drink coffee."[24] The alterations introduced by Guillén Landrián are significant: Whom does this "we all" refer to, beyond blacks and their white counterparts who drink coffee? Who is this "we" in Cuba?

Nonetheless, despite the inclusion of this phrase, the confusion of drums and a turbulent revolutionary multitude do not conclude the film in triumphalist choral ecstasy. The director reproduces the song "The Fool on the Hill" by the Beatles in dangerous proximity to the images of the masses facing Fidel Castro. The censorship of Guillén Landrián's work has often been superficially attributed to the authorities' hasty judgment of this inclusion. Its irreverence in utilizing a song by a rock band prohibited in Cuba at the time tends to overshadow the message of the particular song Guillén Landrián selected. "The Fool on the Hill" resonates with the revolutionary gesture itself, yet it could also serve as a critique of the bureaucratization of the original revolutionary dream fomented by the popular majority.

Such a complex vision of revolutionary society also strikes the viewer of *Desde La Habana ¡1969!* (From Havana, 1969!). Without an explicit explanation, the explosion of images and sounds obstructs any monolithic interpretation, as Guillén Landrián strives to expose the paradoxes of reality through an existential perspective. The phrase "Mother Nature's Son," from another Beatles song, is followed by images of nuclear bombs being dropped on Japan by US armed forces. As if a continuation of the messages initiated by *Coffea Arabiga*, now the music of the Beatles accompanies a denunciation of the crimes in Viet Nam, repressions against demonstrators for civil rights, and government tolerance for the KKK. The United States that permits and commits such deplorable acts is the same country that puts the first man on the moon as a great display of progress. A foregoing debate regarding the pertinence and considerations of development and underdevelopment comes into play here. Guillén Landrián also reproduces the first images of the film *Memorias del subdesarrollo* (Memories of Underdevelopment, dir. Gutiérrez Alea, 1968), which question the meaning of development to the rhythm of black Cubans playing drums. The original idea for these shots, now classics in Latin American cinema, has been attributed to Guillén Landrián (Álvarez, "Pequeño homenaje"), and they certainly coincide with his dizzying aesthetic. In *Desde La Habana*, these images appear linked to the very agricultural labor that would supposedly lead Cuba to overcome the problem of underdevelopment.

The film also exposes the situation prior to 1959 (pseudo-republic, a succession of tyrants, misery, racial segregation), expressing the need for revolutionary triumph. It thus presents history as an indispensable antidote to national oblivion (one of the characteristics of underdevelopment recreated in *Memorias*). Fidel Castro appears yet again at a podium, in a diatribe about the deaths of Ernesto Guevara and Camilo Cienfuegos, revolutionary commandants who had shared leadership with him until that point. The film also presents Castro urging people to join the coffee campaign, as well as technical and productive commentaries on coffee farming and various testimonies on Cuban society before and after 1959. A sense of absurdity dominates the film and penetrates the compressed distance between destruction and the creation of a new world. Another Beatles line, "Everybody's got something to hide except me and my monkey," serves as a refrain throughout the movie. Except for existence itself, which is irreducible since it can only be had or lost, the meaning of everything remains mysterious. Reality is not flat but chaotic. And this nervous disorder serves as the basis of Guillén Landrián's films. To accept his schizophrenic perspective is to renounce the contemplation of chaos and jump right into it, experience it. His work cultivates doubt rather than indoctrinating or informing. It does not appease the expectations of a government that hoped to vanquish uncertainty and chaos.

Guillén Landrián "was capable of capturing the volatility of the moment and hit rock bottom,"[25] as Olga García Yero recognizes. "An interpreter of his reality," as the filmmaker himself would confess in *Café con leche* (Coffee with Milk, 2003), the documentary in his homage by Manuel Zayas. This attempt to probe the very interstices of existence explains his chaotic cinematic vision of a reality that may appear to be organized under the strictest Marxist codes—structured by revolutionary slogans, ideological manuals, and effervescent discourses—but is in fact always disordered. This perspective does not correspond with the predominant line of thinking on the island during the 1960s and 1970s, when the majority of Cubans dutifully dedicated themselves to the construction of the new society. Guillén Landrián's images are not explicitly counterrevolutionary, but they also do not fully reflect the Cuban that Ernesto Guevara envisioned as well on his way toward becoming the New Man. Julio Ramos indicates as much in his assertion that the filmmaker "produces a cinema against the grain of the politics of the body and of culture established on the basis of Guevara's historical speeches on voluntary work and 'moral' incentives at the beginning of the 1960s" (46).[26]

It was also Guevara who would refer in his treatise to the institutionalization of society as a phenomenon that fit perfectly with the "image of the multitudes marching towards the future," describing it as a "harmonious set of channels, steps, restraints, and well-oiled mechanisms which facilitate the advance, which facilitate the natural selection of those destined to march in the vanguard, and which bestow rewards on those who fulfill their duties and punishments on those who commit a crime against the society that is being built" (373).[27] Such institutions—often presented by the director through a critical and ironic perspective, in documentaries such as *Taller Claudio A. Camejo Línea y 18* (Claudio A. Camejo, Línea and 18th Sts., 1971)—fulfilled their function in the case of Guillén Landrián, whose work was heavily censored. Condemned as counterrevolutionary, he was imprisoned on various occasions, and his health deteriorated considerably until he emigrated to Miami in 1989.

Another resemblance between the work of Sara Gómez and that of Guillén Landrián lies in the fact that messages in their works are not deliberately and exclusively directed toward the black Cuban population. Guillén and Gómez both deal with blackness through their radical problematization of general marginality and the

New Man's formation process within the socialist society. The presence of the black Cuban in their creations is unavoidable, yet this presence is not conveyed through confrontational or vindicatory discourses. In their works, blacks are an inevitable presence in Cuban society, even if the ideal of a raceless nation and the push for ethnic and cultural mestizaje tend to render it invisible.

In prior publications I have analyzed this ethical-aesthetic strategy for expressing the existence of the black through the concept of "occurrence" (Casamayor, 2009), based on the term *ocurrence* developed by Alain Badiou in *Logiques des Mondes* (2006). In the context of my work, occurrence constitutes a particular presentation of racial facticity that ignores notions of otherness in order to register, quite simply, the existence of the black subject within Cuban society. Occurrence facilitates the expression of what it means to be black without conceiving one as other: that is, outside of a relationship of confrontational codependence with whiteness and beyond the tension induced by the question, *To what extent am I myself, and to what extent am I someone else?*

Occurrence is identifiable in documentaries such as *Los del baile* (The Party People, 1965), which is dedicated to popular music, specifically the *mozambique*, a rhythm created by Pedro Izquierdo "Pello el Afrokán" in the 1960s.[28] Of clear African extraction, the *mozambique* was a plebian national rhythm representing the novelty of the times, the popular character of the revolution, and cultural ties to Africa. The *mozambique* also received broad media coverage, possibly as a decoy to divert attention away from the significant exodus of important cultural figures and film celebrities. Additionally, it reflected a political tendency at the time to privilege national musical genres and undermine the influence of rock, simply because it derived from the capitalist system (Moore 182). In 1965, the same year in which *Los del baile* was produced, Fidel Castro even publicly commissioned Pello el Afrokán to compose a song exalting popular participation in agricultural tasks and took particular interest in its recording process (Moore 184). It is no coincidence, then, that this work by Guillén Landrián explodes with the strong percussion of the *mozambique*. However, the intense soundtrack does not express the revolutionary euphoria that ideologically informs the creation and diffusion of Afro-Cuban rhythm. Moreover, in resonance with *Coffea Arabiga*, which denotes a primordial focalization on the coffee producing and consuming society, this documentary takes more interest in bodies in motion— not always dancing the *mozambique*—than in the musical genre per se. It is significant that the work is titled *Los del baile*. The director assembles images of Cubans that are alien to the context of the revolutionary epic: dancing, drinking beers, enjoying carnival. The beauty and abandon of the bodies at the festivity stand out beneath the almost deafening pounding of the drums. Mostly blacks and mestizos, these individuals also appear, calmer and more somber, in domestic scenes. Here the *mozambique* gives way to smooth, taciturn *danzas*, and the camera returns its focus to a black woman making herself up, perhaps preparing herself for the dance. This time, she straightens her hair, leaving it smooth rather than kinky and natural. The film often surprises these black characters absorbed in their thoughts, with a deep, melancholic, and markedly disquieting expression.

While I agree with Dean Luis Reyes's evaluation that in *Los del baile* "it is clear that the ethnographic vocation of the director is not confined to a political or ethnic militancy," the expressions of its black characters are also far from insipid or innocuous.[29] Their gaze is penetrating. It cuts across centuries without stopping at the Cuban context in which the documentary is inscribed. It also appears to present the pain of a wound gaping open since slavery: this gaze represents an enduring melancholy that black Cubans will continue to endure as long as their racial condition is perceived in terms of otherness in Cuban society and culture.

This powerful appeal to the gaze as a critical tool thus represents another striking characteristic of Guillén Landrián's cinematic poetics, steeped in the search for existential depth in Cuban society: a powerful appeal to the gaze as a critical tool. While this gaze is not restrictive to the black characters that appear in his documentaries, my analysis in this article focuses on this use in particular, given its peculiar, unsettling effects. The strategic use of facial expressions in Guillén Landrián's work invokes the theories of Emmanuel Levinas on the irruption of the face in the dynamics of identity construction and of alterity. This philosopher presented the *epiphany of the face* as an expression of experience, something that previously established identities in society can never quite capture. The face becomes a real presence that dismantles the stereotypes, because it exists and appears without ever being invoked, defying the discourses and structures that strive to immobilize it as an established theme, already explained and accounted for and thereby incorporated into the fictions of identity constructed by hegemonic powers. The question is how to insert the gaze of Cuban men and women in the midst of a dance or immersed in their intimate, daily activities, lost in their private emotions, into Guevara's calculated image of the working and combative masses constituted by homogenized new men and women. How can we explain this shade of melancholy in the black faces of Guillén Landrián, within a society that claims to be egalitarian and free of racial discrimination?

Visitation—the term utilized by Lévinas to describe the face's abrupt appearance in a context structured by those invested with the power to determine identities—offsets any pretense of totality. And it does so without delivering speeches or pronouncements. Nonetheless, Levinas's reminder that "the face speaks" helps to explain why the black faces of *Los del baile* are disquieting even in their silence. Levinas also explains that to speak is to come out from behind appearance, from behind the established form, and create an opening (a possibility or opportunity) in the face's own opening (the mouth; physical act of speaking).[30] The intimate, silent, and silenced experience of blacks in Cuba irrupts through these gazes that hold the viewer captive. And it is this elusive presence that confounds the perfect plan for the New Man as sketched by Guevara.

Marginality and racial, social, and economic inequalities in times of revolutionary transformation also reemerge in the film *En un barrio viejo* (In an Old Neighborhood, 1963). Once again sparse in speech and dialogue, this documentary implicitly expresses the complexity of the existential transition toward socialism. A military squadron passes through a humble neighborhood in Havana under the tired or indifferent gaze of its inhabitants dedicated to their daily activities: hanging around at a barber shop, playing dominos, dancing the rumba, or simply contemplating the imperturbable march of the revolutionaries from the balconies above the street. The effect is that of two separate worlds suddenly coexisting in an impoverished neighborhood whose disappearance is supposedly imminent. Also featured are poor children for whom the revolution promises bright futures; white middle-class men being approached by a beggar; and black workers with somber, resigned, or dreamy expressions framed by the camera. Soviet icons appear alongside the Cuban flag, and the lens follows a few white, apparently wealthy residents and women of various ages walking down the street. These characters comprise a panoply of anonymous, voiceless individuals, in whom Guillén Landrián's cinematic sensibility exposes an imposing individuality, in spite of their silent presence, within the popular mass. These are the neighbors: revolutionary people yet full of subtle contradictions, standing still and watching the squadron pass by. Only the sound of the precise, unalterable steps of the squadron on the pavement accompanies its shots. The images of the people, in contrast, are set to music, which primarily alternates between sad ballads and the imposing rhythm of *batá* drums—instruments of Yoruba origin used in the liturgical music of the Regla de Osha and in popular music. Finally, after a series of images of a solid Catholic church, the film turns to a religious ceremony of African origins that combines crucifixes and Afro-Cuban liturgical objects: animals (a small crocodile) utilized in the ceremony along with the flags of Cuba and of the 26th of July Movement. Posters of Fidel Castro and Comandante Camilo Cienfuegos adorn the walls of a humble living room, alongside shrines dedicated to honored gods. We might ask how Marxist doctrine is able to live side by side with Catholicism in this Afro-Cuban religious ceremony. The participants of the liturgical frenzy range from whites to blacks and adults to children (some of whom appear to be awaiting initiation). Are these people the "malleable clay" that Ernesto Guevara hoped to see sprout into the definitive New Man? A caption reading "THE END, but it is not the end" brings the documentary to a close, alluding to an irresolution of contradictions akin to Sara Gómez's perspective. With the destruction of the old neighborhood and erection of a new one, will the New Man appear? What will happen with the faces revealed by the filmmaker in his documentary? Will their complexity also disappear?

After nearly a decade of exile in Miami, Guillén Landrián directed his last documentary, *Inside Downtown*, in 2001, in which he casts an inquisitive look at the social contradictions and marginal individuals hidden behind the appearance of order and luxury, forgotten by the rest of this Florida city. He died two years later, mired in poverty and lacking the recognition he deserved.

Conclusions

The perspectives on revolutionary life adopted by Sara Gómez and Nicolás Guillén Landrián do not coincide with institutional orthodoxy. These two filmmakers bore a keen interest in the experience of traditionally marginalized Cubans within the context of the revolution. Black Cubans thus receive in their work a treatment rarely found in post-revolutionary cultural production. They do not obey the stereotyped image of the black saved by the revolution, in the process of improving himself and becoming the New Man, nor do they position themselves in confrontation with whites. In the cinematography of Gómez and Guillén Landrián, they are only revealed in their day-to-day existence and in the lived experience legible in body movements, gestures, and facial expressions. And this presence could be more compelling than any explicit vindication, since it entails an experience that exceeds the bounds of verbal expression.

Many of their works were censored or criticized by cultural authorities unable to accept chaotic human vitality beyond the scope of ideology. For many years the legacy of both artists remained largely unrecognized, and it was not until the beginning of the 2000s that new generations of Cubans could discover the important message emitted through their films. Since then, the rediscovery of these films has occasioned retrospectives, commemorative films, and diverse research initiatives. The recognition of the relevance and vitality of the cinematic vision of Sara Gómez and Nicolás Guillén Landrián has finally arrived.

Notes

1. "¿Somos un pueblo pequeño que necesitamos unos de otros, necesitamos el esfuerzo de todos y vamos a dividirnos ahora en blancos y negros? . . . ¿Eso para qué serviría sino para debilitar a la nación, para debilitar a Cuba?"
2. "se alzaron en Guerra los cubanos, rompieron desde el primer día de libertad los grillos de sus siervos, conviertieron a costa de su vida la indignidad española en un pueblo de hombres libres." For a more detailed analysis of Martí's interpretations of black Cubans, see Ada Ferrer.
3. "Hombre es más que blanco, más que mulato, más que negro."
4. Guevara writes in "Socialism and Man in Cuba" that "The leaders of the revolution have children who do not learn to call their father with their first faltering words; they have wives who must be part of the general sacrifice of their lives to carry the revolution to its destination; their friends are strictly limited to their comrades in revolution. There is no life outside the revolution" (Los dirigentes de la Revolución tienen hijos que en sus primeros balbuceos, no aprenden a nombrar al padre; mujeres que deben ser parte del sacrificio general de su vida para llevar la Revolución a su destino; el marco de los amigos responde estrictamente al marco de los compañeros de la Revolución. No hay vida fuera de ella) (381).

    Translator's note: Translations from Guevara's speech are my own, though in some cases I have consulted the translation by Brian Baggins printed in *The Che Guevara Reader*, ed. David Deutschmann. Melbourne: Ocean, 2003. Also available online at *www.marxists.org/archive/guevara/1965/03/man-socialism.htm*.
5. As I indicate in my article "Représentations du Noir dans la littérature cubaine des années 1990 et débuts du XXIe siècle," the social relevance of this novel resides in its contribution of a contradictory vision of the process of "improvement" of the black, revolutionary protagonist. Its author, Manuel Granados, was censored, and his novel—runner up for the Casa de las Américas Prize in 1967—was only published thanks to the intervention of Julio Cortázar (Howe 51).
6. The harsh criticism of Rodríguez Coronel serves as an example: "Granados's novel would have been able to deal adequately and directly with the specific problem of a black discriminated against in terms of both class and race—doubly oppressed—if the author had adopted a realist perspective in his treatment of the subject, if he weren't so encumbered by ideological tendencies that overestimate the role of race, which is only one factor to consider within class struggle, and if he had not been so influenced by 'blackness'" (La novela de Granados sí hubiera podido brindar con acierto, de manera directa, la problemática específica de un negro, discriminado desde el punto de vista clasista y racista, doblemente oprimido, si el escritor hubiera adoptado una perspectiva realista en el tratamiento temático y no hubiera estado imbuido por tendencias ideológicas que sobrevaloran el papel de la raza, el cual sólo es un factor a tener en cuenta, dentro de la lucha de clases, si Granados no hubiera estado influido por "la negritud") (155).

7. "Rompí la placenta y nací, grité: ¡Coño, qué es esto! Quedé parado en dos columnas de concreto armado. Mis piernas estaban sobre la tierra."

8. "para construir el comunismo, simultáneamente con la base material hay que hacer al hombre nuevo."

9. "un proceso consciente de autoeducación"

10. "arcilla maleable con que se puede construir al hombre nuevo sin ninguna de las taras anteriores"

11. "ella sí no tiene complejos"

12. "la Señorita Luisa María López y Galaimena, que le decimos Madrina, los nietos de su hermana"

13. "pero no basta"

14. "Un poema cinematográfico que saca del baúl sus cartas de autenticidad, allí donde las familias negras hemos querido esconder nuestras falsas aspiraciones, nuestras mediocres existencias y las pequeñas miserias humanas, como un mal nefando e impublicable."

15. "¿Habrá que combatir la necesidad de ser un negro distinto, superado? ¿Venir a Guanabacoa aceptando una historia total, una Guanabacoa total, y decirlo?"

16. "No cabe duda de nuestra condición antillana. Pero todo esto es casi la leyenda Cuba construido en un sueño. Lo que pasa es que ahí está Santiago. Y entonces, sí, es cierto: Cuba es una isla de las Antillas. ¿Y mulato? Mulato es un estado de ánimo."

17. "Porque Santiago tiene negros que se llaman franceses y bailan un baile de salón al ritmo de una Tumba a la que llaman francesa."

18. "un siglo y medio después, ya a Santiago no le quedan franceses . . . ni cafetales franceses"

19. "el filme más intenso a la hora de incursionar en el reflejo de las llamadas zonas marginales de nuestra sociedad"

20. "valores de la vida moderna . . . genera marginalidad y promueve relaciones sociales paralelas que son la antítesis de la integración racial."

21. Nephew of the National Poet, Nicolás Guillén Batista, the filmmaker manifested some discomfort over the connotation that these familial ties could have in his work (Reyes).

22. "los negros en el cafetal como mano de obra. / los negros. / ¿cómo? /¡¿los negros?! / si / los negros."

23. "en cuba, todos los negros y todos los blancos y todos tomamos café."

24. "Ay, Mamá Inés, todos los negros tomamos café."

25. "Fue capaz de captar la teluricidad del instante y tocar fondo."

26. "realiza un cinema a contrapelo de las políticas del cuerpo y de la cultura elaboradas a partir de los históricos debates guevaristas sobre el trabajo voluntario y los incentivos 'morales' a comienzos de la década del 1960."

27. "En la imagen de las multitudes marchando hacia el futuro, encaja el concepto de institucionalización como el de un conjunto armónico de canales, escalones, represas, aparatos bien aceitados que permitan esa marcha, que permitan la selección natural de los destinados a caminar en la vanguardia y que adjudiquen el premio y el castigo a los que cumplen o atenten contra la sociedad en construcción."

28. On the musical particularities and social significance of the *mozambique* rhythm in revolutionary Cuba, see Moore 181–85.

29. Dean Luis Reyes also recognizes the transgressive nature of these expressions, yet his analysis focuses on a question of history and falls short, in my opinion, of appreciating their existential dimension: "These gazes compel us to contemplate our own: are we merely integrative cogs in the process of history or are we, rather, shaken by its headwind?"

30. "L'épiphanie du visage est *visitation*. Alors que le phénomène est déjà . . . image, l'épiphanie du visage est vivante. Sa vie consiste à défaire la forme où tout *étant* quand il entre dans l'immanence—c'est-à-dire quand il s'expose comme thème—se dissimule déjà" (51–52).

Works Cited

Álvarez, Sandra. "Pequeño homenaje a un gran documentalista." *La Jiribilla* VI (335). 6–12 Oct. 2007. Web. 15 March 2012. *www.lajiribilla.cu/2007/n335_10/335_32.html*.

———. "Sara Gómez: De cierta manera feminista de filmar." Masters Thesis. Universidad de la Habana, 2008.

Badiou, Alain. *Logiques des Mondes*. Paris: Éditions du Seuil, 2006.

Benítez Rojo, Antonio. "La tierra y el cielo." *El escudo de hojas secas*. La Habana: Unión, 1968. 9–30.

Carbonell, Walterio. *Cómo surgió la cultura nacional*. La Habana: Yaka, 1961.

Carpentier, Alejo. *La consagración de la primavera*. La Habana: Letras Cubanas, 1978.

Casamayor, Odette. "Confrontation and Occurrence: Ethical-Esthetic Expression of Blackness in Post-Soviet Cuba." *Latin American and Caribbean Ethnic Studies* 4/2 (2009): 103–35.

———. "Représentations du Noir dans la littérature cubaine des années 1990 et débuts du XXIe siècle." *Cahiers des Anneaux de la mémoire* 6/7 (2005): 269–84.

———. *Utopía, distopía e ingravidez: Reconfiguraciones cosmológicas en la narrativa post-soviética cubana*. Frankfurt/Madrid: Iberoamericana-Vervuert, 2013.

Cofiño, Manuel. *Cuando la sangre se parece al fuego*. La Habana: Unión, 1975.

De la Fuente, Alejandro. *A Nation for All: Race, Inequality, and Politics in Twentieth-Century Cuba*. Chapel Hill: U of North Carolina P, 2001.

Deutschmann, David, ed. *The Che Guevara Reader*. Melbourne: Ocean, 2003.

Enciclopedia popular cubana. Havana: ICAIC, nd.

Fernández, Nadine T. *Revolutionizing Romance: Interracial Couples in Contemporary Cuba*. New Brunswick, NJ: Rutgers, 2010.

Fernández Robaina, Tomás. *El negro en Cuba (1902–1958)*. La Habana: Ciencias Sociales, 1994.

Ferrer, Ada. *Insurgent Cuba: Race, Nation and Revolution, 1868–1898*. Chapel Hill: U of North Carolina P, 1999.

Fulleda León, Gerardo. "¿Quién eres tú, Sara Gómez?" *La Gaceta de Cuba* 4 (July-Aug. 1999): 42–46.

García Borrero, José Antonio. "Sara Gómez (1)." *Cine cubano, la pupila insomne*. N.p., n.d. Web. 13 Oct. 2011. *cinecubanolapupilainsomne.wordpress.com/2007/03/18/sara-gomez-1*.

———. "Sara Gómez (2)." *Cine cubano, la pupila insomne*. N.p., n.d. Web. 13 Nov. 2011. *cinecubanolapupilainsomne.wordpress.com/2007/03/18/sara-gomez-2*.

García Yero, Olga. "Desde Camagüey, 2009: Más de cuarenta años después." In "Nicolás Guillén Landrián en la mirada de Olga García Yero." *Cine Cubano, la pupila insomne*. 16 March 2009. Web. 9 January 2015. *cinecubanolapupilainsomne.wordpress. com/2009/03/16/nicolas-guillen-landrian-en-la-mirada-de-olga-garcia-yero*.

Gómez, Sara, dir. *De cierta manera*. ICAIC, 1974. Film.

———. *En la otra isla*. ICAIC, 1968. Film.

———. *Guanabacoa: Crónica de mi familia*. ICAIC, 1966. Film.

———. *Iré a Santiago*. ICAIC, 1964. Film.

————. *La isla del Tesoro.* ICAIC, 1969. Film.

————. *Una isla para Miguel.* ICAIC, 1968. Film.

Gónzalez Pérez, Tomás. "Memoria de cierta Sara." *Afrocuba: Una antología de escritos cubanos sobre raza, política y cultura.* Eds. Pedro Pérez Sarduy and Jean Stubbs. San Juan: Editorial Universidad de Puerto Rico, 1998. 109–17.

Granados, Manuel. *Adire y el tiempo roto.* La Habana: Casa de las Américas, 1967.

Guerra, Lillian. *Visions of Power in Cuba: Revolution, Redemption, and Resistance, 1959–1971.* Chapel Hill: U of North Carolina P, 2012.

Guevara, Ernesto. "El socialismo y el hombre en Cuba." *Obras (1957–1967).* Havana: Casa de las Américas, 1970. 367–84.

————. "Socialism and Man in Cuba." Marxists.org. n.d. Web. 9 January 2014. *www.marxists.org/archive/guevara/1965/03/man-socialism.htm.*

Guillén Batista, Nicolás. "Prólogo a Sóngoro Cosongo." *Obra poética I, 1922–1958.* Ed. Ángel Augier. Havana: Letras Cubanas, 2002. 92.

Guillén Landrián, Nicolás. *Coffea Arabiga.* ICAIC, 1968. Film.

————. *Desde La Habana. ¡1969!* ICAIC, 1969. Film.

————. *En un barrio viejo.* ICAIC, 1963. Film.

————. *Inside Downtown.* Village Films, 2001. Film.

————. *Los del baile.* ICAIC, 1965. Film.

————. *Taller Claudio A. Camejo. Línea y 18.* ICAIC, 1971. Film.

Gutiérrez Alea, Tomás. *Memorias del subdesarrollo.* La Habana, ICAIC, 1968. Film.

Howe, Linda S. *Transgression and Conformity: Cuban Writers and Artists after the Revolution.* Madison: University of Wisconsin Press, 2004.

Lévinas, Emmanuel. *Éthique et infini: Dialogues avec Philippe Nemo.* Paris: Le livre de poche, 1982.

Martí, José. "El Plato de Lentejas." *Obras completas.* Vol. 3. Havana: Editorial Nacional de Cuba, 1963. 26–30.

————. "Mi raza." *Obras completas.* Vol. 2. 298–300.

Medin, Tzvi. *Cuba: The Shaping of Revolutionary Consciousness.* Boulder: Lynne Rienner, 1990.

Moore, Robin D. *Music and Revolution: Cultural Change in Socialist Cuba.* Berkeley: University of California Press, 2006.

Ramos, Julio. "Cine, cuerpo y trabajo: Los montajes de Guillén Landrián." *La Gaceta de Cuba* 3 (May-June 2011): 45–47.

Reyes, Dean Luis. "Nicolás Guillén Landrián: El iluminado y su sombra." *Tension lia.* 6 Nov. 2004. Web. 9 January 2015. *tensionlia.blogspot.com/2007/02/nicols-guilln-landrin-el-iluminado-y-su.html.*

Serra, Ana. *The "New Man" in Cuba.* Gainsville: UP of Florida, 2007.

Uxó, Carlos. *Representaciones del personaje del negro en la literatura cubana: Una perspectiva desde los estudios subalternos.* Madrid: Verbum, 2010.

Zayas, Manuel, dir. *Café con leche (Un documental sobre Guillén Landrián).* Havana: Escuela internacional de Cine y Televisión, 2003. DVD.

4

Realism in Contemporary Afro-Hispanic Drama

Elisa Rizo

Contemporary Afro-Hispanic drama offers a breadth of images that at first might be judged unrelated.[1] Take, for instance, the Afro-Uruguayan families evicted from their homes in Jorge Emilio Cardoso's *El desalojo en la calle de los negros* (The Eviction on the Street of the Black People, 1992); the Costa Rican mestizo of humble origins trying to scale the social ladder while confronting a greedy oligarch in Quince Duncan's *El trepasolo* (The Lone Climber, 1993);[2] or the Equatorial Guinean people trying to sort out the capricious rules imposed by a dictatorial regime in Juan Tomás Avila Laurel's *Los hombres domésticos* (Homeboys, 1992).[3] When seen together, such images provide a thematic spectrum that cuts across discourses of identity, geographic locations, and specific local circumstances. Yet, these dramas engage in a specific mode of analytical poetics that are rooted in the oral and written traditions of the African diaspora and that convey a twofold message of solidarity and solutions to problems. Through the examination of the above-mentioned plays, I submit that Afro-Hispanic drama published during and after the 1990s conveys a highly analytical form of realist depiction. While this realism is in alignment with previous models of aesthetic representation put forward by Hispanic intellectuals of African descent, contemporary Afro-Hispanic realist drama is also characterized by transethnic and transnational outlooks, that is, by a cosmopolitan perspective that corresponds to the globalized context in which these works were produced.[4]

Far from being a naïve report of facts and circumstances, the realist style of the dramas by Cardoso, Duncan, and Avila surfaces as an analytical tool to dismantle power relations imbedded in the modern state and its supporting structures (social, cultural, or economic). Indeed, a characteristic of realist Afro-Hispanic contemporary drama is that it critiques an ambiguous paternalistic rhetoric generated by the state that simultaneously declares concern and imposes limitations to civilians' rights and freedoms.[5] Furthermore, when reading Afro-Hispanic realist drama employing Foucault's framework of power relations, one finds a consistent focus in these plays on such processes as the differentiation of peoples (by ethnicity, by tradition, or by other means), the objectives of those exercising power over others (to maintain their status or to ensure economic gain, for example), the manner in which power relations are put in practice (through laws, military force, surveillance, etc.), and the ways in which these relations of power are institutionalized, made effective, and maintained.[6] That is, Afro-Hispanic realist drama underscores the multilayered forces at work within power relations.

Subsequently, this dramatic corpus signals a critical detachment from state narratives. As these dramas address concrete challenges endured by communities or individuals, they also convey alternative ways of looking for solutions outside of designs imposed by the state. Moreover, these plays facilitate the formulation of community or individual inquiries in a way that fosters the transformation of a situation of oppression, despair, or frustration into gates for reflection and vindication. But this analytical model is not new in the discursive traditions of the African diaspora. As Jerome Branche reminds us, "the act of revisiting a moment of rupture or loss in order to reflect and, ultimately, to reach liberation from oppressive systems is one of the basic principles of the discourse of identity in the African diaspora" (31).[7] For this scholar, such community-based response to outside impositions has resulted in a type of "solidarity capable of transcending both whitening efforts in social, political, economic, and cultural alignments, and narrow Afro-centric perspectives" (op. cit. 39). Indeed, *malungaje poetics*, the term coined by Branche to describe this mode of transmitting information and seeking solutions, is a recognizable feature of realist Afro-Hispanic drama. Malungaje poetics and its history of resisting the effects of power structures can be identified in the cosmopolitan trend of ethical, social, historical, and political analysis presented in this dramatic corpus.

To be sure, the type of community-based epistemology that Branche identifies as the poetics of *malungaje* is visible in other proposals by Afro-Latin American intellectuals, especially during the second half of the twentieth century. Take, for instance, the concept of "popular theatre for identification" advanced by Afro-Colombian writer Manuel Zapata Olivella in the 1970s. His proposal demanded an activist-research approach on behalf of artists and anthropologists engaged in promoting theatrical practices that truly served disenfranchised communities. As Zapata Olivella stated:

> Si no se pone suficiente atención a las divergencias de criterio, tratando en todo momento de comprender y respetar el punto de vista de la comunidad, se asumiría la actitud común del manipulador, que subestimando el pensamiento de la comunidad, o rechazándolo de plano, trata por todos los medios de imponer los suyos propios. Los resultados son conocidos, en esto no se trata de entender y aprender la cultura tradicional, sino de destruirla y colonizarla. (61)

> If we don't pay enough attention to the differences of judgment, if we don't make a consistent effort to understand and to respect the community's point of view, we could end up adopting the attitude of the manipulator, who underestimates the community's way of thinking. Or, we could even go as far as rejecting the

community's knowledge and trying to impose our own. We have seen the results of such enterprises: instead of understanding and learning from a traditional culture, they end up destroying and colonizing traditional cultures.

Embracing an ethical commitment to facilitating the inward processes of community reflection and decision-making, Zapata Olivella's research team recorded the oral wealth of black, indigenous, and mestizo communities across Colombia. His strategy involved researching and archiving legends, myths, music, dance, mask making, and other embodied expressions containing local epistemologies (71). For Zapata, social change had to be community driven:

> [Los] cambios no pueden ser otros que los sentidos realmente por la comunidad y no los impuestos desde fuera por fuerzas distorsionadoras. Si tales cambios no arrancan de la esencia misma de los intereses comunitarios, de los intereses tradicionales, no tendría que acudirse a un teatro fundamentado en las raíces históricas del pueblo. (71)

> [The] changes cannot be but those that are truly felt by the community; they cannot be imposed by outside forces with distorting views. If change does not stem from the essence of communal interests, from traditional interests, we could not aspire to propose a theatre based on the historical roots of the people.

Because the "theatre for popular identification" is committed to the liberation of all marginalized peoples, one could think that this concept is not directly rooted in the history of the African diaspora, as the poetics of *malungaje* are. However, the ethical and epistemological nature of Zapata's method of self-discovery and liberation is in alignment with *malungaje*'s proposal of identification and solidarity.

Malungaje poetics can also be traced in Quince Duncan's 2005 proposal of *afrorealismo*, a theorization of the identity discourse existent in works by black writers in the Americas. For Duncan, *afrorealism* comprises the assertion of elements such as the voice of Afro-Americans through the use of afro-centric terminology, the avowal of African symbolism, the vindication of the historical memory of the African diaspora, the concept of ancestral community, and the development of an inward community view. All of these characteristics, according to Duncan, work in tandem with the objective of searching and affirming an African-based identity, which had been historically denied and distorted (Duncan, *El Afrorealismo*). While Duncan's theory centers on literary writing in general, and not only theatre, it reveals a common trend within Afro-Hispanic literature: fostering a sense of community to achieve solutions, such as protecting a group's collective memory and identity.

My approach to contemporary Afro-Hispanic drama is informed by two dialogues, which, in spite of having been developed in different contexts, involve the elements of social justice and realist depictions. On the one hand, I consider the above-mentioned discursive and literary theories of community liberation advanced by Branche, Zapata Olivella, and Duncan. On the other hand, I look at the recent discussion of realisms in the literature produced by minority groups (not only of African descent) across the world. Duncan's proposal, for example, coincides with several aspects of the discussions about philosophical and literary realism, especially in regards to building identity discourses. The Costa Rican author's ideas are in alignment with those of Santya P. Mohanty, a leading scholar in contemporary realism, who has stated that:

> Realists about identity argue . . . that the future of progressive social struggles depends on greater clarity about the ways in which identity claims are justified, clarity about where and why such claims are valid, and where and why they are specious. Realists propose that we take the epistemic content of experiences and identities of minoritized groups seriously, since they contain alternative (buried or explicit) accounts of the world we all share. The development of objective knowledge about society grows out of an engagement with such alternative perspectives. ("Realist Theory")

Realism, then, emerges as a literary model in alignment with a larger concern for global social justice, which, as de Sousa Santos reminds us, is only possible through the attainment of "global cognitive justice" (xix). Again, that commitment to justice is present in the theorizations by Duncan but also in those proposed by Zapata Olivella and Branche. Equally, the type of realist depictions that I identify in contemporary drama by Afro-Hispanic writers is in alignment with both conversations in that it links literature to social justice. While Afro-Hispanic realist drama exhibits points in common with the poetics of *malungaje* defined by Branche, especially those referring to a discourse of liberation not limited to identity discourses (such as limiting afro-centrisms, for example), it differs from the other two proposals. On the one hand, Zapata's "theatre for popular identification" was informed by anthropological work done in specific communities to salvage culture-based ways to achieve solutions. On the other hand, Duncan's "afrorealism" calls for the literary depiction of the challenges pertaining exclusively to the communities of the African diaspora. Different from Zapata's "popular theatre for identification," contemporary realist Afro-Hispanic dramas attend to the formal requirements of Western theatre while informing their plays from communal experience and an awareness of external structures of oppression. Unlike Duncan's afrorealism, this realist dramatic corpus, while grounded by the same strategy of community and solidarity, also attends to issues not exclusive to black communities.

Moving toward a model with which to approach realist Afro-Hispanic contemporary drama, I suggest considering the concept of *scenarios of becoming*. Here, I am borrowing Diana Taylor's definition of "scenario,"[8] which describes the reenactment of an established plot in a given situation with the possibility of rearticulating its value, hence providing that situation with new meaning in a new context. For Taylor, in scenarios, "Social actors may be assigned roles deemed static and inflexible by some. Nonetheless, the irreconcilable friction between the social actors and the roles allows for degrees of critical detachment and cultural agency" (29). The potential for "scenarios" to break fixed categories is matched here with the concept of "becoming," explained by Deleuze and Guattari as a process of movement resulting from alliances that cut across fragmentations imposed in a given space (238–39). Thus, identifying a "scenario of becoming" in a realist drama (by Afro-Hispanic writers or others), would indicate first, the portrayal of a great pressure imposed by power relations, and, second, a movement out of such pressure through solidary actions fostered by analysis (i.e. the conceptual connection of concrete issues with deeper historical, social, political, or economic dimensions). Hence, the term "scenarios of becoming" refers to dramas (and other cultural expressions) that exhibit transversal movements across established hierarchies and restrictions imposed by the state or other entities in order to free people from imposed subjectivities.[9]

The Eviction on the Street of the Black People and the Redesigning of Space Distribution in the Capital City

The concept of "scenarios of becoming" allows the necessary flexibility to approach the variety of contexts addressed in contemporary realist Afro-Hispanic drama. Take, for instance, *The Eviction on the Street of the Black People* (1992) by Afro-Uruguayan playwright Jorge Emilio Cardoso (1938–), a dramatist and narrator devoted to the strengthening of the identity discourse of the Afro-Uruguayan community (Lewis, *Afro-Uruguayan Literature* 104). Cardoso locates *The Eviction* in the Montevideo of the 1970s to unveil specific mechanisms of control imposed by the state regime of the time (a military dictatorship) over the Afro-Uruguayan community. Specifically, Cardoso illustrates how, through a paternalistic discourse, the regime executed a fragmentation of the urban space in the capital city on the bases of social and racial identification, which directly affected black Uruguayans living in centrally situated rental housing. At first sight *The Eviction* could be read as a simplistic drama that denounces the state-imposed strategies used to eliminate the presence of black people in a central neighborhood of Montevideo. A closer analysis, however, reveals the incident of the eviction through its connection to a deeper issue: the ongoing omission of black Uruguayans from the discourse of national identity. In alignment with the model of scenarios of becoming, *The Eviction* is not limited to only denouncing the problems of the Afro-Uruguayan community at a certain historical moment, but it also provides a critical reflection of the problem from an alternative perspective. This is mediated by a community based communicative code: Candombe, a traditional practice that proves to be the key to the survival of the group's sense of identity.

Cardoso's play identifies the legal procedures followed by the state in order to remove Afro-Uruguayans and other mixed-race peoples inhabiting old rental housing, or *conventillos*. As discussed by Lauren Benton's socio-historical study of the 1970s evictions in Montevideo, the regime instituted housing laws that either prohibited the rental of certain buildings (due to their supposed poor conditions) or elevated the rental prices (which forced poor residents out of buildings), effectively engaging in a process of race and class differentiation veiled by a rhetoric of public safety. Such rhetoric justified the inspection of many buildings by a "technical team" that, in turn, certified the need for dislodging hundreds of families to the former city stables (Benton 42–44). Seen retrospectively, the contrast between the regime's ostensibly protective rhetoric and its action of displacing families to quarters meant for animals emphasizes the hypocrisy of the regime's implementation of "citizen safety."

As Benton also notes, the evictions occurred at a time when life in Montevideo's conventillos had increasingly become synonymous with poverty. Living in a conventillo had also come to signal the ownership of an important cultural hub built around Candombe, the musical and performatic tradition developed during colonial times among urban free and enslaved blacks.[10] In fact, during the first half of the twentieth century and all through the military regimes, the image of *conventillo* residents as "piteously poor" but also as people able "to transcend poverty" through Candombe rituals may have been perceived as a challenging gesture to authority (39). This relative independence of conventillo life with respect to the state's control during the 1970s might have "[played] an important role in the implementation of government policies toward central-city slum housing and in determining the balance of forces between conventillo residents and the state" (op. cit. 40).

The ambivalent image of the conventillo residents as the city's poorest and as the creators of a unique cultural expression is at the core of the movement across power relations in Cardoso's play. *The Eviction* portrays the interactions between the residents of the conventillo in the days prior to their forced departure to their new dwellings. Throughout the play, Candombe music, dance, and song emerge as a unique language shared by the community, igniting a collective memory and a sense of identity independent from state control.

As the play begins, the stage directions describe the interior of a conventillo apartment. An older woman, Doña Coca, melancholically fans herself in front of the TV as she waits for Fausto, her husband, to return from work. Soon, Kaulícoro, her idealist nephew (whom the couple has adopted as their son) appears on the scene. When he realizes his aunt's sadness, he teases her about the "good old times" and eventually cheers her up, convincing her to dance with him:

> KAULÍCORO. (*Va al radiograbador y pone un cassette de Candombe.*) A ver, aquí le
>   pongo un Candombe. . . . Hágame una demostración.
> DOÑA COCA. ¡No! ¡No! ¡Qué locura! Estos son otros tiempos . . .
> KAULÍCORO. ¿De qué otros tiempos me habla? El Candombe es eternidad.
>   ¡Vamos! Yo le hago el gramillero . . . (*toma la escoba de la cocina.*)
> DOÑA COCA. Me puede atacar la artrosis . . .
> KAULÍCORO. Le doy unos yuyos y se la curo. ¿Para qué soy el médico de la tribu?
> DOÑA COCA. Está bien. ¡Si me buscan me encuentran! (*Toma el abanico que está
>   sobre la mesa, levanta el ruedo de la falda con la mano izquierda y se pone a
>   bailar*). (9–10)

> KAULÍCORO. (*Goes to where the tape player is and plays Candombe music.*) Let's see,
>   here is a Candombe. . . . Show me how it's done.
> DOÑA COCA. No! No! This is silly! These are different times . . .
> KAULÍCORO. What do you mean "different times"? Candombe is eternal. Come
>   on! I will be the broomsman . . . (*He gets the broom from the kitchen.*)
> DOÑA COCA. Oh, I should mind my arthritis . . .
> KAULÍCORO. I'll give you some homeopathic pills. I am the doctor of the tribe,
>   after all!
> DOÑA COCA. All right. You asked for it. (*She takes the fan that she has left on the
>   table, grabs her skirt with her left hand, and begins to dance.*)

With this dance, the characters reenact a traditional performance of Candombe, headed by the *mama vieja* (the old mother), played by Doña Coca, and the *escobillero* (or broomsman), by Kaulícoro, who also reveals himself as the *gramillero* (the herb doctor). With this, *The Eviction* inserts a revision of a recent chapter in Montevideo's history enabled by Candombe poetics. Through this performatic language, the community asserts its identity, analyses its situation, and claims independence from the state's power relations.

While Candombe is the principal venue used to assert the community's identity, *The Eviction* presents other ways in which the characters build a sense of distinctiveness independent from the rules established by the official discourse. One is the call for a revision of national history. Throughout the play, several characters refer to the contributions made by Afro-Uruguayans to the formation of the country. There is great pride among the townspeople regarding the participation of black soldiers who made it possible for the national hero, Artigas, to win the war of independence. As Anselmo, the leader of the community, reflects:

> ANSELMO. [P]ero en este país no se respeta el pasado. O sino, vea quien se ha ocupado de nosotros: con nuestro sudor creció la Colonia; durante la guerra por la independencia fuimos al frente, pero nunca nos reconocieron nada. (30)
>
> ANSELMO. [B]ut there is no respect for the past in this country. Who has ever taken care of us? We made the riches during the colonial times with our sweat, and during the war of independence we fought at the battlefront; but they have never recognized our work.

Desolately, the conventillo residents who listen to Anselmo know that the idea of revising the role of Afro-descendants in Uruguayan history is not a possibility in a nation where the government is trying to remove their presence from Montevideo's centrally located buildings. Confronted with the persistent rejection of blacks from Uruguayan national identity, Kaulícoro opts for claiming an African identity. However, the reality of the eviction makes this proposal seem ridiculous to other characters. For example, Ebolova, his girlfriend, states:

> EBOLOVA. ¿Por qué te empeñas tanto en buscarme otras patrias? ¡Yo ya tengo una y bien orgullosa que estoy!
>
> KAULÍCORO. Porque eres africana. Esa es tu tierra. Ese es tu pueblo. Y allí, hay una casa esperándote. . . . No te gustaría estar allí, y conmigo . . . así abrazados . . . ¿este momento?
>
> EBOLOVA. ¡Ay! ¡Kaulícoro! Yo vengo tan cansada del ensayo y del calor, pero tan cansada, que lo único que me falta para morirme es justamente eso; ¡irme a África con tigo a que me piquen los mosquitos! (16)

> EBOLOVA. Why do you insist on finding me other homelands? I already have one, and I am proud of it!
>
> KAULÍCORO. Because you are an African. That is your land. They are your

people. And there is a home waiting for you there. . . . Wouldn't you like to
be there with me, hugging each other, right in this moment?

EBOLOVA. Come on Kaulícoro! I am very tired after that rehearsal, and it is so
hot. . . . The last thing I need is going to Africa with you, to be bitten by
mosquitos!

Ebolova, a cabaret dancer, criticizes Kaulícoro's idealism, and with this act also sheds
light on other sources of their community's concerns: their poverty, their marginalization from society, and their reduced opportunities. Furthermore, this notion of an
African identity is proven to be unpopular among most conventillo residents, who
consider the problems at hand more urgent, including the racist practices being enforced by the state. Doña Martina, a middle-aged woman, points to the racism influ-
encing their removal:

DOÑA MARTINA. ¿No entienden nuestra situación? ¿que estamos
desamparados? . . . ¿que nos arrancan de nuestros hogares por culpa de
algún mandamás que no quiere negros en el barrio? (23)

DOÑA MARTINA. Don't you realize our situation? Don't you see that we have
no options? . . . Don't you see that they are kicking us out of our homes
because some big boss doesn't want blacks in the neighborhood?

Through each of the dialogues among neighbors, Cardoso's play brings attention to the multiple causes of the community's situation: poverty, racism, historical silencing, and even the law. However, the references to Candombe spread
throughout the play effectively affirm the community's cultural independence.
The play closes with a Candombe song improvised by some youngsters at the
moment of their eviction:

Y mientras que aquí aguardamos . . .   And while we wait . . .
el momento de partir,   for the moment of departure,
congreguémonos a oír   let us congregate to hear,
su tañido de añoranza   the melancholic drums,
que nos dará una esperanza   that will provide hope
para poder resistir. (25)   to be able to resist.

Even though the material problems of their displacement are not solved through
Candombe, the play shows the community's successes gained by the persistence
of collective memory and mutual help. Within the framework of scenarios of becoming, elements such as collective chants and dances of Candombe performed in
strategic moments during the play underscore that the evicted blacks are the living
archive, the embodiment of an epistemology that resides outside of the boundaries set by state laws. The survival of the community's identity, despite their
detachment from their traditional space, emphasizes their independence from the
state's control.

The Lone Climber and the Violent Theatricality of Social Order

Similar to *The Eviction*, Quince Duncan's *The Lone Climber* (1993) uses housing as a lens for social analysis. The power relations examined here are not, however, based on race but rather on class. As noted above, Duncan has dedicated a great part of his oeuvre to legitimizing the Afro-Costa Rican identity and to defending the rights of Afro-descendants throughout Latin America. Nonetheless, in *The Lone Climber*, Duncan submits questions that move beyond racial discrimination, such as the following: What social, political, and economic forces regulate the possibilities of class mobility? Is the concept of class mobility a mirage created by the democratic discourse of the national state?

Contextualized between the 1980s and early 1990s in Costa Rica, *The Lone Climber* brings attention to the huge gap between social classes in Latin America. Its plot signals the theatricality of social order, national identity, and class belonging by delving into the dynamics of an upper-class neighborhood.[11] Thus, the main focus of Duncan's play is not the power relations imposed by the state *per se* but those structures enhanced by the upper class that have contributed to the maintenance of the status quo. Underlying the mechanisms of social exclusions, the plot displays confluent scenarios of corruption, bribery, surveillance, and manipulations created by the affluent in order to maintain their privileged status. Although the scenario of becoming in this play actually depicts a failed intent of upward mobility in the socioeconomic hierarchy, *The Lone Climber* effectively points to the factors that harness such movement, and hence it prompts critical reflection.

Throughout its seven scenes, *The Lone Climber* narrates the story of Carlos Morado, a humble newspaper salesman who, after winning the lottery, decides to put his money away by buying a fancy home. His intention is not to live like a rich man but to continue with his humble lifestyle until it is time to sell the house once his only son reaches a mature age. The play highlights the commotion Morado's arrival causes among neighborhood residents. All along, Morado has to endure the label assigned to him from the beginning: a criminal.

During the first scene, Morado is arrested for entering his new home with his son. Soon we learn that Don Emilio, the neighbor who had him arrested, has a twofold agenda: on the one hand, a vocal commitment to reinforcing "social order" and, on the other, a particular approach to his "right" to protect his own interests (he had planned to buy the house before Morado's sudden arrival). In his prejudice, Don Emilio makes use of all the power relations available to him in order to eject Morado from the neighborhood. With Don Emilio's actions, the play suggests that maintaining a social status is the result of a carefully orchestrated process involving hypocrisy, corruption, manipulation, and deceit. All aspects of the public and private converge in the activities of Don Emilio and other upper-class characters as they navigate their power network: they contribute money to electoral campaigns to influence the government and even use sexual acts as a means to influence and secure liaisons. As Don Emilio states to his maid while she is serving him coffee:

> DON EMILIO. No me gusta que nada me estorbe. ¿Entiende? No me gusta que
> nada se me oponga. Cuando poseo algo lo defiendo y cuando quiero algo
> lo tomo. (*Toma a la Empleada por la cintura. La muchacha se deja dócilmente . . .*)
> Necesito tu ayuda; quiero que te hagás amiga de la señora de Morado.
> Necesito saber todo de ellos. Todo lo que se pueda. (*La besa en una oreja y la
> muchacha se conmueve . . .*) (25)

> DON EMILIO. I don't like it when things get in my way. You hear me? I don't like
> to have any opposition. When I possess something, I defend it, and when I
> want something, I take it. (*He takes the maid by the waist. The girl lets him without
> resistance.*) I need your help; I need you to become friends with Morado's
> wife. I need to know everything about them. Everything you can. (*He kisses
> her on the ear and she reacts with excitement.*)

Accordingly, Don Emilio's notion of social order also connects with his opinion on
national politics. To him, the national government cannot be trusted with understanding how things should be, and it is up to him to take social and political matters
into his own hands. First, he tries explaining the rules of social behavior to Morado.
Don Emilio invites his new neighbor for a cup of coffee under the guise of apologizing
for having him arrested when they first met. During their meeting, he points Morado
to the series of gaps between his behavior and what is expected from people residing
on that street.

> DON EMILIO. Uno tiene cierta imagen de la gente que vive en este barrio, cierto
> concepto. Y uno ve la gente en la calle y puede decir, éste vive en tal barrio
> y estos otros viven en tales otros barrios. Uno espera que los dueños de
> una casa como ésta, que se yo, sean gente como uno . . . si me disculpa el
> ejemplo tan personal. (39)

> DON EMILIO. There is a certain image of the people who live in this
> neighborhood, a certain concept. So that, when you are out in the street
> you can just tell: this person lives in such-and-such neighborhood, and
> these other people live in so-and-so other place. One expects the owners of a
> house like this one to be, I don't know, to be more like me . . . if you would
> excuse me for the rather personal example.

This interaction reveals a series of social codes that differentiate both men. From linguistic registers to clothing and even pastimes, these seemingly superficial markers
of class constitute important and fixed division lines for Don Emilio and the other
upper-class characters in the play. Moreover, their status depends on the continuation
of those distinctions. The social divide between these two men only increases as the
dialogue continues. The scene reveals that, to Don Emilio's disbelief, Morado is simply
not interested in keeping up appearances (40), in selling the house for half-a-million
profit, as Don Emilio offers (48), and, ultimately, in making more money. At the end
of this dialogue, Morado recognizes Don Emilio's intention of removing him from the
neighborhood and expresses with dignified sincerity:

MORADO. No queremos más dinero, Don Emilio. No necesito más. Mientras
tengamos salud mi vieja y yo, no necesitamos más . . .
DON EMILIO. Pero Morado, no entiendo su razonamiento. He manejado dinero
toda mi vida, y se de lo que le estoy hablando. Agarre esta plata.
MORADO. Así es la vida (*se pone de pie*). No hay trato. (52)

MORADO. We don't want more money, Don Emilio. We don't need more
money. As long as we have good health, my wife and I, we won't need
more . . .
DON EMILIO. But Morado, I don't follow your argument. I have handled money
my whole life. I know what I am talking about. Take this money.
MORADO. Such is life (*He stands up*). There is no deal.

Morado's disinterest in Don Emilio's formula for success highlights the contrast between both men's values, and by extension, the values cherished by their respective
social classes. Realizing that he cannot manipulate Morado with offers of protection
and financial advice, Don Emilio turns to a set of schemes based on crime accusations
with no evidence in order to frame his neighbor.

At last, Don Emilio decides to end the power struggle with the newcomer by simply destroying his name and property. Through a sophisticated plan, he has his maid
and guard file charges against Morado for narcotraffic and possession of weapons and
explosives, and he also secures the placing of bombs inside Morado's home. All of this
results in the cancellation of Morado's agency: not only is his home destroyed and his
freedom taken away (due to the false accusations), but he also loses his only son in the
explosions.

Duncan's play shows Morado's failed attempt to defy social structures. The notion
of a "scenario of becoming" is shown in the character's unfulfilled desire to transgress
a sense of social order. Through Don Emilio's schemes, *The Lone Climber* illustrates
the logic supporting classism. With each scene, as Don Emilio's criminality becomes
clearer, so too do Morado's impeccable ethics. In this representation of "the poor versus the rich," Duncan inverts class stereotypes in Costa Rican culture to call for a
revision of the established notion of a social morality that has permitted so much inequality. In the end, *The Lone Climber* does not offer a solution but rather delivers the
necessary elements for a critique of Costa Rican classism and the blueprint of the areas
most in need of social transformation.

Scenarios of Becoming across the Atlantic: Connections between Latin America and Africa

As we have seen in Cardoso's *The Eviction on the Street of the Black People* and Duncan's *The Lone Climber*, Afro-Hispanic realist scenarios of becoming can take forms as
diverse as the local context to which they refer. But what are the characteristics of such
scenarios outside of Latin America? Within the contextual differences and themes that
concern dramatists on the African continent, it is possible to identify a similar plot
pattern that highlights the issues affecting society.

Similar to the two Latin American dramatists examined above, many contemporary African intellectuals are concerned with delving into social problems, especially those related to national, ethnic, and linguistic identities. Indeed, given the history of recently imposed geopolitical boundaries, first by colonial powers and then by national governments, the affirmation of ethnic histories within African countries emerges as a key issue. As stated by Justo Bolekia Boleka in *Aproximación a la historia de Guinea Ecuatorial* (Toward a History of Equatorial Guinea):

> Los nuevos estados africanos, basados en el modelo occidental europeo, buscaban la homogenización etnocultural de sus súbditos (¡y no ciudadanos!), según las directrices de sus antiguos amos. Las distintas nacionalidades africanas etnolingüísticamente definidas exigían, y siguen exigiendo, el reconocimiento de sus identidades culturales. (156)

> The new African states, based on the Western European model, sought the ethnocultural homogenization of their subjects (and not citizens!), according to the guidelines of their former masters. But the African nations, already defined by ethnicity and language, demanded, and they continue to demand, the recognition of their cultural identities.

Per this intervention, Bolekia points to the marginalization, displacement, and silencing of certain groups due to residual power relations from colonial times that still today affect the social dynamics in Africa. It is logical to think that, like the Afro-Latin Americans Cardoso and Duncan, African dramatists also regard national identity discourses as a core element in the formation of contemporary theatre. These ideas, in combination with a reformulation of embodied indigenous traditions (oral tradition, rituals, dance, music) create what Frances Harding coined as a "theatre of development," which includes the articulation of an African voice, affirmation of agency, control over narrative structures, and encounters of different social groups that otherwise could not engage in dialogue (Tomás-Cámara xxxiii). The identity politics conveyed by this definition of "theatre of development" bear a resemblance to Zapata Olivella's and Duncan's theorizations of literary activity (dramatic and non) in the Americas. Concerning discourses of identity, however, Nigerian dramatist Femi Osofisan points to a new element when he proposes the term "Post-Negritude" to explain how, in contemporary African drama and literature: "all the strategies we employ . . . are attempts to confront, through our plays, our novels and poetry, the various problems of underdevelopment which our countries are facing, and of which the threat of alienation and the potential erosion of ethnic identity constitute only one of the outward signals" (3).

Osofisan stresses the importance of providing critical tools for participation in a self-reflective criticism about Africa's infrastructural challenges, which to him stands among the many challenges caused by globalization. Without a doubt, African intellectuals' and dramatists' attentiveness to identity politics is not only restricted within their national realms. This interest in developing a relational understanding that includes the local and the global is clear in Ngũgĩ Wa Thiong'o's proposal of a "globalectical" approach to reality and texts: "Globalectical reading . . . involves declassifying theory in the sense of making it accessible—a tool for clarifying interactive connections and interconnections of social phenomena and their mutual impact in the local and global space, a means of illuminating the internal and external, the local and the global dynamics of social being" (61).

It is with this rejection of fixed and imposed categorizations such as geopolitical divides and linguistic differences that Wa Thiong'o calls for the identification of similitudes with other people's situations, departing from one's own local experience. Wa Thiong'o's call for liberation from essentialist and limiting identity discourses is in alignment with other calls coming from Afro-Latin America, such as Branche's malungaje poetics. In fact, put together, the notions of globlalectics and malungaje poetics signal a movement among intellectuals from both sides of the Atlantic toward a truly cosmopolitan dialogue, beyond racial, ethnic, class, or national affiliations. Furthermore, the notion of a globalectic reading suggests that we can establish connections between situations, albeit distant in context.

With this in mind, we could identify several historical processes that place Spanish American contemporary realists and their Hispanic African counterparts in a parallel geopolitical location. At first sight, these two regions share a Spanish colonial past. During the twentieth and twenty-first centuries, these spaces have experienced the economic intervention of the United States. Furthermore, we find that some colonial practices used to control people of certain ethnic or social groups have persisted in the dynamics of the modern states of Latin America and Africa.

Homeboys: Undraping the Farce of National Belonging in Equatorial Guinea

While the first two plays observed have dealt with internal forms of domination that keep racial and social groups in their place, the following Equatorial Guinean drama goes on to address the issues posed by global domination while fostering local community building solutions. Similar to Cardoso and Duncan, Juan Tomás Avila Laurel (1966–) has combined a literary career with political activism. A nurse by training and an editor and cultural promoter during his tenure at the Spanish Cultural Center in Malabo, Avila Laurel has increasingly gained recognition outside of Equatorial Guinea both as a writer and activist. *Homeboys* (1992), one of Avila Laurel's early works, clearly shows the prodemocracy agenda that has come to define the rest his oeuvre. In fact, this play also carries the distinction of being the first Equatorial Guinean drama that presents a direct criticism of Teodoro Obiang, in power since 1979. While earlier poetry, essays, and narratives written by Equatorial Guinean writers in exile had been openly critical of dictatorial regimes of the national eras, dramatic writings created inside of the country—due to censorship—had showed only implicit criticism. Conversely, the critique presented in *Homeboys* is not only limited to local politics; it also conveys a deeper criticism of relations of power that extends beyond the national realm into global politics.

Published before the 1995 discovery of large oil reserves in Equatorial Guinea, *Homeboys* does not address the dual process by which over the last twenty years this nation has become one of Africa's major oil producers and its president, Teodoro Obiang, one of the richest men in Africa. With its realistic depiction of the daily situation of Equatorial Guineans during the early 1990s, however, this play constitutes a valuable point of reference for contrasting the shape of state institutions and living conditions before and after the oil boom. As of 2015, the results of the comparison show little improvement, if any.

At first glance, *Homeboys* describes the issues of poverty, impunity, and failed institutions that defined the reality of the country in the 1980s and early 1990s. A second look at this seven-scene play unveils the state's strategies that effectively control and even paralyze the actions of the population in Equatorial Guinea. At the core of the power relations represented in the play are the practices of nepotism and corruption. To start, these are visible in the ethnic divide between the Fangs of Mongomo (the hometown of the president) and the rest of the national ethnic groups, including other members of the Fang ethnicity, the Bubis, the Ndowes, the Creoles, the Bengas, and the Annobonese (Avila Laurel's group). As the play begins, we find a humble and crowded home inhabited by Irgundio, a Fang from Mongomo, with his wife, his children, his two brothers, and their respective families. The description of fights between family members, who are made desperate by the lack of opportunity to find their own homes, reveals a more profound problem: the extended situation of crisis across a population that lives in poverty with a general sense of uncertainty. Impunity is another issue posed by Avila Laurel in this play. By the second scene, we learn that Irgundio has displaced another family in order to occupy the house where he and his extended family live. The rightful owners, from another ethnic group, have been evicted thanks to Irgundio's connections in the government. The son of the previously dispossessed family knocks at the door, oblivious to the fact that his parents have been ejected from their home. Shocked, he has a hostile encounter with Irgundio:

> IRGUNDIO. (*Coge unos papeles que están en unos cajones.*) ¿Ves, chico, estos papeles? Toma, léelos y así sabrás de quién es la casa. ¿Cómo crees que un funcionario del gobierno estará en la calle mientras que un borrachero está disfrutando de la casa? Además, no pagaba . . .
>
> EL JOVEN. Sea lo que fuera, estoy seguro de que pagaba. Además, yo conozco a muchos que deben más de dos años y no pagaban, no porque carezcan de dinero sino porque llevan marca en la cara. No se les toca: pero a otros, basta que deban dos meses para que . . .
>
> IRGUNDIO. (*Irritado*) ¡Salte! ¡Salte de mi casa! Así sois los que salís de España. Así habláis de política para que luego digáis que os persiguen porque habéis estudiado, cuando no sabéis nada. ¡Toma! (*Coge su maleta y lo echa.*) Vete a buscar a tus padres y déjame, que no me quiero enfadar. (174)

> IRGUNDIO. (*Takes some papers out of a drawer.*) See these papers, boy? Come on, take them and read them and you will find out who owns this house. How can you even think that a bureaucrat would be homeless while there is a drunk enjoying this place? Besides, he missed several payments . . .
>
> THE YOUNG MAN. Whatever! I am sure that he paid. Besides, I know many people who owe more than two years of payments, and that it is not because they don't have money, but because they have a mark on their faces . . .

IRGUNDIO. (*Upset*) Get out! Get out of my house! You are just like all those who
return from Spain. You talk politics so that you can complain that they are
after you because you have studied . . . but you know nothing. Take this!
(*Takes his suitcase and pushes him out.*) Go and look for your parents and leave
me alone. I don't want to get upset.

By referring to the "mark on their faces" the young man brings attention to the privileges enjoyed by the Fang of the village of Mongomo and, consequently, to the nepotism practiced by the regime. Furthermore, this character returning from Spain also
introduces another dimension, namely, that of the Equatorial Guinean dependence
on foreign aid. For many Equatoguineans during the 1980s and 1990s, one of the few
options for obtaining an education was through scholarships funded by the Spanish
Government Cooperation Agency (AECID).

By pointing to the international aid made available to the population, *Homeboys*
also reveals the juxtaposition of state politics with international politics. This becomes
more evident in the following scene when Proculo, one of Irgundio's brothers, suffers a mysterious illness, which propels a set of arguments and worry among family
members. After some debate, the sickly brother is taken to a witch who is unable to
cure him. This situation frames the appearance of Frantz Weber, a European physician
working for the humanitarian organization Doctors Without Borders. As the doctor
assesses Proculo's symptoms, the patient explains that he works for the National Radio as a news anchor and that he has been suffering from acute headaches after work.
Frantz asks to read the news that Proculo delivers at the radio and states:

FRANTZ. Estas informaciones son falsas; con la repetición diaria de ellas por la
radio, crea en un sujeto sensible una repulsa o aversión a unas versiones
que de antemano conoce como contrarias a la realidad. Eso le puede hacer
enfermar y hasta morir. (182)

FRANTZ. This news is false; its daily repetition on the radio creates in a sensitive
individual, who knows well that this news is contrary to reality, a repulsion
or aversion. This situation can make him sick, and even cause him death.

Frantz's openly critical comment on the regime irritates Irgundio so much that he
takes the Luxembourgian doctor to a traditional judge, who, in turn, decides to forward the case to the military police. At the police station, Frantz faces charges of inter-
vening in domestic politics and hears over and over that the president is "the defender
of the supreme power" (190). Astonished and irritated by the outrageous accusations
and by the cult to the president's figure, the doctor defends himself with certain arrogance, pointing to Africa's underdevelopment and dependence on Europe. During his
interview with Lieutenant Melchor at the police station, Frantz asserts:

FRANTZ. Mire usted, hace cinco siglos que ya se hablaba de democracia en
Europa, mientras que apenas había estados en África sino una mezcolanza
de pueblos. Como ya le dije, la civilización actual habla el europeo.

MELCHOR. Cada país es el dueño de su destino, por eso, no hay nada que
   justifique la injerencia en . . .

FRANTZ. Perdone, no sólo usted, sino la mayoría de las autoridades africanas
   apelan a la injerencia en los asuntos internos, ¿pero qué es lo que llaman
   asuntos internos? Este país, y lo digo sólo para citar un ejemplo, pertenece
   a la ONU y por eso recibe ayuda de cualquier organismo dependiente de
   la ONU, como es la OMS, la UNICEF y otros. Anualmente cada país
   tercermundista pide y recibe ayuda por valor de muchísimos millones de
   dólares. (190–91)

FRANTZ. Look, people were already discussing democracy in Europe five
   centuries ago; back then, there were just seminal states in Africa along with
   a mish-mash of peoples. As I already said, civilization currently speaks
   European.

MELCHOR. Each country is the owner of its destiny; therefore, there is nothing
   that justifies the interference in . . .

FRANTZ. Excuse me, not only you, but the authorities of most African countries
   object to interference in internal affairs. But what exactly do you mean by
   internal affairs? This country, and I say this just to cite one example, is a
   member of the UN and, therefore, receives help from all the UN's agencies,
   such as WHO, UNICEF, and others. Every year, every single third-world
   country asks for and receives help worth millions of dollars.

Frantz's response highlights the disconnect between the Equatorial Guinean government's request for help to care for its people and its demand for no intervention despite a lack of transparency in national politics. Predictably, his words are interpreted
by the police as an open act of offense to the national government, which prompts
the doctor's incarceration. This scene, however, directs the reader's attention to the
conflict in the European discourse about Africa that, on the one hand, offers humanitarian help while, on the other hand, does little to prompt change in that continent's
circumstances. Ambiguities like these have resulted in global hierarchies of wealth and
labor distribution in the current global economy. As Ramón Grosfoguel, attending to
the conceptual model advanced by Latin American thinkers Anibal Quijano, Enrique
Dussel, and Walter Mignolo, explains: "We went from the sixteenth century characterization of 'people without writing' to the eighteenth and nineteenth-century characterization of 'people without history,' to the twentieth-century characterization of
'people without development,' and more recently, to the early twenty-first-century of
'people without democracy.'"

    Frantz's lecture on Africa's reliance on European aid makes clear that Avila Lau-
rel's critique of power relations extends to global politics as well. At the same time,
Homeboys looks deep inside the silenced opinions of Equatorial Guineans to suggest
that, despite being located on the periphery, the inhabitants of that country wish to
have a working democracy. The play, however, also indicates the factors that silence
and restrict citizen action. This aspect is shown in the scene previous to the visit to the
police station, when Irgundio first took Frantz to the traditional judge. In doing this,
Irgundio was following the constitutional rules that claim to honor Bantu traditions

by assigning judges or "chiefs" in different neighborhoods to take care of familial issues. Since Irgundio also presented charges of adultery against Frantz (with no apparent reason), his case qualified as a domestic problem. It is noteworthy that the visit to the chief reveals how even this character, a tenant of tradition, is discontented with the current status quo. In spite of his fear of the government, the chief shares his opinion with his secretary after he has forwarded Irgundio's case to the police:

JEFE. Si resulta que después de nuestras acciones el asunto llega al Presidente o al embajador del país al que pertenece el blanco, los sicarios querrán lavarse las manos y vendrán por mí. ¿Sabes lo que pasaría si se informara por una emisora extranjera que un jefe tradicional multó y expulsó a un súbdito de donde sea?; las autoridades de este país harían como si nunca tiraron una piedra.
SECRETARIO. Eso es verdad. Por eso los blancos tienen tanta cara. Son como ciudadanos superiores. . . . Este país será peor que Sudáfrica si la cosa no cambia.
JEFE. Este país se hundirá si no salimos a la calle a pedir el cambio.
SECRETARIO. ¿Crees que no nos balearán si lo hacemos? En este país está prohibida la huelga.
JEFE. No sólo la huelga. También se prohíbe la charla, la danza e incluso se prohíbe vivir.

CHIEF. You don't understand. If it happens that after our actions, the case reaches the ears of the president or the ambassador of the white man's country, the mercenaries would want to wash their hands of it and come after me. Do you know what would happen if they were to transmit on a foreign radio station that a traditional chief charged and banned one of his own? The authorities of that country would act as if they had never thrown a stone.
SECRETARY. This country will be worse than South Africa if things do not change.
CHIEF. This country will go down if we do not get out in the streets to demand a change.
SECRETARY. Do you think they would shoot us if we try? Strikes are prohibited in this country.
CHIEF. Not only strikes. They also prohibit conversations, dancing, and even living.

This dialogue acknowledges the state's violence over the population and the extreme discontent of the people. Moreover, it calls attention to the fact that the government paradoxically presents itself as protector of traditions but is in reality more a protector of foreign interests in the national territory. To be sure, the fact that the chief suggests a protest signals what is needed: a negotiation of tradition and modernity.

By delving into local politics (ethnic divisions, corruption, and disrespect for traditions) within the framework of global dynamics, *Homeboys* portrays the competing economic, ethnic, national, and cultural forces that effectively control and even paralyze the actions of the population in Equatorial Guinea. The "scenario of becoming" in this drama, rather than portraying transgressive actions, consists in the realistic depiction of the elements that determine the national circumstance. Thus, the drama strives to pose questions that give a sense of order to a seemingly chaotic situation.

Challenging Power Structures in Realist Afro-Hispanic Drama from Latin America and Africa

The three plays analyzed above convey a systematic way of looking at the particular characteristics of power relations that have resulted in the subjugation of specific communities. This approach includes realistic descriptions of contexts, peoples, and practices, and it delves into different ways in which certain groups can be differentiated and systematically marginalized. In Cardoso's play, the very moment of the Afro-Uruguayans' eviction from their homes constitutes the framework with which to address the multiple ways in which black Uruguayans have been excluded. His drama also pays homage to Candombe's power to foster solidarity and spiritual resistance. In Duncan's play, the tragic ending to Morado's dream of social mobility highlights the entrenched power relations surrounding social differences in Costa Rica and the intersection of economic class and cultural affiliations therein. Lastly, Avila Laurel's play delves into the violence delivered by a neocolonial regime that defends the interests of the few and relies on the deformation of traditional practices, a strategy that results in the identity crisis plaguing the population in Equatorial Guinea.[12]

Seen side by side, the plays by Cardoso, Duncan, and Avila Laurel respond effectively to the problems posed by national and global structures of power, which go from corruption and nepotism to capitalist classism and homogenizing discourses of identity. Thus, Afro-Hispanic realist drama calls for a truly cosmopolitan engagement beyond local or national boundaries. Furthermore, the realistic style presented by these dramatists urges an understanding of the specificities of local circumstances within a global context as an alternative to seeing them through external, master narratives which only provide deranged images of their communities' situations. Pertaining to a literary tradition with longstanding poetics of resistance, realist Afro-Hispanic contemporary drama, at least as shown in these three plays, emerges as a model for critically reading an established world order.

Notes

1. Afro-Hispanic drama is understood here as the corpus of plays written by black writers in Spanish-speaking Latin America and in sub-Saharan Spanish-speaking Africa. Albeit a reduced corpus, more texts are being made available; an example is the recent anthology *Del Palenque a la escena: Antología crítica de teatro afro-latinoamericano* (Jaramillo and Cook, eds).

    Although not dealt with in this essay, it is important to keep in mind that besides written dramas, Afro-Hispanic theatre includes a long-standing set of performatic artistic expressions within African and Afro-Latin American communities, from comparsas, to musical groups, to rituals, to theatre companies, among many other expressions.

2. Dorothy Mosby's translation of the title (see Place, Language and Identity in Afro-Costa Rican Literature, 120).

3. Marvin Lewis's translation of the title (see *An Introduction to the Literature of Equatorial Guinea*, 88).

4. Here, I follow Appiah's definition of cosmopolitanism.

5. My definition of paternalistic state power is informed by the concept of "pastoral power." With origins in medieval times, this term refers to a commitment of a Christian authority to the "salvation" of its subjects. In "The Subject and the Power" Foucault states that the "pastoral power" is a type of power relation that has been successfully transformed and adopted in modern states (208–26).

6. These mechanics of power relations are posed by Foucault, ibidem.

7. All translations from Spanish to English in this essay are mine, unless otherwise noted.

8. This concept has been proven immensely valuable in approaching reformulations of identity discourses in theatre. For example, Christen Smith has combined Taylor's concept of "scenario" with Mary Louise Pratt's concept of "contact zones" in an insightful analysis of race relations as portrayed in Brazilian street theater.

9. This understanding of scenario is in alignment with the concept of "transversal tactics" by performance theorist Brian Reynolds. The concept of transversal tactics refers to actions that transgress given (or even imposed) subjectivities or territories toward inclusive dialogue to solve problems (3).

10. In 2009, UNESCO inscribed Candombe on the Representative List of the Intangible Cultural Heritage. Candombe has since been embraced by the government of Uruguay as a national symbol.

11. Here, I follow Juan Villegas's definition of theatricality: "a means of communicating a message by integrating verbal, visual, auditive, body, gestural signs to be performed in front of an audience. The perception of the message is intended to be received visually. The message is ciphered according to codes established by the producer's or receiver's cultural systems. . . . a given theatricality implies a system of 'theatrical' codes which are integrated in the cultural system and the social and political context" (316–17).

12. For a study on the idea of tradition in Equatorial Guinea's official cultural politics, see Rizo (2009 and 2010).

Works Cited

Appiah, Kwame Anthony. *Cosmopolitanism: Ethics in a World of Strangers*. London: Norton, 2006.

Avila Laurel, Juan Tomás. "Hombres domésticos." *Letras transversales: Obras escogidas de Juan Tomás Avila Laurel*. Ed. Elisa Rizo. Madrid: Verbum, 2012. 171–94.

Benton, Lauren A. "Reshaping the Urban Core: The Politics of Housing in Authoritarian Uruguay." *Latin American Research Review* 21.2 (1986): 33–52.

Branche, Jerome. "Malungaje: Hacia una poética de la diáspora africana." *Poligramas* 31 (June 2009): 23–48.

Bolekia Boleká, Justo. *Aproximación a la historia de Guinea Ecuatorial*. Salamanca: Amarú Ediciones, 2003.

"Candombe and its Socio-Cultural Space: A Community Practice." *Intangible Cultural Heritage*. UNESCO. 2009. Web. 23 Jan. 2014. *www.unesco.org/culture/ich/index. php?RL=00182*.

Cardoso, Jorge Emilio. "El desalojo en la calle de los negros." *Obras Escogidas*. Montevideo: Tradinco, 2008.

Deleuze, Gilles, and Feliz Guattari. *A Thousand Plateaus*. Minneapolis: U of Minnesota P, 1987.

Duncan, Quince. "El Afrorealismo: Una dimensión nueva de la literatura latinoamericana." *Istmo*. N.p., 25 Jan. 2005. Web. 5 Dec 2013.

———. "El trepasolo." *Teatro para el teatro*. Vol 4.2. San José: Teatro Nacional, 1993. 9–85.

Foucault, Michel. "The Subject and the Power." *Michel Foucault: Beyond Structuralism and Hermeneutics*. Eds. H. Dreyfus and P. Raibow. Chicago: U of Chicago P, 1983. 208–26.

Grosfoguel, Ramón. "Decolonizing Post-Colonial Studies and Paradigms of Political-Economy: Transmodernity, Decolonial Thinking, and Global Coloniality." *TRANSMODERNITY: Journal of Peripheral Cultural Production of the Luso-Hispanic World* 1.1 (2011): N. pag. Web. 5 June 2011. *escholarship.org/uc/item/21k6t3fq*.

Jaramillo, María Mercedes, and Juana María Cordones Cook, eds. *Del Palenque a la escena: Antología crítica de teatro afro-latinoamericano*. Bogotá: Universidad Nacional de Colombia, 2012.

Lewis, Marvin A. *An Introduction to the Literature of Equatorial Guinea: Between Colonialism and Dictatorship*. Columbia: U of Missouri P, 2007.

———. *Afro-Uruguayan Literature: Postcolonial Perspectives*. Lewisburgh: Bucknell UP, 2003.

Mohanty, Satya P. "Realist Theory." *International Encyclopedia of the Social Sciences*. 2008. Web. 9 Dec. 2013. *www.encyclopedia.com*.

Mosby, Dorothy. *Place, Language and Identity in Afro-Costa Rican Literature*. Columbia: U of Missouri P, 2003.

Wa Thiong'o, Ngũgĩ. *Globalectics: Theory and the Politics of Knowing*. New York: Columbia University Press, 2012.

Osofisan, Femi. "Theater and the Rites of 'Post Negritude' Remembering." *Research in African Literatures* 30.1 (1999): 1–11.

Reynolds, Brian. *Performing Transversally: Reimagining Shakespeare and the Critical Future*. New York: Palgrave, 2003.

Rizo, Elisa. "La tradición en el teatro guineoecuatoriano." *PALABRAS: Revista de la Fundación España-Guinea Ecuatorial, Madrid, España* 1.1 (2009): 147–54.

———. "Políticas culturales, formación de la identidad hispano-africana y 'El hombre y la costumbre.'" *Discursos poscoloniales y renegociaciones de las identidades negras*. Eds. Clément Akassi and Victorien Lavou. Marges 32. Perpignan, France: PU de Perpignan, 2010. 201–13.

Smith, Christen. "Scenarios of Racial Contact: Police Violence and the Politics of Performance and Racial Formation in Brazil." *E-Misferica* 5.2 (Dec. 2008): N. pag. Web. 12 Dec 2013. *www.emisferica.org*.

Sousa Santos, Boaventura de, ed. *Another Knowledge is Possible: Beyond Northern Epistemologies*. London: Verso, 2007.

Taylor, Diana. *The Archive and the Repertoire: Performing Cultural Memory in the Americas*. Durham: Duke UP, 2003.

Tomás-Cámara, Dulcinea. "Apuntes para un teatro africano." *I. Vi-Makomè. Teatro: África negra en escena*. New York: Ndowe, 2012. 7–67.

Villegas, Juan. "Closing Remarks." *Negotiating Performance: Gender, Sexuality, and Theatricality in Latin/o America*. Eds. Diana Taylor and Juan Villegas. Durham: Duke UP, 1994. 306–20.

Zapata Olivella, Manuel. "Proyecto para desarrollar un *Teatro Popular Identificador*." *Latin American Theatre Review* 9.1 (1975): 55–62.

5

Bojayá in Colombian Theater

Kilele: *A Drama of Memory and Resistance*

María Mercedes Jaramillo
Translated by Emma Freeman

K*ilele* is a term of African origin used in the region of the Atrato River in the department of Chocó situated on the Pacific coast of Colombia. It means fiesta, rebellion, rowdiness, celebration, song and noise; but it is also a cry, a lament, and a moan for those who have died, victims of the violence that ravages this region. It is a word that inspires those who continue to resist the war in the face of Colombia's internal conflict (*Kilele* 158)[1]. *Kilele* is also a theatrical work that pays homage to the victims of the massacre of Bojayá, the perpetrators of which were the guerrillas of the José María Córdoba front of the Revolutionary Armed Forces of Colombia (FARC) acting under orders from Commander Jhonover Sánchez Arroyave, also known as "El Manteco." The tragedy took place on May 2, 2002, when guerrilla fighters made the decision to use cylinder bombs when bullets failed to stop the assault by paramilitaries from the Bloque Elmer Cárdenas, commanded by Freddy Rendón Herrera, alias "El Alemán."[2] The explosion caused the violent deaths of dozens of Afro-Colombians who had taken refuge inside the church of Bellavista, the capital of Bojayá municipality. The gas cylinders destroyed the church where 450 members of the community had sought shelter. It was an act that caused the deaths of seventy-nine people, forty-eight of whom were minors. A further 167 people were injured, and 5,771 people were displaced as a result.

Historical Context

The crime of Bojayá is not an isolated event but rather the culmination of an attack on the civilian population that began in December 1996. The Colombian paramilitaries, with the undisguised complicity of the army and the police and with the consent of certain private investors, began to occupy the region of Atrato. They subjugated the Afro-Colombian and indigenous peoples of the region with the pretext of "ending subversive activities." As noted by Jesús Alfonso Flórez López, what their penetration of the area produced were "masacres, desapariciones y desplazamientos forzados" (massacres, disappearances, and forced displacement) (qtd. in Gómez Nadal 11).

The Pacific coast, isolated since colonial times from the center of the country, has been besieged in recent years by both national and foreign companies interested in the large-scale exploitation of its timber and mineral reserves, resources that have long been taken advantage of by the region's inhabitants using traditional, low-impact methods. The paramilitaries and guerrillas emerged on the scene looking for new sources of funding, to the cost of the communities and their resources. These armed groups were able to take advantage of the absence of the state and its institutions, as well as the vulnerability of the communities, and competed with each other for resources, the local economy, and control of the territories; thus, a conflict originated between armed actors to control the extraction of minerals and timber from the area. According to Paco Gómez Nadal, companies specializing in the extraction of minerals and timber have proliferated in the region without any form of legal authorization. In such a situation, armed groups exercise absolute control, whether by charging so-called "vaccines" or "war taxes"[3] as the guerrillas do, or through direct threats made by the entrepreneurs and frontmen working for the paramilitaries (15).

The growth in the region's extraction economy has been simultaneous with the rise in the cultivation of illicit crops and the African oil palms used to make palm oil. These are radical changes that have altered the local environment, and traditional sources of employment have disappeared. The plundering of the land, pollution, illegal business deals, harassment of the local population, and presence of outsiders with no respect for the values of the local Afro-Colombian and indigenous peoples have all contributed to the fragmentation of communities and the displacement of the native population to cities such as Medellín, Cali, and Quibdó. The illegal crops have brought the typical problems of narcotrafficking in addition to food scarcity; worse still is "la penetración de la mentalidad mafiosa, en la que todo se vale para conseguir el dinero rápido y fácil" (the penetration of a mafia mindset, in which anything is permissible in the pursuit of quick and easy money) (Gómez Nadal 15). A further problem, which has grave consequences for the inhabitants of these areas, is the legalization of this sacking of the land in Bojayá, in the Carmen de Darién, or in the rivers of the Curbaradó and Jiguamiandó regions, "donde se implantó a sangre y fuego el cultivo intensivo de la llamada palma africana. Despojo que se ha podido documentar antes las instancias judiciales y administrativas, pero cuya restitución aún no se ha podido hacer efectiva" (where the intensive cultivation of the so-called African oil palm was introduced with blood and fire. A pillaging that it has been possible to document before the judicial and administrative authorities, but whose restitution has still not been made effective) (14).

The Massacre of Bojayá

The massacre took place in the context of armed confrontations between the FARC's José María Córdoba front and the Bloque Élmer Cárdenas of the United Self-Defense

Forces of Colombia (AUC). Both groups were determined to maintain control of the area and its access to the Atrato River, the fastest-flowing and third most navigable river in Colombia, and an indispensable transport link for the traffic of arms and narcotics:

> El mismo río que les regalaba los peces y el líquido bendito para alimentar el cultivo les trajo un día a los hombres de las armas. Llegaron en canoas con sus fusiles, sus odios y su falta de piedad. Prometían arrebatar a sangre y fuego aquellas tierras a sus dueños. (Ardila Arrieta)

> The same river that gave fish and blessed liquid to nourish cultivation, one day brought men with guns. They arrived in canoes with their rifles, their hatred, and their lack of mercy. They promised to snatch the lands from their owners with blood and fire.

Free access to the river is essential for the community; it is both a source of life and the most important transit route for the people in the area. Giving a different use to the river and controlling the movement of people along it impedes exchange, festivities, and the tasks of everyday life. It also changes "las relaciones familiares y de compadra-zgo. En ese contexto, las dinámicas de la guerra son demoledoras, pues amenazan con exterminar la cultura y desde luego, su gente" (family relationships and friendships. In this context, the dynamics of the war are devastating because they threaten to exter-minate the culture and with it, its people) (*Bojayá* 121). César Romero states that by the end of April 2002:

> [L]os disparos ya hacían parte de los sonidos habituales de la selva que custodiaba el río Atrato. Los intercambios del fuego cruzaban el río de lado a lado y las FARC presionaban el despliegue de los 200 paramilitares que bajaron del norte del departamento del Chocó, evitando, sin nadie saber por qué, el retén militar sobre el río Atrato en el municipio de Riosucio.

> Gunshots were already part of the everyday sounds of the jungle that watched over the Atrato River. The exchanges of fire crossed the river from one side to the other as the FARC pressured the deployment of two-hundred paramilitaries that came down from the north of Chocó department, carefully steering clear of the military checkpoint by the Atrato River in Riosucio municipality, although nobody understood why.

The conflict between the guerrilla forces and the paramilitaries was inevitable; the authorities and the people were aware that the two groups had come to take control of the area. It was an anticipated confrontation. When the crucial moment arrived, children, women, and the elderly took refuge in the church, the only cement structure that could resist the bullets. Others escaped into the jungle (Ardila Arrieta). When they saw the guerrillas, the paramilitaries began to hide between the houses to the south of Bellavista, and the inhabitants abandoned their wooden homes in order to shelter in the church, where numerous families were arriving. Others took refuge in the house of the Augustinian missionaries. Nevertheless, they were unprepared for the gas cylinders that were to be used against them. The first cylinder thrown destroyed a house right in the center of Bellavista; the second fell a little farther away, behind the health center, without exploding; the third destroyed the roof of the church and exploded on impact with the altar inside.

A woman who works as a street vendor, selling bags at the traffic lights in Bogotá, lost her father and her brother in the explosion in the church. Consequently, like many other people from the area, she was forced to look for a new life in the city. Her testimony, collected by Juan Sebastián Serrano Soto ten years after the bloody event, demonstrates the atmosphere of fear in which the community lived even before the tragedy took place:

> El párroco del pueblo, el padre Antún y otros líderes del pueblo trataban de movilizar a la población para que resistiera al conflicto de forma pacífica. Les leían a los armados un documento llamado Declaratoria de Autonomía, en el cual les exigíamos como comunidad el respeto por la población civil. También se habían colgado en la iglesia del pueblo unas banderas blancas y a la entrada ese cartel que decía: "Siga pero sin armas." Era nuestra forma de resistir, aunque servía de muy poco. Cada día se regaba más sangre. (Serrano Soto)

> The parish priest, father Antún, and the other community leaders tried to move people to resist the conflict peacefully. To those who were armed, they read a document called the Declaration of Autonomy, in which they urged them as a community to respect the civilian population. They also hung white flags in the village church, and a sign at the entrance, which read: "Enter, but unarmed." It was our form of resistance, although it was not much use. Each day more blood was spilled.

The devastating event was a landmark in a long trajectory of violence experienced by the Colombian people. It was indicative of the deterioration of the armed conflict and the escalation of the problems suffered by the Afro-Colombian and indigenous communities of El Chocó. The armed groups' terrorist act violated all the standards of International Humanitarian Law by ignoring the obligation to protect the civilian population and is one of the most barbaric crimes committed by the guerrilla fighters against an innocent civilian community. The guerrilla fighters and the paramilitaries failed to respect the church as a sacred place and a traditional place of refuge during a time of war. It was precisely the profound religiosity of the Chocó people that led them to believe that they would be safe in the church. The cynicism and lack of consideration for the local population became evident when Freddy Rincón (El Alemán), commander of the paramilitaries, blamed the Bojayá parish priest, Antún Ramos, for having concentrated the people within the church.[4] All around the church paramilitaries had taken shelter among the civilian population. The diocese and the Afro-Colombian and indigenous populations protested the accusation made by the ex-commander. For their part, the guerrilla forces confirmed that the massacre had been a tactical error, "un daño involuntariamente causado" (harm involuntarily caused) (*Bojayá* 15).[5] It is also necessary to emphasize that the army took no measures to protect the population of the area, as noted by a survivor of the massacre who was quoted by Salud Hernández in the newspaper *El Tiempo*: "Esta tragedia se ha podido evitar pero el Estado solo entra a un pueblo cuando han matado a un poco de gente" (This tragedy could have been avoided, but the State only intervenes in an area once people have already been killed) (qtd. in *Bojayá* 9).[6] The OAS, the UN, and the Catholic Church all condemned the massacre as a crime against humanity and blamed the FARC, the paramilitaries, and the army (*Bojayá* 264–65)[7]. The families themselves had to participate in counting and identifying the dead. The remnants of the tragedy are still visible in the old empty houses located by the river and in the mutilated bodies of the survivors. Many of the victims were mothers, people central to community and family life, a loss of great importance to the community given their status as the family's emotional axis. The survivors now face significant difficulties in taking over the domestic roles and rituals that these mothers carried out (*Bojayá* 94)[8]. The mothers of the community structure daily life and provide a continuity that permits the development of the other members of the family. Furthermore, the disappearance of the elderly causes enormous disruption to the community, as they are the guardians of traditional knowledge, medicine, healing methods, and worship of ancestors. With them, the bridges to the past disappear. On the other hand, the deaths of so many children robbed the community of the possibility of a harmonious future (*Bojayá* 121). Upon seeing the catastrophe, Antún Ramos, the parish priest of Bojayá, prayed that the parishioners were not all dead, "Vi gente despedazada, sin piernas, ni manos . . . cabezas regadas, sangre, mucha sangre. Inclusive aprecié ciudadanos corriendo mutilados" (I saw people in pieces, without legs, without hands . . . split heads, blood, lots of blood. I even saw mutilated people running) (Gómez de los Ríos 73–74).

El Chocó

The massacre of Bojayá was a decisive moment for the reorganization of control in the territory and for a change of strategy from the Colombian state. Today there is a military and police presence in the area, although there has been no reduction in human-rights violations. There is no right to freedom of expression, as Uli Kollwitz of the Life, Justice, and Peace Commission affirms (Gómez Nadal 71).

> Para los boyajaceños en la masacre hacen eclosión los silencios, los olvidos y las deudas históricas de Colombia con sus minorías étnicas y en especial con las comunidades afrocolombianas. Las injusticias del pasado se entrecruzan con las injusticias del presente. (*Bojayá* 21)

> For the people of Bojayá, in the massacre hatch the silences, the forgetfulness, and Colombia's historical debts to its ethnic minorities and particularly to the Afro-Colombian communities. The injustices of the past intersect with the injustices of the present.

On November 28, 1966, the Nadaísta poet Gonzalo Arango, in a letter to his brother Benjamín, denounced the negligence of the Colombian state in abandoning the area of El Chocó, which became an object of national attention only once a tragedy had devastated the region. The tragedy to which Arango referred was the fire that destroyed Quibdó. It is worth reproducing part of his letter, as almost five decades after the poet described this depressing panorama, the situation of the Chocoan people is no better:

> Quibdó siempre existió ahí, y soy testigo de su miseria aterradora, en los límites de la pesadilla. Alguna vez, en mis crónicas de viaje, denuncié la desesperanza de un pueblo que sobrevive en condiciones infrahumanas, degradantes para una sociedad civilizadora que ostenta títulos democráticos y cristianos.
>
> Pero nadie, ni el pueblo, ni el Estado, ni los políticos reaccionaron ante estos testimonios. No era más que literatura inofensiva, aventuras de la imaginación, Gonzalo que es loco. . . . Nos hemos oxidado por la indiferencia, el egoísmo y el desprecio. Nuestros sentimientos sólo despiertan de su letargo culpable cuando son sacudidos por el terror. . . . Yo sé que cuando Quibdó desaparezca de las primeras páginas de los periódicos, de la pantalla de televisión, y la desgracia no sea más una noticia para la avidez y el sentimentalismo del público, entonces el Chocó volverá a desaparecer del mapa, cercenado, condenado a su negritud sin porvenir. Un manto de indiferencia y olvido caerá inexorable, con sus lluvias eternas, sobre la desolación de ese territorio. . . . Nadie volverá a pensar en Quibdó, en su pobreza, en su desamparo. Y esa indiferencia futura—y no sus escombros—es lo que constituye para mí el drama de su situación actual; que el Chocó es un drama eterno. El de antes del incendio, el de después, el de siempre. Y ese drama, hermano, no se resolverá con una estera de caridad, ni con un tarrito de leche Klim, ni con un recital nadaísta. Porque después de la estera y el tarrito de leche, ¿qué? Ése es el problema: lo que vendrá. O sea, la impunidad del hambre, la desesperación, la negra nada. Estoy seguro de que cuando leas esta carta, el Chocó habrá vuelto a la "normalidad," es decir, a su miseria ancestral, a la injusticia. Y la injusticia, todos sabemos, no es noticia de primera página. Ella es nuestro modus vivendi, la apatía, el conformismo, el sálvese quien pueda. (Arango)

Quibdó always existed, and I was witness to its terrifying misery, which was like a nightmare. Once, in my travel journal, I denounced the despair of a people that survive in subhuman conditions, conditions degrading for a society that boasts of being democratic and Christian.

But nobody, not the people, not the state, not the politicians reacted to these testimonies. It was nothing more than inoffensive literature, adventures of the imagination, crazy Gonzalo. . . . We have become rusted with indifference, with selfishness and disdain. Our feelings only awake from their lethargy when they are shaken by terror. . . . I know that when Quibdó disappears from the front pages of the newspapers, from the television screens, and the tragedy is no longer news for the public's greed and sentimentalism, then El Chocó will disappear once more from the map, amputated, condemned to its blackness without future. A blanket of indifference and forgetfulness will inevitably fall, with its eternal rains, on the desolation of this region. . . . Nobody will think again of Quibdó, in its poverty, in its neglect. And this future indifference—and not its rubble—is what for me constitutes the drama of its current situation; that El Chocó is an eternal drama. That of before the fire, that of after, that of forever. And this drama, brother, will not be resolved with a mat of charity, nor with a jar of Klim milk, nor with a Nadaísta recital. Because after the mat and the jar of milk, what? That is the problem: what comes after. That is to say, the impunity of hunger, of hopelessness, of black nothing. I am sure that when you read this letter, El Chocó will have returned to "normality," that is, to its ancestral misery, to injustice. And the injustice, as we all know, is not front-page news. It is our modus vivendi, apathy, conformism, all saving their own skin.

The ancestral misery and injustice that Arango spoke of continue to prevail in the region. What has changed are the actors. El Chocó is now a bounty of war for the illegal armed groups, and its inhabitants who defend their territories and its traditional uses are considered an obstacle to the "development" of the area. The riches of its timber, mines, and waterways are in the sights of investors only seeking to get rich quick without concern for the environmental impact, the destruction of enormous biodiversity of every square kilometer, or the displacement of the autochthonous population.

News from Bojayá

Among the official reports that recount what happened in Bojayá are those of the United Nations' High Commissioner for Human Rights, the Ombudsman's Office of Colombia, and the Office of the Inspector General of Colombia. The last one, "Bojayá, la guerra sin límites" ("Bojayá, the War without Limits"), was published in 2010 by the Historical Memory Group of the National Commission on Reparations and Reconciliation and is a detailed follow-up to this tragic episode. Another document that stands out is *Los muertos no hablan* (The Dead Don't Speak) by Spanish journalist Paco Gómez Nadal, who visited the area recently as a result of the massacre and illustrates the indelible mark left on the psyches of the survivors. In the prologue to the 2007 edition, Gómez Nadal rightly states: "Cuando la memoria de la muerte se diluye, el tormento de los vivos arrecia. Mientras el impacto de la muerte permanece en la conciencia colectiva, los vivos tienen posibilidad dc hacerse notar" (When the memory of a death is diluted, the torment for the living intensifies. While the impact of a death remains in the collective consciousness, those who survive also have a possibility to be noticed) (21). For this reason memory is an indispensable mechanism for creating a better future. Reconciliation does not entail forgetting. To forgive is not to forget; to forgive is to permit a future.

Bojayá in Colombian Art

The bloody episode at Bojayá attracted national attention due to the scale of the barbarity as well as the scant presence of the state and its institutions in the region. Non-governmental organizations, journalists, sociologists, playwrights, painters, and many other intellectuals have taken up the event in order to look for solutions and explanations and above all to condemn those responsible. The incident is also the subject of a variety of artistic works that explore the individual history behind the newspaper reports. These are cultural expressions that lend meaning and importance to these lives and deaths, as well as registering the history and traditions of a people. For example, Freddy Sánchez Caballero painted *La muerte de los Santos Inocentes* (The

Death of Blessed Innocents) in order to show images of daily life as well as the violence wrought against the Afro-Colombian and indigenous people (*Bojayá* 298). Juan Manuel Echavarría has taken up the subject of Colombian violence by inviting wounded soldiers, guerrillas, and decommissioned paramilitaries to express their experiences of war through painting. Echavarría opened the doors of his studio to them so that they could capture their memories of armed warfare with a brush. The work *La guerra que no hemos visto* (The War That We Did Not See) is a stunning testimony to the suffering and brutality caused by the war. The massacre of Bojayá is one of the themes from the war as seen by the culprits themselves, and *Del gatillo al pincel: Memoria gráfica de la guerra* (From the Trigger to the Brush: A Graphic Memory of War) is a collection of paintings exhibited in the Bogotá Museum of Art.[9]

In 2012 the groups Génesis and El Malpensante premiered the piece *Bojayá: Los cinco misterios de un genocidio* (Bojayá: The Five Mysteries of a Genocide), a work that "como hecho ético, propone un rotundo no olvido de la tragedia nacional, no para mortificarnos como pueblo, sino para no cometer los mismos errores, y aún más, para vigilar que el Estado y los que gobiernan no los comentan de nuevo" (as an ethical act, proposes emphatically that we not forget the national tragedy, not to torment ourselves as a people, but so as not to commit the same mistakes, and further still, to ensure that the state and those that govern us do not commit them either) (Gabokú). The drama brings together African and European customs with music that helps to remember the event without falling into sentimentality and pity. The creators, with the support of Afro-Colombian actors and the dramaturgy of Roberti Vargas, make plain how much Afro-Colombians have to contribute to the national culture.

The people of Chocó also impart their own version of events by composing songs to denounce armed groups and the corruption that spreads throughout the area. These compositions used to recall incidents from times of slavery and of life in the *palenques*.[10] Now the songs focus on the here and now and point to the Chocoan politicians for their poor government, their corruption, and their evident "whitening" (Gómez Nadal 34). With good reason, Gómez Nadal states that the region's reality has meant that the traditional songs composed for funeral rites are now dedicated to denouncing the situation with which the inhabitants of Chocó are confronted. One such song is composed by María Mercedes Porras, an elderly woman who sings *alabaos* in the Atrato, in which she narrates the history of black people in the area. It speaks of the original kidnapping of the Africans during the slave trade and how they were brought here to work in the jungles and rivers, and even of how many of them were brainwashed into whiteness. The people also show in their songs the sorrow that afflicts them, as in Porras's poem that condemns the "whitening" and the collaboration of some native inhabitants with their oppressors.

Another song denounces the opportunism of the new arrivals and investors who are foreign to the traditions of the native communities whose culture had a minimal impact on the ecology of the Pacific jungle region. The new economic actors only see the area as a source of riches, and consequently, they endanger the biodiversity that the Afro and indigenous communities have long used sustainably, lacking the heavy machinery and power saws that extract resources at such a dramatic rate. It expresses the desire of the indigenous people and the Afro-Colombians to live in peace and to be respected, adding that Chocoan culture allowed for the preservation that is today called biodiversity, and laments the irony that violence is inflicted upon them although they were the ones who protected and defended mother nature here (Gómez Nadal 35).

Other members of the community have also elaborated their testimonies in dance and works of theater that were collected by Inge Kleutgens with the local people.[11] For its part, the diocese of Quibdó made use of its national and international network to produce reports recalling the events. The academic sector has also offered support through dissertations and theses that have served to document this tragic event (Gómez Nadal 16).

Kilele

The volume *Ese Atrato que juega al teatro* (Playing at Theatre in the Atrato Region, 2008) contains eight scripts and was compiled by Inge Kleutgens with the support of the diocese of Quibdó, whose members, it is well known, are the only ones who have always formed part of the Chocó region. The texts were produced through *creación colectiva* (collective creation) with the men and women of the tributaries of the Atrato, and they gather together the memories and lived experiences of these communities. One of these works is *Kilele: Una epopeya artesanal* (Kilele: A Homemade Epic) written by Felipe Vergara[12] from the Grupo de Teatro Varasanta. Vergara and Catalina Medina conducted theater workshops in different areas of the region in order to collect testimonies that were then dramatized in *Kilele* and that tell the story of Bojayá. The piece was inspired by diverse imaginaries of the armed conflict, by testimonies, by truths only half-spoken, by the ambition and arrogance of those responsible for the violence. As Vergara puts it:

> Surgió de los relatos de muchos velorios y novenas truncadas, de lágrimas prohibidas y de muertos insepultos. En fin, tomó su forma gracias al brillo misterioso que tienen los ojos de quienes cultivan la resistencia. *Kilele* es un viaje obligado de los desplazados y de los viajes prohibidos de alguien que quiere retornar a su pueblo. Una lucha por la libertad en condiciones en las que parece imposible alcanzarla. (*Kilele* 158)

> It emerged from accounts of many wakes and novenas cut short, of forbidden tears and unburied bodies. In the end, it found its form thanks to that mysterious gleam in the eyes of those who cultivate resistance. *Kilele* is the forced journey of those displaced and the forbidden journeys of someone who wants to return to their home. A struggle for liberty in conditions in which it seems impossible to achieve it.

The play begins with an allegorical scene where sinister gods—who represent the leaders of the armed groups—are callously putting out 119 candles, unconcerned with respecting *El Ángel de la muerte* (the angel of death).[13] Noelia, Élmer, Manisalva, and Castaño playfully count the extinguished candles, a macabre game that alters the destiny and livelihood of the community. They are the representatives of the guerrillas, the paramilitaries, and the army. Their conversations reveal how the conflicts began and the emergence of the AUC as a response to the abuses of the guerrillas. In their wake they leave only death, destruction, and displaced people. The community is left abandoned, inhabited by ghosts who wander by the river. The piece dramatizes the history of the region from the moment in which the inhabitants began to be harassed by the armed groups. *Kilele* condemns the neglect of the state, the collaboration of the army with the paramilitaries, and the abuses of the guerrillas. The *bojayaceños* are alone and at the center of a struggle between economic interests that mine the resources of the region and displace the community. The massacre was the climax of this struggle and brought national and international attention to the region. The play also acknowledges the presence of a number of NGOs common to disaster areas and humorously denounces the ineffectiveness of many of them:

> UNA MODELO. La organización MODÈLES SANS FRONTIÈRES,
> OTRA MODELO. Que significa Modelo sin Fronteras
> OTRA MODELO. Se ha sentido muy deprimida por la tragedia ocurrida aquí
> OTRA MODELO. En el pueblo de los 119 muertos
> OTRA MODELO. Por eso venimos a abrazar a los sobrevivientes. (*Kilele* 179)

> A MODEL. The organization MODÈLES SANS FRONTIÈRES,
> ANOTHER MODEL. That means Models without Borders
> ANOTHER MODEL. One that's felt really depressed about the tragedy that happened here
> ANOTHER MODEL. In the town of 119 dead
> ANOTHER MODEL. That's why we've come to embrace the survivors.

Many of the acts of solidarity undertaken by the organizations dedicated to international aid remained caught up in image campaigns. In pursuing the publicity that would justify their presence, at times they failed to resolve the communities' most urgent, and least visible, problems. In El Chocó, the NGOs dedicated themselves largely to questions of culture and the environment rather than resolving the population's basic needs (Gómez Nadal 118), a fact that is rightly denounced by the play.

After the explosion, the psychological and emotional damage became evident in the deterioration of overall mental health. The people had experienced extreme situations of threat, destruction, and personal and collective loss that had injured the fabric of social and family life to the detriment of the sociocultural models that are indispensable for the structure of the community (*Bojayá* 89). Some of the characters of *Kilele* represent victims who have gone mad but cannot forget the massacre. They express pain and hopelessness and ask why alcoholism, unemployment, and misery have overtaken the region: "SANTA TECLA. Aquí no hay gente ya. ¡Lo que hay aquí es la jedionda maldad! ¿Me oyen? Después de la explosión en la iglesia la gente se fue toditica" (SANTA TECLA. There are no people here anymore. What is here is the stench of evil! Can you hear me? After the explosion at the church the people left one and all) (*Kilele* 171). These are words that confirm the fears of parish priest Antún Ramos: "SAN JOSÉ. Dicen que la cabeza no nos funciona bien. Pero si esto fuera cierto tendría que haber una razón para que hubiera tanto demente en el Atrato" (SAN JOSÉ. They say that our heads are not working right. But if that were true there would have to be a reason why there was so much dementia in Atrato) (*Kilele* 171). Further on it is declared: "¡Por eso es que ahora nosotros andamos andrajosos! Algunos, incluso nos hemos aficionado a la bebida" (That's why we are so ragged! Some of us have even turned to drink) (*Kilele* 173).

The visible imprint of violence on the lives of the characters is shown on their bodies and in the space they inhabit; their starting point is the territorial marking of tragedy. Bojayá condenses representations of the war and establishes itself in the imaginary. The acts show the degradation, the destruction, and the human suffering that the war has left behind it. Bojayá presents a map of the *guerra sin límites* (war without limits) (*Bojayá* 21). This tragedy is the real, deep Colombia, divided by a war for land that annihilates rural communities and ethnic minorities: "La presencia militar ha colocado a la población en una situación de dependencia frente a las armas, pues la seguridad no resulta del desmonte efectivo de las estructuras que generan la violencia" (The military presence has placed the population in a situation of dependency on arms, given that security does not follow an effective dismantling of the structures that have generated the violence) (*Bojayá* 82–83). For this reason security is perceived as something fragile that disappears as soon as the army retreats from the area.

The play follows the structure of classical theater, and many of the characters fulfill the roles of tragedy. For example, the unequal conflict between armed men and the civilian population of Chocó evokes the confrontation between the gods and human beings in Greek theater; the desperate efforts of the men and women to control their destiny clash with the whims of the gods/armed men who rule over life, goods, and individual and community land and whose designs take no account of individual or community welfare. The chorus of parasoled women recreates the voices of the people, gives their opinion of the armed men, and above all, cries for the desolation of the survivors:

> RUTH. Por aquí han pasado los hijos de todos los dioses. Por eso nosotros no creemos ya en mesías. . . .
> FELICIA. Los primeros que vinieron fueron las tropas Noélidas [la guerrilla].
> RUTH. Eran criaturas paridas por una diosa a la que llamaban Noelia, la vieja.
> FELICIA. Iban a mi pueblo a descansar, pero también querían adoctrinarnos en su fe. Decían que nuestros dioses habían muerto. Y parecía cierto, porque hacía tiempo, que ni San José ni Santa Rita oían nuestras súplicas. De nada valían mandas ni secretos. Esa gente decía que sus dioses sí amaban a los pobres y nos iban a sacar de la miseria.
> BRÍGIDA. Pero un día sus jefes, sus sacerdotes o quienes fueran, empezaron a exigir sacrificios. Un cerdo de vez en cuando, un par de gallinas de tiempo en tiempo, un bulto de arroz semana de por medio; nada que no pudiéramos sobrellevar. (*Kilele* 178)

> RUTH. Through here have passed all the children of the gods. That's why we no longer believe in messiahs. . . .
> FELICIA. The first ones to come were the Noélidas troops [the guerrillas].
> RUTH. They were creatures born of a goddess called Noelia, the old one.
> FELICIA. They would go to my village to rest, but they also wanted to indoctrinate us in their faith. They said that our gods were dead. And it seemed so, because neither San José nor Santa Rita had heard our pleas in

a long time. Neither vows nor secrets did any good. These people said their
gods loved the poor and that they would rid us of our poverty.

BRÍGIDA. But one day their bosses, their priests, or whoever they were, began
to demand sacrifices. A pig now and then, a pair of chickens from time to
time, a bag of rice every few days; nothing we couldn't endure.

But the demands of the guerrillas kept increasing, and they began to recruit young
people from the community, who at first went with them voluntarily given the lack
of employment or future offered by their home. As the women say, they wanted to
"sacudirse el aburrimiento," "distraerse con la guerra," and "evitar el hambre" (shake
off the boredom, distract themselves with the war, and escape hunger) (*Kilele* 178).
This initial interest disappears, however, and the people begin to fear the guerrillas
because they take the youngest ones as soldiers and to work in the plantations in the
north (*Kilele* 278). Then the paramilitaries and the army appear, also recruiting young
people for their respective troops. This is expressed in the play as follows:

FELICIA. A mí me dijeron que los sacrificaban a sus dioses.
RUTH. Noelia, la vieja exige sacrificios humanos.
FELICIA. Igual que Élmer [un paramilitar] y Manisalva [un militar].
BRÍGIDA. Todos los nuevos dioses son iguales.
FELICIA. Iguales pero diferentes.
FELICIA. Comenzaron a llevarse muchachos por la fuerza y cada vez más y más
jovencitos. (*Kilele* 178–79)

FELICIA. They told me that they sacrifice them to their gods.
RUTH. Noelia, the old one demands human sacrifices.
FELICIA. Same as Élmer [a paramilitary] and Manisalva [a soldier].
BRÍGIDA. All the new gods are the same.
FELICIA. The same but different.
FELICIA. They've started to take the young people by force, and the ones they
take they are getting younger and younger.

This dialogue among the women of the chorus reveals the feelings of the people of El
Chocó; for them, the armed groups of left and right, legal or illegal have committed
the same abuses in their villages. Their mistreatment is the same though their ideology
is different. For this reason the community rejects them and treats even the state's
own forces with suspicion. The complicity between the landowners, the army, and the
paramilitaries made possible the looting and annihilation of the communities of the
region. The *boyajaceños* are aware of this conspiracy, and this leads Santa Tecla to say:

Los noélidas y los manisalvas . . . ¡maldita sea mi boca! ¡maldita sea mi boca!
Esos . . . esos . . . peludos lo destruyeron todo. Pero no estaban solos, no, estaban
amangualados con todos los nuevos dioses y sus lacayos . . . Aquí entre nos, la
verdad, que acá abajo hay un montón de porquería, pero si uno no la mira pa'llá no
sabe que está ahí . . . En cambio lo que hay arriba es peor que porquería y lo peor es
que uno no puede dejar de verlo. (*Kilele* 171)

The noélidas and the manisalvas . . . damn my mouth! damn my mouth! These . . . these . . . fools who destroy everything. But they are not alone, no, they're employed by the new gods and their lackeys. . . . Between us, honestly, here below there is a load of filth, but if you don't look that way you don't know it's there. . . . On the other hand, what's up above is worse than filth, and the worst is you can't help looking at it.

Autonomy, freedom of expression, and movement are severely restricted by the presence of the violent groups. Livelihoods are held back or fail because access to natural and economic resources is frustrated by the irresponsible invaders, who murder the inhabitants and pillage the community of its goods. The armed men appropriate their lands and replace subsistence farming with palm-oil crops in order to enter the global biofuels market.

El Viajero (The Traveler), a central character of the play, condemns this act: "El pueblo de mis abuelos no existe. Donde había casas ahora solo hay palmas. Las palmas sagradas de los nuevos dioses. Ellos se alimentan con su jugo" (The village of my grandparents no longer exists. Where there were houses now there are only palm trees. The sacred palms of the new gods. They feed off their juice) (*Kilele* 194). For his part, Élmer (the paramilitary leader) sings a song of his own creation "Colombia, tierra mía, mía, mía" (Colombia, my land, mine, mine, mine), whose verses tell the story of the plundering of the communities of the Pacific: "Quitamos una casita, ponemos una palmita" (We get rid of a little house, we put up a little palm tree). His performance is attended by his friends: ranchers, businessmen, and politicians who have nominated him head of the *Grupo de Empresarios Exitosos por la Paz* (Group of Successful Entrepreneurs for Peace). His friend and accomplice Manisalva is also there, he who throws a stone and then hides his hand and is the companion of the "incursiones nocturnas, y de las desapariciones fortuitas" (nighttime raids and fortuitous disappearances) (*Kilele* 162–63).

Manisalva/Manosalva is the representative of the army. As in a *roman a clef*, the names of the characters point to the people who were involved in these events. For example, colonel Orlando Pulido Rojas was the commander of the Batallion Alfonso Manosalva Flórez of the IV Brigade, who gave assurances that there were no armed men in the village when the people of Bojayá requested protection (*Bojayá* 76); the dog Castaño indicates the recognized paramilitaries, brothers Vicente and Carlos Castaño. In the play Manisalva is the goddess of security and an expert in disguises and in detecting collaborators. Finally, Élmer introduces Noelia with well-chosen words that synthesize the long history of the Colombian guerrillas:

[V]ieja contradictora, motivadora de conflictos y debates eternos, mujer de recio carácter y animadora de mil batallas, diosecilla terca, sin cuyos deliciosos desmanes de fuerza bruta me hubiera sido imposible emprender el proyecto agroindustrial con el que desde 1996 hemos traído progreso y desarrollo a estas tierras y luz a estas gentes. (*Kilele* 163)

Contradictory old woman, instigator of eternal conflicts and debates, woman of fierce character and inspiration of a thousand battles, stubborn little goddess, without whose delicious excesses of force it would have been impossible for me to undertake the agro-industrial project with which since 1996 we have brought progress and development to these lands and light to these people.

El Viajero navigates the river, returning in search of his family, and like Ulysses or Aeneas, descends into the world of the dead, searching for his wife Tomasa and his son Polidoro, both victims of the explosion. With each person that he finds he strikes up a similar conversation, which serves to emphasize the magnitude of the tragedy. Some respond in monosyllables; others recount the events. The survivors also tell him the fate of his family: "SANTA RITA. Viajero, oye tú, Tomasa ya no está más con nosotros, tu hijo Polidoro ya no está más con nosotros. Yo misma lo rearmé enfrente de la iglesia, cada cuerpecito con su manita, con su cabecita" (SANTA RITA. Traveler, hey you, Tomasa isn't with us anymore, your son Polidoro isn't with us anymore. I put him back together myself in front of the church, each little body with its little hand with its little head) (*Kilele* 172).

El Viajero is the connection between the past and the future; in undertaking the journey along the river that connects life to death, he seeks to recover his present (his wife) and his future (his son). The desolation of the present, of the inescapable *now*, obliges him to face up to his destiny and become the hero that makes possible a future for the survivors of Bojayá. The future is glimpsed the moment el Viajero/ the hero no longer lives only to satisfy his immediate needs, but foresees the needs of the future. He affirms:

Hay tiempo de nacer y tiempo de morir. Tiempo de dar muerte y tiempo de dar vida. Tiempo de edificar y tiempo de llorar. Tiempo de abrazar y tiempo de alejarse de los abrazos. Tiempo de odio y tiempo de amor. Tiempo de Guerra y tiempo de paz. Tiempo de gala y tiempo de luto. (*Kilele* 195)

There is a time to be born and a time to die. Time to kill and time to give birth. Time to build and time to cry. Time to hold each other and time to let go. Time to hate and time to love. Time for war and time for peace. Time for celebration and time for mourning.

An affirmation that encapsulates the practices and knowledge that maintain the social order of the Afro-Colombian communities and which help them to face conflicts, organize ceremonies, celebrate rites of passage, prepare the land for cultivation, and conserve their traditions.

The chorus of souls articulates the long genealogy of el Viajero and demonstrates his status as a legitimate inhabitant of the region, a representative of the community, and the inheritor of the Mina, the founders of the palenque where slavery was resisted:

CORO DE ÁNIMAS. Makerule, príncipe de los Minas en el Congo engendró a Mateo Mina. Él fue esclavizado, pero resistió y mató a catorce hijos de los dioses castellanos antes de fundar el palenque de Tadó. Él concibió a Sando Mina y él a su vez a Ateneo Mina que sabía el secreto para hacerse invisible. (*Kilele* 177)

CHORUS OF SOULS. Makerule, prince of the Minas in the Congo gave birth to Mateo Mina. He was enslaved but resisted and killed fourteen sons of the Spanish gods before founding the palenque of Tadó. He conceived Sando Mina and he in turn Ateneo Mina, who knew the secret of making himself invisible.

The series of descendants continues through Sinecio Mina, Satanás, who according to legend was immune to bullets and was able to liberate many slaves from Cauca. The genealogy ends with el Viajero, who is the son of Eneida Mina Aponsá and the Atrato River, a fact which lends him a supernatural status, a sense of belonging in the territory, and a legitimate authority; he is not a recent arrival whose power is based on arms and intimidation. The words of the Atrato surprise el Viajero, but the river tells him of his family's qualities: "Por parte de madre su destino está ligado a la desobediencia, a la rebeldía y a la ciencia de los Mina; por mi parte está ligado con el destino del río, con el de los dioses que antiguamente se movían por él y con el de todos los muertos que he tenido que arrastrar" (On your mother's side your destiny is linked to disobedience, to rebellion, and to the expertise of the Mina; on my side you are linked to the destiny of the river, to that of the gods who in ancient times moved along it and with it, all the dead who I have had to bear) (*Kilele* 177).

The genealogy of el Viajero is his hero's mark. To belong to the caste of the Minas is the recognition that he requires to become a leader and a model for men that will continue his lineage. The feats of his ancestors make him worthy of this enterprise. El Viajero can construct a future by recognizing his past, but in order to do so he must communicate with his ancestors, who know his extraction and who encourage him to follow the traditions and fulfill the funeral rites abandoned in the war. For this journey to the underworld he must take warm herbs that will allow him to speak to the dead and to know his destiny. This is an indispensable rite of passage that will sustain him in his new role. He is the leader of an ethnic group that is identified with a history, a territory, and a culture with collective rights (*Bojayá* 90).

The territory is conceived of from a perspective that is at once historical, sacred, and symbolic. It is the home of their ancestors, inhabited by powerful spirits whose role is to look after and preserve the community. In this imaginary the territory itself is a mother; it is origin and end, where the people live and children are brought up; it is the legacy of the "reborn." It is not a place only to plant, but also to make a home and to do daily tasks. In this place the umbilical cord and the placenta are buried, and a natural relationship with the life cycle is established (*Bojayá* 112–13):

Dicen que el territorio es como parte de uno mismo, y así tiene que ser, porque uno es tierra. Y dicen que uno donde nace lo sepultan, lo que es parte de uno es el ombligo, y mi ombligo está enterrado en esta tierra. Y entre nosotros acá eso es una tradición. ¿Por qué no me dio por irme para otra parte . . . ? Por mi ombligo. (Nubia Bello 84)

They say that the territory is a part of you, and so it must be, because we are earth. And they say that you are born where they will bury you, what is part of you is the umbilical cord, and mine is buried in this land. And among us here, this is a tradition. Why didn't I go elsewhere . . .? Because of my umbilical cord.

The village will be founded anew in another place, far from the places filled with spiritual power that should not be mauled over by people foreign to their cultural tradition (*Bojayá* 113). This new village will also be far from the river that gave them life but also brought them death.

The search for his descendants and the survivors leads el Viajero to his destiny as the guardian of traditions. In him the past, the present, and the future are fused together. The classic texts that tell of the destruction of Troy and the founding of Carthage are repeated in the twenty-first century in Bojayá. The legitimate inhabitants defend their right and confront the invaders who replace their homes with palm trees, trade life for death, and violently snatch the territory which is theirs, as proved by the history of the Mina. It is for this reason that Bojayá and Bellavista are the *lugares de memoria* (places of memory) that, according to Joël Candau, reinforce the connections by which a people recognize themselves. They are places where memory is embodied (113). Therefore, it is around them that "la nación se hace o se deshace, se tranquiliza o se desgarra, se abre o se cierra, se expone o se censura" (the nation is made or unmade, it is in peace or torn apart, it opens or it closes, it expresses itself or it censures itself) (Candau 111). It is the upheaval and the condemnation that these places evoke that unites the victims of violence and the descendants and leads them to reconstruct homes with those who are able to recover this common memory, dialect, and destiny.

The *boyajaceños* display their exhaustion with the celebrations that take place on the anniversaries of the tragedy. The new inhabitants of Bellavista continue suffering the ravages of war. The paramilitaries and the guerrillas continue to be present in the region, and the government only comes on anniversaries to politicize the event, though they still haven't solved the basic issues that afflict the population, such as unemployment, lack of opportunities, inadequate housing and education. Many of these chance visitors ridicule the traditional practices of the Afro-Colombian and indigenous communities; their insensitivity and ignorance are another form of cultural violation: "Así, ni autoridades, ni dioses, ni ancestros, parecían detentar el poder suficiente para detener la guerra, lo que llevó a cuestionar su eficacia y vigencia, y de este modo se afectó también las creencias y certezas construidas históricamente" (So, neither the authorities, nor the ancestors, seemed to hold sufficient power to stop the war, which led to a questioning of their efficacy and validity. In this way the historically constructed beliefs and the certainties were affected) (*Bojayá* 111).

The victims want to establish a sanctuary for the memory of the massacre that will allow them to process their pain, work through it, and be reconciled with their dead "para que no deambulen en el mundo reclamando su lugar" (so that they do not wander in the world demanding their place in it) (*Bojayá* 296). In order for the community to achieve the equilibrium necessary to eradicate violence and to recuperate the traditional use of the river and their lands, it is necessary to cleanse them of blood. As a woman from the region states, evoking a nostalgic and idealized version of the past, for them the river is dead: "ahora solo lo usamos para transportarnos y no para saciar otros deseos como el bañarse, pescar, lavar los platos, cepillar la ropa, . . . ¡Y eso era una felicidad! La una cantaba, la una echaba un verso, la otra echaba un chiste . . . todas esas cosas ya se acabaron . . ." (now we only use it for transport and not to satisfy other needs such as bathing, fishing, washing dishes, washing our clothes, . . . That was happiness! One would sing, another would throw in a verse, another a joke . . . all these things have ended now) (*Bojayá* 109).

The *bogajaceños* need certainties in order to plan for the future, and above all guarantees that allow future generations to remain in the territory of their ancestors. Only in this way can they develop social, cultural, economic, and political projects that generate a sense of community identity and belonging. Through music, painting, song, oral traditions, and rites that articulate and interweave ancestral components with contemporary ones, memory and history are safeguarded and become the basis for an identity.

Kilele is a drama that gives a voice to the shattered community, harassed by violent armed groups that have abused thousands of Colombians. The protests of the survivors, the photographs, the families' accounts of the victims, and the complaints of the displaced all primarily seek a response from the government and a solution to the conflict; however, with the passage of time, they become vehicles for spiritual communication and bonds of social cohesion. The survivors must continue with their lives, in spite of what has happened and the persistent imprint of pain on their bodies and their memories. The collective is the mechanism that will allow them to recuperate their solidarity and foment local resistance (*Bojayá* 287). The mutilated Christ of the church in Bellavista has become a relic and a symbol of the damage and the immense suffering of the survivors of the massacre who, like this figure of Christ, also wear the brutal consequences of the war on their bodies.

The Alabao and the Gualí: Rituals of the Dead

The *alabao* and the *gualí* are the poetic elegies that are sung during the wakes for adults (*alabao*) and for children under seven years old (*gualí* or *chigualo*) and that join African religious traditions with Catholic practices and invoke "entidades espirituales africanas como el Muntu (unidad entre vivos y muertos), al Ikú (orishá que viene en busca de los difuntos) o al Kulonda (el ancestro)" (African spiritual entities such as Muntu [unity between the living and the dead], Ikú [an orisha who comes to seek the dead], or Kulonda [the ancestor]) (Gómez Nadal 34).

At the end of *Kilele,* candles are lit for the typical funeral rites of the region that were not celebrated after the massacre because of the continuing confrontations between the paramilitaries and the guerillas, which provoked enormous anxiety within the community. The dead, according to African customs, continue wandering unable to find peace since they were not properly buried with the *alabaos, gualíes,* and other funeral rituals appropriate for children, adults, and the elderly. The survivors must abandon the area without fulfilling this sacred duty, thus upsetting the necessary processes that will allow the children who have died to be transformed into cherubs and guardian angels and the adults into protecting ancestors. The rituals of the dead are essential in order to help their souls on the path to the other world. The songs, prayers, and responsories help to process the sadness and to quell fears (*Bojayá* 102). The *alabao* and the *gualí* aim to spin harmony between the living and the dead and are rites of passage that allow souls to go beyond, where they will aid and watch over the living. There they become the venerated ancestors of African culture:

> Los velorios no los pudimos hacer, sacar su muerto pasearlo por las calles y enterrarlos, tocó en bolsas porque no había cómo comprar y hacer ataúdes y a ninguno se le pudo enterrar como es debido . . . las tradiciones de cantarle, rezarle, pasearlo por el pueblo, que son nuestras costumbres, ni siquiera a los chiquitos pudimos hacerles nada . . . Es que ni siquiera llorarlos, porque estábamos huyendo para salvarnos los pocos que quedábamos, y hasta la enfermedad le puede quedar a uno de no llorar a sus muertos. (Testimonio, taller de memoria histórica, Bellavista 2009). (*Bojayá* 101)

> We couldn't do the wakes, the taking out of our dead into the streets before the burial; they had to be put in bags because there was no way to buy or make coffins, and not one of them could be buried in the proper way . . . the traditions of singing, praying, walking them through the streets that are our customs, we couldn't even do it for the little ones . . . We could not even cry for them, because those of us that were left were fleeing to save our own lives; not crying for the dead can make one ill. (Testimony from a historical memory workshop, Bellavista 2009).

One of the strategies used by the armed groups against the Afro communities was to prevent the traditional funeral and novenary rituals that were fundamental for the community in constructing indestructible ties of fraternity and solidarity among themselves. For this reason, as Gómez Nadal points out, they made sure that:

> los cadáveres no aparezcan, o aparezcan seccionados, toman medidas para que no se pueda velar a la víctima durante los nueve días que manda la tradición. En algunos casos, como cuando el cadáver «viaja» por los ríos, la situación es vergonzante para las propias comunidades, ya que ven pasar frente a sus casas cuerpos que no pueden recoger, porque hacerlo los señalaría de colaboradores de alguno de los grupos armados. (108–09)

> the bodies do not appear, or they appear in pieces; they take measures to make it impossible to hold a wake for nine days as is dictated by tradition. In some cases, as when a body "travels" on the river, the situation becomes embarrassing for the communities; they must watch bodies pass in front of their houses without being able to collect them, because to do so would implicate them as collaborators of one of the armed groups.

Jaime Arocha Rodríguez, one of the most recognized experts in Afro-Colombian culture, confirms in "Desarraigo forzado" ("Forced Uprooting") that the fact of not having been able to bury the dead as they should has an *impacto mortal* (fatal impact) on the culture, given that it breaks one of the most revered traditions of Afro-Colombian communities:

En las mañanas y tardes y atardeceres y noches siguientes, los hijos del Atrato, con los nervios en punta, sentían que sus muertos no se encontraban en paz. "Los velorios, el novenario, los alabaos, las oraciones, los adulatorios y los responsorios, rituales propios de los negros, se habían quedado sin realizar." Las cantadoras, sobre todo, sabían más que nadie lo que significaba pasar por alto esos protocolos mortuorios. "Los 48 niños masacrados, por otra parte, se habían quedado sin el 'guali,' esa costumbre africana, conocida también como 'chiguala,' en la que el cuerpo sin vida del pequeño es alzado de mano en mano mientras se canta, se baila y se juega con él." Era así como las comunidades negras festejaban al niño que, muerto, se escapaba de la esclavitud. Ahora, no habían tenido la ocasión de festejarlos por haberse librado del infierno de la guerra.

In the following mornings and afternoons and evenings and nights, the sons of Atrato, with their nerves on edge, felt that their dead could not find peace. "The wakes, the novenary, the alabaos, the prayers, the adulations, the responsaries, all the rituals of the Afro-Colombians, had remained uncompleted." The singers knew more than anyone what it meant to overlook these rituals of the dead. "The forty-eight massacred children, on the other hand, remained without the 'guali,' that African custom also known as 'chiguala,' in which the child's lifeless body is lifted and passed from hand to hand while the people sing, dance, and play with it." In this way the Afro communities celebrated the child, who in death had escaped slavery. Now, they had been unable to celebrate for the children who had freed themselves from the hell of the war.

The play, then, is a funeral rite that tells the story of the community and of the victims. El Viajero dies after completing his mission to celebrate the *guali* and the *alabao* that bid farewell to the dead and through which they say goodbye to their home:

> ÁNIMA. ¡Setentisiete levantamientos de tumba![14]
> ÁNIMA. ¡Apaguen las velas!
> ÁNIMA. ¡Retiren las mariposasnegrasdepapel!
> VIAJERO. ¡Quiten los velones!
> ÁNIMA. ¡Adiós a los adornos!
> ÁNIMA. ¡Adiós! . . .
> (Las Ánimas entran al valle de José.) (*Kilele* 197)

> SOUL. Seventy-seven new tombstones inaugurated![15]
> SOUL. Put out the candles!
> SOUL. Take away the black paper butterflies!
> TRAVELER. Take away the thick tallow candles!
> SOUL. Goodbye to the adornments!
> SOUL. Goodbye!
> (The souls enter the valley of José.)

Kilele takes up the cause of modern historiography in defending the place of traditionally excluded sectors in the story of human development and revealing the social prejudices and political interests which they have had to confront. This piece casts light on our historical and public moment, as well as the private lives that it permits us to imagine, and fills a gap in official history. Michael Millar in "Popular Theatre and the Guatemalan Peace Process" recognizes that:

> La naturaleza fecunda del proceso de contar produce una historia que lleva más a la acción que a la revelación estéril de hechos del pasado. Al proveer un reto a los años de silencio, esta práctica muestra maneras afirmativas de contradecir la tendencia de la cultura dominante y del discurso político en favor de una interpretación de la historia más universal. El foco localizado en experiencias únicas y compartidas de individuos y comunidades facilita un mejor entendimiento de las circunstancias presentes y por lo tanto una voluntad de trabajar por la transformación social en los nuevos espacios provistos por el proceso de paz y de democratización.

> The generative nature of this storytelling process produces a history that leads to action, rather than a sterile revelation of past events. In providing a challenge to years of silence, this practice shows an affirmative means of countering the tendency of dominant cultural and political discourse to favor more universal interpretations of history. The focus placed on shared and distinct experiences of individuals and communities facilitates a much greater understanding of present circumstances and therefore a willingness to work for social transformation within the new spaces provided by the processes of peace and democratization. (110)

Individual memory is the foundation of resistance; it is a weapon against forgetting and preserves details and images that are brushed aside by the historian. Memory is individual, and history is collective, as Pierre Nora puts it, but memory illuminates history by presenting the face of human experience. Laura Ardila Arrieta also defends the importance of historic memory as a part of the whole that is often left out: "Si no hay espacio para la verdad y la memoria no hay espacio para las soluciones" (If there is no space for the truth and memory, there is no space for the solutions). Memory brings forth anguish and pain, but it is also a source of resistance. For this reason sentence C 370 of the 2006 Constitutional Court established that:

> la verdad tiene una dimensión colectiva que consiste en el derecho de las sociedades de conocer su propia historia, elaborar un relato colectivo relativamente fidedigno sobre los hechos que la han definido, y tener memoria de tales hechos. Para ello, es necesario que se adelanten investigaciones judiciales imparciales, integrales y sistemáticas sobre los hechos criminales de lo que se pretende dar cuenta en la historia. (*Bojayá* 233)

> the truth has a collective dimension that consists of the right of societies to know their own history, to elaborate a relatively reliable collective account of the events that have defined that history, and to remember those events. To this effect, it is necessary to move forward with impartial, comprehensive, and systematic legal investigations into the criminal acts which these histories attest to.

In the play *Kilele*, the life and dignity of Afro-Colombians is celebrated, and the tragedy is mourned. It is at once a memorial to the grievances suffered and a call to unite and to resist their apparent *destino fúnebre* (mournful destiny), as its creators themselves declare.

Notes

1. *Kilele* appears in the volume Ese Atrato que juega al teatro. The play will be cited using only the title of the drama itself.
2. The FARC used gas cylinders as bombs in a number of regions throughout the country.
3. Translator's note: In Colombia these terms refer to the "revolutionary taxes" or protection money extorted from rural populations by the FARC.
4. According to the diocese of Quibdó, in the basin of the Atrato and its tributaries there were at least six-hundred civilians killed and twenty thousand displaced by Freddy Rendón Herrera, known as "El Alemán," a nickname he received for his enthusiasm for order and discipline while he was commander of the Élmer Cárdenas Bloc. Among the many horrific crimes this group of paramilitaries committed are the burning of villages, the murder of pregnant women, and playing football with the heads of their victims. El Alemán was also involved in politics and was one of the creators of the political project Urabá Grande, United and in Peace. According to him, with this project the paramilitary self-defense groups would be able to locate their representatives in different local governments and departmental assemblies throughout Antioquia, Chocó, and Córdoba. El Alemán and his brother, Daniel Rendón Herrera, alias "Don Mario," were requested for extradition from the United States at the beginning of August 2009; the former for the crime of narcotrafficking and the latter for financing terrorist organizations. On October 16, 2009, El Alemán was sentenced by the Second Criminal Court of Antioquia to fourteen years in prison for conspiracy to commit aggravated crime and for the murder of a minor who was executed by paramilitaries on January 18, 2005. He is currently in jail and presenting free testimonies before the district attorneys of Peace and Justice in Medellín ("'El Aléman,' Freddy Rendón Herrera").
5. Freddy Rendón cynically blamed Antún Ramos for the massacre and implicated members of the church, who had been the guardian angels of the communities of Atrato, as responsible for these tragic deaths. Not everyone is content with the placard installed by the army, on which is stated that the place where the FARC massacred children, elderly people, and defenseless civilians, whom they turned into human shields, will never be forgotten. Many feel that the army forgets to mention that the paramilitaries attacked the long-suffering community both long before and after the massacre. They themselves are still not in agreement about how much memory and how much forgetting they need, how to remember and live with the profound pain of burying their relatives without the traditional rituals, and how to endure the indelible physical and spiritual imprint that the massacre has left on them (VerdadAbierta.com).
6. On May 1, 2010, Laura Ardila Arrieta stated that: "The central responsibility lies with the FARC and in this sense it has been a diligent legal process. There are two guerrilla combatants serving thirty-six years in prison each for these acts. Likewise, there are other parties who have been accused of participating. With respect to the 'paras,' there have been a number of confessions. In fact, El Alemán in one of his own free testimonies admits to having participated. Nevertheless, among them there are none that have been sentenced. Nor has there been justice with respect to the Army who, by action or

omission, were involved in what happened, as has been indicated by the Office of the United Nations' High Commissioner for Human Rights. . . . There are three armed actors that participated, by action or omission, but there has only been effective legal action against one of them. Furthermore, there is a debt of justice for the crimes that were committed during ten years of violence. Who should be cited for the thousands of forced displacements? These are very important debts of justice. With respect to reparations, it was a slow process of recognition for the victims." At this time the victims of the massacre have still not received adequate help, they remain without employment options, and what is worse still, violence and armed groups operating outside of the law continue to be active in the area.

7. Pedro Alfonso Albarado Zabaleta, alias "Mapanao," died in the bombing of a FARC encampment on February 22, 2012; he was implicated in the events at Bojayá. The government has now sentenced twenty-one guerrilla combatants for this crime.

8. See Virginia Gutiérrez de Pineda, Familia y Cultura en Colombia. Bogotá: Instituto Colombiano de Cultura, 1975.

9. The works can be seen at www.lasillavacia.com/historia/4630.

10. Translator's note: Communities of previously enslaved individuals.

11. A German artist and teacher who has worked on the subject of armed conflict in different communities in Central America, Kleutgens began the work with a number of playwrights from the river communities who shared their experiences as inhabitants of the region.

12. Felipe Vergara wrote the text in 2004 and received numerous prizes such as the Playwriting Fellowship and the 2005 National Creation Fellowship. The piece was directed by Fernando Montes and was presented in the Festival Iberoamericano, in the Festival of Bogotá, and has been on tour to various states throughout the country.

13. It has been difficult to establish the exact number of victims because many bodies were left in pieces. In a document from December 2011, Gonzalo Sánchez stated that there were seventy-nine and not 119 victims, although he did not clarify how many children died. "La errónea apreciación se debió a que el desmembramiento de cuerpos esparcidos generó confusión. Los fragmentos de un mismo cuerpo, recogidos en distintos lugares fueron contabilizados como de diferentes víctimas fatales. Hay pues errores que forman parte del horror de la Guerra" (The erroneous calculation was the result of the dismemberment of the scattered bodies, which caused confusion. Fragments of the same body, collected from different places, were counted as different fatalities. These are thus errors that form part of the horror of the war) (Sánchez qtd. in Durán Núñez).

14. The seventy-seven candles point to a different total number of victims and demonstrate how difficult it was to count the dead.

15. Translator's note: The levantamiento de tumba is a practice specific to the Afro-Colombian communities of El Chocó. It is the final farewell ritual for the deceased person's soul and takes place on the last day of novenary (nine-day mourning period). As part of the "raising of the tomb," a new shrine is built and songs are sung to seal the departure of the deceased.

Works Cited

Arango, Gonzalo. "Choco en llamas." Cromos [Bogotá], 28 Nov. 1966: 10–12. Biblioteca Virtual: Biblioteca Luis Angel Arrango. www.banrepcultural.org/blaavirtual /periodismo/ reporta1/repor13.htm.

Ardila Arrieta, Laura. "Bojayá, herida que no cierra." *El Espectador* [Bogotá].
  Comunican S.A., 1 May 2010. Web. 8 April 2012. *www.elespectador.com/impreso/
  articuloimpres0201015-bojay a-herida-no-cierra.*

Arocha Rodríguez, Jaime. "Homobiósfera en el Afropacífico." *Revista de Estudios Sociales*
  [Bogotá] 32 (2009): 86–97.

———. "Desarraigo forzado." Bogotá, DC. 20 Oct. 2007. Web. 28 Apr. 2012. *especiales.
  universia.net.co/galeria-de-cientificos/antropologos-sociologos-politologos-y-afines/jaime-
  arocha/desarraigo-fo.html.*

*Bojayá: La guerra sin límites. Informe del Grupo Memoria Histórica de la Comisión Nacional de
  Reparación y Reconciliación.* Bogotá: Taurus, 2010.

Candau, Joël. *Antropología de la memoria.* Trans. Paula Mahler. Buenos Aires: Nueva Visión,
  2002.

Durán Núñez, Diana Carolina. "En Bojayá fueron 79, no 119: Gonzalo Sánchez." *El
  Espectador* [Bogotá]. Comunican S.A., 12 Dec. 2011. Web. 5 May 2012. *www.
  elespectador.com/impreso/judicial/articulo-314712-bojaya-fueron-79-no-119.*

Ese Atrato que juega al teatro, Libretos de ocho historias para teatro. Creación Colectiva,
  Coordinación Inge Kleutgens. Vol. 2. Quibdó, Colombia: Diócesis de Quibdó, Editorial
  Nuevo Milenio, 2008.

"'El Alemán,' Freddy Rendón Herrera." *VerdadAbierta.com: Conflicto Armado en Colombia.*
  N.p., 7 Jan 2009. Web. 18 June 2012. *www.verdadabierta.com/component/content/
  article/36-jefes/716-perfil-freddyrendon-herrera-alias-el-aleman.*

Gabokú. "Teatro Invisible: Bojayá: Los cinco misterios de un genocidio." *El Espectador*
  [Bogotá]. Comunican S.A., 28 May 2012. Web. 19 June 2012. *blogs.elespectador.com/
  teatroinvisible/2012/05/28/bojaya-los-cinco-misterios-de-un-genocidio.*

Gómez de los Ríos, Sara. "El miedo a vivir entre la guerra: Testimonios de víctimas de la
  masacre del 2 de mayo de 2002 en Bellavista, cabecera municipal de Bojayá, Chocó."
  MA thesis [Periodismo]. Universidad de Antioquia [Medellín (Col.): Facultad de
  Comunicaciones], 2008.

Gómez Nadal, Paco. *Los muertos no hablan: Edición Bojayá, una década (2002–2012).*
  Medellín: Editorial Nuevo Milenio, 2012.

Gutiérrez de Pineda, Virginia. *Familia y Cultura en Colombia.* Bogotá: Instituto Colombiano
  de Cultura, 1975.

Hernández Mora, Salud. "Más cornadas da el hambre." *El Tiempo*: 12 May 2002. Web. 17
  June 2012. *www.eltiempo.com/archivo/documento/MAM-1336921.*

Millar, Michael. "Popular Theatre and the Guatemalan Peace Process." *Latin American
  Theatre Review* 39.2 (2006): 97–116.

Nora, Pierre. "Entre memoria e historia: La problemática de los lugares." *Cholonautas.* IEP:
  Instituto de Estudio Peruanas, n.d. Web. 5 Feb. 2012. *cholonautas.edu.pe/memoria/nora1.pdf.*

———. "Between Memory and History: Les Lieux de Mémoire." *Representations* 26 (1989):
  7–24.

Nubia Bello, Martha, et al. *Bojayá, Memoria y Río: Violencia política, daño y reparación.*
  Bogotá: Universidad Nacional de Colombia, 2005.

Romero, César. "Bojayá: De la muerte al emblemático abandono." *Bojayá: Una década.*
  Wordpress, 30 May 2012. Web. 18 June 2012. *bojayaunadecada.org/2012/05/30/bojaya-
  de-la-muerte-al-emblematico-abandono.*

Serrano Soto, Juan Sebastián. "La última vez que vi Bojayá." *La silla vacía.* N.p., 2
  May 2012. Web. 2 May 2012. *www.lasillavacia.com/historia/la-ultima-vez-que-vi-
  bojaya-33025.*

"Tragedia en Bojayá, Chocó" [Fotos de Bojayá]. *El Tiempo*. Casa Editorial El Tiempo, n.d. Web. 21 May 2012. *www.eltiempo.com/Multimedia/galeria_fotos/colombia4/tragedia-en-bojaya-choco-_11663781–5*.

VerdadAbierta.com. "Conflicto Armado en Colombia." N.p., n.d. Web. 18 June 2012. *www.verdadabierta.com/nunca-mas/2728*.

6

Uprising Textualities of the Americas

Slavery, Migration, and the Nation in Contemporary Afro-Hispanic Women's Narrative

Lesley Feracho

In contemporary Afro-Hispanic literature the importance of a cultural, economic, and political development of the collective is often represented through physical, psychological, and symbolic movements as a navigation of cultural roots and contemporary strategies of individual agency and collective mobilization. Such negotiations occur not only between these discourses but also with states of belonging that engage transnational movement; be it to a nation, to a diasporic community, or positionings between both. As Antonio Tillis notes: "For Latin America, the colonial encounters and subsequent waves of migration form the foundation for social interaction and bartering of cultures, as peoples and their endemic traditions underwent a process of transculturation in the colonial, postcolonial, and transnational space" (3). For black women writers in the Americas, and the Hispanophone Americas in particular, the development of subjectivity and agency on both an individual and collective level in these transculturated, transnational spaces occur amid a "historical background of displacements and disjunctures. . . . Their literature is fragmentary and discontinuous; it is characterized by silences and lacunae—what Cocco de Filippis calls 'Feminine Parentheses'—in its evolution" (DeCosta-Willis xxvii). Such movement is also part of the ways in which black women writers employ a range of cultural, political, and discursive strategies in a process of redefinition and in many cases contest imperialist structures and patriarchal discourses of power while crossing ideologies and structures of domination. These challenges to hegemonic structures and discourses are also part of a negotiation of inclusion and exclusion, connecting the racial and gendered collective with the nation. As Homi Bhabha notes in his analysis of the narration of the nation:

> The marginal or "minority" is not the space of a celebratory, or utopian, self-marginalization. It is a much more substantial intervention into those justifications of modernity—progress, homogeneity, cultural organicism, the deep nation, the long past—that rationalize the authoritarian, "normalizing" tendencies within cultures in the name of the national interest or the ethnic prerogative. In this sense, then, the ambivalent antagonistic perspective of nation as narration will establish the cultural boundaries of the nation so that they may be acknowledged as "containing" thresholds of meaning that must be crossed, erased, and translated in the process of cultural production. (4)

For Afro-Hispanic women writers in general and black women writers in particular, such interventions against a homogenizing, normalizing (post)modernity cross and challenge national boundaries through a variety of discursive and cultural strategies. Discussions of these strategies through which they assert an individual and collective engagement with discourses of race, gender, class, and the like are often framed as navigations seen through the lens of postcolonial discourse. However, scholars such as Carole Boyce Davies propose alternative ways of theorizing black feminist practices that challenge the relegation of black women's voices to objects of study. As such, understanding these processes calls for a framework that is not fixed, but rather migratory, crossing ethnic, national, geographic or temporal boundaries. These "migratory subjectivities" demonstrate how "the subject is not just constituted, but in being constituted has multiple identities that do not always make for harmony. . . . Migrations of the subject refers to the female subject refusing to be subjugated. . . . Migratory subjects suggests that black women/s writing cannot be located and framed in terms of one specific place but exist/s in myriad places and times, constantly eluding the terms of the discussion" (36).

One such strategy of contestation for Afro-Hispanic women—and specifically black women writers of the Hispanophone Americas, particularly within the postcolonial and transnational moments within which they create, which also serves as a creation of spaces of resistance—is what Boyce Davies posits as "uprising textualities": "I propose to identify the meaning implicit in 'uprising' to reformulate a host of textualities, which seek to destabilize the established knowledge/authoritarian bases. It is a new resistance to imperialism, which eschews colonial borders, systems, separations, ideologies, structures of domination" (108).

Such a practice is an alternative theorization and understanding of black feminist practices that challenges the limiting "master narratives" and marginalization that she identifies as part of postcolonial theory. For Mary K. DeShazer, this use of writing as a site of resistance can also be a bridge connecting the text to action, similar to the ways in which praxis binds theory and practice. This connection can also be understood as "a poetics of resistance" in which "writers participate in resistance by inscribing it" through poetry and prose (311).

Afro-Hispanic women writers, like their Anglophone and Francophone counter-parts, for example, have found the articulation of female experience and strategies of resistance and agency to be a continuous process that engages not only the socio-historical present but also an understanding of the past—questioning the marginali-zation of certain voices while reclaiming them as important to individual and collec-tive identities. One such way in which this linking of past and present has occurred is through an exploration of the roots of the African diaspora, particularly through representations of slavery in texts that George Handley defines as "postslavery texts" and Angelyn Mitchell categorizes as "liberatory narratives." According to Handley, while writing by black women has engaged memory and dialogue with the past as a catalyst for reformulations of identity, these literary representations of slavery not only imagine untold histories from within the plantation but also examine the importance of genealogies: "I primarily want to emphasize the ideological thrust of those works of literature that, although written after the demise of slavery, return to slavery's past in a genealogical exploration of its deep, historical roots in order to understand its relationship to the present. . . . genealogy expresses a deep sense of historicity as well as points to a path of liberation from the past" (3,14).

This pursuit of "liberation from the past" to which Handley refers is also present in Angelyn Mitchell's typology of these narratives. She uses the term *liberatory narratives* to classify these contemporary texts in the African American literary tradition that engage the period of chattel slavery "in order to provide new models of liberation . . . and is focused on the protagonist's conception and articulation of herself as a free, autonomous and self–authorized self. . . . their primary function indeed is in describ-ing how to achieve freedom" (4). While Mitchell's term is originally used for African American texts, her study in particular addresses the contemporary engagement with the female experience of slavery as it provides strategies for freedom though agency and autonomy that is relevant for understanding black writing, and in this study, black women's writing, throughout the Americas.

Contemporary Afro-Hispanic women writers (as well as those of Brazil), have found the articulation of women's experience under slavery and beyond as a powerful tool not only to emancipate their hidden stories but also as points of connection with larger strategies of agency that cut across race, gender, and class. In this essay I contrast the representations of slavery and the slave past in the works of three Afro-Hispanic women writers—whom I here incorporate into a larger canon of black women writers—of Cuba, Ecuador, and Puerto Rico as a means of exploring the intersection of the jour-ney from and between the past and present, particularly through the confrontation of the slave past, as a strategy of contestation. Through a study of the legacy of slavery on black women's journeys in María de los Reyes Castillo Bueno's Cuban testimonial *Reyita: The Life of a Black Cuban Woman in the Twentieth Century* (1997), in dialogue with Luz Argentina Chiriboga's historical novel *Jonatás y Manuela* (1994) and Dahlma Llanos-Figueroa's generational study *Daughters of the Stone* (2009), I analyze how the individual subject's migration (physical, psychological, symbolic) coupled with an on-going engagement with a collective memory of slavery can also serve as an assertion of the female subject's citizenship and a counter to and expansion of exclusionary conceptions of the nation. I highlight the importance of memory and particularly (re) membrance in this process by applying Karla Holloway's definition of (re)membrance as a textual feature present in black women's writing, here extended to black women writers of the Hispanophone Americas. As Holloway notes: "a *(re)membered* text privileges ways of organization that support the processes of memory as an accurate and appropriate means towards figuring one's history. In this way, those black and female voices that have been excluded from Western historiography tell and (re)member their own stories using their own means of recovering these experiences" (13).

While connected to the use of myth as a form of recovery of memory, the positing of memory as "culturally inscribed . . . and a tactile path toward cultural recovery" that can also facilitate the temporal movement between past and present can provide a useful framework for understanding how black women writers of the Hispanophone Americas use memory to challenge exclusionary histories (Holloway 25).

For these contemporary black women writers, therefore, the memory of slavery is part of the larger project of recovery and contestation that I examine in this essay. In particular, I propose a framing of these projects through what Chicana feminist Chela Sandoval defines as "oppositional consciousness": "a *'topography'* of consciousness in opposition . . . the set of critical points around which individuals and groups seeking to transform oppressive powers constitute themselves as resistant and oppositional subjects. . . . They provide repositories within which subjugated citizens can either occupy or throw off subjectivities in a process that at once both enacts and yet decolonizes their various relations to their real conditions of existence" (267).

In this response to hierarchical discourses, "the subordinated group claim their differences from those in power and call for a social transformation that will accommodate and legitimate those differences, . . . to affirm subordinated differences through a radical societal reformation" (269). As articulated here, this consciousness is a process of navigation and contestation with the most revolutionary action being that of "social transformation and societal reformation." While the writers analyzed here do not necessarily engage in this final representation of "oppositional consciousness," Sandoval's model illustrates the strategic links of contestatory practices that can exist between women of color by proposing a negotiation of subjectivities and processes of decolonization that is an especially useful tool for highlighting the complexities of black women writers' strategies of resistance and redefinition.

As I have noted, an understanding of the relation of black women to the nation as articulated in their contemporary twentieth and twenty-first century texts' dialogue not only with sixteenth to nineteenth-century colonial systems and institutions of slavery but also with nineteenth-century narrative representations, nowhere more prominent in the Americas than in Cuba. For example, both Gertrudis Gomez de Avellaneda's and Cirilo Villaverde's reflections of the social and political national discourses of nineteenth-century Cuba in their antislavery novels, *Sab* (1841) and *Cecilia Valdés* (1882), respectively, while seemingly exploring the end of slavery and the possibilities of egalitarian society, in reality maintained racial and gendered hierarchies. Flora González Mandri compares *Cecilia Valdés* with the more recent trilogy on slavery produced during the second decade of the Cuban Revolution by Cuban director Sergio Giral (*El otro Francisco* [1974], *Rancheador* [1976] and *Maluala* [1979]), noting that both Villaverde and Giral "create female characters who are determined by a nationalist domineering patriarchal gaze. They define the mulatta not only as a child of a black parent and a white parent, but also as exceptionally beautiful and sensual, and often doomed" (13). It is in the early decades of the twentieth century when Afro-Hispanic writers—particularly Cuban—together with Cuban ethnographers engaged in an intellectual movement which, as Darien Davis notes, "emphasized the contribution of the African to Western culture; . . . as important as the Spanish in the forging of *cubanidad* or *Cuban-ness* . . . to emphasize the unity of blacks and whites in the forging of the Cuban community—a community that was culturally mulatto" (152). However, while serving as an important step in the representation of black subjectivity, the problematic incorporation of at times exoticized representations of race and gender demonstrated the need for further nuanced and critical representations.

Such was the case with Esteban Montejo and Miguel Barnet's *Biography of a Runaway Slave* (1966), written in the early stages of the Cuban Revolution, which represents an individual and collective history of the marginalized and marks the beginning of testimonial literature. At a time of social resistance and renewal, as William Luis notes, this text engages oral performance elements, privileges myth and religion over written literature and history, and represents an alternate history of the Cuban nation wherein the black marginalized object becomes a historical subject, connecting slave communities' cultural practices and resistance strategies to later manifestations of the fight for freedom (475, 477). One result is the inscription of the black Cuban population within the larger national reconstruction. However, while Montejo and Barnet's text represents the black Cuban as a historical subject, contemporary Afro-Hispanic women writers (as well as filmmakers and artists) produce works that serve not only as creative outlets but also as a platform to contest Montejo and Barnet's decidedly masculine discourse of nation building. As González Mandri notes, these women "represent black women as independent subjects who challenge the patriarchal gaze" (13).

Such a project is undertaken less than twenty years later in Morejón's seminal poem "Mujer Negra/Black Woman," written in 1979 and published in the collection *Parajes de una época*. As an example of Boyce Davies's "uprising textualities," this epic poem chronicles the physical and emotional journey of several generations of black women from the Middle Passage through enslavement in Cuba to their political participation as Cuban women in the revolution of 1959. As Lorna Williams and RoseGreen-Williams state, it is "a rewriting of Black history according to the teleology of revolution. . . . Morejón . . . invests her persona with an activist's consciousness of her historical contribution to the Cuban economy" (132–33).

In this epic poem, the physical and symbolic migrations of the poetic voice beginning with the Middle Passage continue in the Americas, ultimately representing the generations to follow who engage in an "oppositional consciousness" by "throwing off subjectivities" that mark them as enslaved. Through the journeys wherein these subjects "rebelled, walked, rose up and worked on and on," identities formed under conditions of oppression become sites of developing rebellion and agency. Lorna V. Williams notes that, as a representation of the development of the Cuban nation, "Morejón provides a feminist reading of Cuban history by breaking with the patriarchal model and having her persona postulate her engagement in the political enterprise of securing the island's freedom through her participation in the wars of independence and the Revolution" (133). "Mujer negra" addresses the absence of the female historical subject in *Biography of a Runaway Slave* in two ways: by emphasizing the role of the racialized and gendered other—the black woman—as representative of Cuban and African descended cultural and political acts of resistance, and by expanding perspectives on the nation's construction to include black Cuban women, who were integral participants in the collective struggles for independence and autonomy.

Just as Morejón's textual uprising traces the roots of Cuban women's resistance from slavery to national revolution, María de los Reyes Castillo Bueno's 1997 testimonial to her daughter (Cuban historian Daisy Rubiera Castillo) chronicles a black Cuban woman's complex navigation of gender, race, class, and citizenship in the twentieth century, from its first decades through the Cuban Revolution. Often contrasted with Esteban Montejo and Miguel Barnet's germinal 1966 testimonial *Biography of a Runaway Slave*, *Reyita: The Life of a Black Cuban Woman* was once described as the first Cuban testimonial to analyze marginality and national identity through a gendered analysis and, according to Paula Sanmartín, "constitutes the closest narrative we have of Black Cuban women's life from a protagonist with direct knowledge of the experience since the period of slavery" (115).

It is nonetheless Reyita's life, spanning the political mobilization of the Independent Party of Color in 1910 and its subsequent destruction in the Massacre of 1912, through the Garvey movement's presence in Cuba in the 1920s and the Cuban Revolution of 1959, demonstrating her complex relationship to Cuban nationality, particularly under an ideology that saw racial (dis)identification as divisive. As Sanmartín notes, Reyita's testimony is "both integrated into and separated from official revolutionary discourse," a navigation that tensely juxtaposed internalization of racial hierarchies with the use of writing to relay experiences of marginalization, silencing, and their resistance by trying to "find a voice and a discourse that allows them to transform themselves into active and articulate historical agents . . . capable of contesting dominant discourses" (116).

Given the complexity of Reyita's "self-inscription in history," I would like to demonstrate her representation of a complex "oppositional consciousness" through her relationship to discourses of race, gender, and class that dialogue with and at times contradict Cuban revolutionary ideology. In particular, I highlight a genealogy of resistance through Reyita's memories of her grandmothers' experiences in slavery, presented as strategies of survival that serve as the seed not only for her political engagement focused on national loyalties but also specifically for her community work. Such a relationship between the individual and collective connects the personal and the political, exemplifying what Sanmartín defines as a specifically gendered nationalism: "The stories of active resistance portrayed in the *testimonio* represent more than domestic struggles, but instead present Black Cuban women as an example of 'maternal nationalism.' . . . Reyita's struggles show that the Black female (m)other presents a challenge to a stable homogeneous national identity of which it is, nevertheless, a necessary constituent" (129–30). At the same time, this complex relationship to nationhood demonstrates Reyita's consciousness of 1) Cuban racial politics and inequalities and 2) the interlocking marginalizations of race, class, and gender that manifested themselves in her concrete actions within the poor and in some cases black Cuban community.

In Reyita's testimonial, the importance of women during slavery is highlighted in the first chapter through the stories about her mother's and paternal grandmother Tatica's experiences. The stories told by her grandmother about her relationship to her homeland, her enslavement, and her strategies of survival and resistance serve a dual function: as a means of connecting her with a past—both in Africa and in Cuba—and as a model of resistance to oppression, which she would emulate with her own actions both politically and through community involvement. Similar to Morejón's positing of Cuban women as historical subjects, Tatica's stories highlight a still rare woman-centered representation of slavery. As we see in Reyita's retelling of her grandmother's memories of enslavement, carefully balanced with examples of survival, the recounting of migrations is important in charting these female subjects' navigations of systems of oppression, as well as their strategies of resistance through the maintenance of family ties, acts of political involvement, and religious beliefs. As Reyita recalls, remembering the stories Tatica shared about her enslavement with her two sisters: "Nunca tuvo bien claro cómo fue que se las arreglaron las tres para permanecer unidas; y cuando hablaba de eso, daba gracias a una persona que yo no sabía quién era-y que luego comprendí que era su Dios" (20–21) (I never understood exactly how the three of them managed to stay together; when she talked about it she'd give thanks to someone I didn't know, and who I later understood was their god) (25). The reference to "their god" underscores the importance of African-derived religious systems that would later become part of the foundation for syncretic practices such as Santería.

Not only do Reyita's memories recount Tatica's descriptions of the capture, the sale of slave women, and the sexual abuses and rape to which they were also vulnerable, but they also focus on the role of these women as historical agents, either alluding to or explicitly referencing their participation in the fight for Cuban independence. It is in these moments of historical agency where movement becomes an important strategy that unites physical migrations with the "migratory subjectivities," who refuse subjugation and challenge masculine scripts of national independence through female movement for survival and political participation. One such example can be seen when Tatica goes to the hills with her husband Basilio in his war with independence forces for Cuban autonomy. In this struggle for autonomy it is her daughter Isabel and paternal grandmother Mamacita who are identified as *Mambí* (belonging to the Cuban independence fighters):

> Tu abuela junto con sus tres hijos pequeños se unió a los familiares de los mambises. . . . Mi abuela, quien lo había seguido a la manigua, después del Pacto del Zanjón, regresó a Santiago. . . . Cuando comenzó la Guerra del 95, . . . Mamacita no se quiso ir con papá Panchito y se incorporó a la lucha con todos sus hijos. (Rubiera Castillo 30, 38–39)

> Your grandmother, along with her three small children joined up with the families of the *Mambí*. . . . My grandmother, who had followed him [Antonino] into the resistance, returned to Santiago after the Zanjón Pact. . . . When the War of 1895

began, . . . Mamacita didn't want to go with Papa Panchito, and she joined the insurrection with all her children. (Castillo Bueno 33–34, 41–42)

In all these cases, all three women, as female members of the Mambises, move to different sites of insurrection, at times in defiance of the movement of their male partners, thus destabilizing the paternalistic construction of revolution and the fight for independence as a strictly masculine endeavor. Subsequently, these stories and examples of women's subjectivity are what later inspire Reyita to her first conscious example of oppositional consciousness through her involvement with the Garvey movement. As she explains: "Ese amor que mi abuelita me inculcó por su tierra natal influyó mucho en mi determinación de incorporarme al movimiento de Marcus Garvey–para irme para Africa—, cansada de ser discriminada por negra" (22) (This love for her homeland that my grandma instilled in me had a big influence on my decision to join Marcus Garvey's movement—to go to Africa—tired of being discriminated against for being black) (26–27). This developing consciousness was initially sparked when Reyita was a child during the 1912 massacre of members of the Independent Party of Color, a moment which, according to Aline Helg, "achieved what Morúa's amendment and the trial against the party in 1910 had been unable to do: put a definitive end to the Partido Independiente de Color and made it clear to all Afro-Cubans that any further attempt to challenge social order would be crushed with bloodshed" (194). When Reyita witnessed the false arrest of her Aunt Manga (then President of the Lady's Auxiliary of the Independent Party of Color) for her political activity, along with the oppression and deaths of protesting black Cubans in the massacre, which is also known as the Race War of 1912, she became acutely aware of the falsity of Cuba's espousal of racial democracy.

As a black woman during the Cuban Revolution, Reyita navigated her awareness of racial injustice with her perceived responsibilities as a Cuban. Sanmartín notes: "In her struggle for self-representation, Reyita's strong black consciousness enters into conflict with . . . commonplace ideas about motherhood and revolutionary ideology" (130). Thus, her political activity through the Literacy Campaign, the Revolutionary Defense Committee, the Federation of Cuban Women, and other activities in defense of Black Cubans is uncomfortably placed alongside her justification for marrying a white Cuban man in order to provide a better life free of discrimination for her children. However, these tensions can be seen not as obscuring but rather as underscoring the importance and complexity of Reyita's navigations and the ways in which her community involvement did contest dominant discourses about race, gender, and class while exemplifying how "in their struggle to live with dignity Afro-Cubans adopted an assortment of strategies" (Dore 6). Such is the case with Reyita's different projects for economic advancement and to provide for her family: her home restaurants (*tren y cantinas*), the plans that allowed her to install electricity as well as purchase a radio and car, and her religious practices of *espiritismo/spiritism*. According to Aline Helg, this demonstrates how Afro-Cuban racial political practice adopted hidden strategies, given that the Cuban government's actions against political parties were based on racial mobilization, as was the case with the Independent Party of Color. All of these actions were part of Reyita's process of independence: "El tiempo pasaba. Yo iba despertando. . . . Por tanto comencé a hacer una vida, hasta cierto punto, independiente a la del viejo" (87) (Time went by. I was awakening. . . . So I began to make a life, up to a certain point, independent of your old man's) (85).

This awakening, here seen in her recognition of the gendered racial politics of patriarchy and power in the interpersonal relationships played out in the private space of the home, is part of an oppositional consciousness which is particularly revealed in Reyita's community involvement through her work with prostitutes and their children. It represents the beginning of a consciousness that, while not fully completing this revolutionary strategy through a call for social reformation, does explicitly recognize and respond to structures of inequality. For Reyita, her role as caregiver to the children of the prostitutes in the Plaza del Mercado neighborhood is not just an extension of her familial duties as mother but is also motivated by her awareness of unequal racial, class, and gendered discourses in the Cuban nation, representative of what Sanmartín has defined as her embodiment of "maternal nationalism":

> Muchas de esas mujeres no eran malas. Diría que casi todas fueron víctimas
> del sistema imperante en nuestro país. . . . Pero todas eran unas desgraciadas,
> marginadas, discriminadas. . . . Yo no cobraba nada por cuidarlos, solamente que sus
> madres me ayudaran con la alimentación de sus hijos. . . . Lo que me inspiraba . . .
> era mi sentido de la humanidad y los tristes recuerdos de mi niñez. (72–73)

> Lots of those women weren't bad. I would say almost all of them were victims of
> the system prevalent in our country. . . . They were all wretched, marginalized and
> discriminated against. . . . I didn't charge for taking care of them, just as long as
> their mothers helped. . . . What inspired me . . . was my feeling of humanity and
> sad memories of my own childhood. (71–72)

The motivations of Reyita the narrative voice (in collaboration with her daughter Daisy) for her community activism at times intersect with the textual representation of Reyita. While the narrator recognizes the unequal discourses and explains her actions through maternal instincts and humanitarian concern, the text's structure places her community caregiving within a genealogy of women who in different moments in Cuban history identified dominant discourses of race, gender, and class alongside the marginalizations they created, and through their actions they contested them. Such a lineage goes back through her Tía Manga to her grandmothers under slavery, emphasizing a common link: their destabilization of dominant discourses through the (re)membrances of migrations and actions that posit their historical agency and in part create "liberatory narratives" within the construction of the Cuban nation.

Just as Morejón's textual uprising traces the roots of Cuban woman's resistance and the developing subjectivity from slavery to national revolution, so too does Castillo Bueno's *testimonio* situate Reyita's beginning oppositional consciousness in an at times uneasy co-existence with her sense of maternal nationalism that seemingly upholds the racial, gendered, and class foundations of Cuban nationhood. In a similar complex interaction of opposition and expansion of the nation, Luz Argentina Chiriboga's 1994 novel *Jonatás y Manuela* represents women's experiences under slavery as counterhistories, models of resistance carried out through later generations. In this historical novel, the seeds of revolution in Ecuador are not found in the historical figure of Manuela Saenz, lover of Latin American liberator Simón Bolívar (also known as the *libertadora del libertador*) and activist in her own right, but date back to the examples of resistance represented by the enslaved female family members of Saenz's slave—and later her companion—Jonatás. Unlike many historical novels, Chiriboga's representation of the early period of Ecuadorian and African diasporic culture focuses on the marginalized voices of the women. Chiriboga's "gynocentric vision," according to Rosemary Feal, "produces an Afrocentric counternarrative to the grand historical novels of Latin America"(25). In chronicling the complex relationship of these two women within larger contexts of resistance and independence, Chiriboga creates a "liberatory narrative" through the strategies embodied by Jonatas's grandmother, a slave in the Americas, which are later fully realized in her granddaughter's collaborative struggle for freedom. Their development as oppositional subjects serves as a counter to limiting gendered, racial, and class discourses, represented on both an individual (in terms of gender and racial norms) and collective (for both blacks and the nation) level.

Ba-Lunda, Jonatás's grandmother, who opens the novel named after her granddaughter, represents the remembrance of ancestral ties as key to understanding the history of displacement, trauma, navigation, survival, and resistance that marks the life of the female slave in the Americas and is established as foundational in the later development of the Ecuadoran nation. Torn from her country and her lover, Jabí, physically and emotionally violated as a slave, and renamed Rosa Jumandi, Ba-Lunda's adherence to her spiritual beliefs and desire to protect and unite her family are the beginning of her consciousness of opposition through a challenge to the colonial discourses that would silence her: "Rechazó aquel nombre, no entendió por qué se lo imponían, . . . No contentos con quitarle la libertad, ahora le quitaban su nombre" (34) (She rejected that name, and couldn't understand why they forced it on her, . . . Not satisfied with taking away her freedom, now they were taking away her name) (translation mine). Her contestation of her powerlessness is enacted by rejecting the name forced on her by the slave owners and seeking strength for retribution from the African god Oddán to whom she prays.

Although Ba-Lunda's attempts to poison the priest and replace the forced migration of her ancestors with her own planned escape do not result in her ultimate freedom, her resistance is later embodied, not in her daughter, who marries a slave trader in order to acquire a more secure place in post-slavery Ecuadoran society, but in her granddaughter Jonatás. Here Chiriboga's protagonist from early childhood draws on storytelling as (re)memory and recovery of her ancestor's experiences: a narration of the crossing of the colonial boundaries as a resistance to silencing and a form of cultural preservation. When Jonatás is bought by Manuela Saenz's father to serve as a companion to his daughter, the two develop a relationship of companionship that challenges the young Manuela's relationship of subservience to her mistress. United by the absence of their respective mothers and the desire to challenge limiting notions of gender and race, Jonatás's use of (re)memory is as a tool to introduce the young Manuela to African-centered traditions and stories. These narratives, when combined with Jonatas's childhood games as *musis* fighting the

Spaniards, serve as communal resistance and seeds for later liberatory activities the two will undertake.

Along with their continuing affirmation of their position as subjects, such actions and agents of resistance to enslavement form the basis of the development of Jonatás and Manuela's "oppositional consciousness": a liberatory strategy wherein coalitions across ethnic and class lines are formed with not only Manuela but also other indigenous subjects to fight for societal transformation. For example, Jonatás and Manuela's planning of and participation in raids for materials and arms to free slaves embody movement as counter to the colonial structures that would keep them in place. In her accepted travels with the slave Natán through the market in service to their mistress, Jonatás's encounters with other slaves and mulattos are the seed for her continued struggles for their liberation, leading to her union with other blacks and indigenous subjects to obtain materials needed to finance their freedom:

> Al recorrer las dos esclavas los mercados, las plazas y las cantinas de Lima, conversaban con los africanos y los mulatos; al escuchar los bandos con las promulgaciones de nuevas ordenanzas, Jonatás empezó a sentir una apremiante necesidad de organizar también allí algunos grupos musis. . . . Separaron y envolvieron en sacos los badajos, . . . los seis zafaron la campana mayor. . . . Jonatás, al juntar sus manos y su rostro a los rostros y a las manos de los indios, ayudándolos a sostener el peso, sintió a los aborígenes como sus hermanos. (152-53, 157)

> While the two slaves were going through the markets, the plazas, and cantinas of Lima, they spoke with the Africans and mulattos; upon hearing the proclamations with the promulgations of new orders, Jonatás began to feel a compelling need to also organize there some groups of *musis*. . . . They separated and wrapped up the clappers in sacks, . . . the six untied the larger bell. . . . While Jonatás united her hands and her face to the faces and hands of the Indians, helping them to support the weight; she felt the aborigines were her brothers. (translation mine)

Their physical crossing of the religious space of the church by this multiracial, multigendered coalition in order to steal the bell represents an equally important crossing of gendered and racial norms as a challenge to the colonial discourses that would objectify and exclude them from citizenship. These coalitions demonstrate the development of "resistant and oppositional subjects," whose early counters to the oppressive colonial structures soon develop into the awareness of the need to fight for independence on all its fronts, leading Jonatás and Manuela to extend their liberatory projects abroad. Here again, physical migration through the Spanish colonies is also a union of these spaces, in shared struggles to free not only the slaves but also colonies of New Granada (Peru, Ecuador) from Spanish domination in 1822: "En el trayecto, liberan esclavos y convencen a curiosos para que marchen con ellas y se enrolen en el ejército independentista" (166) (On the way, they liberate slaves and convince the curious to march with them, and they enlist in the army for independence) (translation mine). The combinations of these migrations and struggles for independence demonstrate a similar movement as seen in both Morejón and Reyita: the representation of the gendered black excluded object as historical subject and a key contributor in the development of the nation. Chiriboga's position of Jonatás's struggle against limiting racial and gender norms within a larger anticolonial project exemplifies the complexity of the liberatory project through a "narration of the nation" that highlights the boundaries that not only contain these desires for freedom but are also contested by them. The folding of Jonatás's pursuit of autonomy as a black female subject within the larger national project mirrors both Morejón's and Castillo Bueno's black female subjects who become the defenders of the Cuban Revolution. This is simultaneously placed alongside the positing of national liberation as necessary for all peoples to be truly independent, represented by the interconnectedness between orality, the freedom of slaves, and women's physical and symbolic movement as foundations for national independence from colonization.

The final example of a "liberatory narrative" wherein the female subject engages in the development of an "oppositional consciousness" is the generational novel *Daughters of the Stone* by Puerto Rican writer Dahlma Llanos-Figueroa. In her novel, Llanos-Figueroa begins the journey of individual and collective navigation and resistance through the figure of Fela, a slave brought to the plantation just as the text begins, in mid-nineteenth century Puerto Rico. Through the novel's matrilineal focus—presenting each female descendant, from Fela through her daughter Mati to her daughter Conchi, whose daughter Elena gives birth to the line's last descendant, Carisa—each woman deals with her responses to oppression, individual developments of subjecthood, and the possibilities of maintaining traditional ties to African-based ways of knowing while navigating contemporary discourses of progress and modernity. Such journeys, here represented through remembrances that present female-centered histories, are transmitted through storytelling and symbolic embodiments of cultural memory represented by the stone Fela brings from Africa to Puerto Rico and passes down to each generation. I draw upon Jeannette Rodriguez and Ted Fornier's definitions of memory, expanded to include archaeologist Jan Assman's definition of cultural memory, which inhabits the "outer dimension of human memory," embracing "memory culture" and "reference to the past":

> Memory culture is the process by which a society ensures cultural continuity by preserving, with the help of cultural mnemonics, its collective knowledge from one generation to the next, rendering it possible for later generations to reconstruct their cultural identity. When we speak about cultural memory, we are including in this definition two distinct characteristics: (1) the survival of a historically, politically and socially marginalized group of people, and (2) the role of spirituality as a form of resistance. (1)

This cultural memory serves to articulate not only a shared past, including shared trauma, but also an active continuation of a cultural legacy where spirituality is in constant tension with the development of the modern nation.

As this analysis will demonstrate, the connection established between the enslaved Fela and her great granddaughter Carisa through the cultural memory initiated under slavery becomes the model for Carisa's use of writing as a liberatory narrative that engages in a form of resistance to assimilating forces of progress and is also a means of continuing to assert their agency as subjects. Llanos-Figueroa's representation of cultural memory exemplifies the narration of the boundaries of the nation, crossing and contesting the marginalizing and limiting visions of Puerto Rican national identity predicated on specific hierarchies of race, gender, and class. According to Maritza Quiñones Rivera, this contradicted the idea of equality through *mestizaje* that the *gran familia puertorriqueña* (great Puerto Rican family) espoused (177). As Quiñones Rivera states: "To publicly acknowledge racial difference is a threat to the island's class- and color-blindness where individuals—regardless of their social, economic and racial/ethnic background—are ostensibly able to realize their potential and obtain social mobility. Afro-Puerto Ricans have to negotiate their blackness silently, while protecting their Puertoricanness, their common denominator, in an often antagonistic racial environment. On the island the politics of difference are silent, subdued and embedded within imaginary nationalist discourses" (163).

In this way, Llanos-Figueroa's protagonists continue and expand on Morejón's, Castillo Bueno's, and Chiriboga's projects of emphasizing black women as historical subjects whose agency and resistance not only challenge but also expand the definition of the nation.

Having been forcefully migrated away from her life in Africa and her plans for a family with her lover, Imo, Fela's belief in the destiny of her motherhood as well as in her need to atone for her sins to Mother Oshún lead her to navigate the slave society, not as victim but as subject in opposition to colonial structures of control and enslavement. This is most clearly represented through her constant guarding of a magical stone originally used in Africa in her attempt to conceive. Fela refuses to cede to the hierarchies of the slave plantation and instead chooses to affirm subjectivity and control through her own body and her relationship with the slave owner Don Tomás. This use of the body and maternity as a site of cultural preservation and resistance dialogues with the complex historical navigations of slaves, and particularly female slaves, for control and a sense of subjectivity under an institution that consistently divested them of any value.

Fela's negotiation of the racial and gendered discourses of objectification as a site for subjectivity and agency is especially enacted through her body. This black, female body, historically represented as economic commodity, the producer of future objects of labor and sexual object, was also the physical embodiment of white male desire and fear. As Mayra Santos Febres notes, the inferiorization of the slave took on an especially sexual nature in the case of the black woman:

> Dicha definición inferiorizante del esclavo se basaba en una "explotación" que no era tan sólo de índole económica, ni psicológica. Era también de índole sexual. La existencia de indieras y corrales de negros evidencían cómo capataces y amos violaban a las jóvenes esclavas para satisfacerse sexualmente y, de paso, impregnarlas con nuevas "piezas" para vender en el Mercado. . . . La práctica de tener sexo o violar a mujeres esclavas fue muy común en las Américas. De ellas nacieron poblaciones enteras sobretodo en el Caribe. ("El color de la seducción" 120)

Such an inferiorizing definition of the slave was based on an "exploitation" that was not only of an economic nature, nor psychological. It was also of a sexual nature. The existence of Indian women and corrals of blacks was evidence of how the overseers and masters raped young slaves to satisfy themselves sexually, and, as such, impregnate them with new "pieces" to sell in the market. . . . The practice of having sex or raping female slaves was very common in the Americas. From that practice entire populations were born, especially in the Caribbean. ("The Color of Seduction," translation mine)

Llanos-Figueroa establishes this objectification of the black female body early on in her representation of the sexualization of Fela by the prominent white men in the village, both businessmen and slave owners alike:

The white men who habitually sat there drinking aged rum or discussing the buying and selling of crops stopped their conversations and turned to watch Fela move up the opposite side of the street. They watched all women, but the daring of their commentary depended on the complexion of the women's skin. . . . She chose to ignore the lust that dripped from the corners of the men's mouths. She could feel their eyes on her skin. . . . Their eyes searched out her waist, her thighs, the dark secrets they imagined lay within the folds of her skirt. These men smelled like overheated irons left unattended. . . . Looking away, she pulled herself up straight, more contained within herself, beyond them. (39)

In this brief scene the objectifying gaze highlights Fela's positioning as both commercial product, similar to the crops and other products the businessmen frequently traded, and sexual property to be desired, explored, and ultimately conquered. The exploration of the female body, here further defined by race, acquires additional symbolic import when placed within the history of the metaphors of colonization and particularly of European conquest of the African continent and the Americas.

This symbolism of domination is, however, countered by Fela's subtle physical act of resistance. As Santos Febres notes in her application of Nelly Richards' analysis of the body as performative strategy and discourse of signification to the Caribbean context, the body is a site that is not only constructed and enacted upon, but also used as a tool of contestation:

La incorporación de la sexualidad funciona entonces como dinámica de reformulación simbólica de las categorías de la identidad. . . . La presencia del cuerpo en la literatura caribeña suele señalar hacia otro espacio de contención y negociación literaria-la que define al cuerpo como la frontera entre lo social y lo íntimo . . . escribir sobre el cuerpo (o a través del cuerpo) también significa hacer constar la existencia de dos tipos de conocimiento—el conocimiento interno, y el conocimiento de cómo el poder actúa sobre la existencia misma de ese cuerpo. ("Los usos de Eros" 88–89)

The incorporation of sexuality therefore functions as a dynamic of the symbolic reformulation of the categories of identity. . . . The presence of the body in

Caribbean literature tends to point to another space of contention and literary negotiation—that which defines the body as a border between the social and the intimate . . . writing on the body (or through the body) also means recording the existence of two types of knowledge—the internal knowledge, and the knowledge of how power acts upon the very existence of that body. ("The Uses of Eros," translation mine)

The Caribbean author, which I extend to include the Caribbean diasporic author, through the narration of, or through the body itself, brings to light the complex interaction of two types of knowledge that also reflect the question of object and subject: 1) an understanding of the body as affected by discourses of power and 2) an inner revelation of the self.

In this sense, the black female body was not solely an example of the violation, objectification, and victimization of the female subject. What Santos Febres calls the "experience of the body" could also be an important site of the development of her historical subjectivity:

Es por medio de una profunda experiencia del cuerpo que se llega a la subjetividad—a través del descubrimiento de las coordenadas del cuerpo, de sus contextos históricos, orgánicos, sociales y sexuales . . . la liberación y la sabiduría que obtiene el sujeto son propuestas como armas importantes para la aceptación propia y para la liberación de opresiones que siempre definen al cuerpo como objeto de otros, como imagen del deseo de otros. ("Los usos de Eros" 90)

It is through a profound experience of the body that one arrives at subjectivity—through the discovery of the coordinates of the body, of its historical, organic, social and sexual contexts . . . the freedom and wisdom that the subject obtains are proposed as important weapons for self-acceptance and for the freedom from oppressions that always define the body as the object of others, as an image of others' desire. ("The Uses of Eros," translation mine)

In the protagonist Fela's case, the continuation of this knowledge of the self, through the body, is exemplified through her physical change in posture as a response to the sexual stares of the white businessmen and plantation owners. In defiance, she uses her body as a symbol of her refusal to be objectified, a gesture through which she both recognizes yet attempts to place herself "beyond" the social, economic, class, race, and gendered discourses of power at play in the gaze upon her.

A second way in which the black female body contests the objectifying, exploitative discourses of power is through an assertion of her worth outside the economic through her role as the creator of future generations of not only labor, but more important, of Afro-descendants that would help define the identity of the Americas. When placed in the context of the complex sociocultural ramifications of the relationship between master and slave, the black female subject's role as mother of future populations, of "entire populations of the Caribbean" for example, demonstrates an additional lens through which the violence can be understood.

The development of a counterdiscourse of historical subjectivity in the midst of violence is one theme that can be seen in various writings of black Hispanic women writers. As an illustration, I would like to briefly return and reconnect to one I have previously noted: Morejón's "Mujer Negra." When her singular vision of the black woman's journey from slavery to Afro-Cuban citizen and active historical agent is placed alongside Llanos-Figueroa's representation of the development of the Afro-Puerto Rican historical subject, the portraits of the black woman, particularly her response to enslavement and colonization, reveal important elements of the plantation experience and the strategies of survival. It is important to note that the complexity of this resistance, both psychological and physical, is the subject of several other poems by Morejón, such as "Amo a mi amo" ("I Love my Master"), in which, as Mariela A. Gutiérrez points out: "The woman in 'Amo a mi amo' is alone, all alone, away from her land, away from her people, separated from her gods, . . . she has become *Nothing* through slavery. The woman in this poem embodies the state of exile, solitude, slavery and violation in which the African female found herself during three centuries of European colonialism. For her, there is only one way of transcending this situation: by transforming her nightmare into a positive vision of freedom" (216).

In "Mujer Negra" the violence of colonialism, enacted on the female body, is reworked by the female subject on the path to freedom over the course of centuries. One telling contrast can be seen when the relationship of Morejón's enslaved with her slave master, a nobleman she refers to as "His Worship," is specifically placed alongside Llanos-Figueroa's representation of Fela's relationship with Don Tomás. As Morejón's epic poem progresses, the female subject negotiates violence, exploitation, and the objectification it engenders, here represented by her purchase by His Worship and the resulting sexual relationship she is forced to endure, resulting in a son who, as additional property, is objectified like his mother. As C. RoseGreen-Williams has noted in her study of Morejón's text:

> The persona of "Mujer negra" foregrounds, not the victimhood and martyrdom of her enslavement, but her strength and indestructible capacity for survival. Subtlety, indirection and ellipsis are the means employed to convey protest against her slave experience. The line, "Bordé la casaca de Su Merced y un hijo macho le parí" (1.13), is more powerful in its impact because the disconnection between the act of embroidering for her master and the result of bearing his child points starkly to the reality of sexual exploitation of the Black woman which is imminent in the history of slavery. (191)

As Morejón's black female subject declares:

Su Merced me compró en una plaza.
Bordé la casaca de Su Merced y un hijo
    macho le parí.
Mi hijo no tuvo nombre.
Y Su Merced, murió a manos de un
    impecable *lord inglés*.
Anduve. (200)

His Worship bought me in a public square.
I embroidered His Worship's coat and bore
    him a male child.
My son had no name.
And His Worship died at the hands of an
    impeccable English lord.
I walked.

The juxtaposition of the physical labor of embroidering and forced childbearing is heightened by the disconnection and exploitation RoseGreen-Williams notes. However, Morejón's use of the autobiographical voice in recounting the exploitation and the consequences point to the ways in which survival negotiated both objectification and agency. Here amid the exploitation is the female voice—recounting not only the violence and invisibility, but also the ways in which these power dynamics were subject to shifts, as exemplified by the seemingly powerful master's death at the hands of another nobleman. What is also telling of the subject's recounting is the juxtaposition of marginalization and voice—the exploited subject whose son is invisibilized is placed at the center of her story through the focus on her first-person narration of events. The foregrounding of her firsthand account of her enslavement and survival is taken one step further following His Worship's death, when the female subject again engages in another action in her quest for freedom: her declaration "Anduve" (I walked), which when placed alongside the other short verses—"Me rebelé / Me sublevé / Trabajé mucho más / Me fui al monte / bajé de la Sierra" (I rebelled / I rose up / I worked on and on / I left for the Hills / I came down from the Sierra") (200, 202)—are, as Gutiérrez notes, a part of "a continuous motion that purposely emphasizes the slave woman's feelings of rebellion, coupled with an indomitable perseverance that persists throughout the four centuries covered in the poem" (213).

Similarly, in *Daughters of the Stone*, Fela's relationship with Don Tomás exemplifies the enslaved black woman's vulnerability to the objectification, exploitation, and sexual violence of the slave master and the complex, myriad strategies she utilizes for survival and resistance. Here, Fela's counter to the imposition of Don Tomás's desire is an assertion of agency. She claims control of her body, placing the sexual exploitation that has been historically part of the colonial experience within the context of the strategies used by Afro-descendants, including the continuation of religious beliefs through cultural memory. As she emphatically declares: "Maybe the goddess was guiding her down this path. . . . At least this time she would have as much to do with what was about to happen as he did. She would not be taken. This time it would be her choice. . . . Fela felt nothing of what was occurring with her body. . . . She sent her senses beyond this place. . . . She would join Imo and the others. Oshun would be appeased and the ancestors would welcome her" (46–47, 49).

Fela's determination to wrest control of her body from Don Tomás—to give the sexual act a meaning outside of victimization and exploitation, to serve as a means to create a child who would be given a purpose and name—connect her with history and memory in a way that contrasts with the relationship between the enslaved black woman and His Worship previously highlighted in Morejón's text. Her decision to psychologically distance herself from her physical exploitation and in so doing assert a sense of agency is in strict contrast with the silence she had previously experienced. Llanos-Figueroa's recognition in a contemporary narrative of the complex relationship between discourses of power and agency in the colonial context, especially as represented through voice and silence, exemplifies Elleke Boehmer's emphasis on the importance of the postcolonial text as a reversal of silence: "This is perhaps one of the key distinguishing features of the postcolonial: the acting out of paradox, the conversion of imposed dumbness into self-expression, the self-representation by the *colonial body* of its scars, its *history*. . . . Representing its own silence, the colonized body speaks; uttering its wounds, it strives to negate its muted condition. This is ideally speaking a process not of reclamation only, but, importantly, of self-articulation, reconstitution through speaking one's condition" (131).

At the moment of her sexual encounter with Don Tomás, Fela uses her body and memory as reclamation and a representation of physical and psychological wounds. She recalls the first time she was silenced at the hands of both her slave master who raped her and the mistress of the plantation, who removed Fela's tongue for daring to demand punishment for her violation. It is a physical silence she later turns into a sign of strength, using her body as a means of control and psychologically seeking refuge in "an internal world that ran parallel to the one in which everyone else existed" (Llanos-Figueroa 52).

Fela's negotiation of the power structures that were part of the colonial slave society point to a recognition of an inner knowledge that links her to the African community she was forced to physically leave behind. Her self-articulation as subject is partly through a recognition of her role as an agent of a spiritual destiny established by the orisha Oshun. Consequently, the psychological trauma Fela experiences, represented as a guilt resulting from her separation from her family, is one articulation of the impact of displacement on African descendants as a result of the Middle Passage. At the same time, her determination to turn the historic, social, and sexual contexts operating on her body into tools for recognition of subjectivity and resistance to oppression also connect Fela to the processes of spiritual survival and continuity for African descendants in light of the disconnections and displacements of slavery.

Part of this survival links African-descended spiritual practices with the transferal of cultural values, here symbolized by the stone's journey. It is physically passed on from Fela to her daughter Mati and ultimately to Carisa, representing a migratory subjectivity that demands that each woman be understood in the context of a larger matrilineal ancestry that dialogues with the contemporary socio-cultural, economic forces of progress. Each transferal of the stone occurs after moments of silencing of traditional beliefs (whether it be under the pressures of modernity or under the trauma of familial loss) and is the beginning of a line of traditional beliefs that each daughter wrestles with as she navigates her cultural and spiritual legacies within a constantly changing world.

With each generation, Fela's descendants find themselves navigating the legacy of their gifts and the responsibilities of cultural preservation with the modernization of the island. However, for each woman, Mati, Conchi, and Elena, there is a moment of realization of the power of these traditions, of the need to recover and protect this cultural memory as a recuperation of a history that provides a source of strength in the face of trauma and loss, and as a resistance to homogenizing, silencing discourses of progress. Elena's daughter Carisa becomes the embodiment of the journey of not only the stone but also the cultural memory it represents, bringing the traditions, stories, and powers it holds full circle. Through her act of (re)membrance, chronicling the stories of her female ancestors, she engages in an "oppositional consciousness" that recognizes not only the values of these voices, but also the forces of oppression that make their continuation so difficult.

Her friendships with an elderly African American and a Jewish woman who foster her desire to create stories of female subjects silenced by history are challenged by the historic opposition within the Americas of the African, marginalized as primitive in Anglo-European representations of civilization and later progress. It is a belief she confronts in the elementary-school teachers in the United States who echo the belief that African cultural traditions as they developed in the Americas and any valorization of them are counter to modernity: "But we're Americans now, modern and educated. Here we believe in science. No need for superstitions anymore. That's what we call progress" (253). In a similar representation of the role of education in socialization and the promotion of these binary discourses, Llanos-Figueroa places a similar condemnation in the mouth of a college professor who criticizes Carisa's decision to write about "semiliterate, poverty stricken people who have no past and even less of a future" (272).

The beginning of Carisa's awakening is seen in her response to the silencing of ancestral beliefs as discourses of value in a modern world: returning to Puerto Rico as a journey of (re)membering and reconnection in order to move forward. The stories of the women from her childhood reaffirm the sense of community she had lost, allowing her time to heal and find an individual textual voice built on collective stories of suffering and strategies of survival, engaging through her writing in an example of Boyce Davies's "uprising textuality" that simultaneously serves as a liberatory narrative. The continued development of her "oppositional consciousness," still in early stages, is also a metafictional contemplation of the role of the writer in the preservation and continuation of tradition and culture by historically excluded groups. As she notes of the meetings with these elderly women in Puerto Rico: "I woke up thinking of the tales, and the pen in my hand moved and kept on moving. I couldn't write quickly enough to capture all the words that swirled around my head. I took their stories and nurtured them, blended them with my own, and let them simmer" (286). Retelling these stories counters national structures of exclusion by linking earlier (re)membrances of her ancestors with later female subjects placed on the margins of their nation's history.

Nonetheless, Carisa's development of an "oppositional consciousness" and psychological and social awakening is continued when she meets and begins to work with the Puerto Rican photographer María Luisa. Through María Luisa's friendship and mentorship, Carisa is opened up to the awareness of the realities of social injustice on the island and the limiting visions of the Puerto Rican nation that marginalize racial and class difference despite the national discourse of racial and class equality. These encounters, placed alongside the visual documents of difference represented in María Luisa's photographs and Carisa's stories of her African ancestry recounted as a child in the homogenizing US school system and continued as a returning daughter of the island in search of her (second) roots, exemplify a textuality of uprising, a narrative of liberation that serves as an example of active opposition to the "real conditions of existence" that surround her on the island.

Ultimately, this journey of liberation takes Carisa beyond the borders of her Puerto Rican and North American identities, compelling her to journey to West Africa as a continuation of her search for reconnection, linking her identity as storyteller to her ancestry through her vision of Oshun: "She knows I am watching. When she turns her face to me I see that the Lady has my face" (323). The stories begun with Fela's physical and cultural journey to the Americas become the subjects and voices that her great granddaughter shares in the final postscript—a metafictional and symbolic recognition of her link to tradition and the continuation of this cultural memory to the reader: "I am a teller of stories. . . . It is who I am. . . . And now I give them to you."

From Reyita's female ancestors to Ba-Lunda and Fela, continuing with Jonatás and Manuela's revolutionary activism and Carisa's work as a writer, Castillo Bueno, Chiriboga, and Llanos Figueroa present texts that embody Bhabha's narration of the nation as a migratory and liberatory contestation of exclusionary, marginalizing discourses. Through the incorporation of (re)membrance and oral performance and the continued trope of the journey, they create "oppositional subjects" whose critical liberatory narratives contest oppressive structures while, in the texts of Castillo Bueno and Chiriboga, demonstrating the complexity of such challenges as their subjects both enact and throw off limiting discourses. Such works of (re)membrance link the historical subjectivity of the Afro-Hispanic woman in struggles for independence and agency with previous projects as a contextualization of the resistance and agency strategies contemporary Afro-Hispanic women writers use in order to promote selfhood and challenge and expand marginalizing definitions of national identity.

Works Cited

Bhabha, Homi K. "Narrating the nation." Introduction. *Nation and Narration.* Ed. Bhabha. London: Routledge, 1991. 1–5.

Boehmer, Elleke. *Stories of Women: Gender and Narrative in the Postcolonial Nation.* Manchester: Manchester University Press, 2005.

Boyce Davies, Carole. *Black Women, Writing and Identity: Migrations of the Subject.* London: Routledge, 1994.

Castillo Bueno, María de los Reyes. *Reyita: The Life of a Black Cuban Woman in the Twentieth Century.* Durham: Duke UP, 2000.

Chiriboga, Luz Argentina. *Jonatás y Manuela.* Ecuador: Abrapalabra Editores, 1994.

DeCosta-Willis, Miriam. "This Voyage Towards Words: Mapping the Routes of the Writers." Introduction. *Daughters of the Diaspora.* By DeCosta-Willis. Kingston: Ian Randle Publishers, 2003. xvi–xlii.

DeShazaer, Mary K. *A Poetics of Resistance: Women writing in El Salvador, South Africa and the United States.* Ann Arbor: U of Michigan P, 1994.

Dore, Elizabeth. "Afro-Cuban History from Below." Introduction. *Reyita: The Life of a Black Cuan Woman in the Twentieth Century.* By María de los Reyes Castillo Bueno. Durham: Duke UP, 2000. 1–18.

Feal, Rosemary. "The Legacy of Ba-Lunda: Black Female Subjectivity in Luz Argentina Chiriboga's *Jonatás y Manuela*." *Afro-Hispanic Review* 17.2 (Fall 1998): 24–29.

González Mandri, Flora. *Guarding Cultural Memory: Afro-Cuban Women in Literature and the Arts*. Charlottesville: U of Virginia P, 2006.

Gutiérrez, Mariela A. "Nancy Morejón's Avenging Resistance in 'Black Woman' and 'I Love My Master': Examples of a Black Slave Woman's Path to Freedom." *Singular like a Bird: The Art of Nancy Morejón*. Ed. Miriam DeCosta-Willis. Washington DC: Howard UP, 1999. 209–19.

Handley, George. *Postslavery Literatures in the Americas: Family Portraits in Black and White*. Ed. James Arnold. Charlottesville: UP of Virginia, 2000.

Helg, Aline. *Our Rightful Share: The Afro-Cuban Struggle for Equality 1886–1912*. Chapel Hill: U of North Carolina P, 1995.

Holloway, Karla F. C. *Moorings and Metaphors: Figures of Culture and Gender in Black Women's Literature*. New Brunswick: Rutgers UP, 1992.

Llanos-Figueroa, Dahlma. *Daughters of the Stone: A Novel*. New York: Thomas Dunne Books, 2009.

Luis, William. "The Politics of Memory and Miguel Barnet's *The Autobiography of a Runaway Slave*." *Modern Language Notes* 104.2 (1989): 475–91.

Mitchell, Angelyn. *The Freedom to Remember: Narrative, Slavery and Gender in Contemporary Black Women's Fiction*. New Brunswick: Rutger's U, 2002.

Montejo, Estaban, and Miguel Barnet. *Biography of a Runaway Slave*. Willimantic: Curbstone Press, 1994.

Morejón, Nancy. "Mujer negra / Black Woman." *Looking Within/Mirar Adentro: Selected Poems/Poemas Escogidos, 1954–2000*. Eds. Juanamaría Cordonés-Cook and Gabriel Abudu. Trans. Kathleen Weaver. 200–203.

———. "Amo a mi amo / I Love My Master." *Looking Within / Mirar Adentro: Selected Poems/Poemas Escogidos, 1954–2000*. Eds. Cordonés-Cook and Abudu. Trans. David Frye. 196–99.

Quiñones Rivera, Maritza. "From Trigueñita to Afro-Puerto Rican: Intersections of the Racialized, Gendered and Sexualized Body in Puerto Rico and the US Mainland." *Meridians: Feminism, Race, Transnationalism* 7:1 (2006): 162–82.

Rodriguez, Jeannette, and Ted Fornier. Introduction. *Cultural Memory: Resistance, Faith and Identity*. Austin: U of Texas P, 2007.

RoseGreen-Williams, C. "Re-writing the History of the Afro-Cuban Woman: Nancy Morejón's 'Mujer negra' in *Singular like a Bird: The Art of Nancy Morejón*. Ed. Miriam DeCosta-Willis. Washington, DC: Howard UP, 1999. 187–200.

Rubiera Castillo, Daisy. *Reyita sencillamente (Testimonio de una negra cubana nonagenaria)*. La Habana: Instituto Cubano del Libro, 1997.

Sandoval, Chela. "US Third World Feminism: The Theory and Method of Oppositional Consciousness in the Postmodern World." *Feminism and Race*. Ed. Kum-Kum Bhavnani. Oxford: Oxford UP, 2001. 261–80.

Sanmartín, Paula. "We Dreamed of an Archived World: Family Feuds and the Continuous Revision of History in Simply, Reyita." *Reclaiming Home, Rewriting Motherhood, Rewriting History: African American and Afro-Caribbean Women's Literature in the Twentieth Century*. Eds. Verene Theile and Marie Drews. Cambridge: Cambridge Scholars, 2009. 114–38.

Santos Febres, Mayra. "El Color de la seducción." *Sobre piel y papel / over skin and paper*. San Juan: Ediciones Callejón, 2005. 119–24.

———. "Los usos de Eros en el Caribe." *Sobre piel y papel / over skin and paper.* San Juan: Ediciones Callejón, 2005. 82–93.

Tillis, Antonio. Introduction to Part I. *Critical Perspectives on Afro-Latin American Literature.* Ed. Antonio D. Tillis. New York: Routledge, 2012. 3–4.

Williams, Lorna. "The Revolutionary Feminism of Nancy Morejón." *Singular Like a Bird: The Art of Nancy Morejón.* Ed. Miriam DeCosta-Willis. Washington, DC: Howard UP, 1999. 131–52.

7

Disrobing Narcissus

Race, Difference, and Dominance
(Mayra Santos Febres's Nuestra Señora de la noche
Revisits the Puerto Rican National Allegory)

Jerome Branche

> We might concede, at the very least, that sticks and bricks *might* break
> our bones, but words will most certainly *kill* us.
>
> —Hortense J. Spillers

The death by gunshot wounds of Isabel Luberza Oppenheimer (b. 1901), of the city of Ponce, Puerto Rico, on January 3, 1974, generated an unprecedented outpouring of commentary in the private and public spheres, the significance of which vainly strove to match up to the reality of her larger-than-life profile and her impact on the national imaginary of the island nation.[1] That the scandal value of the killing was "off the charts," so to speak, is easily attributable to the fact that "Isabel la Negra," as she was commonly known, ran two of Ponce's most notorious brothels, one in Barrio San Antón, and the other in Barrio Maragüez. These were frequented not only by prostitution's more ordinary patrons, but also by politicians of rank, by the important men in Puerto Rico's world of business and finance, by elements of the priesthood, and by notables in the underground economy of the drug trade. Indeed, although the Wikipedia entry for her name documents her demise as that of an "innocent bystander of a drug related homicide," the more current and more salacious speculations regarding Luberza's dramatic departure saw it as a result of direct involvement, on her part, in the nefarious business of illegal narcotics, or as an equal, and predictable perhaps, result of her participation in the high-stakes ventures of the island's powerbrokers. In this regard, Mayra Santos Febres, her most recent literary re-creator, would, in referring to the event, conclude through the anonymous voice of public opinion that "La Negra *traficaba secretos*" (La Negra *trafficked in secrets*) (343, emphasis added). Luberza, the person/a in question, however, had branded herself and her primary place of operations rather differently from the vernacular label and all that it connoted. Her San Antón establishment bore the suggestive title of *Elizabeth's Dancing Place*, claiming thereby an element of caché in the Anglicization of the name Isabel, and through "Dancing Place" re-signifying, ostensibly, the Spanish cognate *Salón de baile* (ballroom), or any such equivalent that might designate the physical structure. The "Elizabeth" in *Elizabeth's Dancing Place*, particularly considering the presence of the US military bases upon the island and the broader modernizing trajectory that had developed with the American takeover back in 1898, presumably also signaled an intention on her part to push back against the particular derogatory connotations inherent in the slur-containing moniker of *Isabel la Negra*.

For a black woman of humble origins in post-slavery Latin American society, exposed to the double standards of racism and patriarchy and integrally involved in sex work, any search for caché or respectability would undeniably be a monumental undertaking. Considering the decades-old, racially tinged practice in public life of excoriating prostitution and prostitutes, in the context of a liberal Great Puerto Rican Family, or *gran familia*—a cornerstone of which was female virginity and wifely fidelity and whose public policy applications included pathologizing and imprisonment for hundreds of women—and a larger cultural tradition that had fashioned a demonized construct of black female sexuality, respectability and harlotry, as embodied in the likes of Isabel, were diametrically opposed concepts.[2] In other words, in the early twentieth-century context of Puerto Rican society, a merciless intersection of inherited gender, class, and racial hierarchies would render access to decency and honor, following the prevailing cultural code, all but illusory for Isabel Luberza, that is, notwithstanding her acquired material wealth and her generosity to the church, charitable causes, and aspiring and settled politicians. An unmistakable indication of her status as social and cultural "outcast," quotidian vernacular registers of condemnation apart, is to be seen in the fact that the corpse of the deceased was denied the benefit of the customary vigil or *velada* in the local Catholic Church upon her death. If social chatter and the newspaper gossip column play a regulatory role in establishing and confirming acceptable values and behaviors and can be regarded as "transitory" discourses,[3] it can be argued that in established literary publications and film, there is a heightened potential for permanence or for long-term projection and reification of these same values. Given Luberza's notoriety, therefore, it comes as no surprise not only that her passing should almost immediately produce two short stories and a feature-length film in Puerto Rico, but also that race, sexuality, morality, and most of all, negative difference in the context of the imagined national community should be the primary themes with which these narratives are concerned. The short stories in question are "La última plena que bailó Luberza" ("The last plena that Luberza danced") by Manuel Ramos Otero (1975) and "Cuando las mujeres quieren a los hombres" ("When women love men") by Rosario Ferré (1976), and the film is the unsubtly titled *Life of Sin*, directed by Efraín López Neris (1979). In what follows,

I revisit the short stories, along with the thematically related *El entierro de Cortijo* ("Cortijo's funeral") by Edgardo Rodríguez Juliá (1983), to see how they interpellate Luberza Oppenheimer and black subjectivity in general in Puerto Rico, and as a way of assessing Santos Febres's revision of the Luberza story against a dominant narrative that is basically characterized by the exotic, the erratic, and the reductive.

Literary race in Puerto Rico has its most salient point of reference in the work of Luis Palés Matos, one of the three canonized and most regularly anthologized poets of the *negrista* or *afroantillana* poetic movement of 1925–1945. The other two are Emilio Ballagas and the bi-racial Nicolás Guillén, both of whom were Cubans, although many other regional poets published their own collections in the genre. Puerto Rican Fortunato Vizcarrondo and Manuel Del Cabral of the Dominican Republic are good examples of these, as are other poets in the Caribbean and further afield in Latin America, who signed on, with fewer contributions, to the primitivist vogue radiating outward from European cultural and aesthetic circles.[4] *Negrismo*, remembered in Latin American literary historiography as part of the regional expression of the *vanguardia*, helped legitimate blackness as a topic for literary contemplation against a Hispanophile postcolonial culture whose hardest edge would be expressed in 1937 in the Dominican Republic by dictator Leonidas Trujillo's massacre of some twenty thousand Haitians in an infamous episode of ethnic cleansing, with repercussions that extend to the present.[5] In Cuba, the so-called "race war" had already been won for whiteness since 1912 with the elimination of the *Partido Independiente de Color* and thousands of its followers.[6] In its wake, a mere four years later, Felipe Pichardo Moya's poem "La comparsa" ("The carnival procession") winced at the sight of a mass of black bodies participating in an innocent street carnival. By 1937, under the impetus of noted Afrologist Fernando Ortiz, the earlier ban on these street *comparsas* would be reversed, leading to their re-appearance in Havana. The premise at that point was that, in spite of their inherent barbarity, these manifestations of black culture were good for Cuba's incipient tourist industry, besides being a potentially valuable element of the national folklore (Branche 1998, 2006).

For the 1930s generation of Puerto Rican intellectuals, engaged as well in the topic of race in the national community, the anxiety of whiteness did not require the material enforcement that took place in the neighboring island nations. With Puerto Rico under foreign domination, the leading voice of the cohort, Antonio Pedreira, would lament the utilitarianism that seemed to accompany the North American incursion of 1898 and the decline of the inherited Greco-Roman sense of high culture. His *Insularismo: Ensayos de interpretación puertorriqueña* (1934), in its recoil from the reality of racial intermixture, which he punned amounted to racial confusion (45), would, however, evoke an old dream of white racial purity for Puerto Rico that went as far back as the migratory policies that under the 1815 colonial *Cédula de Gracias* encouraged Europeans to settle on the island, and thereby redress the island's demographic balance following the Haitian revolution. Subsequent declarations over the ensuing decades would erase a black demographic past and foreclose future black immigration by making a self-fulfilling prophecy of philologist Augusto Malaret's declaration that Puerto Rico was the "whitest of all the Antilles."[7] In this context, Palés Matos's vindication of black culture as an intrinsic element of the Puerto Rican national community in his famous interview in 1932, though hardly original in the framework of *negrista* politics, puts that poet in line with the few contemporary progressive thinkers on the matter, although, as was vigorously pointed out subsequently by his compatriot Isabelo Zenón Cruz, his designation of Puerto Ricans of African descent as living "with us," unwittingly reifies the Euro-centered notion of a Puerto Rican polity, along with the implication that blacks are a marginal, if not aberrant, presence in the island community.[8] Given the centrality of the question of the white patriarchal order as it structured the Puerto Rican *gran familia* at the turn of the nineteenth century and insisted on women's subordination and cultural and genetic whitening, or *blanqueamiento*,[9] it is clear that Isabel Luberza's life trajectory is emblematic of larger historical processes. In re-writing her story, Santos Febres symbolically revisits the moment of transracial coital intimacy that brought about the mestizo Puerto Rican nation, not only to remind us of the narcissism and naked humanity of the presumptive emperor-patrician, but to question the dominant construct of the bourgeois nuclear family in the context of a postcolonial and post-slavery society, and in so doing, reassert the centrality of the black woman to the imagined national community of Puerto Rico.

Afroantillanismo and the Palesian Imprint

The morphology of *negrismo*, or the architectural structure of sound and sense in what was a mainly poetic movement, revolved around the music, dance, and orality of the Afro-Latin American folk tradition. It involved a heightened attentiveness to the black body, whether in its performance of aspects of this tradition—a street carnival or a ritual couple's dance, for example—or simply in the varied dimensions of the daily life of black people, such as a fruit vendor pushing his cart down the street, a washerwoman scolding her child in public, or a mother singing a lullaby.[10] The black subject's voice, his or her skin color or physiognomy, and particularly the female figure as a hyperbolic sign of sexuality all became common motifs that rendered the genre predictable and stereotypical in its depiction of black subjects. In a genre ostensibly about blackness but whose practitioners were mainly white, we see also, in the local Puerto Rican context, a narrative space created for nostalgic excursions into the recent (Spanish) colonial past, in which *negros* and *negras* assumed the subservient roles that would shore up a contemporary white sense of self, over and against the racial and political diminishment imposed by the new US imperial regime. These "plantation fantasies," as they have been dubbed by Kelvin Santiago-Valles (67), merged with narrations of the present to help fix a blackness that was at once local and dismissively marginal. One of the principal referents in this regard is Palés Matos's 1937 poem "Majestad negra" (in López Baralt 536), which presented the hyperbolized black female, here known as Tembandumba, as an object of libidinal speculation and penetration and mocked her pretended majesty with exaggeratedly formal language, while at the same time infantilizing her entourage and the celebration as a whole. Part of the epistemic fallout from this depiction is the poem's subsequent integration into the school curriculum in 1935, its presence there over decades, and, in the final analysis, the artist's contribution to the shaping of social consciousness vis-à-vis this subject, particularly insofar as the black demographic presence in it is signaled mainly through reference to the *cocolos*, Afro-Caribbean immigrants who hail from the neighboring islands or from faraway Africa and who accompanied the carnival queen. Tembandumba's ensemble and its performance, in other words, are projected as being more alien and exotic than they are intrinsically Puerto Rican. The carnival queen as icon, on account of her ample bodily proportions, like the nineteenth-century Hottentot Venus before her, would have numerous narrative offspring to populate the genre. Similar black women would also become commonplace in the musical genres that developed over time in the Hispanic Caribbean alongside the written poetic word.

Robin Moore has identified the Cuban *son*, the conga, and the rumba, popularized internationally as part of the burgeoning music industry of the interwar decades, as integral aspects of the larger Cuban *vanguardia*. Indeed, from as early on as 1930, Nicolás Guillén's book of poems, *Motivos de son,* inspired by the vernacular musical form, established the trans-generic connection in which many of his *son*-poems were put to music.[11] *Negrista* or Afro-Cuban (primitivist) art also included Amadeo Roldán's ballet pieces *La Rebambaramba* (1928) and *El milagro de Anaquillé* (1929) and Wilfredo Lam's famous totemic painting and ceramics. In similar fashion, the Afro-Puerto Rican *plena* would be the musical vehicle for many local *negrista* poems, even as it also enjoyed international diffusion and renown over the ensuing decades. The incursion into black cultural spaces by such classically trained white artists as Amadeo Roldán and Alejandro García Caturla, which Robin Moore described as part of the process of "nationalizing" blackness in Cuba, has its analogue in the poems and more particularly in the editorial packaging of the *negrista* genre, a procedure that lasted for half a century from the 1930s through the 1980s, as has been analyzed elsewhere (Branche 2006).[12] In the mid-1970s in Rio Piedras, a section of the young generation of writers organized around the journal *Zona de carga y descarga* ("Loading and unloading zone") decided to turn away from the pessimism and the concern for linguistic and formal correctness of the Pedreira era. They would find a ready cultural palimpsest in Palés Matos's long-formulated idea of *afroantillanismo* and participate in a renewed and faddish involvement in Afro-Puerto Rican cuisine, music, history, and patterns of speech.[13] In the works under study, the *plena* functions as both a unifying symbol and a metonymical framework through which this "black" narrative flow might be channeled.

In Palés Matos's 1952 "Plena del menéalo" ("The menéalo plena") (in López Baralt 613), the poet charts a cynical response to the disheartening development of Puerto Rico's becoming a Free Associated State of the United States. Mercedes López Baralt describes it as "the most political of his Afroantillean poems,"[14] as the poet uses the figure of the erotic *mulata* to simultaneously bewitch and incense the (presumably puritanical) North American incursionist. In her deployment as a sort of cultural shield for the besieged island, and as a black woman, the *mulata* has been symbolically brought in from the margins by the putatively "nationalist" bard to defend the nation and its culture at this juncture of the imperialist takeover. The *mulata*'s symbolic relevance, moreover, is applicable region-wide considering the repeated episodes of invasion and domination already registered by midcentury, by the United States, in neighboring Cuba, Haiti, and the Dominican Republic. It is noteworthy, though, that in spite of the anti-imperialist tenor of the poem and the supposed acknowledgement of the black female subject, the basic role of Palés Matos's protagonist, Mulata-Antilla, has not changed. She is depicted here as whore and neocolonial prize for the Americans, alongside the material losses occasioned to the island by the governmental and economic takeover. Palés Matos's use of the vernacular vehicle of the *plena* to make his political statement is also to be noted as part of the apparatus of the extended *negrista* cultural aesthetic. The *plena*, a musical and dance form that developed out of the *bomba* in Ponce and the Afro-Puerto Rican coastal communities at the beginning of the twentieth century, had been unapologetically linked to prostitution and to bordellos by the guardians of high culture and propriety in Puerto Rico.[15] Given the cultural and epistemic linkage between black femininity, the *plena*, and prostitution, it is not surprising to find its reappearance, along with the associated moral judgment/s, in the works in question as they imaginatively create stories centered on the life of Isabel Luberza Oppenheimer. Both Rosario Ferré's title "Cuando las mujeres quieren a los hombres" and the first of her two epigraphs are taken verbatim from longstanding *plenas*, although the actual story she fashions has nothing to do with music.[16] In "La última plena que bailó Luberza," Manuel Ramos Otero also uses it in a similar way: as motif for his narrative about the last day of the life of the protagonist. Edgardo Rodríguez Juliá, as well, in his quasi-ethnographic report a few years later on his visit to the funeral of famous *plena* musician Rafael Cortijo, takes the opportunity to digress into myriad aspects of local literary blackness. That is to say that with the larger *afroantillana* or *negrista* narrative canvas behind them, these writers all coincide in making Elizabeth Luberza Oppenheimer the "living" and symbolic nucleus in an ontological aggregate on blackness and black femininity in what is really a colonially inflected onlooker's script aimed largely at marking negative racial difference within the (still colonial) national storyline.

If Rodríguez Juliá's write-up on the Cortijo funeral ceremony, which we can visit only briefly here, assumes a sense of objectivity since he was consciously "documenting" a historical event in which he participated, the same cannot be said for the other two writers whose point of departure was that of an ex post facto, fictional re-creation around the life of the other well-known deceased individual. For Ferré, taking into account the *Zona de carga y descarga* literary initiative, her short story about Luberza promised to be "a great experiment." Ramos Otero is also recorded as saying, prior to adding to public opinion on the topic of the (in)famous *ponceña*, that he "didn't know anything about her" (qtd. in Mullen 90). Doubtless, the *plena* provided a metonymic platform for the two writers as they proceeded with their individual forays into a world that was more or less unfamiliar, not least because of the class difference that separated them from the subject in question. From Ferré we get an optimistic attempt at a gendered transracial reconciliation that uses the strategy of the double to tie together the fortunes of black and white women and see them as equally vulnerable to the machinations of white male privilege, or the quid pro quo of submission and sexual availability, through the domineering figure of the husband/lover in early twentieth-century Puerto Rico. By the end of the story the two women are made to magically merge into each other as they recognize their mutual condition, even though the wife has fallen into poverty and madness, while the paramour has displaced her as the benefactress and social butterfly. "Nosotras," concludes the narrative, "tu querida y tu mujer, siempre hemos sabido que debajo de cada dama de sociedad se oculta una prostituta" (We, your lover and your wife, have always known that there is a prostitute hidden beneath every high-society lady) (23). In collapsing the difference of class and race here, Ferré has made a significant advance upon the feminist ethic of the *gran familia* of earlier decades, which saw an irrevocable dichotomy between "proper" (white) wives and mothers and the "disreputable" (darker) women (Suarez Findlay 21).

Describing "Cuando las mujeres quieren a los hombres" as a "feminist manifesto," as one critic does, however, seems a bit of an overstatement.[17] Despite the apparent acknowledgement of commonality between the two women, and despite the cultural logic that would place the prostitute at the negative end of the spectrum of decency and respectability, the moral register of the women's responses and experiences under the domineering and now absent Ambrosio reveals a clearly asymmetrical accounting as it is outlined. While as readers we are invited to be sympathetic toward the wife, there is hardly as much compassion elicited for the paramour. Luberza, the white and dutiful *señora* (here even Isabel's last name has been appropriated in the short story, and she is simply dubbed *La Negra*), has been cruelly betrayed by the philandering husband, and her efforts to retain his attention and affection have been to no avail. In her desperation she has sought recourse in the wifely folk wisdom of generations of her foremothers, and she eventually loses faith in that most powerful of social attributes in the colony, her white skin, before finally abandoning her umbrella and capitulating to the melanophilia of Ambrosio and the dominant males of the society and, of course, inviting sunburn thereby (Ferré 36, 39). In a purportedly supreme act of contrition and solidarity, she even flagellates her own body, as she prays for her rival and usurper to return "al camino del bien" (to the path of righteousness) (39). But aside from a writerly nod to Isabel's past as a deprived black child with a longing to grow up and be like the beautiful blond woman on the arm of the gentleman on the patio of the imposing big house that she used to pass by daily (30), there is little such acknowledgement of Isabel's vulnerability on account of her race and gender. Nor is there a corresponding sense of openness to the creation of a possible persona in the subject, who might elicit some element of empathy from the reader. It is her sense of acquisitiveness, rather, that is suggested as she approaches Luberza (the wife) in order to discuss converting the house that they have both inherited in equal proportion into a grand bordello. Looking forward to the future, Isabel is determined that "De ahora en adelante nada de foquinato de mala muerte, del mete y saca por diez pesos, los reyes que van y vuelven y nosotras siempre pobres" (From now onward, no more cheap fucks in this dump, in and out poking for ten pesos, kings who come and go while we stay poor) (34). As their identities—lady and tramp, saint and sinner—converge in one of the more intensely lyrical passages of the story, it is clear that it is the prostitute/procuress who gets the heavier epistemic weighting, as whoredom, the oldest profession, traverses time and space through metaphors of powerful and alluring female sexuality that extend from the immediate cultural past (Tembandumba), through Old Testament references (Salomé, the Queen of Sheba), almost to the Garden of Eden and the (original) Fall of "Man":

> Isabel la Rumba Macumba Candombe Bámbula; Isabel la Tembandumba de la
> Quimbamba, contoneando su carne de guingambó por encendida calle antillana,
> sus tetas de toronja rebanadas sobre el pecho; Isabel Segunda la reina de España,
> patrona de la calle más aristocrática de Ponce; Isabel la Caballera Negra, la única en
> quien fuera conferido jamás el honor de pertenecer a la orden del Santo Prepucio de

Cristo; . . . Isabel Luberza la Católica . . . la santa de las Oblatas; . . . Isabel la Perla
Negra del sur, la Reina de Saba, the Queen of Chiva, la Chivas Rigal, la Tongolele,
la Salomé, girando su vientre de giroscopio en círculos de bengala dentro de los
ojos de los hombres, meneando para ellos, desde tiempos inmemoriales, su crica
multitudinaria y su culo monumental, descalabrando por todas las paredes, por
todas las calles. (25–26)

Isabel the Rumba Macumba Candombe Bambula; Isabel, Tembandumba de la
Quimbamba, shaking her okra-stew meat on the hot Antillean street, her breasts like
half-grapefruits on her chest; Isabel the Second, Queen of Spain, patron of the most
aristocratic street of Ponce; Isabel the Black Lady Knight, the only one to have ever
received the honor of belonging to the Order of the Holy Foreskin of Christ; . . .
Isabel Luberza the Catholic One . . . the Saint of Oblation; . . . Isabel the Black
Pearl of the South, the Queen of Sheba, the Queen of Horns, the Chivas Regal,
Tongolele, Salome, gyrating her gyroscope waist in Bengali circles into the eyes of
men, shaking for them, from time immemorial, her all-may-come pussy and her
monumental ass, spreading disaster on all the walls, through all the streets.

Insofar as the historical Isabel Luberza is assimilated by this narrative into a succession of black and *mulata* temptresses of the Hispano-Caribbean lyrical tradition, who
pose a threat to the integrity of the colonial and neocolonial Christian nuclear family,
Ferré's narrative joins the slavery era writers before her in a post-slavery episode of
negative myth-making.[18]

There is a more troubling aspect in this character's representation, however. To
the extent that Isabel, like her literary predecessors, is made the scapegoat in a series
of sexual exchanges whose ultimate source of control resides in the white postcolonial
male, the true nature of the latter's power goes understated. That Ambrosio has continued to be such a source of angst for both his lover and his wife even years after
his death attests to this power. Ferré's Isabel, within the post-slavery sexual economy
of Puerto Rico, is both compliant and complicit with the white husband in what
turns out to be a peculiar narrative manipulation of the post-emancipation libidinal universe. Historically, enslaved black women and girls were the designated sexual
initiators for the young men of the planter class. Lactating black mothers in slavery
also served as surrogates, mammies, and nannies, for the latter during their infancy
and childhood. Ferré's Isabel (*La Negra*) seems to reprise both of these roles, for the
white sons *and* their fathers in the post-slavery scenario of twentieth-century Puerto
Rico. And her collusion in this aberration is worthy of note. It is revealed in the ethic
of maternal protection and care that is articulated as she facilitates the social code of
white male virility by massaging the insecure pride of the young males and preparing
them for the appropriate husbandly performance in the marital sphere (Ferré 32). This
lyrical merging of the roles of mammie and whore in the same person/a for the same
individuals would invoke the taboo of incest, albeit indirectly, or raise the question,
for the young men, of unresolved Oedipal yearnings, were she their "real" mother. The
sexual drama among Oedipus and his parents resuscitated by Freudian psychoanalysis,
however, revolves around the axis of marriage: that of the original marriage between
the parents of the infant prince, Oedipus, and his "accidental" marriage to Jocasta,

his mother the queen, after he unknowingly kills his father, Laius. Since neither paradigm, on account of the element of marriage, would apply to the *negra* of slavery or post-slavery in Hispano-Caribbean societies, projecting Isabel as both "wet nurse" and subsequent sexual "instructor" to her former "sons" places her somewhere between bizarrely conscious pedophilia and the mute sexual "thingification" of the slave and social outcast whose humanity is not considered as mattering within the dominant cultural index. It adds, besides, several degrees to her debasement as prostitute. According to the narrative, however, there is no doubting the role that has been foisted upon her, which she has apparently accepted. Her sexual preparation of her young charges would be careful, loving, and complete, executed without fear of harm from the "vagina dentata" that has haunted the male psyche the world over:

> porque en los brazos de Isabel la Negra todo está permitido, mijito, no hay nada prohibido . . . y el placer es lo que nos hace dioses, mijito . . . escondido entre los brazos de Isabel la Negra nadie te va a ver, nadie sabrá jamás que tú también eres débil y puedes estar a la merced de una mujer . . . aquí a nadie va a importarle que tú fueras un enclenque más, meado y cagado de miedo entre mis brazos, porque yo no soy más que Isabel la Negra, la escoria de la humanidad. (33)

> because, son, in Isabel La Negra's arms, anything goes, nothing is forbidden . . . and pleasure is what makes us gods, my son . . . hidden in Isabel La Negra's embrace no one is going to see you, no one will ever know that you too are weak and can be at the mercy of a woman . . . here no one will care if you are just another weakling, pissing and shitting yourself with fear here in my arms, because I am only Isabel La Negra, human scum.

She would be equally conscious of protecting her young wards from falling into the disgrace of homosexuality by assuring their virility and thereby the continuance of the patriarchal order:

> para que sus papás pudieran por fin dormir tranquilos porque los hijos no les habían salido mariconcitos . . . porque los hijos que ellos habían parido eran hijos de San Jierro y de Santa Daga . . . teniendo cuidado de no apretar demasiado mis piernas podadoras de hombres, un cuidado infinito de no apretar demasiado los labios, la boca devoradora insaciable. (32)

> so that their dads can finally rest easy because their sons did not turn out to be little fairies . . . because those sons that they brought into the world were sons of Saint Iron and Saint Dagger . . . taking care so as not to squeeze her man-pruning thighs too hard, taking infinite care to not contract her labia too much, her insatiable, devouring mouth.

Ferré's Isabel, in a word, despite the gesture toward oneness implied in the technique of the double, does not, in my reading, break with the dichotomous rendering of good and evil as it is embodied in black and white racial subjectivity. The narrator's stream of consciousness, through which we access the women, covers an authorial omniscience that has opened little room for frank dialogue and the voice of the "Other." There is, after all, no real rapprochement without the intention of equality.

Ferré's colleague from the *Zonda de carga y descarga*, in his rendering of the Luberza story, dispenses with the Tembandumba imagery in its aspect of youthful allure and specular attractiveness. Manuel Ramos Otero opts, instead, for the protagonist as an older woman, and his account sets out to cover the last day in the life of Luberza. The mandatory reference to the illegality of sex and drug trafficking and of corruption in high places is very much in evidence in his version, as are the experimental structuring of the account (seven segments from 6:30 am to 1:59 am) and the clever use of stream of consciousness in the narrative outlay of the story. Neither the wife nor the errant husband makes an appearance, though, so that both the narrator's and the reader's attention are focused more fully on the protagonist and her emporium. However, the Palesian trace, as indicated, is also present. It is there in the age-old repudiation of the black presence in Western culture, and in this case, the rejection is not limited to contemporary society but projects diachronically backward to the period before the nation was conceived. Ramos Otero's loose adaptation of previous Palesian motifs operates from two identifiable bases: from that of the jocularly expressed corruption of Christianity that is implied when it comes into contact with Africans and African-derived religion, as we see in the Palés Matos poem "Ñáñigo al cielo" ("Nañogo in Heaven") (in López Baralt 550), and in the other, more secular dimension conveyed in his anti-Haitian poems. In these the Haitian postrevolutionary aristocracy of Henry Christophe's court is ridiculed for mimicking French upper-class dress and behaviors.[19]

Isabel Luberza, accordingly, is hunchbacked, malodorous (the sweat from her armpits is tinged with the smell of sulfur),[20] has a menacing aspect, and walks with a cane. When we meet her she has come to the Monsignor with the intention of "buying" the kingdom of heaven (Ramos Otero 49), and her cynicism is of such that she is prepared, should the churchman quibble, to withdraw with her checkbook and take her proposition to any of the many Protestant denominations conspicuously present in Puerto Rico (50). If for the reader her boldfaced attempt at bribery at the beginning of the story is not sufficiently discordant in ethical terms, our attention is immediately caught by the fact that the handle of her walking stick is adorned by a nest of vipers, as a second symbol, along with the reference to sulfur, that associates her with the devil and evildoing. The Afro-descendant Luberza, then, is clearly bent on deceit, and it is the purpose of the narrative to expose her as a religious impostor. She is therefore immediately shown praying to and making offerings to Ochún, to Changó, to Obatalá, and to Eleguá—all African deities that have survived the Middle Passage and resurfaced in syncretic form in the Caribbean. Luberza's apparent involvement in the two cultural worlds is not an embrace of cultural syncretism on the part of her literary interpreter, however. On the contrary, it is a rejection by him of *mestizaje* in its many forms, and this to a degree that was not even apparent in his precursor Palés Matos's famous interview. Luberza is also revealed to be a secular impostor. Although she had sought in life some measure of prestige in naming her place of business Elizabeth's Dancing Place, in this iteration of her story, the appropriation of English is mocked by the narrator, who re-brands her *Frau* Luberza, in unveiled allusion to the German slave-holding family from whom he intimates she gets her last name. To remove any doubts about this, he offers on her behalf a flashback to her infancy on the coffee plantation and the big house, from whose windows emanated the strains of Beethoven and in which her mother, like her mother before her, had wrested their respective masters from the arms of their respective wives (52). For Luberza, then, the text suggests that sexual exploitation or whoredom, more than having their determinant in social conditions, are natural and essentialized features of black womanhood, and her choice of profession needs no further explanation. Like the atavism to which all black people are subject, according to this nineteenth-century racist perspective, it exists beneath the veneer of civilization that the protagonist exhibits through her pretended affinity for classical music, here represented in Beethoven's Mass in C major Op. 86, which she plays in her ostentatious limousine (52).

Ramoso Otero's Isabel Luberza turns out to be a de-feminized and grotesque cultural fraud and criminal, whose heartless moneymaking enterprises include slave trading and drug running, and whose practice of power inside her brothel includes a minute and omniscient management of the (professional) sexual performance of her employees that combines equal parts prurience and sadism. In repeating that Frau Luberza knows and feels and hears and sees everything, as she walks the corridors in nightly "panoptic" inspection of the rooms and their inhabitants (Ramos Otero 63–66), the text unerringly points not only to her power lust but also to the irreparably repugnant evil that she represents. It is only logical, from this standpoint, that appropriate punishment be visited upon her, in the form of the four assassins who, like the four horsemen of the apocalypse, destroy her body in graphic and gory detail, bringing her, even before she succumbs to inevitable death, into vivid awareness of the eternal hellfire that awaits (67).

The Belabored Body

There is a much-evoked reference in the cultural study of the Caribbean made by the late Antonio Benítez-Rojo in his influential book *The Repeating Island: The Caribbean and the Postmodern Perspective* that alludes to the purportedly peculiar gait of two old black women in his Havana neighborhood on the occasion of the Cuban Missile Crisis of 1962. Something that the writer was hard put to describe but which was communicated through their manner of walking assured him that the impending apocalypse threatened by this particular manifestation of the Cold War would not in effect take place. This was so because the competing ideologies of the superpowers, he went on to suggest, and the nuclear holocaust that they entertained, were inimical to Caribbean culture: "These are ideological propositions articulated in Europe which the Caribbean shares only in declamatory terms," he stated, adding that notwithstanding the region's persistent poverty, its residents are "fucked [-up] but happy" (10). Even if we accept the role of "intuition" as "valid" in the writer's assessment on the averted disaster, one is hard pressed to understand how this insight might be connected to the sexuality or the conversation of the two female passers-by, that is, to their walking "in a certain kind of way" as the text asserted (10). "There was a certain kind of ancient and golden powder between their legs," he mused, "a scent of basil and mint in their dress, a symbolic, ritual wisdom in their gesture and in their gay chatter. *I knew then at once that there would be no apocalypse*" (10, stress added). What quality of intimacy, one is prompted to ask, is presupposed when the subjectivity of unfamiliar black women is deemed accessible to the white Creole writer in this way? Of what does the familiarity consist? Would white Creole women of the Caribbean offer the same psychic safety from Western-originated nuclear annihilation? On what grounds can he claim to speak for the poor and powerless in Chicago as he went on to do, or of all the "unfortunate" of the Caribbean? Although a full analysis of these questions is beyond the purpose of the present discussion, it is sufficient to remark on the speaker's assumption of power that the declaration reveals, his presumed (transracial) prerogative or "right to write," and the associated specular and historical practice upon which this writing is based. Recently George Yancy, in the wake of distinguished postcolonial critics' writings on the topic of coloniality's scopophilia vis-à-vis the black body, has reminded us regarding the resultant textuality that "In this way the Black body appears as something *it is*, rather than as something that *is done* to it" (7, stress in the original). Considering the narrative interpretations in the case of Afro-Puerto Rican Isabel Luberza, it is easy to understand the position taken by her compatriot, Mayra Santos Febres, as she also approached the subject three decades later.

In taking up the topic for her 2006 novel, Santos Febres shows that she is acutely aware of the power of narrative to make its fictionalized reality "permanent" and of the way the alienating discourse of coloniality, in both its international and national registers, interpellates her as an individual.[21] Her statement in a recent interview, that black women are seen in this tradition as "toda carne y nada de cerebro" (all meat and no brain) and that it is "casi imposible" (almost impossible) to break out of the stereotype of the kitchen, sex, and folklore created by the white lettered class in Latin America, has motivated her to speak in her work from her own sense of honesty and experience, to confront this episteme, and in so doing, to uncover its narcissistic and self-serving intentions (Celis 249). As we are reminded by Eileen Suárez Findlay, the construct of white femininity's respectability in Puerto Rico at the turn of the century was premised on the corresponding degradation of the island's non-white women. It is from a position of empathy and of identification vis-à-vis the subject in question, therefore, that Santos Febres can declare that: "en última instancia yo soy Isabel La Negra" (Isabel la Negra, in the final analysis, is me), adding that the infamous public figure is also Puerto Rico and the rest of the Caribbean, extending thereby the metaphor of domination and s/exploitation (7). In *Nuestra Señora de la noche*, the only extended novelistic treatment of the Luberza story, the position assumed is not that of an apologist, but rather one that makes a humanizing gesture through its critique of the subject's demonization, her subjection to the Manicheism of Judeo-Christian religiosity, and the double standards that proceed therefrom under the patrifocal framework. By focusing on Isabel in her infancy, in her childhood, in puberty, and as a young female in a crushingly hostile social environment, Santos Febres's perspective sheds light on the precariousness of the lives of those Puerto Ricans outside of the framework of the bourgeois nuclear family and on the material and psychological cost imposed on these "others" who, by their exclusion, maintain that framework as a structural and ideological dominant. In creatively exploring the period *before* Luberza becomes a public figure, her account also takes the reader *beyond* the parameters established by the earlier narratives, in that it reveals important aspects of the everyday lives of the non-white working poor and the variety of their occupations in the sense of their too-often overlooked importance to the larger economy. This creative engagement with the personae of the period also highlights the quality of kinship that existed among the black community of Ponce, its ethic of solidarity and survivalism. And just as importantly, it revisits the atmosphere of creativity and cultural syncretism that produced the *plena*, the national music generated out of the mix of local and regional Afro-descendants from the neighboring islands. Isabel Luberza's mother, after all, was a West Indian, an "inglesa" (Englishwoman) according to the novel (37). Her presence, though minimal, is not only of cardinal importance in terms of the concept of the (African) diaspora, but it is also crucial as an overlooked but contributing component of the nation.

My discussion of Luberza from the perspective of a "belabored" body intends to signal not only the epistemic violence suggested in the OED meaning of "belabor" as "to beat with words," already outlined above in part. It wishes to highlight also the excesses contained in the labor practice of black females in pre- and post-Emancipation Puerto Rican society. Censuses in the early decades of the twentieth century recorded non-white women as being engaged primarily in domestic pursuits, in work that linked them directly to the division of labor of the slavery era. This included washing, ironing, cooking, cleaning, and taking care of infants, the elderly, and domestic animals, and serving as untrained midwives, nurses, hairdressers, and manicurists (Crespo 33). It is important to note here that there were no government regulations in existence to guarantee either a minimum wage per day/hour or how long the working day might last. On the latter, Crespo adds that: "Some women did not work for pay, but for an equivalent, for example, in the form of room and board. Additionally domestic work was situated in an intermediate position between the spheres of the public and the private and resulted in women submitting to an unending work day" (33). Negrista poet Palés Matos's generic description of the black woman as a "animal doméstico" (domestic animal) and Evaristo Ribera Chevremont's as "mansa bestia" (tame beast)[22] thus articulate a perception, even if unfeeling in its nonchalance, that is based on the reality of these women's exploitation. At the intersection of the public and private spheres in which the women were inserted also lay their usage as "mistresses" by their employers, a practice that continued into the early twentieth century (Crespo 38). Crespo observes that with the advent of manufacturing that accompanied the US intervention between 1899 and 1930, white women would gain relatively greater access to factory jobs than their black and *mulata* counterparts. The existential matrix out of which possibilities of or for agency might emerge for this group, then, as reflected in the novel, is constituted in the degree to which their lives were overdetermined by labor and its vertical and horizontal associations. It is labor and labor relations in the post-slavery society that decide for these women (to return to the earlier reference to Yancy's comments on narrative discourse) what their bodies *are* or *become*, vis-à-vis what they are *made into* by narrative.

While sex is the focus of Ramos Otero's short story as his narrator follows Luberza on her nightly inspection and eavesdrops with her on the brothel's women at work—the ubiquitous animal imagery is present as Mirtelina is reported to be breathing heavily and, "como si fuera una vaca" (like a cow) (64)—and Benítez-Rojo creates an incomprehensible pubic explanation as to why the Cuban Missile Crisis did not end in nuclear war, there is, with Mayra Santos Febres, a body image that is much more germane to the personhood of the black woman. The black washerwomen, among whom Isabel Luberza spends an early apprenticeship on the banks of the Portuguese river where they worked, are depicted as robust and hardworking, dignified and graceful as they confront the challenge of making a living. Even as they banter or sometimes bemoan their condition, they are also combative as they speculate on how to wrangle better remuneration for their effort, all the while fashioning a vernacular culture recognizable as their own, both to themselves and to outsiders. It is significant that the quality of complexity that obtains in the young Isabel's personhood is narrated in contiguous scenes that speak to labor, to the body, to her identity, and to her destiny. It is on the occasion when her godmother Madrina Maruca points out how important it is to get to the riverside before the other washerwomen cloud the water with soapsuds that she sees her biological mother for the first time; a dark woman with cornrows and a wash basket atop her head, who walks and balances it in such a way that nothing falls, according to the text, and whose ample womanly hips are belied by hands made as strong as a man's through her daily mission (35). The physical and mental fortitude of the group of laundresses is reiterated as they are pictured washing the heavy garments, laying them out in the sun to bleach, and finally transporting them on their heads on the long walk back to San Antón:

> Adelante iba Madrina Maruca balanceando el inmenso lío de ropa en la cabeza. Derechita como un pájaro zancudo, hundía sus piernas largas en el camino, tensaba su cuello oscuro . . . De espaldas, su Madrina y la otra lavandera parecían la misma persona, repetidas. Carne oscura, dos enormes fardos de ropa en la cabeza, blusas de algodón, falda de estampados o en gingam. Ambas caminaban midiendo cada paso con el vaivén de sus caderas. Aunque iban a buen tiempo, casi no levantaban los pies descalzos del piso, agarrando el ritmo perfecto para el balance de su carga. Así caminaban todas las lavanderas que Isabel había visto en su vida. Así era, incluso, el caminar de aquella mujer que Madrina le había dicho que era su madre. (35–36)

> Madrina Maruca went ahead balancing the enormous bundle of clothes on her head. As erect as a long-legged bird, she dug her long legs into the trail, tensing her dark neck . . . From behind, her godmother and the other washerwoman looked like the same person, identical. Dark skin, with huge bundles of clothes on their heads, cotton blouses, cotton print or gingham skirt. They both strode measuring each step with the cadence of their hips. Although they kept a good pace, they almost didn't lift their bare feet off the ground, catching the right rhythm to keep their load balanced. That's how all the washerwomen whom Isabel had seen in her life walked. That was how that woman who Madrina had told her was her mother walked too.

The older women's direct and indirect intentions of apprenticeship toward Isabel are not to be taken as their endorsement of a similar trajectory of overwork and hardship for her. This much is clear as she is advised, in the same scene, to "never become a washerwoman, [for] that is no kind of a life for anyone" (No te hagas lavandera. Esto no es vida para nadie) (36). The care and concern embedded in the admonition, I suggest, speak to a larger issue of community and collaboration that is both transgenerational and translocal. The co-mothering (*comadrismo*) of which she is the recipient is the gendered expression of Afro-diasporan slavery and postslavery practice of mutual recognition and solidarity, which I have called elsewhere *malungaje*.[23] It has its origins in the slave-ship survivors (*malungos*) who have created out of their shared misfortune a sort of fictive kinship that helps them confront the racial dictatorship in its many challenges in slavery and postslavery society. A *malunga* ethos is in evidence in Isabel's life from the beginning, as her *cocola* immigrant mother is forced to give her up to Teté Casiana at the tender age of forty days in order to follow the trail of the sugar-cane harvest (Santos Febres 37). It is in evidence when Maruca identifies her from among the other children being cared for by Casiana, a(n other) foster mother, to raise her as her own, and reappears later when Demetrio, the labor organizer and school teacher, teaches her to read and write in his rustic schoolroom. Community kinship and solidarity is again apparent as Lorenza, the older maid with whom she serves in the house of the white Doña Georgina, shares her expertise as a former seamstress with the young Luberza. It is significant that here, in her first direct contact with the white world, the gait associated with labor is not the dignified stride that the young Isabel had observed among the washerwomen. That air of independence is replaced by the bowed head and the submissive step required by hierarchy in the "big-house." As the servant-in-training, part of her mandatory performance would be to walk "five paces behind" Lorenza, "with the soup bowl or the dishes of food in her hands" (cinco pasos detrás, con la fuente de sopas o el servicio de vituallas cn las manos) (78). She would eventually have to leave on account of the attempted rape by Doña Georgina's husband.

The limitations faced by the women of her condition constitute the experiential context that leads her to conclude, at one point, that "life is war" (268), and it is the loss of her husband to military redeployment in Panama that forces Luberza to take in sewing and washing to keep her house and eventually venture into small-scale business involving the sale of illegal liquor and the rental of rooms for sexual liaisons. For the women in her milieu, she muses, it is the specter of "hunger" and "misery" (hambre . . . miseria) (262), that propels them into sex work, that is, in spite of the moral condemnation of prostitution and in spite of the arbitrarily imposed Hygiene Regulations under which they could be arrested and hospitalized for up to eighteen months (163). Isabel's terse dialogue with Demetrio reveals that she, like they, also sees it as a source of independence and emancipation given the labor market and the current marriage contract of husbandly control (264). Certainly her own status as paramour to the white, upper-class Fernando Fornaris played no small role in her "rejection" of their son, sending him to the father for his care and upbringing.[24] Although *Nuestra señora de la noche* does not set out to be an apologia for prostitution, as indicated above, the social and cultural contradictions that are highlighted by the life and the post-mortem chatter around Isabel Luberza offer Santos Febres an opportunity to critically review these contradictions. In so doing, she takes creative recourse, as did Rosario Ferré before her, in the literary strategy of the double. For Santos Febres, Isabel's double is not Fornaris's white wife, however; it is Montse, María de la Candelaria Fresnet, the black caretaker and general maid at the religious sanctuary at Hormigueros. Montse is the surrogate mother of Isabel's son. She had been charged with raising young Rafael Roberto by his father. As a *religiosa*, the role is both cathartic and catalectic for Montse; cathartic in the sense that raising Rafael Roberto relieves her anxiety and sense of incompleteness at not having children of her own, and catalectic in the sense that the job, by its very nature, simultaneously reinforces this sense of incompleteness. It becomes the source of her eventual madness. The sexual restrictions imposed on Montse by her religious vows, and the slowly growing hysteria that her celibacy makes compulsory, allow her to be Santos Febres's symbol for the argument against sexual repression and the view of eroticism as sinful. This subtheme is reinforced by Montse's fanciful identification of herself as the mythical Black Virgin caring for the Christ child ("Virgen negra con hijo blanco en el regazo" eg. 53). Their metaphorical doubling is articulated by Isabel as assertive, empowered, and upwardly mobile while Montse is submissive, isolated, and long-suffering; where Isabel is dismissive of the purported phallic power of "white males" and makes them pay for their pleasure/s, Montse lives in the thrall of her religious fantasy in which she is a Virgin in the (Holy) Trinity, with Fernando as God the Father (or *el Amado*), and Rafael Roberto as God the Son (*el Hijo*), or as *el Nene*, as the book sometimes refers to him (eg. 245). In combination, the two figures, Isabel and Montse, bring together the dichotomy of whore and virgin. Through them, and through the novel's overt allusions to the biblical Mary of Egypt and Mary Magdalene, sinners-turned-saints, Santos Febres reminds her readers of historical antecedent and the Christian value of forgiveness and redemption and suggests hypocrisy in the contemporary local church's condemnation of Isabel Luberza.

In addition to her allusion to the existence of black virgins and former "women of sin" in the history of Christianity, Montse is important to the narrative because she represents non-conformity with the notion of the nuclear family as dominant and other family models as aberrant. Hortense Spillers's insights into African American families in the wake of the Moynihan report refer us to slavery's commodification and objectification of black bodies and their susceptibility to disruption and dispersal, as well as the implications within the regime for black family bonding and parenting. Rafael Roberto Fornaris's situation in post-Emancipation Puerto Rican society is not unlike that of untold numbers of slavery era bi-racial children, often the product of colonial rape, whose parents lived a perpetual mis-recognition on account of their social and racial difference. His resulting racial "orphanhood" and social alienation would prove the bane of his existence as a young man, and slights over his provenance and racial pedigree would often get him into fights. This is the context in which Montse's constant care and affection for Rafael Roberto become emblematic of the novel's argument that true motherhood, as proposed also by Spillers, is not necessarily sourced in biology: "Madre," as Montse often points out to Rafael Roberto, "es la que cría" (The one who raises you is your mother) (9). The younger Roberto's situation offers an interesting counterpoint to that of his biological mother, Isabel Luberza, who was also raised by a surrogate, Madrina Maruca. Luberza's "orphanage," however, is attenuated by her belonging to an extended *malunga* family. As in the previously indicated examples, she is able to count on their support even as an adult, when, for example, Demetrio Sterling mobilizes the comrades of the union of tobacco workers to assist her in setting up her Twelfth Night decorations at the Dancing Place. On that occasion she recognizes her long connection to Demetrio and refers to him as "family" (118). The scene is important also for what it reveals, in terms of an atmosphere of black community and collaboration, for the young Luis Arsenio Fornaris, the (white) legitimate son of the older

Fornaris, who had come for the entertainment offered at Elizabeth's emporium. At the end of the evening he is reluctant to leave:

> Era tiempo de marcharse. Pero Luis Arsenio no quería irse. Había sido testigo de algo, de un vínculo sin nombre. Habia atestiguado otra manera en la que la sangre se anuda, otros lazos que pueden configurar alianzas profundas . . . Aquella noche hubiera dado cualquier cosa por ser un jornalero más; cualquier hijo de vecino, realengo y sin nombre. No llevar el que llevaba y que lo enclava a su estirpe, a su casta. Hubiera dado cualquier cosa por permanecer entre las paredes del Elizabeth's Dancing Place hasta que el mundo de afuera lo llamaba se hiciera polvo y viento. (119)

> It was time to go. But Luis Arsenio did not want to leave. He had seen something; it was a linkage that had no name. He had been witness to another way for blood to come together, other bonds that can shape deep alliances . . . That night he would have given anything to be just another laborer; just a regular guy, without anything special behind his name. To not carry the thing that nailed him to his clan, his caste. He would have given anything to stay inside the walls of Elizabeth's Dancing Place till the world that was beckoning to him from outside became dust and wind.

If we could see Luis Arsenio's revelation in terms of a disavowal of the colonial caste system and the patriarchal order and a desire for transracial incorporation into the extended black (*malunga*) family, it would constitute an argument on the part of Santos Febres for an alternative to the dominant (Eurocentric) national imaginary. The historical importance of black subjectivity to the culture and economy of Puerto Rico had long been argued for by José Luis González in his, for some, controversial essay "El país de cuatro pisos" ("The four-storied house") (1980). To González's original proposal, which vindicated Afro-Puerto Ricans on the basis of their slave-era contribution, we might add progressive black settlement from the West Indies over the course of the nineteenth century and the early twentieth century, a "fifth" tier, as it were, and an idea to which the novel seems to be alluding.[25] These Caribbean *cocolo* migrants have been belatedly recognized as crucial in the evolution of the music and dance genre of the *plena*, now recognized as the "national' music, out of the preceding genre of the *bomba*. Not surprisingly, the legendary Joselino (Bumbum) Oppenheimer, the first of an impressive line of Ponceño and Puerto Rican *pleneros*, makes an appearance in the work. His appearance is in the context of a grassroots, working-class dance, organized by Demetrio Sterling and held at the *centro obrero*, or labor-union hall (Santos Febres 161).[26] The narrative takes care to underscore the importance of the *plena* as a vehicle for social commentary and critique, as a crucible for creativity and black Atlantic leisure, and as an expression of the essential mobility of Afro-diasporan culture.[27] There is an unavoidable element of poignancy to the fact that at one point, Isabel, a "no-whereian,"[28] orphaned by diasporic shifts but cognizant of the rhyme and the rhythm infused into the *plena* by the West Indian settlers, wonders if Bumbum Oppenheimer himself might not be a relative of hers:

Bumbún era músico de batey, de barrio bravo. Oirlo entre toque y toque daba deleite, con ese ritmo que le arrancaba de los cueros de chivo prensados sobre una horca de madera. . . . La voz de Bumbún era el pregón que contaba lo que pasaba en el barrio, noticias que no salían publicadas ni en el Aguila no en La Democracia ni en ningún periódico. Lo requerían por todo el litoral, en bailes que se celebraban en los bateyes de Vista Alegre, y La Joya del Castillo, o en el mismo Barrio Bélgica. . . . El también emigró de las islas inglesas, como la madre de Isabel. Quizás hasta fueran familia. (161)

Bumbum was a musician from the sugar refinery, from the tough neighborhood. It was a real rush to hear him play, with that rhythm that he tore out of the goatskin stretched across a wood frame . . . Bumbum was the loudspeaker that told everyone what was going on in the barrio, news that would not be published either in *El Aguila* or in *La Democracia* or in any newspaper. All along the coast they wanted him, in dances at the Vista Alegre refinery, and the Joya del Castillo, or even in the Barrio Bélgica . . . He too was an immigrant from the English islands, like Isabel's mother. It was even possible that they might be related.

The *plena* as metonymic platform for racial ventriloquism in the context of Puerto Rican *antillanismo*, and as pre-text to Santos Febres's re-writing of the story of Isabel Luberza Oppenheimer, is relevant, finally, not only by what is revealed through a close reading of the short stories that deal with the topic of her life and death. One notes that even the ostensibly objective "chronicle" penned by Edgardo Rodríguez Juliá on the occasion of the funeral of the inimitable *plenero* Rafael Cortijo (1928–1982), in providing what can only be seen as another Palesian walk through black-defined spaces in that poet's "Esta noche he pasado" ("Tonight I walked through") (in López Baralt 257), is again careful, as were the aforementioned writers, in signifying Luberza through reference to the *plena*, to keep a clear distance between his narrative "I" and the black people under his writerly gaze. And this is so even when the speaker acknowledges a certain "oneness" with the subject, as in Palés's "sus/mis cocolos" (her/ my cocolos) in the Tembandumba poem, or his "Mi Antilla" (my Antilla) of "Plena del menéalo" (613–17). The ambivalence of identification, the trepidation of association, and a certain distanced paternalism sourced in the assumption of speakerly superiority all come through along with the Palesian trace, as Rodríguez Juliá approaches the lower-class public housing area of Río Piedras, the Caserío Lorréns Torres, where Cortijo lived. One need hardly go beyond the chronicler's decision in *el entierro de Cortijo* to ride a cab instead of facing the possible theft of his own automobile had he driven himself (12), or his repeated invocations of canonical literature,[29] or his gratuitous references to the bodily abundance of the black females—there is even a sex scene whose over-the-top articulation leads to a heart attack on the part of the portly white male visitor to his black kept woman—to recognize in this narrative a repeat of a familiar formula on racial difference (62–66).

In the face of *afroantillanismo*'s extended expression of "backyard Orientalism" (Guisti Cordero 65), what Santos Febres has offered in *Nuestra señora de la noche*, I propose, is a counter narrative that is conscious of the ontological aggregate to which it stands in opposition, both in terms of gender and race, yet is firm in its national/istic stance. *Nuestra señora* articulates another *gran familia*; one that has emerged out of black diasporan relocation but which is potentially reconciled with the rest of the Puerto Rican nation on the grounds of equality, as emblematized in the mutual recognition of the two sons of Fernando Fornaris, as they bear, together, the remains of Isabel Luberza at her funeral. If the most radical question posed in the tortuous decade of national soul searching of the 1930s was that of the mulatto poet Fortunato Vizcarrondo, "Y tu agüela, a'onde ejtá?" ("Where's your grandmother?"), Santos Febres brings the rhetorical challenge one generation closer by asking instead, "Who's your momma?" Inscribed within her national allegory is the challenge of having a symbolic mother whose social and moral pedigree explodes traditional Western precepts of female worth and respectability and has but the scantest regard for the colonial dominant.

Notes

1. Guillermo Irrizaray's study ratifies this "espacio icónico" (iconic space) that she occupied 209.
2. See Eileen J. Suárez-Findlay on the liberal project of the *gran familia* and the US-backed persecution and internment of sex workers and those deemed to be carriers of venereal disease, often through the informal workings of gossip, in the early part of the twentieth century.
3. See Jörg Bergmann on gossip's regulatory function in society.
4. The early anthologies of Emilio Ballagas (1934, 1946) and Ramón Guirao (1938) were followed in the 1970s by a series of similar collections.
5. See, for example, Susy Castor, *Migración y relaciones internacionales (El caso haitiano-dominicano)*. On September 23, 2013, the Constitutional Court of the Dominican Republic decided, through its TC/0163.13 decision, that children of undocumented immigrants in the country, going back as far as 1929, cannot have Dominican nationality. As a result, tens of thousands of Dominicans of Haitian ancestry were rendered stateless. See Rocío Silverio, "Protests Hit Dominican Republic's expulsion of Haitians."
6. See, for example, *Los independientes de color: Historia del Partido Independiente de Color* by Serafín Portuondo Linares.
7. Governor Rafael Hernández Colón reportedly declared in 1988 that the black contribution to culture in Puerto Rico was "irrelevant." In the 2000 census some 80.5 percent of Puerto Ricans self-identified as racially white. See Arlene Torres 286, Isar Godreau 171, and Branche (2006) 187.
8. The 1932 interview was with Angela Negrón Muñoz. See also Isabelo Zenón Cruz 47.
9. Eileen Suárez-Findlay 58.
10. The anthologies by Guirao, Ballagas, and more recently Jorge Luis Morales, among others, replicate this rich but paradoxically limited repertoire.
11. See Marilyn Miller's "Palomas de vuelo popular: Los poemas de Nicolás Guillén más allá de la hoja blanca," for example.
12. See Robin D. Moore. *Nationalizing Blackness: Afrocubanismo and Artistic Revolution in Havana, 1920–1940.*
13. See Juan Guisti Cordero's "AfroPuerto Rican Cultural Studies: Beyond *cultura negroide* and *antillanismo*."
14. "el más politico de todos los poemas afroantillanos de Palés" 613.

15. Juan Flores quotes from a 1929 authority who declared that the *plena* "arose in the brothels, it was born *in the most pestilent centers of the underworld* where harlots hobnob with the playboys of the bureaucracy" (90, emphasis added).

16. "La puta que yo conozco / no es de la china ni del japón / porque la puta viene de ponce / viene del barrio de san antón" (The whore that I know / is neither from China nor Japan / because the whore is from Ponce / she is from the San Anton neighborhood) (22).

17. See Mullen 91.

18. The tradition goes back to at least 1845, the date of Francisco Muñoz del Monte's "La mulata." See also Vera Kutzinski in this regard.

19. See Branche (2006) 185–211.

20. "sudor de azufre." Ramos Otero 50.

21. My perspective here sees coloniality as a transhistorical phenomenon that was replicated by the lettered classes in Latin America during and after the colonial period proper and manifested in political ideology and public policy, most notably under the long shadow of Positivism, into the twentieth and twenty-first centuries, as suggested above.

22. In the poems "Pueblo negro" (in López Baralt 533) and "La negra muele su grano" (in Morales 54), respectively.

23. See *The Poetics and Politics of Diaspora: Transatlantic Musings* 1–18.

24. The judgment by critic Rubén Ríos Avila of Isabel as a "mala madre" (bad mother), makes no mention, as is wont to happen in these cases, of the father's role in the dynamic 75.

25. See Jorge Luis Chinea's *Race and Labor in the Hispanic Caribbean: The West Indian Immigrant Worker Experience in Puerto Rico, 1800–1850* in this regard.

26. Oppenheimer was himself an agricultural worker, a plowman by day, and by night a musician.

27. See Paul Gilroy, *The Black Atlantic: Modernity and Double Consciousness*.

28. The term in the Anglophone Caribbean vernacular refers to an individual with no fixed affiliation among the Protestant denominations, or alternatively, of no fixed place of abode.

29. Rodríguez Juliá invokes the notorious Palesian description of Puerto Rico as "burundanga," or a ugly admixture of worthless things, mainly on account of the black demographic, as he situates his narrator among the residents of the *caserío*, paraphrasing Coleridge's Ancient Mariner, lost and alone at sea, with his life in imminent danger: "Barroco, barroco, por todos lados y solo un Mont Blanc para escribir" (Baroque, Baroque everywhere and only one Mont Blanc to write with) (25). There is a similar allusion to Conrad's *Heart of Darkness* (57).

Works Cited

Ballagas, Emilio. *Mapa de la poesía negra Americana*. Buenos Aires: Editorial Pleamar, 1946.

———. *Cuaderno de poesía negra*. Santa Clara, Cuba: Imprenta La Nueva, 1934.

Benitez-Rojo, Antonio. *The Repeating Island: The Caribbean and the Postmodern Perspective*. Trans. J. E. Maraniss. Durham: Duke UP, 1996.

Bergman, Jorg. *Discreet Indiscretions: The Social Organization of Gossip*. New York: Aldine de Gruyter, 1993.

Branche, Jerome. "Negrismo: Hibridez cultural, autoridad y la cuestión de la nación." *Revista Iberoamericana* 188–189 (1998): 483–504.

———. *Colonialism and Race in Luso-Hispanic Literature*. Columbia: Missouri UP, 2006.

———. *The Poetics and Politics of Diaspora: Transatlantic Musings.* New York: Routledge, 2015.

Castor, Susy. *Migración y relaciones internacionales (El caso haitiano-dominicano).* Mexico: Facultad de Ciencias Políticas y Sociales, UNAM, 1983.

Celis, Nadia V. "Apéndice: 'Mayra Santos Febres: El lenguaje de los cuerpos caribeños.' Conversación con Nadia V. Celis." *Mayra Santos Febres y el caribe contemporáneo.* Eds. Nadia V. Celis and Juan Pablo Rivera. San Juan, Puerto Rico: Isla Negra Editores, 2011. 247–70.

Chinea, Jorge Luis. *Race and Labor in the Hispanic Caribbean: The West Indian Immigrant Worker Experience in Puerto Rico, 1800–1850.* Gainesville: U of Florida P, 2005.

Crespo, Elizabeth. "Domestic Work and Racial Divisions in Women's Employment in Puerto Rico." *Journal of El Centro de Estudios Puertorriqueños* 8.1–2 (1996): 30–41.

Ferré, Rosario. "Cuando las mujeres quieren a los hombres." *Papeles de Pandora: Cuentos.* New York: Vintage, 2000. 22–41.

Flores, Juan. "The Insular Vision: Pedreira and the Puerto Rican Misère." *Divided Borders: Essays on Puerto Rican Identity.* Ed. Juan Flores. Houston: Arte Público, 1993. 13–57.

Gilroy, Paul. *The Black Atlantic: Modernity and Double Consciousness.* Cambridge, Massachusetts: Harvard UP, 1996.

Godreau, Isar. "Folkloric 'Others': Blanqueamiento and the Celebration of Blackness as an Exception in Puerto Rico." *Globalization and Race: Transformations in the Cultural Production of Blackness.* Eds. Kamari Maxine Clarke and Deborah Thomas. Durham: Duke UP, 2006. 171–87.

González, José Luis. "El país de cuatro pisos." *El país de cuatro pisos y otros ensayos.* Río Piedras, Puerto Rico: Ediciones Huracán, 1980.

Guirao, Ramón, ed. *Orbita de la poesía afrocubana 1928–37 (Antología).* Havana: Ucar, García y Cía, 1938.

Guisti Cordero, Juan. "AfroPuerto Rican Cultural Studies: Beyond *cultura negroide* and *antillanismo.*" *Journal of El Centro de Estudios Puertorriqueños* 8.1–2 (1996): 56–77.

Irrizaray, Guillermo. "Pasión y muerte de la madama de San Antón: Modernidad, tortura y ética en *Nuestra Señora de la noche.*" *Mayra Santos Febres y el caribe contemporáneo.* Eds. Nadia V. Celis and Juan Pablo Rivera. San Juan, Puerto Rico: Isla Negra Editores, 2011. 206-25.

"Isabel la Negra." *Wikipedia: The Free Encyclopedia.* Web. 1 May 2014.

Kutzinski, Vera. *Sugar's Secrets: Race and the Erotics of Cuban Nationalism.* Charlottesville: UP of Virginia, 1993.

López Baralt, Mercedes. *La poesía de Luis Palés Matos, edición crítica.* San Juan, PR: Editorial de la Universidad de Puerto Rico, 1995.

López Neris, Efrain. Dir. *A Life of Sin,* (1979). Film.

Miller, Marilyn. "Palomas de vuelo popular: Los poemas de Nicolás Guillén más allá de la hoja blanca." *Lo que teníamos que tener: Raza y revolución en Nicolás Guillén.* Ed. Jerome Branche. Pittsburgh: Instituto Internacional de Literatura Iberoamericana, 2003. 245–69.

Moore, Robin D. *Nationalizing Blackness: Afrocubanismo and Artistic Revolution in Havana, 1920–1940.* Pittsburgh: U of Pittsburgh P, 1997.

Morales, Jorge Luis. *Poesía afroantillana y negrista (Puerto Rico-República Dominicana-Cuba).* Rio Piedras, PR: Editorial de Universidad de Puerto Rico, 2000.

Mullen, Edward. "Interpreting Puerto Rico's Cultural Myths: Rosario Ferré and Manuel Ramos Otero." *The Americas Review: A Review of Hispanic Literature and Art of the USA* 17.3–4 (1989): 88–97.

Muñoz del Monte, Francisco. "La mulata." *Poesía negra de América [Antología]*. Eds. José Luis González and Mónica Mansour. México: Ediciones Era, 1976. 164–68.

Negrón Muñoz, Angela. "Hablando Con Don Luis Palés Matos." *Luis Palés Matos y su trasmundo poético*. Ed. José de Diego Padró. Río Piedras, Puerto Rico: Ediciones Puerto, 1973. 85–92.

Palés Matos, Luis. *Poesía (1915–1956)*. Barcelona: Editorial Universitaria Universidad de Puerto Rico, 1971.

Pedreira, Antonio S. *Insularismo: Ensayos de interpretación puertorriqueña*. Ed. Mercedes López-Baralt. San Juan: Editorial Plaza Mayor, 2001.

Pichardo Moya, Felipe. "La comparsa." *Poesía negra de América*. Eds. José Luis González and Mónica Mansour. México: Ediciones Era, 1976. 75–76.

Portuondo Linares, Serafín. *Los independientes de color: Historia del Partido Independiente de Color*. Havana: Editorial Caminos, 2002.

Ríos Avila, Rubén. "La virgen puta." *Mayra Santos Febres y el caribe contemporáneo*. Eds. Nadia v. Celis and Juan Pablo Rivera. San Juan, Puerto Rico: Isla Negra Editores, 2011. 71–77.

Rodríguez Juliá, Edgardo. *El entierro de Cortijo*. Rio Piedras, Puerto Rico: Ediciones huracán, 1983.

Santiago-Valles, Kelvin. "Populism in World-Historical Context: The Poetics of Plantation Fantasies and the Petit Coloniality of Criollo Blanchitude." *Race, Colonialism, and Social Transformation in Latin America*. Ed. Jerome Branche, Gainesville: UP of Florida, 2008. 59–90.

Silverio, Rocío. "Protests Hit Dominican Republic's Expulsion of Haitians." *IACenter.org*. International Action Center [New York], 24 Oct. 2013. Web. 11 May 2014. *www. iacenter.org/haiti/haiti-dr121713*.

Spillers, Hortense J. "Mama's Baby, Papa's Maybe: An American Grammar Book." *Diacritics* 17.2 (1987): 65–81.

Suárez Findlay, Eileen J. *Imposing Decency: The Politics of Sexuality and Race in Puerto Rico, 1870–1920*. Durham: Duke UP, 1999.

Ramos Otero, Manuel. "La última plena que bailó Luberza." *El cuento de la mujer del mar*. Rio Piedras, Puerto Rico, 1979. 49–68.

Santos Febres, Mayra. *Nuestra señora de la noche*. New York: Rayo, 2006.

Torres, Arlene. "La gran familia puertorriqueña 'ej prieta de beldá' (The Great Puerto Rican Family is Really Really Black)." *Blackness in Latin America and the Caribbean: Social Dynamics and Cultural Transformations*. Eds. Torres and Norman E. Whitten, Jr. Bloomington: Indiana UP, 1998. 285–306.

Yancy, George. "Colonial Gazing: The Production of the Body as 'Other.'" *Western Journal of Black Studies* 32.1 (2008): 1–15.

Zenón Cruz, Isabelo. *Narciso descubre su trasero: El negro en la cultura puertorriqueña*. 2 vols. Humacao, Puerto Rico: Editorial Furidi, 1975.

Bilingualism, Blackness, and Belonging

The Racial and Generational Politics of Linguistic Transnationalism in Panama

Ifeoma Kiddoe Nwankwo

Canonical and contemporary scholarship on the linguistic complexities of Latin American-descended populations, especially in the United States, focuses primarily on the juggling of English and Spanish as its central issue. This paper builds on such scholarship, identifying race (particularly, responding to racism and articulating racial collectivism) as a factor in Afro-Latin American cultural producers' decisions about which language to use and when. These public published figures' work suggests that language use, for them, is not only a reflection of their community's migration histories, but also a way of demonstrating their right to national belonging while connecting themselves to broader racial and cultural identities that go beyond the borders of their nation-states. Transnational code-switching, then, serves as a means of naming and countering the discrimination that has for so long been fundamental to Latin American nation-states' treatment of Afro-descended communities.

This chapter centers on two Panamanian-West Indian cultural producers as case studies: poet-scholar-activist Carlos Russell, who came of age in Brooklyn on the frontlines of the US Civil Rights Movement alongside Dr. Martin Luther King Jr., and Danger Man, a hip hop and reggae en español artist born in 1972. Transnational code-switching in their work makes an argument about the significance of West Indian ancestry for Panamanian West Indians of different generations, posits multilayered notions of national and transnational community, and, by extension, challenges mainstream Panamanian ideas of what rights this population has to such self-definition. Their decisions about whether and how to employ West Indian vernacular, standard Spanish, standard English, and US African American vernacular are not just decisions about idiom, but, more significantly, about conceptualizing oneself and one's community as bound to the Panamanian nation as part(s) of an international Caribbean diaspora or as facets of global Blackness undergirded by the spread of US African American political thought and cultural forms.

As Trinidadian-Canadian writer Dionne Brand reminds us, "no language is neutral."[1] Language is an aural archive of an individual's or a community's histories, memories, and relative valuations of disparate cultural referents. Precisely because it is such a rich repository, language has been a key entry point for scholarly and creative writing on the Caribbean people.[2] It features particularly prominently in writing that addresses the impact of colonialism and migration on Afro-Caribbean peoples' identities and is used variously as both evidence of the impact and as a weapon against it. Lillian Allen illustrates this clearly in the final line of one of the poems in her collection *Women Do This Every Day* when she states: "Dis word is my weapon" (17). Eddie Baugh documents this beautifully in his 2010 W. P. Ker Lecture "'The Pain of History Words Contain': Language and Voice in Anglophone Caribbean Poetry," noting that "the development of Caribbean poetry has involved a creative exploration of the resources and tensions of a heterogeneous cultural heritage. . . . This process has been centrally a drama of language" (18). Similarly, Carolyn Cooper celebrates the new generation of Caribbean writers by stating that "Caribbean writers can now talk as they write because the languages of the region . . . both English and various Creoles—are their natural inheritance, the raw materials of their craft . . . the Caribbean writer now speaks with the absolute authority of a man or a woman who has found the true-true self" (16).

Pioneering Jamaican writer-performer Louise Bennett's poem "Amy Son" foregrounds language acquisition as it tells a story about Jamaican labor migration to (and back from) Panama (*Jamaica Labrish* 204). After praising the migrant for being "in the pink of form" when he returns to Jamaica, the poem's speaker goes on to cheerfully list the material goods he has brought back with him: a "walkin' stick," a watch, a long gold necklace, a bed, and gold teeth.[3] The bulk of the story about the items with which the migrant laborer has returned, however, centers on language—his new "Spanish twang." As the speaker tells of the migration and return of "Amy('s) son," she proudly specifies several of the words that are now in his vocabulary (as she hears them): "wappin-passero," "malos dame," "habla expanol," "bonos nochos parasol," and "chikita, what muchos grandos change." By the end of the story, she decides to create and share her own Spanish twang, saying how pleased she is to see him do so "muy exibonos well."[4] The acquired vocabulary functions here as a synecdoche for all of "Amy son's" experiences in Panama, highlighting his new affinity for goods and language acquired during his time there. Within the space of the poem, the homefolks comment on his newfound "foreign twang." Their comments make them part of the story of this migration to a degree that conventional historical writing about the migration has not. Their words *about* his new words shed light on their views of what going to Panama means, their expectations about what should happen there, what the markers of success are, what should be brought back, and what migration should mean or do for him as well as for them.

More specifically, the speaker's affinity for the migrant's "Spanish twang" suggests that she sees international engagement as a desirable accouterment that along with or, it seems, even more than material goods acquired abroad is a marker of success—of the fact that one is getting on "muy exibonos well." As such, the poem stands as a literary embodiment of Kamau Brathwaite's indexing of the centrality of both migration "in fact" and migration "by metaphor" to West Indian life and identity: "the desire (even the need) to migrate is at the heart of West Indian sensibility—whether that migration is in fact or by metaphor" ("Sir Galahad" 26). As Bennett's poem illustrates, language is one of the key ways in which Caribbean people migrate "by metaphor" and make sense of the roots and results of their "in fact" migrations.

There is a noteworthy divergence, however, between the discourses on the languages of populations from the formerly Spanish Caribbean and those from the formerly British Caribbean. Writing on the language of people descended from the formerly Spanish Caribbean—and especially the scholarly writing—frequently foregrounds the concept of bilingualism and focuses on contemporary bilingualism among US Latinos.[5] This bilingualism is largely attributed to Latin Americans crossing, re-crossing, or being crossed by Anzaldua's *la herida abierta* (the US–Mexican border) or Negron-Muntaner's *el charco* (the "puddle" between the United States and Puerto Rico) and is frequently tied to a biculturalism positioned as both a catalyst for and evidence of the productive and destructive possibilities of these crossings.

In terms of scholarly studies, "Spanish/English Speech Practices: Bringing Chaos to Order," an article published in *The International Journal of Bilingual Education and Bilingualism,* best illustrates this orientation. The author, Almeida Jacqueline Toribio, mounts an intensely assertive challenge to the idea that the bilingualism of heritage Spanish-English bilinguals in the United States is a marker of linguistic deficiency and sets about disproving that prevailing wisdom. She speaks of "bilingual ability" rather than deficiency in one language or the other and posits bilingualism as "redundancy reduction" rather than a loss of either language (144).

Tato Laviera's poem "my graduation speech" uses a poetic representation of code-switching (i.e. changing language mid-sentence; inserting whole clauses in the other language) to dramatize the linguistic situation of many Puerto Ricans in the United States. It includes the lines: "I think in Spanish / I write in English / . . . tengo las venas aculturadas" (qtd. in Toribio 145). The speaker has acculturated veins and is juggling two languages, neither of which he (on his own admission) speaks even close to well. Almeida Toribio reads it as a "deliberate use of 'anti-aesthetic' language to render an enactment and commentary on the linguistic dilemma of Puerto Ricans in the U.S." (145).

Writing on the language of people from the formerly British Caribbean, in contrast, often emphasizes the historical roots of the region's Creole languages, particularly African ancestry, slavery, and colonialism. Edward Kamau Brathwaite's concept of "nation language" exemplifies this trend. For him it is "influenced very strongly by the African model, the African aspect of our New World/Caribbean heritage. English it may be in terms of its lexicon, but it is not English in terms of its syntax . . . rhythm and timbre" ("History of the Voice" 266). Leaning on the work of Glissant, he goes on to say that "nation language is a strategy used by the slave to disguise his personality and to retain his culture" (267).

Through her character "Aunty Roachy," Louise Bennett celebrates Jamaican "dialec'" as evidence of our African forefathers' cunning evasion of our European forefathers' attempts to impose Standard English: "But we African ancestors-dem pop we English forefadhers-dem . . . an disguise up de English Language . . . in such a way dat we English forefahders-dem still couldn understan what we African ancestors-dem was a talk bout when dem wasa talk to dem one annoder!" (*Aunt Roachy Seh* 2). In this approach to describing the genesis of the Jamaican language, she emphasizes the linguistic agency of Africans brought to the Caribbean, lauding their creation of Creole as a way of disguising the English language in ways that would allow them to continue to use their African languages. In this statement, she tells the story of the development of Jamaican Creole using sentence structure and diction that both establish and reiterate language's role as a creator and index of collectivism among the Africans—highlighting the language's role as connector by specifically mentioning their talking to one another in it.

Exemplifying another thread in the discourse on language in the (formerly) British Caribbean, Trinidadian-Canadian writer Marlene Nourbese Philip uses repetition, alliteration, and short lines to poignantly re-enact the language loss, language imposition, and language regurgitation/rejection wrought by slavery and colonial education. Through these literary techniques, Philip actually forces the reader to psychically stutter—to struggle with the words—and by doing so forces the reader's brain to re-enact the speaker's battle with and over language. She writes:

> I must therefore be tongue
> Dumb
> dumb-tongued
> dub-tongued
> damn dumb/tongue. (31–35)

Domination, Philip's speaker illustrates, need not lead to silence, to tongue-*lessness*. On the contrary, the poem gives voice to Caribbean individuals' agency; more specifically, to their creation and claiming of their own tongue that carries their own rhythms (dub) even though it has been oppressed (dumbed). The last line, "damn dumb/tongue" (and particularly Philip's inclusion of the word "damn"), gives the line an intensity that conveys the subject's frustration with and determination to resist the equation of his/her tongue with dumbness.

In his Nobel Prize speech Derek Walcott similarly references Caribbean peoples' battles with and over language. He avers:

> Deprived of their original language, the captured and indentured tribes create their own, accreting and secreting fragments of an old, an epic vocabulary, from Asia and from Africa, but to an ancestral, an ecstatic rhythm in the blood that cannot be subdued by slavery or indenture, while nouns are renamed and the given names of places accepted like Felicity village or Choiseul. The original language dissolves from the exhaustion of distance like fog trying to cross an ocean.

Words like "deprive," "captured," and "subdued" call attention to the forces arrayed against the African and Asian peoples of the region. The words are deadpan and flat compared to the dynamic words he uses to describe the actions of the "captured and indentured tribes": dynamic words like "accreting," "secreting," "epic," "ecstatic," and "rhythm."

Each of the Caribbean writers I have just identified is essentially speaking about "the regular use of two languages," a phrase coined by one of the most iconic figures in the development of scholarship on "Hispanic Bilingualism," linguist François Grosjean, who uses it to define *bilingualism* (1). They are also indexing the development of a linguistic system created out of a need to address the realities of a population (what Otheguy calls "communication innovation"). Philip's and Laviera's poems are attempts to find ways to paint a rich picture of the processes of becoming/being made "tongue dumb"—of having a "dumb tongue." In a similar vein, both Toribio and Brathwaite are pressing for the reclamation of the purposeful power of the languages/ ways of speaking of Caribbean and Caribbean-descended peoples. The differences in emphasis—the tongue-tying created by migration for the formerly Spanish Caribbean and that forced by slavery and colonialism for the formerly British—do not negate these similarities.[6]

The scholarly discourse on African American Language (AAL) converges with that on language in the Caribbean, especially with that on language in the (formerly) British Caribbean, in its explicit attentiveness to the institutional and state-level powers that marginalize "non-standard" languages and their speakers. These scholars call attention to the powers that not only impose and reify Standard English but also deem code-switching, "code-meshing," or any other nonstandard uses of the language to be indicators of dumbness.[7] Documenting the biases in the pedagogical practices of K-12 teachers and disseminating vocabularies and methods teachers can and should use in order to minimize that bias and ensure that all the students in their classrooms can learn have both been recurrent issues in AAL-focused scholarship. Geneva Smitherman's work has been particularly crucial here. In her foundational text "Black Idiom" she notes that "traditionally, the school and its English teachers . . . have simply contended that Black speech was characteristic of ignorance and lack of education" (90). Using multiple sources and languages to illuminate the fatal shortcomings of this traditional belief and the significant weaknesses in the existing scholarship, Smitherman avers: "we bees bout extending the legitimacy of the Black Idiom into America and the world. . . . Language is/has been/will continue to be, if we let it, a tool of oppression" (116). In "Language and Liberation" she calls for a "liberation pedagogy" focused on "determining how to use our language as a medium of instruction to facilitate the children's mastery of literacy and other skills that can be used for our collective advancement" (23). In "Language and African Americans: Movin on up a Lil Higher," she encapsulates her perspective on AAL: "Descendants of Africans enslaved in the United States constitute a nation within a nation, whose collective will can bring about the declaration and acceptance of U.S. Black speech as a language" (193).[8]

Smitherman's work is in conversation with that of scholars in African American literary studies like Karla F. C. Holloway, whose works include *Moorings and Metaphors*, which documents the writing of black women and the way they reflect cultural traditions through language and figures. Smitherman's work and the discourse on

AAL of which her work is a part also resonate with studies by Farah Jasmine Griffin (*Who Set You Flowin,'* 1996), Tony Bolden (*Afro-Blue*, 2003), and Houston A. Baker (*Blues, Ideology, and African American Literature*, 1987). All three scholars have each called attention to the resonances between African American language and music. Also key to the conversation are African American writers, including those discussed in depth by Henry Louis Gates in *Signifying Monkey* (1988), which includes discussions about Zora Neale Hurston and Ishmael Reed. These writers, according to Gates, draw on the surface and deep structures of AAL in order to represent the forgotten or hidden nuances of African American life and culture.

In spite of their similarities, however, the discourses on AAL and Caribbean speech do diverge in the degree to which and the vocabulary through which they explicitly identify racism as a driver of institutional and state-level treatment of the language(s) and their speakers. Race and racism are a given in the writings on and from the (formerly) British Caribbean, since racism was both the driving force behind and the foundation of the very structure of oppression that the writings index, even though they are not always explicitly mentioned. Scholarship on Dominican Americans by writers like Benjamin Bailey and Emilia Maria Duron-Almarza[9] illuminates the potential knowledge to be gained by incorporating considerations of race into scholarship on Latino and Latin American multilingualism.

My point here is not to argue that these communities' engagements with language are exactly the same—there are certainly substantial differences between the communities' pasts and presents as well as between the categories into which linguists may appropriately place each of their "languages" and the terms scholars may use to discuss them: e.g., diglossia with or without bilingualism (Fishman) or bi-dialectalism (Mordaunt). Contrarily, there is much to be gained by bringing the discourses about them into conversation with each other, particularly in terms of the relationship between race and language choice.[10] In light of the convergences and divergences between the aforementioned discourses on American speech/language, I ask: What happens when we factor racial concerns, particularly racism and racial collectivism, into discussions of multilingualism in Latin America?

The remainder of this chapter will focus on Panamanians of West Indian descent, a community whose language use and language shifting demand an analytical approach that draws on all three discourses—the speech of people in and from the (formerly) British Caribbean, the speech of those from the (formerly) Spanish Caribbean, and US African American language and culture—in order to illuminate their complexities. As such, it opens up new avenues for enriching current discourse on identity and language in the Americas and, more specifically, for contextualizing and interpreting the language use of "digital native" generations, whose tongues are not limited to ancestral or state-imposed languages; who draw on languages from faraway places brought to them by media that moves across and without regard to state borders; and who embrace those languages as part of their approach to conceptualizing and articulating their identities. Such phenomena constitute a new manifestation of Brathwaite's migration "by metaphor"—movement which occurs outside the purview of the nation-state. It is this very migration "by metaphor" that is less focused on remembering and/or reconnecting to a historical or cultural past than it is on building and indexing community in the present. Delving into the convergences and, more significantly, the divergences between different generations' approaches to multilingualism helps us better understand the implications of contemporary globalization for the speech and identities of socioeconomically marginalized communities in "our America."

Panamanians of West Indian descent are largely the result of migrations to the Isthmus during the early decades of the twentieth century. The most well-known reason for the migration spike is the Panama Canal, then under construction (from 1904 until 1914).[11] The descendants of those who came have had a complicated relationship with both the Panamanian and US states; one characterized by outright rejection and denial of their rights to Panamanian citizenship (as in the 1941 constitution); both overt and more subtle forms of racial discrimination, which ranged from the Jim Crow system put in place by the US government during the construction of the Canal to the more subtle forms of discrimination that surface often in contemporary life; and a simultaneous circulation of individuals, cultures, and ideas between both nations.

Alberto Barrow and George Priestley's *Piel Oscura Panama* and Barrow's *No Me Pidas Una Foto*, among others, do an excellent job of blending quantitative and qualitative data on discrimination at all levels in today's Panama. Barrow documents the racist attitudes underpinning employers' requests that job applicants submit photographs along with their applications (51). He also decries the "invisibilization" of brown Panamanian women in the public sphere, including on television and in the nation's financial center. Barrow bemoans the fact that, although Panama is an ethnically diverse nation, "In the heart of the financial center this ethnic diversity . . . takes on an extremely Nordic appearance, subsequently looking like another country and not at all like Panama" (En el corazón del Centro Financiero la policromia étnica . . . adquiere un semblante demasiado nórdico, situación que hace pensar que se trata de otro país, distinto al nuestro) (170).

Inextricable from issues of race, language has been a key battleground for this community. Panamanian-West Indian writer-professor Melva Lowe de Goodin, whom I quote here at length, has cogently encapsulated the battles lost and won. She explains:

> You know language very often is used politically. That happens in the US, and all over the world. When we have political entities that are formed out of the conglomeration of people, there has to be one language that serves as a *lingua franca*, and then that language empowers the people who speak it. In the early years of Panama, because of the building of the Canal, the presence of the Americans, the presence of so many English-speaking Caribbeans because of the Canal, English started becoming very pervasive in the society. And this scared the leaders of Panama. Because in our 1904 Constitution, there wasn't anything that said we had an official language. But I think that the fact that English was then becoming such a pervasive language in the society, by the time they wrote the next constitution in 1941 or several laws in between then, we acquired an official language of Spanish, and then it was emphasized that Spanish was the official language. And during those early years there was a lot of discriminatory treatment towards my parents and grandparents and those who spoke English to the point where several generations of West Indian Panamanians have grown up not speaking English because their

parents wanted them to be integrated in society and didn't want them to suffer any discriminatory treatment. So they spoke to them in English only, and they developed very negative attitudes towards English. During the time when we were trying to get control of the Canal there was an anti-American campaign going on. An offshoot of the campaign was those people who speak English were looked [on] not very favorably. So then again you get a generation of people who shied away from speaking English just so that they would fit in politically and integrate to the society. . . . Now that we have control of the Canal, now everybody is seeing the need for English. And we have the unfortunate thing that those of us of Afro-Caribbean descent who had parents or grandparents who spoke English, many of those people didn't give their grandchildren or great grands the language, and those people now are at a disadvantage now at getting jobs and doing well in school. And so you know, we keep getting the short end of the stick so to speak. Because at one time we were so eager to fit in that we shied away from using our mother tongue. And then once we grew up, then we saw that, oh, it's important to know English. (Lowe de Goodin, personal interview, 2007)

Gloria Branch describes the situation this way:

It's sad. Panama should have been a bilingual country . . . from the year one because we were here and we could've input the language to them . . . but . . . due to ignorance and prejudice, mostly prejudice, they overlooked English . . . and how many years after, they're paying, and giving crash courses and being ripped off with some very poor English programs when they could have had it free of cost. (Branch, personal interview, 2008)

Residing as they do (on multiple registers) within and between Latin America, the formerly British Caribbean, and the United States, the linguistic shifts of Panamanians of West Indian descent force us to confront the lacunae in accepted ways of thinking about multilingualism and language contact in the Americas. There is a complexity that we can begin to glimpse in the following translation, found on a sign in a laundromat in a Panama City hotel frequented by tourists and staffed, in part, by young Panamanians of West Indian descent. The sign reads: "Por favor cuando limpie el filtro de la secadora no bote la basura en el desagüe. Please do not clean de lint screen in the drain."

Here is a context that is clearly intended to be bilingual, but there is a third language operating as a palimpsest, one that bursts through in the use of the English Caribbean Creole word "de." The surfacing of "de" ends up undercutting the pretension that there are only two language/cultural systems at work. The writer unknowingly tells on him or herself and, by extension, on Panama itself, unconsciously revealing his/her/its West Indian roots. In the Panama laid bare in this sign, English, as an idiom, is inseparable from West Indian English.

Similarly, language use in this community does not fit neatly into the tongue-tied-by-Spanglish "nation language," the colonial imposition of language, or the racist devaluation of Black speech's conceptual frameworks that dominate scholarly discourses on the American languages discussed earlier. Instead, it illustrates that all these situations can coexist in/on the same tongue, and it subsequently demands an analytical approach that attends to the varying uses of language(s) in and by communities that do not fit neatly into existing frameworks.

In his first poetry collection, for example, Panamanian-West Indian writer-professor-activist Carlos Russell uses language shifting to simultaneously assert the Canal diggers' histories as well as their claim to Isthmian soil and to West Indian cultural specificity.[12] The book's title poem "Miss Anna's Son" begins by listing all the towns in Panama and the Panama Canal Zone in which the speaker has lived. The listing and the words emphasizing his physical connection with these locations—"I walk the streets of" and "I have lived in"—show the speaker as both claiming and laying claim to the towns as part of his history and memory. The fact that each town has/constitutes its own line intensifies the reader's feeling that the speaker has many Isthmian homes. The speaker goes on to list "his" West Indian name(s), positioning himself as a synecdoche, standing in for the entire population of diggers. He also specifies his West Indian grandfather's pronunciation of one of the names.

The poem dramatizes a battle between Spanish place names and English/West Indian family names and uses names as a means of rooting the individuals about which it speaks in Panama while also acknowledging both their and Panama's Caribbean ancestry. By presenting three lists of names, the poem presses the reader to compare them to each other and, in so doing, grapple with the histories and cultural contact they represent. The first list consists of Spanish place names (of places in Panama proper, not in the Canal Zone). The third is comprised of English/West Indian family names. The second is made up of Canal Zone place names that are both in and influenced by English, Spanish, and West Indian (in the middle)—ergo the inclusion of Red Tank and Silver City in the list of place names. As such, it reflects the linguistic and cultural layering of that space and the incorporated communities' collision and collaboration between Spanish, English, and West Indian talk that have all made Panama a linguistic and cultural "between-space."

The poem also calls attention to the cultural and historical layering indexed through the linguistic collision and collaboration and, even more explicitly, to the fact that the layering is part of what makes the speaker's Panamanianness absolutely unquestionable. The speaker is Panamanian by birth, yes, but he is also Panamanian because of the blood, sweat, and tears his ancestors shed to help make the nation strong. The family-oriented vocabulary in the poem, along with a reference to his ancestors shedding "their precious blood," emphasizes the speaker's grounding in Panama. In addition, his mother's name, identified in the book's and the poem's title as "Miss Anna," is referenced in the body of the poem as "Miss Ana," marking his Panama-ized approach to even his mother.

As it moves between languages, the poem establishes several "we" versus "them" oppositions that reinforce the speaker's connection to the Panamanian nation while also expressing his indignation about the racist treatment he receives from both his "latin" countrymen and the US "foreigners." The overarching opposition here is between "we" West Indian-descended Panamanians, "them" (the white US Americans), and the "latins," but another opposition—one between a Panamanian "we" and a US American "them"—is also present. It comes across most clearly in the phrase "a foreign twang" that, because it is used to describe the speech of the "cops whose necks were red," positions the US American cop as an foreigner/outsider and the speaker as a native/insider.

After noting he was chased by "redneck" cops, the speaker calls attention to the racist verbal abuse meted out by the "latins." Russell chooses to use the Panamanian version of the n-word (chombo) instead of the US/English version, emphasizing that the persons doing the name-calling are the "latin" Panamanians. Russell's speaker goes on to recall the pain of the racial hatred expressed by the "latin" compatriots/playmates. Russell's decision to use the Spanish word for the game they he and they were playing together—platillos—also highlights the speaker's connection to the language and the culture of Panama, even while the abuse he remembers mirrors the pain that being in a racist, black-rejecting Panama has brought him and his ancestors.

Elsewhere, Russell also uses language mixing as a means of delineating and invoking a particularly Panamanian-West Indian chronological framework. The poem "The (sic) Dared to Live," for example, reads in part:

> Expressions of yesteryear
> where language was bent
> to bridge the gap
> and echoed new hybrid sounds (5–8)

Throughout the poem Russell represents the blended words West Indian migrants created to speak to and from their multilayered cultural contexts. By representing yesteryear using language mixing, the poem contends that language reflects and structures an approach to marking time in which the creole/patois words and phrases evoke/stand in for a specific PAST moment in time that is treasured and idealized. These words and phrases are synecdochic signifiers of a distinctively Panamanian-West Indian past that is being lost. This chronology surfaces in the perception held by many of Russell's generation and others who proximate that the younger generation(s) have no interest in the language and, by extension, no interest in the culture or history of their forebears.

As the aforementioned quotations from Lowe de Goodin and Branch note, the economic benefits of knowing English have grown exponentially in the last few years; for example, plum jobs in call centers and tourism are available to those lucky few who have some knowledge of English. Unfortunately, as feared by many Panamanian West Indians from and close to Russell's generation, many of the West Indian-descended youth, who would have naturally learned English at home, have no access to these jobs because they turned a deaf ear to the English of their forebears during their childhood. The narrative is that they wanted to be seen as unquestionably Panamanian, so they rejected their ancestral English. However, different forms of English represent different things for the younger generations. West Indian English and culture as they are linked in Russell's mind serve as historical artifacts. However, from the younger generations' perspective, US English is both the present and the future. Historical and present-day language and race-linked/based discrimination notwithstanding, these youth have no problem wanting to learn or connect to it. Indeed, the pasts and presents of racial discrimination make language choice a very complex decision for the younger generations.

In his seminal text *Life With Two Languages*, François Grosjean identifies bilingualism as the product of a social hierarchy in which the marginalized are forced to try to speak the language of those in power: "bilingualism is often a consequence of the contact between two linguistic groups that do not have the same numerical, political, and economic importance" (24). He goes on to say that, barring extraordinary circumstances, "the usual outcome of bilingualism, is a return to monolingualism" (38). Perhaps what is really happening in Panama is a natural language shifting that is complicated by the youth being sandwiched between a Panamanian society that claims to espouse the ideology of "todos somos panameños" (we are all Panamanians), even as it does nothing to curtail ongoing racial discrimination (such as that indexed by Barrow), and an older generation that criticizes the younger ones for denying their West Indian heritage. The lyrics of Panamanian hip hop/reggae artist Danger Man provide some insight into such a phenomenon, which may well be occurring with younger generations.

Danger Man's lyrics, although primarily in Spanish, are generally a mix of Jamaican patois, Spanish, and US African American vernacular, differentiating his music from that of his *reggae en español* forebears like El General, Renato, and Nando Boom, whose music consisted of lyrics that were almost completely in Spanish and sung over the hottest Jamaican dancehall reggae beats. His lyrics are distinguished from Russell's poetry primarily by the predominance of Spanish and his invocation of US American words and forms (which Russell does not do despite the fact that he was actually living in the United States at the time he wrote the poems). The lyrics of the song "Paz y Amor" ("Peace and Love") from the album *First Class* feature English words as fundamental elements of the rhyme, appearing frequently as the anchor words for the lines. Consider, for example:

Esto no es un juego no es un game	[This is not a game it is not a game
Hay muchos que están muertos por plata y por fame	There are many men who have died for money and fame
Y sé que tú te sientes strong	And I know that you feel strong
Quiero decirte que en la calle hay buco manes	And I want to tell you that in the street there are many men
Que tú no le aguantas ni un round. (Blackwood)	Who won't let you make it through even one round.] (Translation mine)

Most of the English words used are Standard English and work to bolster Danger Man's didactic message through their sound (standing out aurally in a sea of Spanish) as well as through their positioning as a point of emphasis. The song displays a range of approaches to juggling languages—some fitting into conventional Spanish Caribbean-focused linguistic frameworks while others do not—from the first line's facing phrase translation; to the second, third, and fifth lines' lexical borrowing; to the lexical adaptation/reworking of the fourth line. In addition, the West Indian originated patois/way of speaking once again bursts through, this time in the word "manes" (pronounced mah-ness), a Hispanicization of the West Indian usage "de man dem." In "Taxi, Taxi," Danger Man lyrically actuates his ancestral connection to Jamaica through vocabulary. The song includes Hispanicized forms of Jamaican creole/patois English words like "taxi boy," "taxi man," and your "shanty [home]": "buay del taxi," "el man del taxi," and "tu chanty." In "Paz y Amor" he references "una shotta" (in Jamaican patois, a "shotter" can be loosely translated as a gangster). His language in these songs reflects the coexisting cultural referents and mentalities also echoed in the content.

In terms of content, "Paz y Amor" is a fascinating and creative mix of what could be characterized as a politically conscious roots reggae political mentality with a "rude bwoy" or "gangsta" hip hop and dancehall one. He goes on to say:

Y ahora escucha la tercera estrofa	[Now listen to the third verse
You know, how much ghetto people them a suffa	You know, how much ghetto people them a suffa
Vendiendo en la calle jugando vivo puro check it	Selling in the street I play life clean check it
Mientras que el gobierno pura estafa y money making.	While the government making money by corruption.]

Danger Man's use of the Jamaican patois/creole phrase "ghetto people them a suffa" conveys a sense of community among the poor and disenfranchised who suffer at the hands of the greedy government—a collectivism that is at once local and transnational. It becomes a distinctively Panamanian tool in the transnationally conscious ghetto-music toolbox.[13] The song continues:

Si no quieres morir cambia tu personality	[If you don't want to die, change your personality
Enséñale a la gente que tú tienes quality	Teach the people that you have quality
Y trázate una meta y ponte tu visuality	And draw up a goal and put on your visuality
Y resale a Dios que el te lo dará facility.	And go back to God who will give you the facility.]

The song's diction and the choice to have these specific words at the end of the lines in English also reveal the multilingual lyricist's craft: his use of his languages is an example of a consciously crafted instance of the aforementioned notion of "code choice" in which bilinguals do not merely switch from one variety to another, but choose one over or along with another depending on the "semantically significant" information they wish to convey. "What distinguishes bilinguals from their monolingual neighbors is the . . . awareness that their own mode of behavior is only one of several possible modes, . . . that there are others with different communicative conventions and standards of evaluation that must not only be taken into account but that can also be imitated or mimicked for special communicative effect" (Gumperz, *Discourse Strategies* 65). By including these words in English, these particular words in which the stress is on the final syllable, and placing them at the end of the lines, Danger Man uses his multilingualism as a tool that enables him to place particular emphasis on the specific concepts he wishes to highlight—personality, quality, visuality, facility. If they were in Spanish, they would blend into the rest of the line and not stand out as much as they do.

In this song (among others), neither English nor Caribbean Creole is, for Danger Man, a way of invoking a lost past (as Russell's poetry did). For Danger Man, English, Caribbean Creole, and US African American vernacular all serve as a way to index, speak to, and carve out a very specific approach to conceptualizing collectivism/

communal identity. It is an approach to communal identity that is at once marked as distinctively Panamanian-West Indian, because of the languages he uses to describe it, and transcultural/transnational, because the terms he uses are often ones that define community based on class status—the common condition of being poor. This condition, rather than a nation-state focused vision of community, is implicitly invoked through collectivity indexing terms like "ghetto people" and the somehow recognizable highlighting of a sense of community rooted in the experience of living in financial poverty and struggling to survive. This is an approach to defining community that recurs in conscious roots reggae and hip hop and, one could convincingly argue, is one of the key aspects of these musical forms that have made them so attractive to black and marginalized communities globally. Danger Man's lyrics, therefore, reflect a transnational linguistic culture that cannot simply be encapsulated in binaries like loss and preservation, or even in bilingualism and monolingualism.

Danger Man often explicitly connects himself to US African American hip-hop culture through diction, syntax, accent, and slightly amended versions of lines and hooks well known to aficionados of US African American hip hop. The song "Baby If You Give It to Me" is one of the clearest examples of this linking and mirroring:

> Yo shit is serious I have to catch a plane
> Out Philly you know what I'm saying
> Cause I heard that D'blasio doing big things
> What's the deal?

His positioning himself as an important person who has to "catch a plane" to a specific city in the United States positions travel to the United States both "in fact" and "by metaphor" as a desired accouterment and an indicator that one is doing "muy exibonos well." In contrast to Russell (who uses English, Spanish, and Caribbean Creole to highlight the community's history in Panama and to call attention to and celebrate the community's distinctiveness vis-à-vis other Panamanians), Danger Man uses US African American vernacular to index his and his crew's links to a transnational racial and cultural community, while also employing Spanish along with Jamaican patois to spotlight their particular brand of Panamanianness. His music positions language and transnational racial community as sources of power and as ways to gain status locally. Moves such as this have been identified in other communities by scholars of global hip hop who have used terms like "connective marginalities" (Osumare) and "resistance vernaculars" (Mitchell) to speak to the ways in which artists from around the world have connected to and/or revised this globalized African American form for their own localized purposes/ends. The artists draw on US African American cultural forms to create their own cultural texts that simultaneously speak to local concerns and link their communities to a global collective.

Danger Man's approach to engaging US African American hip hop in "Baby, If You Give It To Me" shows that he accords it a particularly significant value relative to Jamaican or Panamanian forms. At one point he says: "This ain't no reggae shit. This is real hip hop." Here he is indexing and performing an authentic connection to "real" hip hop and, by extension, to real US African American modes of expression. His valuing of a link with real US African American hip hop extends to links with icons of that culture as well as with objects defined by and within the culture as valuable. The track "Los Envidiosos" includes lines like "Pregúntale a Jay Z, compro mi ropa en Macy's" ("Go ask Jay Z, I buy my clothes in Macy's") and "Pero tú sabes que yo muevo como Biggie Smalls" ("But you know I roll like Biggie Smalls"), which tie Danger Man to two of hip hop's most important icons. The song also includes a performative listing of the material goods in his possession that reinforce his status as "el macho," who is also "un fucking P.I.M.P" who buys his clothes at Macy's. The list of goods includes a Rolex, a Jeep, an earring, and a large diamond ring in particular, as well as "bling bling" in general.

Both Russell and Danger Man use the languages at their disposal in ways they know are recognizable to their audiences and will help them convey their messages to the disparate generations they are attempting to reach. They use movement between languages both consciously and unconsciously to identify, "big up," and communicate a didactic political/social message to the Panamanian population of West Indian descent, while also grounding themselves and their communities squarely in Panamanian terrain. Indeed, indexing and verbally actuating connections with the international features prominently in both men's works. However, the divergence between the particular internationals they reference is telling. The United States appears in "Miss Anna's Son" in the form of the US state (that administers the Canal Zone) and the redneck cops who mistreat the speaker. In Danger Man's lyrics, US Americanness appears through US African American cultural and linguistic practices created in opposition to or in spite of the US state. British Caribbean language and culture surface in Russell's work as the distinctive root through which the speaker defines himself even as he moves between towns on the isthmus and begins to identify himself in and through them. They serve as a means through which Russell seeks to inform or remind his readers of a history he fears they either may not know or may be forgetting. Danger Man also draws on British Caribbean language and culture, positioning them as key building blocks of identity for him and his crew in the here and now. Both Russell and Danger Man use language shifting and international engagement to talk over the institutional and state structures that have marginalized them. They also use language to claim Isthmian soil and culture as their own while reminding everyone, including Panamanians, that the nation has always been a profoundly and fundamentally multiracial and multilingual one, regardless of whether the state chooses to acknowledge that history or reality.

Linguistic and cultural transnationalism, particularly as they surface in Russell's poetry and Danger Man's music, are always already gendered. That gendering inheres in the diction, tropes, and referents as well as in the content of both men's works. These word artists' approaches to articulating pride and the vocabularies through which they express it idealize masculinity and heterosexuality.

The Russell poems discussed earlier in this essay, for example, celebrate the noble (male) Canal builder using a vocabulary that presents his survival struggle as at once a battle fought by and between men and as a fight for masculine dignity. His strength comes not so much from his mother, Miss Anna, as from his male forefathers and his fellow West Indian Canal builders, whose last names he lists individually on their own lines, creating a kind of incantation/chant to and in honor of the builders.[14]

For both Russell and Danger Man, strength (individual and collective) is rooted primarily in masculinity and in a relativist approach to expressing pride. That pride is frequently implicitly or explicitly articulated relative to others, others who are posited as less than and, more specifically, as less masculine than the speaker. This approach is evident in Danger Man's lyrics in terms of masculinity, in general, as well as in terms of sexual orientation, in particular: "you fuckin batty buay" ("Tu No Eres Mi Friend") and "kill the batty buay again toda familia and your friend" ("Saludos Pa Los Boy Del Town"), evincing an all too familiar violent homophobia.[15] Masculine collectivism is, at points, rooted in a common aversion to homosexuality: "big up pa' los gangsta u pa' todos mis fanatics / los manes que no creen en cueco ni en batty" (big up to the gangstas and to all my fanatics / the men who don't believe in homosexuality) ("Taxi Taxi"). Homophobia here shows up, unfortunately, as a key element of validated masculine identity (individual and collective) and as a validated reason for crossing languages. To reiterate and make absolutely clear his opposition to homosexuality, Danger Man combines and connects Panamanian vernacular ("cueco") and Jamaican patois ("batty").

Women factor into this swagger as means and media through which masculinity is negotiated and demonstrated: "Los envidiosos hablan de mí / Pero yo se que todas las guíales van a mi / Tengo mi carro, casa y bling bling / Yo soy un mother fucking P.I.M.P" (The envious ones are blabbing about me / But I know that all the girls are going to me / I have my car, house, and bling bling / I am a mother fucking P.I.M.P) ("Los Envidiosos"). They are also the media and means through which masculinity is, at times, negated: "Haciendo papel de bad buay y fijándote en mí / Y a tu gal la mueve el man del taxi" (You're spending time pretending to be a bad man / and fixating on taking me down / all the while the taxi man is making moves on your girl) ("Taxi Taxi"). The road to strength, significance, and survival is paved with showing superiority in terms of masculinity, attractiveness to women, and possession of material goods. "Los Envidiosos" encapsulates this stance in its concluding lines:

> Is all about the bling bling nigga
> Is all about the bitches nigga
> This is Scaredem Crew nigga.
> What up.

It is more than noteworthy that this encapsulation is done wholly in African American vernacular (orthography included) and is the song that has more explicit references to African American hip hop figures and more tropes from African American hip hop in the rapped core of the song than any of the other songs on the album. It is also the song that most directly mirrors a specific African American hip hop song in its melody. Transnationalism here is not only about individuals blending idioms but also, and importantly, about word artists consuming, blending, and redeploying different communities' tropes, semiotic systems, epistemological frameworks, and, by extension, the ideologies that undergird them in the service of recognition of their and their community's significance.[16] Bilingualism, and especially black bilingualism, is not just about idiom/code switching or even meshing, but also about the blending of vocabularies, images, and tropes that constitute modes of accessing and demonstrating significance, that constitute ways of recognizing and working to employ swagger as a survival strategy. Russell's and Danger Man's multilingualism also, therefore, indexes the transnational movement and/or embrace and/or exchange of particular words as well as of particular notions of masculinity and perceptions of the relative value of specific approaches to articulating, indexing, or describing local rooting and global routing.

The multilingualism in Danger Man's songs is part and parcel of his more general treatment of cosmopolitanism as a particularly valuable kind of "bling bling." It is a key element of his swagger. This fact is especially evident in "Pronto Voy," a song speaking directly to those who would dare to say that Danger Man is not internationally experienced and, more specifically, that he does not know Spain inside and out and has never traveled all over France. Beginning the song with the line "good to fly," he counters those critics by vowing

Pronto voy, poco a poco cabalgando, subiendo la montaña,	[I'm going soon, riding little by little, climbing the mountain
Directo a España voy,	I'm going direct to Spain
Se que algún día me van a conocer.	I know that one day they are going to know me.]

The linguistic transnationalism evident in Danger Man's lyrics, then, is not simply a result of growing up between ancestral cultures but also an index of a broader philosophy about the value of defining oneself as a man of/who knows the world and about the way that crossing languages facilitates the showcasing of that internationalist bling. He is not just mixing idioms or grammatical forms. He is blending ideologies, ethical frameworks, survival strategies, and techniques for calling attention to one's and one's community's significance from different cultures, communities, and geographies. Danger Man's lyrics reveal two elements of his perception of international engagement as a type of bling. The first element consists of familiarity with and mastery of the world, Europe included, and is evident in lyrics referencing his knowledge of Spain and France. The second element consists of the aforementioned referencing and replication of terms and tropes from African American hip hop culture.

Importantly, over the course of the CD, Danger Man blends that showcasing of internationalist bling with a celebration of his local communities and connections, further illustrating that his ultimate goal is to call attention to the significance of not just himself, but his local community. He employs international bling, including linguistic and (linked) cultural transnationalism, as well as machismo in the service of that end. This again reinforces the importance of attending to the reality that Black multilingualism, particularly in public published works, is not simply about switching idioms or linguistic codes or grammars but about making purposeful choices in the service of a goal much bigger than simple communication—of demanding attention to the significance of marginalized individuals and communities. The song "Paz y Amor" illustrates just this, showing Danger Man's concern for the men in his community and his desire to share his advice about the best ways to seek and gain significance. He begins the song by saying: "Crees que eres malo / Deberías escuchar a tu madre / Goza mientras puedas / Pero acuérdate que superman esta en silla de ruedas" (You think you are a bad man / You need to listen to your mother / Have fun while you can / But remember that Superman is in a wheelchair). He goes on to say: "Solo quiero que seas inteligente / y que mis líricas penetren en tu mente / Para que dejes de hacer estupideces / Y vivas toda una vida y no meses" (I just want you to be intelligent / and for my lyrics to penetrate your mind / So that you will stop doing stupid things / and live a whole life not just months). His use of bilingualism as a tool that helps him reinforce his fundamental point—wanting the men in his community to do better—appears in several of the song's lines: "Si no quieres morir cambia tu personality / Enséñale a la gente que tú tienes quality / Y trázate una meta y ponte tu visuality / Y resale a Dios que El te lo dará facility" (Emphasis mine; If you don't want to die, change your personality / Teach the people that you have quality / And draw up a goal and put on your visuality / And go back to God who has given you the facility). Danger Man's treatment of multilingualism as a tool for calling attention to and promoting his and his fellow community members' significance brings to mind dub poet Lillian Allen's powerful statement "Dis word is my weapon" (9). The words from multiple languages along with the tropes, epistemologies, ideologies, and ethical frameworks they index are weapons used by these Panamanian-West Indian word artists and their speakers—weapons to be used against the structures that marginalize them and also, unfortunately at times, against fellow community members deemed less than.

By highlighting the distinctive aspects of the multilingualism of this community that is at once Black, Latin American, West Indian, and has ties to the United States, this essay ultimately expands contemporary scholarly discourse on "Hispanic" bilingualism and multicultural, multilocational Latino identity, carving out a space for attentiveness to Afro-Latino/Latin American communities while also allowing us to see how and where the Creoles from the formerly British Caribbean have themselves become Creolized in diaspora and have connected through and across languages with other African-descended communities, including especially African Americans. As such, they prove the venerable Mr. "Nothing was created in the West Indies" Naipaul wrong again and again (Naipaul 129). The works of Panamanian West Indians like Carlos Russell and Danger Man stand as proof that much has been created in the region and that, furthermore, this work continues to serve as the basis for creation—and re-creation—to this very day.

Notes

1. Dionne Brand, *No Language is Neutral* (1990). Brand's powerfully beautiful collection, including the title poem, explores the physical and psychological traumas, memories, and scars brought about by slavery, colonialism, postcoloniality, and migration in the Americas.

2. Early attempts to document and/or reconstruct the culture and speech of Afro-Caribbean populations in the (formerly) British West Indies have been compiled by Jean D'Costa and Barbara Lalla in *Voices in Exile: Jamaican Texts of the 18th and 19th Centuries* (1989). The materials they present include a pre-meal blessing captured by historian and folklorist H. P. Jacobs (9) and a song documented by J. B. Moreton (12). *The Dictionary of Jamaican English* by Frederic Cassidy and R. B. LePage, as well as Cassidy's *Jamaica Talk: Three Hundred Years of the English Language in Jamaica* (both

published in 1967), represent pioneering attempts to document the distinctiveness of Afro-Caribbean ways of speaking. Claude McKay's poetry collections *Songs of Jamaica* and *Constab Ballads* (both published in 1912), Louise Bennett's *Jamaican Humor in Dialect* (1943), and Roger Mais's *Brother Man* (1954) are among the path-breaking literary works that sought to replicate and represent the voices of everyday Afro-Caribbean people in the early and mid-twentieth century. Also of note are Mervyn Alleyne's pioneering literary, editorial, and critical publications and J. Edward Chamberlin's monograph *Come Back to Me My Language* (1993).

As scholars and creative writers have been documenting and dramatizing the vernacular speech of the British Caribbean, their peers have been doing the same for the (formerly) Spanish Caribbean. Examples include Fernando Ortiz's *Glosario de Afronegrismos* (1924), which also includes the *Diccionario de Afronegrismos*; Nicolás Guillén's *Motivos de Son* (1930) and *Songoro Cosongo* (1931); Alejo Carpentier's *Ecue-yamba-o* (1933); and Ana Lydia Vega's *Encancaranublado* (1982).

3. This focus on material goods recalls the similarly focused Jamaican "Colón Man a Come" folk song that became, for many Caribbean people, a key touchstone for their thoughts about West Indian migrants to Panama. See Rhonda D. Frederick, *"Colón Man a Come": Mythographies of Panama Canal Migration* (2005) for an excellent analysis of its significance.

4. The poem reads, in part:
   Me please fe se him get awn soh
   Muy exibonos well. (Bennett, 1966, 27–28)

5. For more information, see Lourdes Torres, "In the Contact Zone: Code-switching Strategies by Latino/a Writers" (2007); A. J. Toribio, "Convergence as an Optimization Strategy in Bilingual Speech: Evidence from Code-Switching" (2004); Vivian Cook, *Portrait of the Second Language User* (2002); Judith Klavans, "The Syntax of Code-Switching in Spanish and English" (1983); Joshua Fishman, "The Sociology of English as an Additional Language" (1982); J. J. Gumperz, *Language and Social Identity* (1982); S. T. Wagner, "The Historical Background of Bilingualism and Biculturalism in the United States" (1981); and E. Hernandez-Chavez, "Language Maintenance, Bilingual Education and Philosophies of Bilingualism in the United States" (1978).

6. In fact, noting this parallel paves the way for the bridging (and perhaps the destruction) of the divide between the ways we talk about the issues of language that permeate the history and the present of Caribbean people from islands formerly colonized by the British and the Spanish and opens the door for more cross-ethnic, pan-American, or pan-Atlantic frameworks in discussions of language. Focusing on multilingualism in African Diaspora youth and popular culture, in conversation with the work of language specialists like Mary Buckholtz and Ronald Butters, strikes me as a particularly promising approach.

7. For more information, see Vershawn Ashanti Young, "Should Writers Use They Own English" (2010) and "Nah, We Straight: An Argument Against Code-Switching" (2010). See also Vershawn Ashanti Young and Aja Y. Martinez, *Code-Meshing as World English: Pedagogy, Policy, Performance (2011)*, Vershawn Ashanti Young et al, *Other People's English* (2013), and Tracy Weldon "A Reflection on the Ebonics Controversy" (2000).

8. Smitherman bemoans the absence of a "major campaign" on the part of scholars to "go public with our knowledge, to take linguistics and educational research out of ivory—and—ebony towers, and to advocate on behalf of African American youth and their/our language out there in the public trenches" (194).

9. See Benjamin Bailey, *Language, Race, and Negotiation of Identity* (2002), "Shifting Negotiations of Identity in a Dominican American Community" (2007) and "Language Alternation as a Resource for Identity Negotiations Among Dominican American Bilinguals" (2007). See also Emilia Maria Duron-Almarza, "Ciguapas in New York: Transcultural Ethnicity and Transracialization in Dominican American Performance" (2012).

10. In his book *A History of Afro-Hispanic Language* (2005), John Lipski contends that there are no Creolized forms of Spanish and, further, "in contemporary Latin America . . . there is nowhere to be found an ethnically unique 'Black Spanish' comparable to vernacular black English in the U.S." (5). He does document the African influences present in the speech of the Congos in the Republic of Panama, defining their speech as an "Afro-Hispanic Dialect" (Lipski, "The Speech of the Negros Congos of Panama").

11. There were many who migrated to Panama from the British Caribbean for reasons other than working on the Canal. In fact, one could argue that the vibrant West Indian communities that came about on the Isthmus—not just in the Canal Zone, but also in Colon and Panama City—could not have come about without the presence of the seamstresses and tailors, shoemakers, teachers, nurses, those with a leaning toward political leadership, and others who also came to Panama.

12. Poet-scholar-activist Carlos Russell came of age in Brooklyn on the frontlines of the US Civil Rights Movement alongside Dr. Martin Luther King Jr. and is Professor Emeritus at Medgar Evers College.

13. As such, it recalls Halifu Osumare's "connective marginalities" and Russell Potter's concept of a "resistance vernacular," expanded upon by Tony Mitchell.

14. Women in the poems appear as the speaker's and other builders' strong mothers and teachers, as well as the sensually powerful objects of the speaker's and his fellow builders' gazes. Multilingualism, particularly in the poem showing the latter, serves to add emphasis to the speaker's sentiments. In "Glamor Gal," the speaker and his fellow builders are appreciatively ogling a woman he considers so attractive that he and his fellow builders must develop and deploy multilingually influenced neologisms to describe her body and style: "She put on she escudun / and walk with a lot of piquete" (1–2).

15. See Byron Hurt's documentary *Hip Hop: Beyond Beats and Rhymes*; essays by Tricia Davis (2010), Peter Manuel (1998), Mimi Sheller (2005), Niah Stanley Sonja (2005), and Deborah Thomas (2002); and the essay collection *Sex and the Citizen* edited by Faith L. Smith (2011).

16. This formulation is a reworking of and inspired by Houston Baker's discussion of Frederick Douglass's "quest for self-definition" (*The Journey Back* 30) and "the black autobiographer's quest for being" (32); as well as his argument that "from what appears to be a blank and awesome backdrop, Douglass wrests significance" (35) and "by adopting language as his instrument for extracting meaning from nothingness, being from existence, Douglass becomes a public figure" (390).

Works Cited

Allen, Lillian. *Women Do This Every Day: Selected Poems by Lillian Allen*. Toronto: Women's Press, 1993.

Alleyne, Mervyn, ed. *Theoretical Issues in Caribbean Linguistics*. Kingston, Jamaica: Mona-U of the West Indies P, 1982.

Anzaldua, Gloria. *Borderlands/La Frontera*. San Francisco: Aunt Lute, 1987.

Bailey, Benjamin. "Language Alternation as a Resource for Identity Negotiations Among Dominican American Bilinguals." *Style and Social Identities: Alternative Approaches to Linguistic Heterogeneity*. Ed. Peter Auer. New York: Mouton de Gruyter, 2007. 29–56.

———. *Language, Race, and Negotiation of Identity: A Study of Dominican Americans*. SelectedWorks, 2002. Web. 30 April 2014. *works.bepress.com/benjamin_bailey/44*.

———. "Shifting Negotiations of Identity in a Dominican American Community." *Latino Studies*. SelectedWorks, 2007. Web. 30 April 2014. *works.bepress.com/benjamin_bailey/48*.

Baker, Houston A., Jr. *Blues, Ideology, and Afro-American Literature: A Vernacular Theory*. Chicago: U of Chicago P, 1987.

———. *The Journey Back: Issues in Black Literature and Criticism*. Chicago: U of Chicago P, 1980.

Barrow, Alberto. *No Me Pidas Una Foto: Develando el Racismo en Panama*. Panama City, Panama: A. Barrow, 2001.

Barrow, Alberto, and George Priestley. *Piel Oscura Panamá: Ensayos y Reflexiones al Filo del Centenario*. Panamá, República de Panamá: Editorial Universitaria "Carlos Manuel Gasteazoro," 2003.

Baugh, Eddie. "'The Pain of History Words Contain': Language and Voice in Anglophone Caribbean Poetry." *PN Review* 36.6 (2010): 18+.

Bennett, Louise. *Aunt Roachy Seh*. Kingston, Jamaica: Sangster's Book Stores, 1993.

———. *Jamaica Humor in Dialect*. Kingston, Jamaica: Jamaica Press Association, 1943.

———. *Jamaica Labrish*. Kingston, Jamaica: Sangster's Book Stores, 1966.

Blackwood, A. [Danger Man]. *First Class*. Prodigus Entertainment, 2005. CD.

Bolden, Tony. *Afro-Blue: Improvisations in African American Music and Culture*. Urbana: U of Illinois P, 2003.

Branch, Gloria. Personal Interview. 18 April 2008.

Brand, Dionne. *No Language is Neutral*. Toronto: Coach House, 1990.

Brathwaite, Edward. "History of the Voice." *Roots*. Ann Arbor: U of Michigan P, 1993. 259–304.

———. "Sir Galahad and the Islands." *Roots*. Ann Arbor: U of Michigan P, 1993. 7–27.

Buckholtz, Mary. "Language and Youth Culture." *American Speech* 75.3 (2000): 280–83.

Butters, Ronald. "The Internationalization of American English: Two Challenges." *American Speech* 75.3 (2000): 283–85.

Carpentier, Alejo. *Ecue-yamba-o: Historia afrocubana*. Madrid: Editorial España, 1933.

Cassidy, Frederic, *Jamaica Talk: Three Hundred Years of the English Language in Jamaica*. New York: St. Martin's, 1961.

Cassidy, Frederic, and Robert Le Page. *Dictionary of Jamaican English*. Cambridge, UK: Cambridge UP, 1967.

Chamberlin, J. Edward. *Come Back to Me My Language: Poetry and the West Indies*. Urbana: U of Illinois P.

Cook, Vivian, ed. *Portrait of the Second Language User*. Clevedon, UK: Multilingual Matters, 2002.

Cooper, Carolyn. "Islands Beyond Envy: Finding Our Tongue in the Creole-Anglophone Caribbean." *Caribbean Quarterly* 59.1 (2013): 1–19. *Literature Online*. Web. 30 Apr. 2014.

Davis, Tricia. "Generation M: Misogyny in Media and Culture." *Teaching Sociology* 38.4 (2010): 398–99. *ProQuest*. Web. 2 Jan. 2015.

D'Costa, Jean, and Barbara Lalla. *Voices in Exile: Jamaican Texts of the 18th and 19th Centuries*. Tuscaloosa: U of Alabama P, 1989.

Duron-Almarza, Emilia Maria. "Ciguapas in New York: Transcultural Ethnicity and Transracialization in Dominican American Performance." *Journal of American Studies* 46.1 (2012): 139–54.

Fishman, Joshua. "The Sociology of English as an Additional Language." *The Other Tongue: English Across Cultures*. Ed. B. Kachru. Oxford: Pergamon P, 1982. 19–26.

Frederick, Rhonda D. *"Colón Man a Come": Mythographies of Panama Canal Migration*. New York: Lexington Books, 2005.

Gates, Henry Louis Jr. *The Signifying Monkey: A Theory of African-American Literary Criticism*. New York: Oxford UP, 1988.

Glissant, Edouard. *Caribbean Discourse: Selected Essays*. Charlottesville: U of Virginia P, 1999.

Griffin, Farah Jasmine. *"Who Set You Flowin': The African American Migration Narrative*. New York: Oxford UP, 1996.

Grosjean, François. *Life with Two Languages: An introduction to Bilingualism*. Cambridge: Harvard UP, 1982.

Guillén, Nicolás. *Motivos de Son*. Havana: Imprenta y Papeleria de Rambla, Bouze y Compania, 1930.

———. *Songoro Cosongo*. Havana: Imprinta Ucar, Garcia, 1931.

Gumperz, J. J. *Discourse Strategies*. Cambridge: Cambridge UP, 1982.

———, ed. *Language and Social Identity*. Cambridge: Cambridge UP, 1982.

Gumperz, J. J., and Edward Hernandez. "Cognitive Aspects of Bilingual Communication." *Language Use and Social Change*. Ed. W. H. Whiteley. Oxford: Oxford UP, 1969. 111–25.

Hernandez-Chavez, E. "Language Maintenance, Bilingual Education and Philosophies of Bilingualism in the United States." *International Dimensions of Bilingual Education*. Ed. J. E. Alatis. Washington, DC: Georgetown UP, 1978.

Hurt, Byron, dir. *Hip Hop: Beyond Beats and Rhymes*. God Bless The Child Production, 2006. Film.

Holloway, Karla F. C. *Moorings and Metaphors: Figures of Culture and Gender in Black Women's Literature*. New Brunswick: Rutgers UP, 1992.

Klavans, Judith. "The Syntax of Code-Switching in Spanish and English." *Proceedings of the Linguistic Symposium on Romance Languages*. Vol. 14. Chapel Hill, NC: John Benjamin, 1983. 213–31.

Lipski, John. *A History of Afro-Hispanic Language*. Cambridge, UK: Cambridge UP, 2005.

———. "The Speech of the Negros Congos of Panama: An Afro-Hispanic Dialect" *Hispanic Linguistics* 2.1 (1985), 23–47. *Proquest*. Web. 5 April 2011.

Lowe de Goodin, Melva. Personal interview. 15 February 2007.

Mais, Roger. *Brother Man*. London: Cape, 1954.

Manuel, Peter. "Gender Politics in Caribbean Popular Music: Consumer Perspectives and Academic Interpretation." *Popular Music and Society* 22.2 (1998): 11–29. *ProQuest*. Web. 2 Jan. 2015.

McKay, Claude. *Constab Ballads*. London: Watts, 1912.

———. *Songs of Jamaica*. Kingston, Jamaica: A. W. Gardner, 1912.

Mitchell, Tony. "Doin' Damage in My Native Language: The Use of Resistance Vernaculars in Hip Hop in France, Italy, and Aotera/New Zealand." *Popular Music and Society* 24.3 (2000): 41–54.

Mordaunt, Owen G. "Bidialectalism in the Classroom: The Case of African-American English." *Language, Culture, and Curriculum* 24.1 (2011): 77–87.

Naipaul, V. S. *The Middle Passage*. London: André Deutsch, 1962.

Negron-Muntaner, Frances. *Brincando El Charco: An Exploration of Puerto Rican E(m)igration to the United States (1940–1980)*. Philadelphia: Temple UP, 1989.

Nourbese Philip, Marlene. *She Tries Her Tongue, Her Silence Softly Breaks*. Charlottetown, PE, Canada: Ragweed P, 1989.

Ortiz, Fernando. *Glosario de Afronegrismos*. Havana: Imprenta "El Siglo XX," 1924.

Osumare, Halifu. *The Africanist Aesthetic in Global Hip Hop: Power Moves*. New York: Palgrave, 2007.

Otheguy, Ricardo, and Ofelia García. "Diffusion of Lexical Innovations in the Spanish of Cuban Americans." *Research Issues and Problems in United States Spanish: Latin American and Southwestern Varieties*. Eds. J. Ornstein-Galicia, G. Green, and D. Bixler-Márquez. Brownsville, TX: Pan American U, 1988. 203–43. Rio Grande Series in Language and Linguistics. 2.

Russell, Carlos. *Miss Anna's Son Remembers*. Brooklyn, NY: Bayano, 1976.

Sheller, Mimi. "Citizenship and the Making of Caribbean Freedom." *NACLA Report on the Americas* 38.4 (2005): 30+. *ProQuest*. Web. 2 Jan. 2015.

Smith, Faith L., ed. *Sex and the Citizen: Interrogating the Caribbean*. Charlottesville: U of Virginia P, 2011.

Smitherman, Geneva. "Black Idiom." *Negro American Literature Forum* 5.3 (1971): 88+. *JSTOR*. Web. 30 Apr 2014.

———. "Language and African Americans: Movin on Up a Lil Higher." *Journal of English Linguistics* 32.3 (2004): 186–96. *Proquest*. Web. 30 Apr 2014.

———. "Language and Liberation." *The Journal of Negro Education* 52.1 (1983): 15–23. *JSTOR*. Web. 30 Apr 2014.

Sonja, Niah Stanley. "'Dis Slackness Ting': A Dichotomizing Master Narrative in Jamaican Dancehall." *Caribbean Quarterly* 51.3 (2005): 55+. *ProQuest*. Web. 2 Jan. 2015.

Thomas, Deborah A. "Democratizing Dance: Institutional Transformation and Hegemonic Re-Ordering in Postcolonial Jamaica." *Cultural Anthropology* 17.4 (2002): 512–50. *ProQuest*. Web. 2 Jan. 2015.

Torres, Lourdes. "In the Contact Zone: Code-switching Strategies by Latino/a Writers." *MELUS* 32.1 (2007): 75–98.

Toribio, A. J. "Convergence as an Optimization Strategy in Bilingual Speech: Evidence from Code-Switching." *Bilingualism* 7.2 (2004): 165–73.

———. "Spanish/English Speech Practices: Bringing Chaos to Order." *International Journal of Bilingual Education and Bilingualism* (2004): 133–54.

Vega, Ana Lydia. *Encancaranublado*. Río Piedras, Puerto Rico: Editorial Antillana, 1982.

Wagner, S. T. "The Historical Background of Bilingualism and Biculturalism in the United States." *The New Bilingualism: An American Dilemma*. Ed. M. Ridge. Los Angeles: U of Southern California P, 1981. 29–52.

Walcott, Derek. "The Antilles: Epics of Fragment Memory." Nobel Lecture. 7 Oct. 1992. Web. 20 Oct. 2011. *nobelprize.org/nobel_prizes/literature/laureates/1992/walcott-lecture.html*.

Weldon, Tracy. "Reflections on the Ebonics Controversy." *American Speech* 75.3 (2000): 275–79.

Young, Vershawn Ashanti, "Nah, We Straight: An Argument Against Code-Switching." *JAC* 29.1–2 (2010): 49–76.

———. "Should Writers Use They Own English." *Iowa Journal of Cultural Studies* 12/13 (2010): 110–17.

Young, Vershawn Ashanti, and Aja Y. Martinez. *Code-Meshing as World English: Pedagogy, Policy, Performance*. Urbana, IL: National Council of Teachers of English, 2011.

Young, Vershawn Ashanti, et al. *Other People's English: Code Meshing, Code Switching, and African American Literacy*. New York: Teachers College P, 2013.

Racial Consciousness, Place, and Identity in Selected Afro-Mexican Oral Poems

Paulette A. Ramsay

Afro-Mexicans are frequently characterized as a people who, for the most part, are lacking in any understanding of themselves as being of African descent (Gonzalez, *Afro-Mexican Dances* 2). The last two or three decades, however, have witnessed some change in this assessment due mainly to the work of scholars whose research and interactions with Afro-Mexican communities have helped to raise awareness of issues of ethnicity and identity among them. Recognition must be given to the early work of Aguirre Beltrán, the Minority Rights Group, the Instituto Guerrerense de Cultura, and the Dirección General de Culturas Populares in Mexico who pioneered early research into Afro-Mexican ethnic identities and pointed to some attempts at self-vindication.[1] Furthermore, the extensively fundamental and historic work of Fr. Glynn Jemmott among Afro-Mexicans and the results Jemmott's work has borne of raising self-awareness among them cannot be overstated.[2] This chapter is an attempt to uncover ways in which racial and cultural identities are constructed by Afro-Mexicans in their literary and cultural production through oral narratives that overtly and covertly contribute to this objective.

The interdisciplinary field of cultural studies furnishes a particularly useful theoretical standpoint for exploring and interrogating issues related to identity in this chapter because identity has been framed as a concept that figuratively combines the intimate or personal world with the collective space of cultural forms and social relations (Holland et al. 5). This significant concept/definition of identity taken from the field of cultural studies will be invoked in the discussions of how racial consciousness and place in selected Afro-Mexican creative forms advance firm positions about self-formation, self-projection, issues of citizenship, and belonging in Afro-Mexican communities.

The determinate culturally constructed interpretation of identity is advanced by Holland, et al., as an alternative formulation, grounded in practice-activity theories and fieldwork. Furthermore, these theorists regard identity as being constructed in three different contexts: (i) the "figured world," (ii) "relational identities" / "positionality," and (iii) the "space of authoring" (271). "Figured worlds" characterizes the way in which individuals construct reality as they "perceive it or want it to be." A "figured world" is peopled by the figures, characters, and types who carry out its tasks and who also have styles of interacting within distinguishable perspectives and orientations. It refers to a socially and culturally constructed realm of interpretation in which particular characters and actors are recognized, significance is assigned to certain acts, and particular outcomes are valued over others (51–52).

The second context in which identity is considered as being manifested, "positionality," also referred to as "relational identities," involves the individual's sense of social place or entitlement. "Relational identities" are performed in different ways—such as the way people dress, speak, or express themselves and assert who they are. Holland, et al., explains the term as follows: "Relational identities have to do with behavior as indexical of claims to social relationships with others. They have to do with how one identifies one's position relative to others, edited through the ways one feels comfortable or constrained, for example, to speak to another, to command another, to enter into the space of another, to touch the possessions of another, to dress for another, or to enter the kitchen of another" (127).

"Authoring" is denoted as the response of an individual or group to the world and situations they encounter. It is "a matter of orchestration of arranging the identifiable social discourse/practices that are one's resources in order to craft a response in time and space defined by others' standpoints in activity" (275). This term is inferred from Bakhtin's philosophy of dialogism, in which he accentuates the value of dialogue or of individuals being able to counter and respond to "authoritative discourses." Elizabeth White sharply characterizes this philosophy of dialogism in the following manner: "dialogism represents a methodological turn towards the messy reality of communication in all its many language forms. Emphasis is simultaneously placed on the location of dialogue within the heteroglot as the place where opposing forces inter-animate with each other to generate new meaning that goes beyond, and draws from more than the official alone. Inherent within dialogic philosophy is an emphasis on dialogue as an ongoing process of meaning, orality that occurs between people as subjects" (4–5).

These three concepts will be used together to constitute the analytical frame for this chapter, in which I interrogate poems which, I argue, reveal a commanding level of racial consciousness and interaction with the land or region occupied by Afro-Mexicans as their performers or authors unstintingly engage in a complex process of self-fashioning. I propose further that "figured worlds" are created by Afro-Mexican composers or performers of oral poems to advance arguments about their membership in the Afro-Mexican community and in Mexico in general. Relational or positional identities will be dramatized by poems that depict Afro-Mexicans making claims about their entitlement to being regarded in ways that show their place in Mexican society.

The production of these poems will be treated as the dramatization of the authors' understanding of themselves as blacks, their attempts to declare who they are, and their engagement in the intricacies of self-fashioning.

In addition to these ways in which cultural studies construct identity or agency, broad postcolonial theories will be used to underline how the verses proffer a new discourse about Afro-Mexicans and their ethnic heritage. The main aspect of postcolonial discourse on which I will draw is informed by Stephen Slemon's view of a creative revisionism, which involves the subversion or displacement of dominant discourses. This revisionism "challenges the tenets both of an essentialist nationalism which sublimates or overlooks regional differences of an unconsidered multiculturalism (mis) appropriated for the purposes of enforced assimilation, rather than for the promulgation of cultural diversity" (qtd. in Huggan, 357). This is indeed very applicable to the Mexican context, in which all considerations of multiculturality are denied and the discourse of homogeneity promoted.

Racial/Ethnic Pride

In two previous articles in which I discuss Afro-Mexican *corridos* (ballads) and Afro-Mexican folktales, respectively, I argue that although there were no specific references to blackness in any of these oral forms, the racial positions were encased in the striking posturings, which were similar to the attitudes depicted by other groups of blacks in other contexts, specifically in the Caribbean.[3]

However, in many of the *coplas* (verses) in the collections *Alma cimarrona* (Maroon Soul) (Torres Díaz and Reyes Larrea, 1999) and *Callate burrita prieta: Poetica afromestiza* (Be Quiet Black Donkey: Afromestiza Poetry) (Aparicio Prudente, Garcia Casarrubias, and Díaz Perez, 1993), it is clear that the poetic voice speaks from a particular ethnic identity's position of understanding and opines in a structured context best described as a "figured world," which also provides creative reversionings. Attention will be drawn to how this reversioning gives emphasis to both racial and cultural diversity in Mexico. The following lines from the title poem of the collection *Alma cimarrona* imply a poem written as the result of a cognition or percipience of a specific racial heritage and upbringing in a particular geo-political space that is associated with Afro-Mexican inhabitants:

A mí me dicen el negro	They call me the black one
porque una negra me crió,	because I was raised by a black woman,
y por toda la Costa Chica	and all along the Costa Chica
no hay negro como yo,	there is no black man like me,
porque mi nanita chula	because my sweet mother
con buena leche me amantó.	breastfed me with good milk.[4]
("Alma cimarrona" 27)	

There is an unequivocal hint of pride in being identified as a black person, but the persona is even more proud of his incomparable and incontrovertible "pedigree," which he traces to his black lineage and the nurturing received from his black mother. This, of course, implies a longstanding tradition of consciously embracing and celebrating a distinct and unique heritage and way of life.

In the collection *Callate burrita prieta: Poetica afromestiza*, this same effort at self-presentation and self-definition is evident. In the poem "Color," the persona deliberately subverts the stereotypical and dominant discourse about blackness through the projection of positive images. Through the indubious acknowledgement of blackness and elevation of the black male, a new kind of discourse about the black race in general and the black man in particular is advanced. The poem's internal structure simultaneously reveals the tension created by the intentional rejection of the expected Eurocentric, biased choice of a white partner in preference for a black one. Interestingly, the black man is chosen not just for his color, but for the admirable traits he possesses as the one who is gentlemanlike, romantic, and amorous:

De arriba cayó un pañito	A small cloth fell from above
derechito al duraznito	right beside the little peach tree
dejé de querer a un blanco	I stopped loving a white man
por querer un trigueñito	because I love a little black one
tendrá la sangre muy dulce	his blood must be very sweet
y por ser muy hombrecito.	as he's quite a gentleman.
("Color" 20)	

In "Alma cimarrona," racial consciousness is also boldly expressed in the positive depictions of the Afro-Costa Chican female. The desirability of the black Mexican woman is resolutely conveyed in a spirited *copla*, which dispenses with the mainstream tendency to privilege the appearance or physical attributes of lighter-complexioned women over black ones. The persona earnestly communicates a willingness and eagerness to be close to the black woman and to be united in marriage with her:

De tu boca quiero un beso,	I want a kiss from your mouth,
de tu blusa un botón,	a button from your blouse,
darle a tu nombre apellido	I want to give you a surname
y de ti morenita, el corazón.	and to win your heart, black woman.
("Alma cimarrona" 17)	

The persona is obviously proud of his surname, which no doubt indicates his ethnicity, and wants to share this aspect of his unique heritage with the black woman. Evidently his intention toward her is also honorable, as he desires to make her his wife.

Here, it seems that the issue of how Afro-Mexican women traditionally have been objectified and demeaned becomes a site of contestation as this poetic voice seems to give her dignity—a new "positional identity" in which she is worthy of being or becoming someone's legitimate wife rather than a concubine without legal claims or entitlements. According to Jameelah Muhammad:

> Afro-Mexican women generally work as cooks, maids and domestics. Like black men, they are viewed as objects of servitude—overweight, uneducated, illiterate and poor, and speakers of unintelligible Spanish. Yet black women in Mexico cannot seem to escape the myth of being oversexed. Many historians write about Spanish men's desire to have African women as their concubines. In this way, the

black woman's body has become a commodity. She was known as a prostitute in major colonial cities like Puebla and Mexico City. At one point in history the words *negra* and "prostitute" were synonymous. This image has persisted, and is routinely depicted in Mexican comic books. (Muhammad 177)

This seemingly simple proposal by the poetic persona to "give her his name" becomes a powerful and noteworthy attempt to unsettle those disparaging, vocalized constructions of black female identity in Mexico. The idea that the black woman is only good enough to appease the sexual desires of Spanish men, even for monetary gain, is forcefully challenged.

A patently clear restitutive role is intended in the positioning of the black woman in a particularly positive light. She is depicted as one who has the gift of healing and comforting, one who is needed in the life of the black man to make him contented and complete:

Que tundrá mi corazón	What could be wrong with my heart
que no quiere estar conmigo	why it doesn't want to be with me?
yo le pregunto que con quien	I ask it "with who then?"
y me dice que contigo,	and it tells me "with you,"
Por que contigo? Está dolido,	Why with you? It is hurting,
y cuando lo tienes en tus brazos,	and when you have it in your arms,
negrita linda,	beautiful black woman,
se le quita lo adolorido.	all pain is gone.
("Alma cimarrona" 19)	

"Relational identities" / "positionality" seem to be spiritedly dramatized in the black woman's apparently central role in the black man's life, as conveyed by another *copla* in which the persona expresses his preference for death over life without the black woman:

Negra, negra	Black woman, black woman
sin tu amor no me hallo,	without your love I'm lost,
nada, nada me divierte,	I can't enjoy myself at all,
si a ti te quitan el que me	if the one you speak of
hables,	takes you away from me,
a mi me han deseado la muerte	they have wished death upon me
mejor que me parta un rayo	it would be better for lightning to strike me
que yo dejar de quererte.	than for me to stop loving you.
("Alma cimarrona" 22)	

A similar expression of high regard and respect for the black woman is to be found in "Color" from *Callate burrita prieta*. The poetic voice proclaims the black woman as a source of anchoring and stability in his life:

Negra sin tu amor no me hallo	Black woman, without your love I'm lost,
nada, nada me divierte	I can't enjoy myself at all
mejor que te parta un rayo	it would be better for lightning to strike you
para dejar de quererte	so I could stop loving you.
("Color" 21)	

Repetition functions as an important discursive strategy in these two *coplas* to highlight their performative nature and the involvement of different individuals in preserving the oral tradition in the Afro-Mexican community. In one collection, the *copla* is slightly modified, but the essence remains the same and gives authenticity to its origin and significance.

Two other *coplas* in "Alma cimarrona" work together to imply that the Afro-Mexican male has assessed the Afro-Mexican woman as someone who is entitled to a particular kind of treatment, given who she is. She is elevated to a position of regality and one deserving of pampering and the finest in life. Here again, we may draw on the concepts of "the figured world" and "relational identities" to comprehend that great value is being placed on the Afro-Mexican woman. The poetic voice has re-positioned her as one with a social position worthy of regal treatment:

A mi negrita te he de hacer	My black woman, I have to build you
una casita en el viento,	a little house in the wind,
la pared ha de ser de oro	the wall must be of gold
y de algodón el cimienta.	and the foundation of cotton.
("Alma cimarrona" 23)	

This is sustained in another *copla* that speaks to the beauty and regality of the black woman while simultaneously employing contrast as an effective strategy to indicate how other women of less regality should be treated:

A las morenas bonitas	For the beautiful black women,
una corona imperial.	an imperial crown.
a las güeras revolcadas	for the humiliated blonde girls,
una penca de nopal.	a prickly pear pad.
("Alma cimarrona" 35)	

The beauty of the black woman is equally lauded in direct contradiction to traditional discourse, which has characterized her as being unworthy of admiration due to her negroid features:

Bendito sea Dios, Negrita	Praise be to God, black woman
que linda y hermosa te ha hecho	who has made you so beautiful and lovely,
delgadita de cintura	small in waist
y abultadita del pecho.	and voluptuous in breast.
("Alma cimarrona" 24)	

The powerful lyrics of the *décima* (ten-line stanza) "Negrita cimarona" ("Little Black Maroon") in *Alma cimarrona* continue in the same vein as some of the *coplas* discussed earlier. It is without doubt a poem of self-authoring and self-projection, as its architect Reyes Larrea portrays the magnificence of the black female. The poem becomes an embodiment of the dialectics on race, history, and culture and presupposes blackness as a symbol of majesty, even in resistance. The ideology of white supremacy is forcefully challenged in the claim of black superiority in this oral discourse, as the poem connects the Afro-Mexican woman to her African past through her response to the drum, a central instrument in African-derived cultures. The impassioned beat of the drum reverberates in the spirit of Afro-Mexicans and becomes an eternal cadence, awakening the African spirit to alertness:

Ruge el tambor
y mi negritilla se emociona
sale luego a relucí
su alma cimarrona

Negra e' su cabellera
cuculuxte la ingrata,
su cuerpo de sirena
su mirada me mata

Bailar ¡como le encanta!
¿ a qué negra, díganme no?
-Manque sea con charrasca
como quera bailo yo

De tierras muy lejanas
heredó en su piel, el color,
la alegría, la bravura
y bailar con sabor.

Ante nada se ejpanta
e' parte de su cultura
les confieso mij hermanoj
¡el no verla me tortura!

Cuando mi negrita habla,
habla sin temor,
y si es necesario bronquea
¡pelea pa' dejeundé su honor!

Orgullosa ella ejtá
del color achapopotao de su piel
de su cabecita punchuncha
y de esos labios de miel

Si por negra—dice—
me deprecias
no maldigas mi color
entre perlas y diamantes
¡la morena es la mejor!

No maldigo mi mulata
no maldigo tu color,
pue' de no juyirte conmigo
no tendría hoy yo tu amor.
Vengan Diablos y Tortugas,
Toros, Panchos o Minga,
tóquenme un son,
bailaré con mi pardita,
mi machete ejta desvainao
no tenga miedo nadita
nunca ando descuidao
por si alguién me rejpinga.
("Negrita cimarrona,"
Alma cimarrona 69)

The drum rumbles
and my little black girl gets excited
she then goes out to show off
her maroon soul

Her curly hair is black
that little ingrate,
she has a body like a mermaid
her look kills me

How she loves to dance!
To what black woman? Please tell me.
"Even if it is only with a percussion scraper
I dance anyway."

From faraway lands
she inherited her skin, her color,
joy, courage
and she dances with flair.

She's not frightened by anything
it's part of her culture
I tell you my brothers
not seeing her is torture for me!

When my black woman speaks,
she speaks without fear,
and if necessary, she will quarrel with you
she fights to defend her honor!

She's proud
of her tar-like complexion
of her little *punchuncha* head
and of her lips of honey

If because I'm black—she says—
you despise me
don't curse my color
because, of all the pearls and diamonds
the black one is the best!

I don't curse my mulatto woman
I don't curse your color,
because if you didn't run away with me
I wouldn't have your love today.

Let the Devils and Turtles,
Bulls, Panchos, or Mingas come,
play me a song,
I will dance with my mulatto woman,
my machete is unsheathed
I'm not afraid at all
I never walk carelessly
in case someone insults me.
    (translation by K. Henry)

Reyes Larrea unreservedly apotheosizes the black phenotype that mainstream writers and historians have used derogatorily to define Africans and their descendants. These physical features—hair, skin, eyes, and lips—are highlighted, with accolades of appreciation to nullify all tendencies to depreciate them. This way the intransigent strength of the blacks of Mexico belies and reversions the traditional racial discourse perpetuated through colonialism.

The black woman is presented as the epitome of feminine creation: negroid hair—"Negra e' su cabellera" (Her hair is black)—the mention of which implies its beauty. This noticeable feature is highlighted by the persona in celebration of blackness and in depicting a captivating picture of the black woman's body. Notwithstanding, the beauty of blackness is also linked to the boldness of the black woman as caution is given to the irresistible but possibly fatal effect of an encounter with an Afro-Mexican woman who incubates the maroon spirit.

In the effort, deliberate or otherwise, to redeem the image of the black woman, fearlessness and a dauntless fighting spirit characterize her. She is celebrated for her indefatigable spirit of resistance and boldness in the face of terror. These seemingly inborn traits are naturally emergent from the African culture and typify the black woman as possessing prowess in battle, overthrowing the orthodox view on gender dominance in warfare. This stance is personified both in spirit and in speech, but more so, it is actualized in the unstoppable daring that will not retreat from any challenge in defense of honor. Reyes Larrea's *décima* elucidates the historical component attached to the Afro-Mexican legacy of black skin color while presenting blackness as the quintessence of color. At the same time, the *décima* proudly declares Africa as the source and place of black identity formation and the heritage of bravery. The conferring of a rich heritage is embodied in the black skin: richness of color personifying a fertile earth; a spirit of indomitable courageousness; and lastly, the mastery of dance, counterpart to music, enriching Mexico's culture with unparalleled dynamism. The most important aspect to this declaration of beauty, bravery, and pride is reflected in the acceptance of the color of her skin:

De tierras muy lejanas
heredó en su piel, el color,
la alegría, la bravura
y bailar con sabor.

From faraway lands
she inherited her skin, her color,
joy, courage
and she dances with flair.

Cuando mi negrita habla,
habla sin temor,
y si es necesario bronquea,
¡pelea pá dejuendé su honor!

When my black woman speaks,
she speaks without fear,
and if necessary, she will quarrel with you
she fights to defend her honor!

Orgullosa ella ejtá
del color achapopotao de su piel
de su cabecita punchuncha
y de esos labios de miel
("Negrita cimarrona" 69)

She's proud
of her tar-like complexion
of her little *punchuncha* head
and of her lips of honey.

The poetic voice is still mindful of reality and simultaneously admits the irony of the social context in which the Afro-Mexican woman dwells. For, despite his own pride, the *negra* maroon who is depicted as a paragon of racial beauty is also seen as repudiated and despised:

Si por negra—dice—
me deprecias
no maldigas mi color
entre perlas y diamantes
¡la morena es la mejor!
("Negrita cimarrona" 69)

If because I'm black—she says—
you despise me
don't curse my color
because, of all the pearls and diamonds
the black one is the best!

Staunch resistance in the face of black racial discrimination is vociferously expressed in these lines. The intimation is that there is no justification for prejudice and typecasting of people who are black. The persona condemns the contemptuous utterance and rejects the depreciation of the color black and black skin in particular. The black woman is metaphorized as the most prized of all precious stones, including white ones; thus, the ideology of white superiority is once more subverted:

No maldigo mi mulata
no maldigo tu color,
pue' de no juyirte conmigo
no tendría hoy yo tu amor.
("Negrita cimarrona" 69)

I don't curse my mulatto woman
I don't curse your color,
because if you didn't run away with me
I wouldn't have your love today.

Indeed, the dogmas of *mala raza* (bad race) and *mala sangre* (bad blood) entrenched in Mexico's ideological racial construct of *mestizaje* (mixed race) enforce a natural tendency for racial delimitation inherent in this stereotypical treatment of the Afro-Mexican in Mexico. Reyes Larrea uses this form of oral tradition to expose the idiosyncrasies on race in the excerpt which follows. While there is consciousness and appreciation of one's own color, there is also acceptance of another's. It becomes clear that the framework of intelligibility expressed concerning racial identity and color incorporates recognition of difference while making allowance for ethnic syncretism.

"Negrita cimarrona" further captures the centrality of music and dance to Afro-Mexican cultural expression. These artistic expressions exoticize without diminishing Afro-Mexican culture in an untheorized space:

Bailar¡ como le encanta!
¿a qué negra, díganme no?
-Manque se con charrasca
Como quiera bailo yo.

How she loves to dance!
Is she a black woman? Tell me no!
"Even if it's only with a percussion scraper
I dance anyway"

Vengan Diablos y Tortugas,
Toros, Panchos o Minga,
Tóquenme un son,
Bailaré con mi pardita,
Mi machete ejta desvainao
No tenga miedo nadita
Nunca ando descuidao
Por si alguien me rejpinga
("Negrita cimarrona" 69)

Let the Devils and Turtles,
Bulls, Panchos, or Mingas come
Play me a song
I will dance with my brown-skin woman
My machete is unsheathed
I'm not afraid at all
I'll never walk carelessly
In case someone insults me.

The explicit references to *diablos*, *tortugas*, *toros*, and *mingas* clearly signal the persona's familiarity with the performance of specific Afro-Mexican cultural forms and how deeply entrenched are the cultural idiosyncrasies associated with them. All four figures are the main characters in three of the Costa Chica's main dance forms previously referred to. In *La danza del diablo* (Devil Dance) and the Turtle Dance, *Panchos* and *Mingas* dance together to perform serious roles of the masculine pursuit of females, even though all the roles are performed by men disguised as women. In both popular dances, rebellion against the status quo is performed in different ways, as turtles, *Mingas*, and *Panchos* try to overpower each other. Anita Gonzalez explains: "Rebellion in the Turtle Dance is expressed by means of overt sexuality. Generally, the lead Pancho rules over all the dancers, as if orchestrating their mating play. He has the freedom to mount the turtle or the Minga. As in the Devil and Bird Dances he contains the other dancers without being contained himself. The aggressive behavior is much more subdued in this dance, instead the performers disrupt societal norms in their unconcealed lustful behavior" (*Afro-Mexican Dances* 78).

In the *décimas* being studied, the implication of the persona's challenge to these figures is that he is not intimidated by the most sexually potent of those famous for their sexual prowess but is confident of his own physical strength and is determined that no-one can/will challenge his position in his woman's life or his ability to ward them off. The reference to his prepared machete invokes the performance of the dances and the various ways in which females are overpowered in this dance space. This simultaneously conveys his willingness to use force to defend such a challenge. Indeed, he may be seen as projecting more power himself than the *Pancho* figure, who would normally be the one to restrain the other characters who are all drawn from different Afro-Mexican carnivals associated with the Costa Chica.

Indeed, the poems play a crucial role in forging linkages between spatial occupation and definitive identity markers of the people of the coastal regions. Without doubt, this unique poem revises history and problematizes Mexico's racial discourse, in which people of African ancestry are considered to be infinitesimal on the landscape as a result of racial categorization and stigmatization based on the *mestizaje* criterion.

"Pa' mi Nicolasita" ("For my Nicolasita"), in *Alma cimarrona*, is a dedicatory poem that illustrates the concept of the "figured world," seen in the persona's deep love and admiration for the black woman. There is a sense of awe in her beauty, reinforced by the way she is addressed in the first line of the opening *cuarteta*: "¡Ay que mi nita re'bonitilla!" (Oh my beautiful black woman!). Poet Donají Méndez Tello infuses wonderment in the endearment, making the diminutive form of *bonita* a love language. There is finesse in the black woman's gait, and the poet emphasizes it as a captivating yet empowering quality:

Mira nomaj qué sensual caminas	Look how sensual you walk
y me da coraje que te vean los niños	and it makes me angry that the boys look at you
¡Ay mi Nicolasita!	Oh my Nicolasita!
("Pa' mi Nicolasita" 72)	

The poem expounds the depth of love that children exhibit toward their black mothers, alongside the nuances and textualities of relationships. The persona's deep-felt commitment and love is such that he wants to keep his woman away from the world, so he can be with her without interruption:

Te quiero tanto mi negritilla	I love you so much my little black girl
que yo te pongo un bajarequillo	that I will build you a little hut
pa' que ejtemos nomaj los doj solitos.	just for the two of us.
("Pa' mi Nicolasita" 72)	

Amid the portrayal of the black man's quest to win the black woman, the poetic voice also reveals a certain level of communal relations and aspects of the livelihood of the people, solidifying the synchronous duality of an autonomously separated community with a collective culture. The firm implication is that the black man understands the importance of providing for his family and depending on the support of the wider community for keeping the family together. The determination to author self and to project images of blacks in a particular redeeming manner is evident:

¡Júyete conmigo ahora mejmo	Run away with me right now
y ya dejpué que najca el munchito,	and after the baby is born,
se lo levemos a papacitoj.	we'll take him to Daddy.
mira, la veredeta que va a tu casa	Look, the path that leads to your house
acompañándola también ejta	is also being trod by my
mi mula prieta que quiero tanto	brown mule that I love so much
y que me ayuda a cargá el mai.	and which helps me to carry my corn.
Anda mi negra no seaj ingrate	Come on my black woman, don't be
Jùyete conmigo, ni piensej má	disagreeable,
que ejte año si Dios me ayuda	run away with me, don't think about it
toda la siembra del limonar	because this year, with God's help
será pa' nosotroj doj,	the entire lemon harvest
Pa' que tengamos otro munchito	will be for both of us,
y al año, otro, nomaj.	so we can have another baby
("Pa' mi Nicolasita" 72)	and next year, another one, and no more.

Strong racial consciousness is projected in the *coplas* and lyric poems to a sphere of liberation. Black men are positioned to demonstrate that the oppression of Afro-Mexicans stretches across gender lines to include their female counterparts. Each positive address of the black woman, each recognition of her beauty, works to change the way in which black women are perceived and related to and indicates an understanding that any agenda for racial/social legitimation must also include black women. The images or proclamations suggest, moreover, an undertaking that black men and women share a common legacy and history of slavery, colonialism, and racial oppression, which must inform their self-formation.

A decided aspect of self-definition for black men and success in achieving freedom and gaining access to citizenship must involve validating women as well as men and include the group as a whole. The positive images point to possible ways in which black men understand that there is a need for the power positions between them to shift so that they participate less in denigrating black women and more in elevating them—to silence the voices of domination and racism against which black women struggle on an ongoing basis.

Orality, Place, and Identity

The study of postcolonial societies has also given emphasis to the role of orality and place in identity formation. Indeed, the oral forms serve as a testament to Mexico's multiculturality, as well as reveal a consciousness of a collective culture, language, and sensibility used to characterize the Afro-Mexican group and narrate its attachment to a particular region and cultural heritage. The narrators of oral verses and writers of lyric poems in *Alma cimarrona* draw on the versatility of these art forms, *décimas* and *coplas*, to express their understanding of who they are. Indeed, the verses reveal the ways in which they are linked to a particular space/place and identify a group that is obviously aware of its ethno-racial distinctions in Mexico.

One striking feature of the verses in the collection *Alma cimarrona* is the manner in which they reveal a deep interconnection between the land and the African oral tradition. The dedicatory *décima* "Canto a la costa mía" ("Song to my coast") shows affinity to the land and poetically eulogizes the coastal region for its natural beauty, the magnificence of its people, and its regional particularism. Zárate Arango's poetic apostrophe resonates with accolades to the Costa Chica and its coastal environs. This poem pronounces on Afro-Mexican identity as being located in the Costa Chica, and it gives attention to uncovering the linkages that it establishes between the development of racial consciousness and the way in which orality allows for the expression of this self-awareness and facilitates the self-authoring of a figured world. The palm identifies the place and characterizes its natural environs as being unequivocally along the coastline. The palm is a typical feature of beaches and coastal regions, where it thrives unencumbered. It is also a symbolic representation of the strength and resilience of the Afro-Mexican people who inhabit the coastal regions. During colonialism their ethnicity and ethnological differences were key components in predetermining spatial occupation to territories where their skin color or pigmentation tolerated the sun. Over time, their claim to the coastal regions in Mexico has become legitimized with an intimate longstanding relationship.

The line "Del palmar surgió una voz" ("A voice arose from the palm grove") gives vocalization that is potent and resonant in soliciting its request. The palm is represented as a powerful communicative device between the land and its people. There is a specifically directed summons to the poetic persona who acts as the immediate oracle, evident from the ensuing verses, to chant songs to the land—to the persona's Costa Chica. The possessive claim to the land shows intimacy and an attachment to it by its inhabitants. Place is undeniably linked to identity formation, so the poet's musical dedication is not only an expression of but also an extension of identity, embodied in the kaleidoscopic fusion of land and people.

In "Canto a la Costa mía," Nature's involvement in broadcasting the tribute to the territory of Costa Chica lends unmistakable force to this oral form: "El mar arrulló mis versos / en sus olas cadenciosas" (The sea whispered my verses / in its rhythmic waves). The reverence palpable in the homage is conveyed in the gentleness of the sea's lull. In this sense the *décima* serves to poetically fuel the oral tradition through the recognition and praise of regionalism: Costa Chica is particularized to be canonized. The persona reveals space as a reinforcement of place, conveying the message of ownership and intimacy with the land and sea:

El mar arrulló mis versos
en sus olas cadenciosas
a ti Costa Chica mía
te dedico algunas coplas
("Canto a la Costa mía," *Alma cimarrona* 52)

The sea whispered my verses
in its rhythmic waves
to you my Costa Chica
I dedicate some verses

While the failure of mainstream Mexico to recognize the Afro-Mexican coastal zone and its people is forcefully underscored, the "Afro-Mexican" coastal flagship is unmistakably clear in drawing awareness to its own existence. The dedicatory lyrics function as an X-ray that uncovers the injustice of non-recognition. The light advertises the beauty of the Costa Chican region and accentuates the unmistakable pride of place and race. The rhythmic cadences and internal assonances of these lines join in the celebration of black selfhood to establish a unique nationalism and regionalism within the broader spectrum of Mexico's denied racial pluralism to reveal *mestizaje* as a denial of regional alignment and distinction.

Regional particularism is pervasive in "Canto a la costa mía," as defining features of towns and locals along the Costa Chican coast are given prominence; for example, Acapulco is praised for its artistic, svelte *chilena* dancers and its women of "pure coastal blood":

De Acapulco hasta mi tierra
se ha bailado la chilena,
orgullo de sus mujeres
de pura sangre costeña.
("Canto a la costa mía" 52)

From Acapulco to my land
they have danced the chilena,
proud of its women
of pure costeña blood.

Racial pride is marked by the impeccable bloodline of *los costeños* (people from Costa Chica). This conceptualization of *pura sangre costeña* (pure Costeña blood) demystifies and debunks the latent underlying colonial stereotype of *mala raza* and *mala sangre* attached to black ethnicities. Without being intentionally antagonistic, the appreciation of beauty visible in the region speaks volumes to the differences in race in reality, against the backdrop of sameness in perceived reality.

Racial consciousness is linked to place in the suggestion that the distinctiveness of Costa Chican women is attributable to their place of origin. Common and dominant along the coastal region is a gamut of women whose striking beauty is renowned. While the women are celebrated for their beauty, the men are praised for their prowess and bravery: "la cuna de hombres valientes" (the birthplace of brave men) (15 stanza 4). Moreover, the coastal town of Cuajinicuilapa, the area with the largest numbers of Afro-derived people in Mexico, is seen as the birthplace and incubator of outstanding Afro-Mexicans. Black racial identity receives fortitude in these lines, affirming its frame for producing a special type of men and women:

"De Ometepec se pregona tener mujeres
   bonitas,
Cuajinicuilapa arteria donde su sangre se agita,
la cuna . . . de morenas bonitas,"
"Cuajinicuilapa es bello por sus mujeres
   bonitas."
("Canto a la costa mía," *Alma cimarrona* 52)

"Ometepec boasts of having beautiful
   women,
Cuajinicuilapa, the artery where its blood is
   stirred,
the birthplace . . . of beautiful black women,"
"Cuajinicuilapa is beautiful because of its
   beautiful women."

Regional pride and nationhood are signal features among Afro-Mexican coastal communities. Place is praised as the heartbeat, the vital life-giving organ of the people. Reverence and adoration are inspired solely by geographical affinity, so there is a duality in identification of people and place. A sense of being is integrally embedded in place, while there seems to be no separateness between place and people: identity with nationhood becomes synonymous with identity with region. In other words, the geographical region evokes a distinctive identity and character in its people:

San Marcos mi corazón,	San Marcos my love,
te canto por ser costeño,	I sing to you because I'm a *Costeño*,
es la única razón	that's the only reason
del canto de este cuijileño	for the song of this *cuijileño*
("Canto a la costa mía" 52)	

This deep attachment of Afro-Mexicans to their natural environs bears an indelible imprint of racial consciousness: "costeño que soy" (I'm a Costeño) and "moreno del corazón" (black at heart) are, without doubt, treated synonymously. The coast is where their identity is conceived and lived, and an allegiance is forged that surpasses time and the ephemeral to a spiritual realm where the native claim to the coastal region is almost preconditioned to be Afro-Mexican. This is voiced in the request and earnest desire not to be forgotten as a true and committed Mexican of African descent. The community is undoubtedly deeply rooted in the geographical locale:

San Nicolás yo te pido	San Nicolás I ask you
como costeño que soy	like the *Costeño* that I am
que no olvides lo que he sido	not to forget that I have been
moreno del corazón.	black at heart.
("Canto a la costa mía" 52)	

Pride in region highlights pride in nationhood in a consummate climax resonant in the final stanza of the poem. Moreover, the women of the region are made out to be emblematic of the beauty of the region, thereby emphasizing their value to the region and the country:

Cuajinicuilapa es bello	Cuajinicuilapa is beautiful
por sus mujeres bonitas	because of its beautiful women
es un pueblo guerrerense	it is a Guerrero town
¡Orgullo de Costa Chica!	the pride of Costa Chica!
("Canto a la costa mía" 52)	

A similarly enthusiastic ownership of place and the firm suggestion that blackness is linked to the place occupied mainly by blacks in Mexico, is expressed in the following *copla* from the same collection, *Alma cimarrona*:

Soy de puro Costa Chica donde reinan los	I am pure Costa Chica
guerreros,	where the Guerrero people rule,
donde los hombres	where the men
¡son hombres!	are men!
y las mujeres, ¡mujeres!	And the women, women!
Donde no nacen maricas	Where no homosexuals are born
y los que nacen ¡se mueren!	And those that are born, die!
("Costa" 33)	

Here, the persona orchestrates self-formation structured on the knowledge of place of origin and a particular understanding of black sexuality as one that unapologetically embraces heterosexuality. All three contexts—"figured world," "positionality," and "authoring"—are intricately tied to these lines. The persona creates an "as if" world: as if it is a given that once the three factors of place, blackness, and a particular sexual orientation converge, one finds a *bona-fide* Afro-Mexican. A strong sense of entitlement, understood in the context of "relational identity," is evident as the persona implies how he expects to be understood and regarded. The voice of the "I," the author, unmistakably disrupts the official monologic, authoritative discourse of Mexico to author himself in a particular way that is inextricably linked to a particular place and cultural outlook.

The affinity of Afro-Mexicans to the land where the coastal regions are emblematic of Afro-Mexican's ethnicity and cultural identity seems evident in Zapata's "Costa." The poem particularizes the region by identifying their unique features so that place is not just a geographical or spatial reference but an embodiment of human existence, codified by a collective genetic component, determinant of a people and a rich cultural heritage. The opening *cuarteta* (quatrain) reveals a picturesque view of the coast and coastal life. An interconnection between the landscape and the people is immediately distinctive:

Costa canción y caricia	Costa song and caress
borrascosa como el mar	stormy like the sea
donde vive sin matar	where you can live without killing
la vida se desperdicia	life just drifts along
("Costa" 53)	

The affectionate address in line one, buttressed by the musicality of the alliteration, exposes a sense of suavity and subtleness that is immediately compared, paradoxically, to the unpredictable and turbulent quality of the sea: *borrascoso* (stormy). The beauty of the land is also paralleled to the longevity of life, which unravels unhurriedly in a natural trajectory: "donde vivir sin matar / la vida se desperdicia" (where you can live without killing / life just drifts along). The spirit of the coast is consuming and prepossessing of its occupants, and a sense of cultural aliveness and inherent vibrancy underscores the zeitgeist of the coast to the extent that everyone is captivated by its irresistible magnetism:

La costa es pasión que asfixia	The coast is a passion that suffocates
tiene el vicio de bailar	it has the vice of dancing
se entrega todo al amar	it surrenders all when in love
como una ingenua novicia.	like a naive novice.
("Costa" 53)	

The oral tradition is an integral part of the everyday life on the coast and is infused with mundane activities and survival strategies. The stance of the troubadour is militant, dignified, demonstrating the indomitable fighting spirit of African-derived Mexicans. It is this position that becomes a dramatization of what he imagines every Afro-Mexican person is asked to do:

Montado en un cuaco briosco	Mounted on a spirited scrawny horse
pajerero y bailador	frisky and dancing
sale un negro trovador,	out comes a black troubadour,
con un machete filoso	with a sharp machete
para defender su honor.	to defend his honor.
("Costa" 53)	

The image of a proud warrior poised in readiness for battle—"con un machete filoso" and buttressed by the image of the horse on which the black troubadour is mounted—is evoked as evidence of the passion for life among coastal dwellers.

"Costa" depicts a region luxuriant and diverse in resources, people, and culture. Each place is distinguished by its particular feature, resulting in an eclectic blend of definitive racial characteristics that ultimately unites culture and people. Zapata celebrates each coastal region for a particular product for which it is known, suggesting that there are strong linkages between the land and the activities of the Afro-Mexicans.

Pochutla huele a café	Pochutla smells of coffee
y Puerto Angel a marisco	and Puerto Angel of seafood
Pluma Hidalgo es gallo arisco	Pluma Hidalgo is a wild rooster
pelea sin saber por qué.	it fights without knowing why.
("Costa" 53)	

Regional distinction is further embodied in its particular products such as coffee, which is aromatic, potent, and black, reflective of the land and its people. There is also seafood, evoking the arresting scent of the ocean and publicizing the dominant trade and skill of the region. Pluma Hidalgo gives homage to the Afro-Mexican freedom fighter and hero, whose fighting spirit is immortalized in the identity of coastal Afro-Mexicans. The metaphorical comparison underlines the proud nature intricately interwoven with the fighting spirit, and its atavistic appearance produces a constant zeal for revolution unheeded by external factors. The specific reference to Hildago, along with the observation "pelea a sin saber por qué" (fights without knowing why), is perhaps a reference to the manner in which the revolutionary was annihilated as he attempted to bring about equality for Mexicans in the pre-independence period.

"Costa" undoubtedly draws pointed attention to the people of the region in celebration of nationhood, racial pride, and unity. The distinctions among the people of different areas are marked to disrupt stereotypical perceptions of them as one indistinguishable group lacking any specific and distinctive qualities, abilities, or traits. Sola de Vega is therefore recognized for its women, whose exceptional beauty is matched only by their own flamboyance. In contrast, the women of Juquila are noted for their religious dedication and pious acts:

Sola de Vegas es mujer	The town of Sola de Vegas is a woman
muy bonita y veleidosa	very beautiful and fickle
Juquila es mujer piadosa	Juquila is a pious woman
que Milagros sabe hacer.	who knows how to perform miracles.
("Costa" 53)	

Music and dance, palpable art forms of the African legacy, epitomize cultural expression along the Afro-Mexican coastal regions. Both artistic expressions are seen as the heartbeat of the people, and their existence is meaningless without them. They are seen as an outlet, as well as an inborn expression of identity, which unifies the group:

Se puso luego un fandango	Then they played a fandango
un violín y un bajo quinto	a violin and a bajo quinto guitar
cantaba el negro más pinto	the most handsome black man was singing
una chilena de rango,	a famous chilena,
yo lo zapatié en un pango	I tap-danced to it on a river ferry,
y hasta cimbraba el recinto.	and until the area shook.
("Costa," 53)	

Conviviality marks the atmosphere in which Afro-Mexicans perform through music and dance the identity they want to project of themselves. According to Anita Gonzalez, performance allows humans to clarify and articulate their history through embodied expressions, by "becoming" through either masked impersonation or crafted improvisation (Gonzalez, *Afro-Mexican Dances* 2).

The way in which these oral and lyric poems are imbued with rhythmic quality and musicality is undeniable. These qualities not only speak to the African religious heritage of the Afro-Mexican people and how the Afro-Mexicans have preserved aspects of their Afro-derived culture, but they also recall the centrality of these features to the Africans from whom they are inherited. In attesting to the great appeal of music and rhythm to African slaves and their descendants in Latin America during and after slavery, Andrews writes: "Music and dance were healing on almost every level, a balm for body and mind. The graceful movements of dance, movement done purely for pleasure and enjoyment, were the antithesis and direct negation of the pain and exhaustion of coerced labor. And when performed collectively, as they usually were, African sons and dance removed, at least for a moment, the degraded social status of slavery and created alternative, deeply healing senses of person-and-people-hood" (29).

Rhythm, music, and dance made life bearable and provided a modicum of self-alienation. Even after centuries of exposure to the music of Catholicism, Afro-Mexicans obviously still revel in the rhythm of drum, music, and dance. Andrews provides powerful support in his firm assertion:

> One of the central messages of African music is that rhythm lifts us out of the daily grind by transforming consciousness, transforming time, transforming and heightening our experience of the moment. And that consciousness-altering effect is entirely purposeful: in Africa and its New World diaspora, rhythm and music were an essential part of religious observance, particularly in creating the emotional and spiritual conditions for the gods to manifest themselves by possessing and "mounting" their worshippers. Drumming and dance were fundamental elements of African religious ritual; and as Africans adopted Christianity and turned it to their uses, a final way in which they transformed Iberian Catholicism was to inject it with the power of African drums. (Andrews 29)

We have seen then the various ways in which Afro-Mexicans construct identity by creating "figured worlds" in oral and lyric poems. Reality is presented as they understand it and the way they want the wider Mexican society to perceive them. Different cultural identities are performed in the "figured worlds" to manipulate the images projected by Afro-Mexicans of themselves and their region to others. The regions predominantly inhabited by Afro-Mexicans are owned as "spaces of authoring" to allow a range of selected identities, "positional identities," to be created for Afro-Mexicans to assert their own cultural and racial identities, debunk the myths about who they are, and unsettle erroneous accounts of their contributions to and place in the Mexican nation. The suggestions of harmony and connectivity between Afro-Mexicans and the land or region seem to imply the possibility of a similar type of unity and harmony between Afro-Mexicans and the rest of Mexican society.

Furthermore, the new identities serve to debunk the concept of *metizaje*, as defended by Mexico in its official definition of its nation and identity, as one of homogeneity. Their emphases, furthermore, on affirming blackness and regionalism as they speak the one to the other provides ample support to Beíntez-Rojo's claim that "*mestizaje* is nothing more than a concentration of differences" (26). This is to say that the poems, with their various revelations of Afro-centrality, belie Mexico's claim of *mestizaje* as a synthesis or homogeneity. They reveal a level of racial consciousness among the performers and writers of Afro-Mexican poems, and an even greater awareness of the link between the places occupied by Afro-Mexicans and their representation of themselves as being irrefutably Mexican.

Notes

1. See Jameelah S. Muhammad in *No Longer Invisible: Afro-Latin Americans Today*.
2. Fr. Glynn Jemmot. Personal interview. July 2013.
3. See Ramsay in "History, Violence and Self-Glorification in Selected Afro-Mexican *Corridos* from the Costa Chica de Guerrero" and "Establishing an Independent Identity: Afro-Mexican Oral Narratives in the Context of Post-Colonial Criticism."
4. All translations mine unless otherwise noted.

Works Cited

Andrews, George Reid. *Afro-Latin America, 1800–2000*. Oxford UP. 2004.
Aparicio Prudente, Francisca, Adela Garcia Casarrubias, and María Cristina Díaz Perez. *Callate burrita prieta: Poética afromestiza*. Oaxaca, Mexico: Dirección de Culturas Populares, Consejo Nacional para la Cultura y las Artes, 1993.
Bakhtin, Mikhail. *The Dialogic Imagination: Four Essays*. Trans. Michael Holquist. Ed. Carl Emerson. Austin: U of Texas P. 1981.
Beltrán Gonzalo, Aguirre. *La Población Negra de México: Estudio etnohistórico*. México: Fondo de Cultura Económica, 1972.
Benítez-Rojo, Antonio. *The Repeating Island: The Caribbean and the Postmodern Perspective*. Trans. James Maraniss. 2nd Edition. Durham: Duke UP. 1996.
Gonzalez, Anita. "*Imaging the Darker Brother: Critical Performances of Racialized Dance in Mexico*." Unpublished paper. LASA Conference. Rio de Janiero, Brazil. 11–16 June 2009.
———. *Afro-Mexican Dances Between Myth and Reality*. Texas: U of Texas P. 2010.

Holland, Dorothy, et al. *Identity and Agency in Cultural Worlds.* Cambridge, MA: Harvard UP. 2003.

Jemmot, Glynn. Personal interview with author, July 2013.

Huggan, Graham. "Decolonising the Map." Eds. Bill Ashcroft, Garth Griffiths, and Helen Tiffin. *The Post-Colonial Studies Reader.* 2nd ed. London: Routledge, 2005: 355–58.

Muhammad, Jameelah, S. "Mexico." *No Longer Invisible: Afro-Latin Americans Today.* London: Minority Rights, 1995.

Ramsay, Paulette. "History, Violence and Self-Glorification in Selected Afro-Mexican *Corridos* from the Costa Chica de Guerrero." *Bulletin of Latin American Research* 23:3 (2004): 303–21.

———. "Establishing an Independent Identity: Afro-Mexican Oral Narratives in the Context of Post-Colonial Criticism." *The Langston Hughes Review* 16:1–2 (Fall/Spring 1999–2001): 8–17.

Huggan, Graham. "Decolonizing the Map." *The Post-Colonial Studies Reader.* 2nd ed. Eds. Bill Ashcroft, Garth Griffiths, and Helen Tiffin. London: Routledge, 2005. 355–58.

Torres Díaz, Augustia, and Israel Reyes Larrea, eds. *Alma cimarrona: Versos costeños y poesía regional.* Oaxaca, Mexico: Direccion General de Cultura Populares, 1999.

White, Elizabeth. *Bakhtinian Dialogism: A Philosophical and Methodological Route to Dialogue and Difference.* Thirty-eighth Annual Conference of the Philosophy of Education Society of Australasia. 2009. *www2.hawaii.edu/~pesaconf/zpdfs/16white.pdf.*

10

Afro-Uruguayan Culture and Legitimation

Candombe *and Poetry*

Melva M. Persico

The known history of Afro-descendant letters in Uruguay goes back to the early to mid-nineteenth century with the work of Jacinto Ventura de Molina.[1] The existence of a literary culture, however, does not guarantee the legitimation of that culture. Afro-descendants in Uruguay are best known for their contribution to their nation's culture through their participation in carnival and the Afro-derived *Candombe*. This chapter takes a contrastive look at the high level of legitimation the *Candombe* has received in Uruguay as against the relative marginalization of the literature of Afro-descendants in that nation. I will argue that cultural policies in Uruguay grounded in issues related to cultural capital form a basis for this marginalization and therefore limit the ability of writers to negotiate within the field of cultural production. I also argue that *Candombe*'s legitimation mirrors similar instances of state appropriation of Afro-descendant cultural manifestations (particularly music) in other parts of Latin America, for example the Brazilian *Samba*. My arguments highlight the ways in which state appropriation and legitimation of these Afro-derived forms is a way of managing minority cultures so that the dominant culture maintains control. As I compare *Candombe*'s legitimation with that of lyrical poetry, I do not ignore the facts with regard to the lack of popularity of non-performative poetry. This chapter concludes with analyses of the poetry of two Afro-Uruguayan writers, Cristina Rodríguez Cabral and Graciela Leguizamón, in which they challenge hegemonic accounts of history and contemporary social realities in that nation.

As Pierre Bourdieu argues, the uneven nature of the field of cultural production comes about as a result of the various players who participate in the production process. In addition to the initial producers of the cultural product (be they writers, singers, film makers, or artisans, to name a few), various other players at other strata of the field directly or indirectly affect the product that reaches the consumer and the success it enjoys. Agents, publishers, museums, critics, the academy, literary prizes, and a host of other individuals and agencies participate in and have influence on the process. Their contributions help serve as a means by which the cultural product is legitimized. In some cases, official governmental and non-governmental agencies also have an impact on the success of cultural works. Bourdieu notes that within the literary field, the struggles focus on "the power to impose the dominant definition of the writer and therefore to delimit the population of those entitled to take part in the struggle to define the writer" (42). As one reflects on this statement, one could conclude that if the struggles within this field deprive some from participating in the legitimating process, that is, from having the authority to determine what is worthy of being read, these same struggles will also determine who can and cannot be rightly defined as writers. This process of legitimation is not in any way limited to the field of literature, as we shall see. Really, the question of the legitimation of cultural works is closely related to that of cultural capital.[2]

Bourdieu posits that cultural capital can be transmitted and acquired unconsciously during the period of socialization within the domestic setting (48–49). The school system, he asserts, is designed to perpetuate this process, since it is more equipped to endorse and build on the cultural capital students have acquired through their families than to introduce it to those whose socialization process lacked the necessary resources (55). John Guillory, who bases his work on Bourdieu's, focuses specifically on the role educational institutions play in promoting cultural capital. Two key points Guillory raises are central to my discussion. First, that one has to take into account the degree of access to the means of cultural production or lack thereof when one considers issues related to exclusion on the basis of social identity (18, 38); and second, that judgments made with regard to which works are canonical usually take place at the level of educational institutions like schools and universities (28–30). The foregoing arguments relate directly to the issue of cultural legitimacy as they point to the socio-cultural and socio-economic factors that influence the value placed on cultural products.

With respect to Afro-Uruguayan culture, one must examine how the previously mentioned factors are applicable. Arguments that belie the existence of racial discrimination usually lay the blame for discriminatory practices on socio-economic factors. In the case of Uruguay, the 2008 study *Población afrodescendiente y desigualdades étnico-raciales en Uruguay* reveals the close link between education and economic resources. One Afro-Uruguayan university student interviewed by researchers who conducted the study revealed that because of a lack of sufficient financial resources he was forced to pursue a career that was not what he had originally intended. Even though this student was employed during his years of study, and like all those who attend government-run schools and universities in Uruguay, he was not required to pay tuition, he found it a challenge to keep up with the additional costs involved in pursuing a university career, like clothing, books and materials (Somma 163). During a 2011 meeting of the United Nations' Committee on the Elimination of Racial Discrimination, in which it considered the Uruguayan delegations' report, discussions highlighted the correlation between poverty and discrimination and access to education. Even as it commended the country on its current efforts toward eliminating discrimination, the committee noted that in Uruguay:

> from its beginnings as an independent State until well into the twentieth century, discrimination against people of African descent and the descendants of native indigenous peoples was present but invisible. The nation's self-image as a white, integrated, homogeneous society hid great inequalities in opportunities for the effective realization of the rights of those communities. The historical and cultural legacy of people of African descent and indigenous people was considered of secondary importance. ("Committee" par. 9)

Note that the United Nations' committee raised questions with regard to the existence of specialized approaches and education programs geared toward the children of Afro-Uruguayans and budgetary allocations for this population (par. 54). As is to be expected, these issues are of concern to the Afro-Uruguayan community as well. Writer and activist Beatriz Santos Arrascaeta stated in a 2009 interview that the high levels of poverty among Afro-Uruguayans meant that many were in no position to compete educationally with their classmates.[3] Given the high drop-out rates among those of school age, it is no wonder that in a community that faces serious socio-economic challenges, some of the more privileged within society may consider Afro-Uruguayans, as a group, ill-equipped to make valuable cultural contributions in fields traditionally associated with the learned in society, like literature and fine arts. In fact, Graciela Leguizamón, one of the writers whose work I analyze, points out:

> Ni en las escuelas, ni secundaria en los cursos de literatura o de idioma castellano, hay textos poéticos o relatos escritos por un afrouruguayo y sabemos que es a esas edades en donde se forma el niño más allá de adquirir las herramientas básicas para su formación cultural.[4]

> In no school, not even at the secondary level where courses in literature or Spanish are offered, are there to be found poetry texts or stories written by Afro-Uruguayans, and we know that it is at those ages that the child develops beyond acquiring the basic tools for his cultural education.[5]

Leguizamón says further that this lack of knowledge of and exposure to their literary heritage has meant that Afro-Uruguayan writers can only look to those outside their community as referents.[6]

This said, it appears that those in control of the field of cultural production in Uruguay and the rest of Latin America have traditionally made a distinction between an official, cultured literature and works of a literary nature that they see as based in the folkloric, oral traditions of Afro-descendants and indigenous peoples (Rama 121, 131). In highlighting this separation, Ángel Rama seems to be calling for ways in which the latter traditions could be recognized as making literary contributions and also for ways of establishing dialogue between the two (or more) traditions (121–22, 131). Even as I question Rama's use of the term "folklore," I recognize the fact that he made these pronouncements more than thirty years ago. Thus, one may assume that the issues he addressed would now be non-existent; that is, such distinctions between what is considered literature versus folklore, with the former holding sway over the latter, would no longer exist. However, recent research indicates that, at least in Uruguay, Afro-descendant literature still receives inadequate recognition, since in two key areas of legitimation—course syllabi and general literary anthologies—they are yet to be included. In fact, very few writers actually manage to get their work published either locally or abroad (Persico 89, 91). Even those who are published may still be marginalized within the literary field since their works may not be in general circulation.

One example of this is Cristina Rodríguez Cabral's anthology *Memoria y Resistencia* (Memory and Resistance) (2004). The fact that this work is not available in Uruguayan book stores is due in part to the complex nature of the field of literary production, especially seeing that it was published by a small publishing house in the Dominican Republic. Within the complex field mentioned earlier, writers and their works are promoted in various ways, thereby gaining recognition. Rodríguez Cabral's desire for legitimation as a writer is no doubt one of the reasons she left her homeland to study and reside in the United States. Nevertheless, she claims that despite her membership in the Association of Uruguayan Writers, she is still virtually unacknowledged in Uruguay outside of the black community.[7]

The Afro-Uruguayan writer's quest for recognition goes back to the nineteenth century. Jacinto Ventura de Molina could be considered the father of Afro-descendant letters in Uruguay. His writing was varied and included works of an autobiographical nature, petitions to local, governmental, and international sovereigns, as well as legal documents. In colonial Uruguay, Ventura de Molina was ridiculed, and his work was treated with contempt. Fortunately, some of Ventura de Molina's works have survived and are now preserved in Montevideo's National Library. William Acree and Alex Borucki's 2008 publication of some of these writings has now made them available to a wider readership. It is noteworthy that Molina is finally being granted the legitimation he so desperately sought in his lifetime. This has been made possible through the recent scholarship of Acree and Borucki, and also that of Alejandro Gortázar and George Reid Andrews.

Afro-descendant letters in Uruguay continued in the nineteenth and into the twentieth century with the publication of a variety of periodicals like *La Conservación*, *La Propoganda*, and *El Progresista*.[8] The period between the 1930s and 1950s was one of particular fecundity in Afro-descendant letters in Uruguay. During this period journals like *Nuestra Raza*, *Rumbo Cierto*, and *Revista Uruguaya* were among the many periodicals that published the viewpoints and literary works of Afro-descendants in Uruguay about matters related to their own social situation as well as international issues. They also served as channels for the dissemination of Afro-descendant culture and identity. In *Afro-Uruguayan Literature: Post-Colonial Perspectives* (2003), Marvin A. Lewis comments on the important function of these periodicals: "[They] are important, not only because they provided an outlet for Afro-Uruguayan authors to publish, but they also afforded citizens an opportunity to express their opinions about themselves in a society which often denied them the same rights and privileges as to other citizens in the Switzerland of South America" (29).

These periodicals are no longer in existence, and Lewis points to lack of support and apathy on the part of the Afro-descendant collective as reasons for their demise (32–33). It is clear that the social uplifting of the Afro-Uruguayan collective was the goal of the organizations that produced the journals of that era. It is not surprising, though, given their socio-economic condition, that the very ones to whom the journals were directed and to whom the organizations looked for support could not really contribute to the sustained viability of these organs. It does appear that a few from outside the black community did support these journals (Andrews 99). It is relatively safe to surmise, however, that such support was the exception rather than the norm. The literary works of Afro-Uruguayan writers of the period were not deemed worthy of general legitimation. They were only published in the journals of the black press and in anthologies dedicated specifically to Afro-descendant writing like Ildefonso Pereda Valdés's *Antología de la poesía negra americana* (1936).

Despite the challenges it faced, Afro-Uruguayan literature flourished. Writers like Pilar Barrios, Carlos Cardozo Ferreira, and Virginia Brindis de Salas were among those who contributed to the literary tradition of the period (Lewis 78–93). Were theirs perhaps the works that Rama referred to as "folklore"? Many of these works did indeed subscribe to a black aesthetic, rooted as they were in drum culture, with a tendency to invoke ethnic memory and to draw attention to the socio-cultural realities of the history and contemporary experience of blacks in the Americas.

The historical moment in which the black literary tradition was developing in Uruguay is of great significance. The second decade of the twentieth century was a period in which Uruguay was developing its national imaginary as the Switzerland of America, with Montevideo as the Athens of the River Plate region (Blanco 13). There was no place for the descendants of enslaved peoples in this national imaginary. It is quite likely, therefore, that in placing Afro-descendant writing in the category of folklore, those responsible for legitimizing literature at the time were successful in keeping it out of general circulation. These works were therefore not deemed worthy of inclusion in anthologies of the nation's literature; neither were they taught in academic institutions nor published by the mainstream media.

Despite their exclusion from the literary canons of the period, the writers of the mid-twentieth century were anything but insular in their focus. In addition to writing the Afro-Uruguayan social experience, they also treated themes that post-negritude writers continue to explore, like the brotherhood of man ("A la ribera Americana" by Virginia Brindis de Salas) and the global plight of the poor ("Voces sin eco" by Pilar Barrios).[9] Even though contemporary writers do not neglect to focus on issues of identity, ethnic memory, and spirituality they continue to expand their thematic focus to include feminist and other social issues that extend beyond the black community. This leads to further consideration of the degree to which Afro-descendant literature has been legitimized in Uruguay.

Various factors contribute to the level of legitimation literary works receive. Interactions among a variety of agents determine the level of recognition of literary works. Publication by a major publishing house, the receipt of critical attention, and inclusion in the general anthologies of national literature and in course syllabi at the secondary and tertiary levels all contribute to that end. Works that are thus legitimized receive further recognition when they win literary prizes. The question that demands an answer is whether the works of contemporary Afro-Uruguayan writers have as yet succeeded in penetrating the socio-cultural barriers that have heretofore kept them on the fringes of their nation's literary tradition.

The academy grants legitimacy through inclusion in course syllabi and anthologies and through the critical attention it gives these works. These sources of legitimation are, however, limited to certain small sections of the society. So far, Afro-Uruguayan literature has not been able to make a significant impact on that country's literary sector. Is it perhaps because of what one academic refers to as a general disinterest in academic and dominant literary circles with regard to Afro-Uruguayan literature?[10] Afro-Uruguayans and those with an interest in their literature recognize the value of this aspect of their culture. Nevertheless, given the challenges they face, it appears that in cases where Afro-descendants find themselves in positions where they could negotiate or lobby for legitimation, they have chosen to pick their battles, so to speak. Their more pressing negotiations in recent years have been focused on constitutional and other reforms that they feel are more urgent to the overall well-being of Afro-Uruguayans.

Afro-Uruguayan writers, especially poets, are on a continual quest for recognition by the wider society. A survey of anthologies of Uruguayan literature over the last twenty-five years reveals that their work is yet to make its way into general anthologies of Uruguayan poetry and is confined to special interest anthologies like the *Antología de poetas negros uruguayos* (Britos Serrat, 1990) and products of literary workshops. In the area of prose, the situation is a little different. *El cuento uruguayo: Narradores uruguayos de hoy* (Benavides et al., 2002) is one anthology that includes the work of the Afro-Uruguayan writer Jorge Chagas. So far, though, his legitimation has not extended to the Uruguayan Academy. In fact, at least up to 2009, the same could be said for all Afro-Uruguayan writers, since Uruguay's University of the Republic did not include the works of any Afro-Uruguayan writers in the courses on Uruguayan and Latin American literature that it taught from 2006 through 2009 (Persico 96). One could only assume that these years' syllabi reflect a tradition of exclusion from certain sectors of the cultural landscape. Such exclusion may have its roots in the aforementioned cultural capital of dominant society that may manifest itself in a general disinterest in this aspect of Afro-Uruguayan culture, possibly as a result of a lack of understanding of the aesthetics that inform it. The latter point receives more attention later in this chapter.

The uneven nature of "the field of cultural production" is therefore very evident in the case of Afro-Uruguayan writers. Many have not published their works. As one Afro-Uruguayan writer and culture worker states, "many of these writers [live and] die in obscurity" (Leguizamón qtd. in Persico 87). Their personal socio-economic deficiencies and the lack of mediators, whether academics, publishing agents, or political and cultural workers within the Afro-descendant community, are among the challenges Afro-descendant writers in Uruguay face. However, this is not to say that the Afro-descendant literary culture goes totally unacknowledged in Uruguay.

As mentioned above, Jorge Chagas's work is included in *El cuento uruguayo* (Benavides et al.), and he has also won a number of prizes for his works with a historico-biographical focus.[11] In 2003 and 2004, for instance, he was the recipient of national and municipal prizes for his work *Gloria y Tormento: La novela de José Leandro Andrade* (2003) based on the life of the famed Afro-Uruguayan footballer of the early to mid-twentieth century, José Leandro de Andrade. *Pacheco: La trama oculta del poder* (2005), *Banco la caja obrera: Una Historia, 1905–2001 (2009)*, and *Guillermo Chifflet:*

El Combate de la Pluma (2011), works he coauthored with Gustavo Trullen, received honorable mention (in the case of the first of the three) and national literary prizes in the category of unpublished historical essays in the years 2007, 2008, and 2010, respectively. The recognition Chagas has received to date is indeed commendable. However, it contrasts in some ways with that of his compatriots who write poetry. One of these is Miguel Ángel Duarte López.

Duarte López, a poet who writes in Spanish and Portuguese, has published to date at least ten volumes of poetry. Seven of these were published in Uruguay and three in Brazil. He has received literary honors in Brazil (2003, 2004, 2005, and 2009) and Portugal (2000).[12] In 2008, 2009, and 2011 he was one of the recipients of the "Premio Victoria" in Uruguay. These awards are given by a group of non-governmental associations dedicated to the arts and social work. According to the official website of the Premio Victoria, the prizes are awarded in recognition of those who work hard in their fields, seeking in their own ways to transform society, and whose work often goes unrecognized.[13] Subsequent to this private honor, in May 2011, City Councilor Daniel Martínez petitioned the municipality of Montevideo for Duarte López's work to be officially recognized as part of that city's cultural heritage. In November of that very year, while not granting the councilor's initial request on the basis of the non-existence of legal regulations for conferring such awards, the city's executives agreed to declare Duarte López's poetry of municipal interest.[14] This is, of course, an important step in the area of legitimation of Afro-descendant literature in Uruguay, especially seeing that it is from an official source. It is important to remember that writers operate within an uneven cultural field. Many Afro-Uruguayan writers who reside in their homeland may be unable to finance the publication of their own works. They may also lack access to the networks of mediators necessary to propel them into the realm of legitimation. In addition to these socio-economic factors, one cannot ignore the issue of genre. One could rightly question whether the tardiness in Duarte López's recognition is not due to the literary genre in which he expresses himself, namely poetry.

Lyric poetry has always enjoyed an elite status when compared to its more oral, folkloric, performative sister genre. Performative genres of poetry have enjoyed increased visibility especially since the US spoken-word poetry revolution of the 1990s (Arancibia qtd. in Paredes par. 4). Latin America has not been immune to this trend. Medellin's International Poetry Festival in Colombia and the "Festival de Poesía en Voz Alta" organized by the Casa del Lago in Mexico are only two examples of attempts to remove poetry from some of its more hallowed spaces and make it more accessible to a wider audience. The latter festival also strives to showcase the various dimensions of the genre (visual, musical, technological, performative, etc.) as it continues to evolve. The increasing popularity of this kind of poetry may perhaps have an impact on the consumption of published works that may appeal to more elite or academic readerships. This was supposedly the goal of the US spoken-word poets of the 1980s and 1990s (Arancibia qtd. in Paredes par. 4). Reading attitudes and preferences can also affect the legitimation of literary works.

A 2009 survey of cultural consumption in Uruguay reveals that in a society in which 24.5 percent of the population reads various books during any given year, only 10.9 percent read poetry (Dominzaín et al. 49, 51). Short stories and novels are the preferred genres. Given the decreased popularity in the consumption of *any* poetry, it is not difficult to understand the challenges that Afro-descendant writers who seek to compete in this particular field face. Like their forefathers of the nineteenth and early-twentieth centuries, they are attempting to show that they have the cultural capital that allows them to express themselves using a written genre, one that has been the preserve of the "elite." Like that of their forefathers, their work enjoys only limited consumption. However, some may argue that unlike their forefathers, their race has very little or nothing to do with the current level of consumption of their work. Nevertheless, perceptions concerning who is or who is not endowed with the cultural capital necessary to participate in certain fields no doubt continue to play a role in decisions made at the level of the mediators in the cultural field. Also, because there appears to be a preference for the performances of minority cultures, those who engage in other areas of culture not geared toward such performance may find it more difficult to receive legitimation since it tends to be more readily granted to other performance-based cultural forms.

The *Candombe* is a performance-based, Afro-derived musical form that has received the highest level of legitimation possible in Uruguay. The UN report cited earlier draws attention to those aspects of Afro-Uruguayan culture that are readily visible within the society, i.e., drums, dance, and religion (par. 26). This is not to say that it was always a favored genre in that society. A closer look at the evolution of this cultural form indicates that it moved from being taboo to becoming the mainstream of Uruguayan society and culture.

The Africans who were enslaved in Uruguay brought with them various cultural traditions from their continental homelands. Among these was a musical form, linked to a dramatic dance performance, that has survived and evolved and is today considered Uruguay's national music. The *Candombe* is a drum performance that has become an everyday reality of Uruguayan life. In fact, Coriú Ahoranián suggests that by the end of the twentieth century the very word *Candombe* had become synonymous with Uruguayan identity (99). The drum rhythms of this cultural form also provide the foundation for a large part of the country's popular music. *Candombe*'s trajectory has not been without struggle. Argentinian journalist Marie Trigona recounts that police records from the early 1800s reveal efforts on the part of members of Montevideo's white upper class to repress and even ban *Candombe* performances altogether (par. 7). Dominant society's negative view of Afro-descendant cultural manifestations had a profound impact on Afro-Uruguayans, especially those who sought upward social mobility. In *Los Candombes de los Reyes*, Tomás Olivera Chirimiri and Juan Antonio Varese trace *Candombe*'s evolution from the mid-eighteenth to the end of the nineteenth century when it went into a period of decline. They attribute its decline to factors like the large numbers of Afro-descendants who died in the wars of independence and a rejection of Afro-descendant cultural traditions by the younger generations. Their reflection on the latter phenomenon reads: "[L]os jóvenes nacidos libertos, para superar la triste condición de sus mayores optaban por rechazar las prácticas de la raza e imitar las costumbres y bailes de los blancos" (In order to rise above the sad condition of their elders, the youths who were born into freedom opted to reject the practices of their race and to imitate the customs and dances of whites) (44). As they strove to gain acceptance as full citizens in society, Afro-Uruguayans of that generation, no doubt conditioned by the prejudices of dominant society, chose to leave behind the practices and traditions they considered to be hindrances to their quest for socio-cultural acceptance. The cultural capital Afro-Uruguayans acquired through schooling had an impact on how some of these individuals viewed their own cultural traditions. Their editorials in the black press of that era strongly condemned these traditional practices since they saw them as preventing the black population from advancing in society (Ayesterán 154). Such reactions of Afro-Uruguayans who were striving to enter the middle class are not surprising. Indeed, cultural whitening and assimilation into the dominant society were considered essential to overcoming social marginalization.

It is not surprising therefore that some Afro-Uruguayans may have felt they were being pressured to reject these practices. A cursory look at snippets of commentaries from Uruguayan newspapers of the mid to late nineteenth century shows that for the most part, the attitude of dominant society toward *Candombe* drumming and the accompanying festivities in which Afro-Uruguayans engaged during the Christmas season ranged from condescension and sarcasm to outright derision.[15] *Candombe* therefore faced challenges both from within and without the Afro-descendant community. Its survival is due in large part to its accommodation of the changes imposed on it. Various commentators have cited the enactment of municipal legislations in Montevideo in the late nineteenth and early twentieth centuries that were aimed at confining the *Candombe* to carnival festivities.[16] If fact, Abril Trigo sees this phase of *Candombe*'s evolution as one in which it became "a purely recreational dance perpetuated through carnival" (Ayesterán 101–09, qtd. in Trigo 717).[17] *Candombe*'s eventual survival and growth is linked to a number of factors that include its acculturation and commodification beginning in the late nineteenth century, its incorporation into carnival, and its politicization by giving voice to those on whom the dictatorial regime of the 1970s and 1980s sought to impose silence (Trigo 718–25). According to Trigo: "Carnival culture, traditionally kept on the margins of a Europeanized society, thus acquires a legitimacy that transcends the physical and chronological boundaries of carnival. *Candombe* was to be danced and listened to all-year round, in every ball-room, on any radio, on any street corner. *Candombe* trespassed the secluded boundaries of the Palermo and Sur neighborhoods . . . and reterritorialized the whole city" (725).[18]

Trigo goes on to describe Montevideo as "carnivalized" and "Candombezed." She explains how poverty and the dictatorship's negative policies of gentrification helped to force the music out of its original home-spaces and into spaces in which it had previously been severely restricted. She sees this "reterritorialization" as a testimony to the spirit of survival of a previously marginalized culture (725).

The appropriation and commercialization of Afro-derived cultural manifestations is in no way limited to Uruguay. Wherever possible, dominant society manipulates Afro-derived culture to maintain its authority. For instance, as Michael Hanchard points out in *Orpheus and Power*, in societies where a dominant racial group seeks "to *lead* as well as to *rule*," the dominant group sees the rearticulation of the cultural practices of minority groups as vital to their maintaining control. They do this by either accommodating or denigrating these practices (140). In the case of Afro-derived musical forms like the Brazilian *Samba* and Uruguayan *Candombe*, it is evident that their commercialization and nationalization has allowed them to be under the control of dominant society. In this way they are no longer seen as threats to the status quo. Not all are blind to these maneuvers. Graciela Leguizamón is one who questions the objectives behind *Candombe's* appropriation. She wonders whether it is not another form of rendering invisible those she sees as the legitimate owners of this cultural practice.[19]

The *Candombe* that Trigo mentions is not just the drumming but also the popular music that has as its foundational rhythms those derived from the *Candombe* drums. This popular music has evolved tremendously and is now a fusion of rock, pop, soul, and other musical genres. Of note, though, is the trajectory of one of the now most acclaimed Afro-Uruguayan musicians, Rubén Rada, the recipient of a 2011 Grammy award for lifetime achievement in his field. In the early years of his career, Rada faced criticism similar to that directed toward his compatriot of the nineteenth century, Jacinto Ventura de Molina. Aharonián reveals that from the 1960s through the 1990s, "el sutil racismo uruguayo lo segregará como personaje simpático y gracioso, lo confinará a figura admirada por un reducido círculo de consumidores, y no le permitirá alcanzar un público realmente masivo hasta la década del 1990" (Subtle Uruguayan racism would segregate him as a likeable and funny personality, it would confine him to the realm of someone admired by a small circle of consumers, and would not permit him to reach a truly massive public until the decade of the 1990s) (103). Aharonián also mentions that this musical genre is the patrimony not only of Afro-Uruguayans. It has generally been performed and promoted mainly by non-Afro-descendants (100). In similar fashion, *Candombe* (drumming/drum calls) is not confined to the Afro-descendant community. George Reid Andrews, for instance, points out that white musicians and drummers have played a key role in the evolution of *Candombe* since its beginnings as a musical genre (125). Even though, as Andrews notes, large sections of neighborhoods have been drawn to practice sessions and performances since the beginning of the twentieth century, he asserts that even greater numbers of whites began flocking to the *comparsas* from the 1990s through the early 2000s (111–12, 124–25). *Candombe* has become so much a part of Uruguayan culture that beginning in 2006, December 3 has been celebrated in Uruguay as "El Día Nacional de Candombe, la Cultura Afro-Uruguaya y la Equidad Racial" (National Day of Candombe, Afro-Uruguayan Culture, and Racial Equality).[20] Additionally, in 2009 Uruguay successfully submitted "The Candombe and its Socio-Cultural Space: A Community Practice" to UNESCO for recognition on the Representative List of the Intangible Cultural Heritage of Humanity.

The evolution of *Candombe's* legitimation supports Yúdice's position that the economic restructuring, neoliberalism, and globalization of the last thirty-odd years have had an impact on culture so that instead of its previous function as an ideological tool for inculcating "civilized" norms, it now operates as a resource that promotes economic growth and seeks to find resolutions to sociopolitical issues. The result of this new framework in which culture operates sees formerly denigrated minority cultural production playing an important role in the overall well-being of society (Yúdice 9, 17, 25). *Candombe* benefits the Uruguayan society in various ways. For one, it allows Uruguay to present itself as a multicultural society.[21] This multicultural dimension makes the promotion of that country's month-long carnival celebration even more attractive to tourists. Websites that advertise Uruguayan carnival highlight the important role of *Candombe* and Afro-descendant culture in the annual celebrations.[22] For instance, Uruguay's Ministry of Tourism and Sports' website highlights *Candombe's* role in the country's carnival festivities, marketing it as a main component of the country's "cultural tourism" product. A report emanating from the office of the Uruguayan president indicates that in January of 2012, some 470,000 tourists visited the South American nation. This number represents a slight increase over the 2011 figure of 457,000. These visitors contributed $435,000 to the nation's economy ("En enero" par. 2 and 4). The report (written before the end of February) goes on to state that for the first two weeks of February, 197,000 tourists had already visited. It indicates, too, that the above figures did *not* take into consideration those who may have visited for the carnival festivities ("En enero" par. 9). These numbers do show the large percentage of visitors who visit this nation of fewer than three million inhabitants during the carnival months. This previously denigrated Afro-derived cultural form has therefore secured its place nationally and internationally as a legitimate cultural product of Uruguay not only through the resilience of its performers but, more importantly, through its proponents at the official level who recognize its value in supporting Uruguay's economy and its new-found multiculturalism. The superficial engagement of non-blacks in Afro-descendant culture is one way in which the state can manage culture to ensure the maintenance of the status quo. This is, of course, an aspect of the subtle racism that Afro-Uruguayans describe as endemic in their society.

The legitimation of an Afro-derived cultural practice is not unique to Uruguay. The Brazilian *Samba* also moved from marginalization to becoming a symbol of national identity. Even though some of the factors that contributed to the *Samba*'s legitimation are different from those that legitimized the *Candombe*, the interactions and negotiations among musicians and mediators, including intellectuals and government officials, were of vital importance in the nationalization of both of these genres.[23] To cite just a few of the similarities: both genres have their roots in Afro-derived religious-based performances, they were traditionally practiced in poor communities that were home to large Afro-descendant populations, and they were originally repressed by those who had the power to do so. Much of these nations' popular music is strongly rooted in these Afro-derived genres. It was mainly through carnival that these genres were disseminated to wider audiences. In the same way that Uruguay succeeded in having the *Candombe* drum performance recognized on the UNESCO Representative List of Intangible Cultural Heritage, in 2008, Brazil did the same for its Bahian *Samba de Roda*, the form that is believed to be the root of the urban *Samba*. These are but two examples of state support for performance-oriented minority cultural forms.

Afro-Uruguayan responses have been ambivalent to the differing levels of legitimation that the various manifestations of their culture receive. While some are pleased that the *Candombe* has been legitimized and is now readily recognized as the national culture, they feel the true meaning and symbolism behind the form is lost on many who practice it.[24] Some have lamented the lack of such legitimation for other cultural manifestations. In *Multiculturalismo en el Uruguay*, for instance, Javier Díaz of the Asociación de Cultura y Sociedad Uruguaya Negra (ACSUN) states:

> [U]na cosa que no está bien difundida son las letras, tenemos poetisas y dramaturgos afrodescendientes, como Emilio Cardozo, Beatriz Santos, y Cristina Rodríguez Cabral. Ellos son los que actualmente están trabajando. Otra de las manifestaciones

más valederas, que ha traspasado fronteras al igual que las letras son los artistas plásticos.

> One thing people generally do not know has to do with (Afro-descendant) writing, we have Afro-descendant poets and playwrights like Emilio Cardozo, Beatriz Santos, and Cristina Rodríguez Cabral. They are the ones who are working at present. Another of our most legitimate manifestations that has overcome barriers similar to that of our writing is our plastic arts. (112–13)

In similar fashion, historian Oscar Montaño recognizes that linking Afro-descendant culture in Uruguay mainly to carnival and *Candombe* could well be reinforcing stereotypes that limit Afro-descendant culture to song and dance performances. He nevertheless appreciates the cultural education that the *comparsas de Candombe* provide, since they are among the few spaces available to Afro-Uruguayan youths to learn about aspects of their cultural heritage.[25] Recent developments in Uruguay indicate the opening of another avenue for such education to take place, that is, through the *Casa de la Cultura Afro-Uruguaya*, inaugurated on December 3, 2011, in Montevideo. Its objectives are to collect, promote, and disseminate the different manifestations of Afro-Uruguayan culture, and also to provide a place where the community can meet and develop. It seeks to promote the integration of Afro-Uruguayans within society and foster the values of solidarity in fighting against racism and discrimination among the entire population ("Festejos" par. 2). The project was financed by the *Agencia Española de Co-operación Internacional para el Desarrollo* (AECID) (Spanish Cooperation Agency for International Development) with the Spanish Cultural Center playing an integral role in the project's implementation. At the *Casa's* inauguration, Marvin Lewis's *Cultura y Literatura Afro-Uruguaya* was launched. This Spanish-language translation of Lewis's work *Afro-Uruguayan Literature* (2003), supported by Spanish funding, was published under the auspices of a new publishing entity, the *Casa de la Cultura Afro-Uruguaya*. Graciela Leguizamón concludes her review of this publication with the affirmation that the work provides material from an authorized source that could be used to teach Afro-Uruguayan youths about their rich literary tradition ("Una Mirada" par. 9). This boost to Afro-Uruguayan literature is important. The establishment of a publishing entity that will focus on the publication of Afro-Uruguayan works now makes it more possible for works that were previously confined to notebooks and to oral expression to be enjoyed by larger audiences.

Even as one applauds the establishment of the *Casa*, one cannot help but wonder if it may not be another means of compartmentalizing Afro-Uruguayan culture within the society. With regard to the publishing arm, such compartmentalization could only mean further marginalization. It brings to mind a desire Cristina Cabral expressed two years before the *Casa* became a reality that black writing in Latin America would be seen as part of the regional corpus without the classification "afro."[26] I interpret Cabral to be saying that dominant society uses this classification in a restrictive way. It is this type of restrictive classification that has confined the literary production of Afro-descendants to special interest anthologies. Of course, time will be the judge of the success of this publishing arm of the *Casa de la Cultura Afro-Uruguaya*. It will serve as a test of whether the field of cultural production in Uruguay is ready to accept the works this entity publishes as part of the Uruguayan literary corpus and fully engage with them critically and within the academy.

In addition to the issue of mediation, the question of literary aesthetics is sometimes one that dominant society uses to further marginalize Afro-descendant works. The history of black letters in the Americas has its beginnings in the desire among blacks to prove their worth as human beings and as rightful citizens of their societies. They have therefore generally tended not to limit their literary production to subject matter that only treats issues relating to their culture and experiences but have sought also to explore themes like love, death, and nature that some may classify as "universal."[27] Given Uruguay's history with regard to matters of race, it appears that black writers have often not expressed their quarrels with the state in an overt fashion. They have chosen to appropriate the same subtlety that characterizes the racism they face in society on a daily basis as their counter-discourse. In discussing how Afro-Uruguayan women writers treat racial discourse in their work, Graciela Leguizamón asserts that very few adopt an overt discourse of negritude. She explains that one should not see this as a rejection by these women writers of their blackness, but rather as a defense mechanism resulting in part from their acculturation, which has left many of them ignorant of their literary heritage. She explains further:

> Hay varias escritoras y poetas que escriben no desde su lugar como sujeto uruguayas y negras, pero en los textos manifiestan sus sufrimientos, angustias y postergaciones. La voz poética de estas escritoras y poetas, no está lejana de su contexto étnico sino de su situación socioeconómica. Es su contradiscurso contra el status quo al discurso oficial del Uruguay sin tensiones étnico-económicas.[28]

> There are many women writers and poets, who write, not from their place as subject, i.e., black, Uruguayan, but their texts are manifestations of their suffering, anguish, and failures. The poetic voice of these writers and poets is not separated from their ethnic context but rather from their socio-economic situation. It is their counter-discourse against the status quo to Uruguay's official discourse without ethnic-economic tensions.

Leguizamón's comments shed light on those of Carole Mills Young with respect to a change in Cristina Cabral's writing from primarily works that dealt with love and those that were introspective in nature to a style that exhibits greater sensibility to matters regarding gender and race. This change began since her sojourn in Brazil (1988) and her residence in the United States (1997) (Mills Young 220). Cabral herself admits to the tremendous impact life in the United States has had on her psyche. However, she explains that, in reality, many critics tend to focus on her more militant works and that, as such, the greater part of her repertoire that treats themes of love and emotions has been left unexamined.[29] Despite the explanations these writers advance, evidence still exists of a counter-discourse that is less than subtle. I now examine this issue more closely.

Cristina Rodríguez Cabral started writing poetry as a child. Her first volume of poetry "Desde mi trinchera" (1993) was published in Uruguay by Mundo Afro. In 2004 she published "Memoria y Resistencia." Published by Editorial Manatí in the

Dominican Republic, this volume is a compilation of her other (published and un-published) collections. The poems in the latter volume vary in content and form with themes that range from the personal and religious to the political. Rodríguez Cabral currently resides in the United States, where she is a college professor. In the two poems I analyze below, Rodríguez Cabral raises issues pertinent to being an alienated minority in society and takes a revisionist look at the five-hundred-year anniversary of the European arrival in the Americas.

The poem "Montevideo" is structured as a statement of familiarity, followed by a question that captures a feeling of perplexity. It then closes with an affirmation of loyalty. The different perspectives expressed are captured in the unequal lengths of the two stanzas. The verbs in the first stanza are governed by a third person singular sub-ject that creates distance between the speaker and the addressee: a distance that brings about feelings of alienation. The poetic voice speaks directly to the city Montevideo. However, whereas the speaking voice is individual in the first stanza, it changes to a collective voice, expressed through the first person plural, in stanza two. This collective voice pledges loyalty to the city. It seeks to remind the city of the previous close rela-tionship they enjoyed through the use of verbs associated with the stages of life: "nacer, crecer / amar, sufrir, / morir / y resucitar" (to be born, to grow up / to love, to suffer, / to die / and to be reborn) (1. 1–4). The placement of verbs in the infinitive at the end of the first line and in the succeeding lines brings such actions into closer focus. The loss of the close relationship has led to feelings of alienation for which the poetic voice blames the city: "hoy me mira con extraños ojos / me apunta con su dedo crítico / y me condena al exilio" (today it looks at me with strange eyes / it points its critical finger at me / and condemns me to exile) (1. 5–7). The second stanza begins with a question. The poetic persona asks the city why it has changed: "¿Por qué olvidaste / tu antigua sonrisa / de niña mimada / asomándose a la vida?" (Why did you forget? / your old smile / of a spoiled girl / leaning forward towards life?) (1.8–11). The image of a spoiled child on the verge of her coming-of-age suggests that at one time the city was the recipient of attention that aided its growth and development. The nature of the question asked in the above lines, along with the repetition of [a] and [m] sounds in the words, create a plaintive tone that highlights the persona's feelings of aliena-tion. A declaration of allegiance now follows in which the collective voice insists on defending the city, despite being subjected to negative forces: "el horror, la angustia, / y el desencanto" (the horror, the anguish / and the disenchantment) (1.12–13). The city is represented metaphorically in these final lines as a flower. The collective voice pledges to defend each petal of this flower: "no han de ser/obstáculos suficientes / para impedirnos defender / cada pétalo / de tu murguera flor" (they won't be / sufficient obstacles / to stop us from defending / each petal / of your carnival flower) (1.14–18). The description of the city as "murguera flor" could have a variety of interpretations. The adjective *murguera* derives from *murga*. This now popular musical theater is an integral part of the Uruguayan carnival celebrations. The farcical nature of this theater and the elaborate costumes and face painting characteristic of the genre could be a negative criticism of the society, a description of it as a façade or spectacle. [30] Addition-ally, the *murga* has historically been the white working-class contribution to carnival, one that did not allow black participation (Ahoranián 107). The poetic voice therefore seems to be engaged in a further censuring of a society that for centuries has projected a white image of itself. The space of the city is used as a synecdoche to represent the nation, in the same way that the first person of the first stanza is really the collective subject that expresses itself in the second stanza. The alienated victims of the society's negative forces are still determined to claim their places as its citizens by way of their loyalty.

In "500 años después" a poem that purportedly treats the five-hundred-year anniversary of the European arrival in the Americas, the focus of attention is on the contrast between official, state discourse with regard to the country's contemporary reality and life as seen through the eyes of the nation's racial minorities. The work is revisionist in its contestation of the discourse of civilization and progress that supposedly resulted from colonization.

The opening line of the poem puts the spotlight on Uruguay's dire economic state in the late twentieth century. The adjectives *seco* (dry) and *caliente* (hot) coupled with *verano* (summer) emphasize the harshness of the conditions the country and its inhabitants are experiencing. The line that follows adds to the dismal picture with the alliteration that the words *sombrío* and *sombras* create. The nation's capital, Montevideo, is a place of "somber shadows," devoid of people ("sombrío / sombras / vacío de gente"). The two Latin words that comprise the word *Montevideo* mean "I see a mountain/hill." In line three, however, the poet, in repeating this word, divides it into three: "MONTE / VI / DEO." The repetition and capitalization can be read as simply a way of focusing attention on the capital, the seat of power. In yet another reading, the two words that are created by the division of the word *video* result in a religious connotation, since *vi* derives from a word meaning "strength" and *deo* means "by God" or "belonging to God." Regardless of the reading one chooses to accept, it is clear that the discourse that emanates from this location (Montevideo) is considered by those who control it to be of great importance. The nation's official discourse as heard on the radio gives directions on ways of coping with inflation and heralds an end to the nation's economic woes: "Hay que apretarse el cinturón . . . se va a acabar" (We have to tighten our belts . . . it's going to end). The questioning of official discourse is immediate as the line that follows this prediction questions whether indeed it has ended: "- se acabó?" (is it over?) (1.10).

The capital city, pictured in stanza one as hot, dry, devoid of people, and a place of extreme economic pressures, is the place where the festivities to mark the five-hundred-year anniversary of European arrival in the Americas takes place. Stanza two begins with the word *Montevideo* and points out that this city is the headquarters for these festivities. The state's sanctioning of these festivities is linked to its version of the colonial encounter: "500 años de que . . . nos descubrieron / 500 años de que . . . nos civilizaron" (500 years since . . . they discovered us / 500 years since . . . they civilized us") (1.15–16). The use of the object pronoun *nos* indicates that the poetic persona is simply repeating this official version of history. It is clear, though, that the persona does not subscribe to the official discourse and is in fact critical of it. This criticism extends beyond the history of European colonization of the Americas to neocolonial issues as the work alludes to a new colonizing entity, one that has the nation's inhabitants in conditions similar to the indigenous peoples of the fifteenth century: "recibiendo a las carabelas / desnudos, hambrientos, pintados, / con plumas en la cabeza / esperando los nuevos espejitos" (receiving the caravels / naked, hungry, painted, / with

feathers on their heads / waiting for their new mirrors) (1.23–26). The image of naked natives awaiting valueless handouts points to the control modern-day colonizing
entities have over developing nations.

In addition to this critique of neo-colonialism, the poem also draws attention
to the impact of colonization on the land and its people and gives insight into how
little has changed over the five-hundred-year period. In stanza two, for instance, the
land is described as ruined and stained with Indian blood and black sweat: "500 años
después / de arrancado la tierra, / Quinientos años teñidos / de sangre indígena . . . y
de sudor negro" (500 years after / losing the land, / Five hundred years stained / with
indigenous blood . . . and black sweat) (1. 17–20). The verbs *arrancar* and *teñir* are
strong indicators of the atrocities that took place in the name of "discovery" and "civilization." The final two stanzas of the poem suggest that despite the passage of time,
not much has changed over the five-hundred-year period. Those who will celebrate are
described in this way: "como buenos / hijos de . . . inmigrantes y esclavos, / recibiendo
a las carabelas / desnudos, hambrientos, pintados, / con plumas en la cabeza / esperando los nuevos espejitos" (like good / sons of . . . immigrants and slaves, / receiving
the caravels / naked, hungry, painted, / with feathers in their heads / waiting for their
new mirrors) (1.22–26). Throughout stanza two, ellipses draw attention to the official versions of history and allow the discerning reader to fill in the blanks with the
unwritten/silenced versions of colonization and its impact on minorities. In addition
to my observation above regarding the persona's mouthing of the official discourse
about progress and civilization, the ellipses communicate a sarcastic tone. The poem
also suggests that those who act on the dictates of the state and join in the celebration are good citizens: "buenos hijos de . . . la Madre Patria" (good sons of . . . the
Motherland) (1.27) in the eyes of officialdom. Once again the ellipsis separates state
discourse from its criticism. While the state sees those who conform to its dictates
as good citizens, minority discourse condemns them as "hijos de . . ." (sons of . . .).
The condemnatory tone that the ellipsis brings out, in its obvious reference to a well-
known Spanish expletive, makes it clear that non-conformist blacks find themselves at
odds with the state and its official discourse. A post-negritude world-view is evident
in the fact that the work does not limit its focus to blacks. Nevertheless, it does draw
attention to the severity of this group's situation. The final two lines, "Dicen que a los
negros / nos van a lustrar el bronce / de los grilletes y cadenas / que aún conservamos"
(They say that they are going / to polish the bronze of the shackles and chains / that
we blacks still have) (1. 29–32), indicate that blacks are still bound by shackles and
chains. The poem's final words are directly linked to its epigraph, particularly the last
line: "a quinientos años / de la conquista de América / el genocidio indígena / y la
esclavitud africana" (to five hundred years / of the conquest of America / the genocide
of the Indians and the slavery of Africans.)

Cabral's poems therefore speak to the situation of the disenfranchised, alienated,
and oppressed in society. In both poems, the persona is at odds with the state and the
way it presents history or reality. Whereas in the first poem the counter-discourse takes
the form of bringing to light those society has marginalized, in the second, it assumes
a more strident tone as it criticizes official discourse.

The second Uruguayan writer whose work I analyze is Graciela Leguizmón, who
has adopted the pseudonym Gracee Marty. As a writer, broadcaster and cultural

worker, Leguizamón is the creator of the blog *Red de Escritores/as y Creadoress Afro-Uruguayos* (*Redescrea/Redafu*) (Network of Afro-Uruguayan Writers and Creators) and of the project *Libro sin Tapas* (Books without Covers). Leguizamón works tirelessly to promote literature in Uruguay and to bring to light the works of the many whose literary works are unpublished. Her own poems are mainly erotic. She shares her work with the public in her blogs and in hand-made editions that are part of her *Libros sin Tapas* project. She was twice the recipient of the Premio Victoria.[31] In "Sin espejos" the poet moves away from her usual genre to invoke ethnic memory, question history, and reaffirm African identity while at the same time raising questions about the nature of this identity. In four stanzas of unequal length, the poetic persona adopts a collective voice that positions itself in the present, looks back in time to invoke ethnic memory and to question official history, and reflects on the current and future of Afro-descendants in Uruguayan society.

The title of the poem is significant. "Sin espejos" literally means "without mirrors," but this expression can also mean "without role-models." As one reads the poem it is clear that the poetic persona is pointing more to the former meaning than to the latter and is saying that this group of people has not been able to see itself—i.e., really affirm their true Afro-descendant identity—because of what it has been subjected to by dominant society over the centuries.

Stanza one is sixteen lines long, the longest of the poem. It sets the scene in the present and looks back to the past. This stanza begins with a people looking out into emptiness trying to find and make connections with their past. Centuries of history have sought to erase these connections. The present generation has questions with regard to its past: "cómo era la tierra de casa hace milenios, cuál era el sendero del agua / o el prometido rito de la lluvia" (what was the home like milennia ago, what was the waterway / or the promised ritual of the rain) (1. 6–7). Sadly, the questioners do not receive adequate answers. They express their frustration in the words "ya cansada de ensombrecidas respuestas . . ." (already tired of shady responses) (1.16). The reason this group lacks mirrors comes out in line ten, which provides an explanation for their predicament: "si no lo permitieron" (if they did not allow it). The same agents who refuse to allow them to see themselves or know who they are accused of providing a history of shamed silences ("historia es enrojecidos silencios") and shady responses ("ensombrecidas respuestas") (1.16). The ellipses that end stanza one come after the words "ensombrecidas respuestas . . ." They are strategically placed here and in other lines in that stanza. They appear in lines that treat (1) the questioners' queries: "cómo la eternidad en la canción de los ancestros . . ." (what was the eternity in the songs of the ancestors like . . .) (1.8); (2) address the existence of incomplete histories and untold stories: "Son tantos duelos incumplidos, tantos huesos sin su entierro . . ." (so many incomplete mournings, so many unburied bones . . .) (1.9); and (3) highlight attempts to hide the truth, as in the case of the previously quoted line "ya cansada de ensombrecidas respuestas . . ." (already tired of shady responses . . .) (1.16).

The poetic persona expresses the group's challenges as they attempt to reaffirm their identity without adequate knowledge of their past. Their identity is described as uncertain ("incierta") (1.11), and their alienation from the past is emphasized not only in the series of questions posed with regard to the past, but also by means of the affirmation that the only past they possess is that of an oceanic heart ("un corazón oceánico") (1.5). The adjective "oceanic" evokes an image that is closely linked to the African diasporic experience while emphasizing the vastness of the expanse between the current and past situations, as well as the length of time that has transpired since their departure from African shores. Their alienation from their ancestral past is also reflected in the language they now possess. Bearing in mind that language is a marker of ethnic identity, the poetic voice shows that what this group now possesses as language has come about as a result of "migraciones obligadas" (forced migrations) (1.13). The repetition of the word "lengua" in lines thirteen and fourteen, "Migraciones obligadas en la lengua / y nuestra lengua enredada entre mil lenguas" (Forced migrations of the tongue / and our language wrapped up among a thousand languages), only serves to further emphasize ways in which the diasporic experience has affected the identity of those involved.

Those who hold power have now seen fit to lift the veil, so to speak, and allow Afro-descendants more insight into their past. Stanza two, the shortest of the poem, begins with the words "Ahora los faraones remueven las arenas" (Now the Pharoahs stir the sands) (1.17). This present action provides hope for a future reunion of the African ancestors with their descendants: "almas de antiguas africanas en algún puerto / esperan el reconocimiento de los hijos de sus hijos / o de los nietos de sus nietos" (souls of ancient African women await in some port / to welcome the sons of their sons / or the grandsons of their grandsons) (1.18–20). This hope extends into the final stanza. The past, present, and future unite in the eight lines of this stanza. The poetic persona first invokes ethnic memory of the past by referring to the raised voices of those ancestors forced to journey to the shores of the Americas: "de aquellos que también / obligados, en barcos vinieron" (of those who also / came by force in ships) (1.21–22). The punctuation, assonance, and imperfect internal rhyme of "obligados, en barcos" allow for an ominous tone, one that highlights the involuntary nature of the voyage and its tragic outcome. The line that follows presents the image of uprooted wombs: "irreversibles vientres desarraigados" (irreversible rootless wombs) (1.23). This highlights one aspect of the tragedy, drawing attention to the violence, pain, and trauma of their experiences. However, out of this sad past, one from which they emerge with no mementos, they manage to reconstruct a tradition: "que se reconstruyen sin relato, / sin fotografías y sin cuentos" (that they reconstructed without records / without photographs, and without stories) (1.24). The image of the invisible magical eagles, ("mágicas águilas invisibles") (1.24), presents a picture of physical and spiritual fortitude. The eagle's rapid, soaring flight also symbolizes the upward movement that the group hopes to achieve as it moves into the future.

Current and past history are again critiqued in line twenty-six, where the expectation is that this people's history will be brought into the light, out of the distant darkness: "esperando que el viento desempolve / sus historias desde la errante tiniebla" (waiting for the wind to dust the wandering shadows / off of their stories) (1.25–26). Evident here is the contrast between vague, hidden, official history, as critiqued in the first stanza, and one that is more easily seen and in which they can have more confidence. The poem ends with two three-word lines that paint the picture of a hopeful future and provide a contrast with its opening lines, not only because the former are longer, but also because of the sentiments expressed. Whereas at the beginning the personae were pictured looking out into emptiness without mirrors, they are now waiting / expecting / hoping. These last two lines read:

Aquí estamos esperando.	Here we await.
También estamos esperando.	We also hope. (1.27–28)

It is noteworthy that the verb used here, *esperar*, means "to wait," as well as "to hope" and "to expect." Afro-descendants await a future where they can fully affirm their identities. They are also hopefully expecting this to become a reality. The hopeful note on which Gracee Marty ends her poem could be contrasted with the pessimistic tone in Cabral's poems, analyzed above. This may very well be due to the time periods in which these works were written. Whereas Cabral's works were written in the late 1980s and early 1990s, Marty's poem was written toward the end of 2011. The hopeful expectation with which Afro-Uruguayans await a full reaffirmation of their ethnic and cultural identities no doubt extends to the realm of poetry. As one of the many Afro-Uruguayan poets whose work is not included in any major anthology of Uruguayan poetry, Gracee Marty's poem sheds further insight on the history that has had an impact on cultural legitimation and provides a basis of hope for an improved future.

Although the recent developments in Uruguay (such as the various ways in which *Candombe* has been recognized and the establishment of the *Casa de la Cultura Afro-Uruguaya*) seem to point in the direction of greater respect for and recognition of Afro-descendant culture in general, it is important to remember that the way in which a cultural product is consumed plays a crucial role in its legitimation, sometimes even more so than that of its intrinsic quality (Labanyi 15). It is therefore easy to see how *Candombe*, as a product that is consumed in public and private festivities by all strata of the society, is guaranteed legitimacy. *Candombe* in its current form does not question the status quo. In fact, it helps to promote the state's agenda. It allows Uruguay to display its multiculturalism and thereby aids in attracting tourist dollars to the national coffers. The case of literature, particularly poetry, is different. In fact, literature may never be able to attract tourist revenue in the way that carnival and *Candombe* do; therefore, the lack of official legitimation is understandable. Nevertheless, as Gracee Marty's poem suggests, there is hope. Such hope has begun to bear fruit with the Municipality of Montevideo's recognition of Duarte López's works. Additionally, the *Casa de la Cultura Afro-Uruguaya* is committed to developing and promoting the cultural works of Afro-Uruguayans. The fact that this new entity has a publication section augers well for the future visibility of Afro-Uruguayan literature. Additionally, writers like Cristina Rodríguez Cabral, Miguel Angel Duarte, and Jorge Chagas who present their works beyond Uruguayan shores allow for the possibility of what Chagas sees as a probable way for their works to be more fully recognized at home, that is, external legitimation by way of an international literary prize. Until then, however, others like Graciela Leguizamón (Gracee Marty) continue to make these works available to all via websites and personal blogs.

To conclude, it is evident that since the eighteenth century, blacks in Uruguay have striven to show that they possess the cultural capital necessary to produce written works comparable to those of their white compatriots. Their abilities have been constantly denied through open ridicule and the relegation of their work to the realm of folklore, thereby implying that it was not worthy of serious consideration. Poets, especially, seem to have a more difficult time receiving legitimation from official cultural agencies and academic institutions. Despite these challenges and those of a socio-economic nature that many of them face, Afro-Uruguayans continue to produce literary works in various genres. The poems I analyzed above shed light on ways in which Afro-Uruguayan writers challenge a state that has only recently, and in a very limited way, begun taking steps to view their work seriously. Their challenges to the state prove that they do possess the cultural capital necessary to be included in the nation's literary corpus. Do recent developments in Uruguay that are aimed at promoting black culture mean an opening up of the literary field in that country? Or will the Uruguayan state decide to manage black writing so that its survival is only possible through commodification? Only time will provide answers to these questions.

Notes

1. See William G. Acree Jr. and Alex Borucki, *Jacinto Ventura de Molina y los caminos de la escritura negra en el Río de la Plata* (2008) and Alejandro Gortázar, *El licenciado negro: Jacinto Ventura de Molina* (2007).
2. Bourdieu treats this concept in various works, including "Cultural Reproduction and Social Reproduction" (1977), *Distinction: A Social Critique of the Judgement of Taste* (1984), and *The Forms of Capital* (1986).
3. Beatriz Santos Arrascaeta, Personal interview, 27 May 2009.
4. Graciela Leguizamón, "Te daré mi humilde opinión," E-mail correspondence, 7 Dec. 2011.
5. Unless otherwise indicated, all translations are mine.
6. Graciela Leguizamón, "Te daré mi humilde opinión," E-mail correspondence, 7 Dec. 2011.
7. Cristina Rodríguez Cabral, Personal interview, 13 May 2009.
8. The first two periodicals are mentioned in Marvin Lewis's *Afro-Uruguayan Literature: Post-Colonial Perspectives* (2003). George Reid Andrews mentions the latter in *Blackness in a White Nation: A History of Afro-Uruguay* (2010).
9. Marvin Lewis analyzes these poems in *Afro-Hispanic Poetry, 1940–1980* (1983: 14–16, 32–33).
10. Alejandro Gortázar, Personal interview, 26 May 2009.
11. Chagas was also one of Uruguay's representatives at Cuba's 2012 International Book Fair.
12. See blog about Duarte López at *Portal Poeta Blogspot* and his web page on *Red Mundial de Escritores en Español*.
13. *Premio Victoria*. 3 Jan. 2012. <premiovictoria.jimdo.com/premio-victoria/>.
14. The municipality's resolution to consider the petition can be found at *www.juntamvd. gub.uy/es/archivos/decretos/4375–11197.htm*. ("Resolución N⁰·11.197"); see their decision as per Resolution N⁰· 5397/11 at *www.montevideo.gub.uy/asl/sistemas/gestar/resoluci. nsf/0bfcab2a0d22bf960325678d00746391/95485b16811fa76383257961004bea2d? OpenDocument*. ("Resolución N⁰·5397/11").
15. In a section of chapter 2 of Tomás Olivera Chirimini and Juan Antonio Varese's *Los Candombes de Reyes* (2009), they transcribe quotes from the local press that present reactions to Afro-Uruguayan celebrations during the Christmas season.

16. Abril Trigo's "Candombe and the Reterritorialization of Culture" (1993), Oscar Montaño's *Umkhonto* (1997), and Coriú Aharonián's *Músicas populares de Uruguay* (2007) are some who have referred to municipal legislations against *Candombe*.

17. An earlier work, Paulo Carvalho-Neto's "The Candombe, a Dramatic Dance from Afro-Uruguayan Folklore" (1962), records the changes the Candombe has undergone with its incorporation into carnival.

18. The majority of the *Candombe* bands (*comparsas*) were concentrated mainly in the *Medio Mundo* and *Ansina* housing projects located in the *Palermo* and *Sur* neighborhoods of Montevideo.

19. Graciela Leguizamón, "Te daré mi humilde opinión," E-mail correspondence. 7 Dec 2011.

20. December 3 is significant to the Afro-Uruguayan collective. It was on that date in 1978 that on the orders of the military dictatorship, many poor Uruguayans, the majority of African descent, were forcibly evacuated from their homes in the *Medio Mundo* housing project. Shortly thereafter, the buildings were demolished. See also note 17 above.

21. Felipe Arocena and Sebastián Aguiar make a distinction between multicultural societies (those with diverse populations) and multiculturalism (active recognition and acceptance of cultural diversity and the enactment of policies that guarantee the integration of various cultures within the society) in *Multiculturalismo en Uruguay* 15.

22. See, for example, "Montevideo Carnival," *Welcome Uruguay.com, www.welcomeuruguay.com/carnavales/index_i.html* and "Carnival All Year Round," *Welcome Uruguay.com, www.welcomeuruguay.com/montevideo/carnival-museum.html.*

23. See Hermano Vianna's *The Mystery of Samba. Popular Music and National Identity in Brazil.*

24. The observation about the failure of many (whites) who practice *Candombe* to fully understand and appreciate its true symbolism of Afro-descendant culture was made by Graciela Leguizamón in an e-mail correspondence. See "Te daré mi humilde opinion."

25. Oscar Montaño, Personal interview. 26 May 2009.

26. Cristina Rodríguez Cabral, Personal interview, 13 May 2009.

27. In literature, the term "universal" has been used in an exclusionary way to present works that conform to hegemonic aesthetics and values as the norm. For a more detailed discussion of the concept of universality, see Persico, "Counterpublics and Aesthetics: Afro-Hispanic and Belizean Women Writers."

28. See "Te daré mi humilde opinión," E-mail correspondence.

29. Cristina Rodríguez Cabral, Personal interview, 13 May 2009.

30. See Gustavo Remedi, *Carnival Theater: Uruguay's Popular Performers and National Culture.*

31. Leguizamón received this honor in 2008 and 2011.

Works Cited

Acree, William G., Alex Borucki, and George R. Andrews. *Jacinto Ventura de Molina y los caminos de la escritura negra en el Río de la Plata*. Montevideo, Uruguay: Ediciones Trilce, 2008.

Aharonián, Coriú. *Músicas populares del Uruguay*. Montevideo, Uruguay: Universidad de la República, 2007.

Andrews, George Reid. *Blackness in the White Nation: A History of Afro-Uruguay*. Chapel Hill: U of North Carolina P, 2010.

Arocena, Felipe, and Sebastián Aguiar, eds. *Multiculturalismo en Uruguay: Ensayo y entrevistas a once comunidades culturales*. Montevideo, Uruguay: Ediciones Trilce, 2007.

Ayesterán, Lauro. *El folklore musical uruguayo*. Montevideo, Uruguay: Arca Editorial, 1972.

Barrios, Pilar. *Piel negra: Poesías (1917–1947)*. Montevideo: Nuestra Raza, 1947.

Benavides, Washington, et al. *El cuento uruguayo: Narradores uruguayos de hoy*. Montevideo, Uruguay: Ediciones La Gotera, 2002.

Blanco, Blanco Elvira. *La creación de un imaginario: La generación literaria del 45 en Uruguay*. Montevideo, Uruguay: Ediciones del Caballo Perdido, 2007.

Bourdieu, Pierre. *The Field of Cultural Production: Essays on Art and Literature*. Ed. Randal Johnson. New York: Columbia UP, 1993.

———. "The Forms of Capital." *Handbook of Theory and Research for the Sociology of Education*. Ed. J. Richardson. New York: Greenwood, 1986.

———. *Distinction: A Social Critique of the Judgement of Taste*. Cambridge: Harvard UP, 1984.

———. "Cultural Reproduction and Social Reproduction." *Power and Ideology in Education*. Eds. J. Karabel and A. H. Halsey. New York: Oxford UP, 1977: 487–511.

Brindis de Salas, Virginia. *Pregón de Marimorena: Poemas*. Montevideo: Sociedad Cultural Editora Indoamericana, 1946.

Britos Serrat, Alberto. *Antología de Poetas Negros Uruguayos*. Montevideo, Uruguay: Ediciones Mundo Afro, 1990.

"Carnaval." *Uruguay Natural*. Ministerio de Turismo y Deportes. n.d. Web. 12 Dec. 2011. *turismo.gub.uy/index.php/es/uruguay/carnaval*.

"Carnival All Year Round." *Welcome Uruguay.com*. Interpatagonia S.A., n.d. Web. 12 Dec. 2011. *www.welcomeuruguay.com/montevideo/carnival-museum.html*.

Carvalho-Neto, Paulo. "The Candombe, a Dramatic Dance from Afro-Uruguayan Folklore." *Ethnomusicology* 6.3 (Sept. 1962): 164–74.

Chagas, Jorge. *Gloria y tormento: La novela de José Leandro Andrade*. Montevideo: Ediciones La Gotera, 2003.

———. Personal interview. 29 May 2009.

Chagas, Jorge, and Gustavo Trullen. *Banco la caja obrera: Una historia, 1905–2001*. Montevideo: Perro Andaluz ediciones, 2009.

———. *Guillermo Chifflet: El Combate de la Pluma*. Montevideo: Rumbo Editorial, 2011.

———. *Pacheco: La trama oculta del poder*. Montevideo: Rumbo Editorial, 2005.

Chirimini, Tomás Olivera, and Juan Antonio Varese. *Los Candombes de los Reyes: Las Llamadas*. Montevideo: Del Sur Ediciones, 2009.

"Committee on the Elimination of Racial Discrimination Considers the Report of Uruguay." *The United Nations Office at Geneva*. 18 Feb. 2011. Web. 26 Jan. 2012.

Díaz, Javier. "Los Afrodescendientes." Entrevistada por Lil Vera y Juan Cristiano. *Multiculturalismo en Uruguay: Ensayo y entrevistas a once comunidades culturales*. Eds. Felipe Arocena and Sebastián Aguilar. Montevideo, Uruguay: Ediciones Trilce, 2007.

Dominzaín, Susana, et al. *Imaginarios y Consumo Cultural: Segundo Informe Nacional Sobre Consumo y Comportamiento Cultural*. Uruguay: Centro Cultural de España, 2009.

"En enero visitaron Uruguay 470 mil turistas que dejaron divisas por US $435 millones." *Cifras Oficiales MINTURD. Presidencia de la República*. 27 Feb. 2012. Web. 1 Mar. 2012.

"Festejos e inauguración de la Casa de la Cultura Afrouruguaya." *180.com.uy*. 2 Dec. 2011. Web. 23 Dec. 2014.

Gortázar, Alejandro. Personal interview. 26 May 2009.

———. *El licenciado negro: Jacinto Ventura de Molina*. Montevideo, Uruguay: Ediciones Trilce, 2007.

Guillory, John. *Cultural Capital: The Problem of Literary Canon Formation*. Chicago: U of Chicago P, 1993.

Hanchard, Michael G. *Orpheus and Power: The Movimiento Negro of Rio De Janeiro and São Paulo, Brazil, 1945–1988*. Princeton: Princeton UP, 1994.

Labanyi, Jo. "Matters of Taste: Working with Popular Culture." *Cultura Popular: Studies in Spanish and Latin American Popular Culture*. Eds. Shelley Godsland and Anne M. White. Oxford: Peter Lang, 2002.

Leguizamón, Graciela. "Una Mirada sobre el libro *Cultura y Literatura Afro-Uruguaya*." *Perspectiva Afrodescendiente*. 11 Dec. 2011. Web. 24 Mar. 2012. *perspectivaafrodescendiente.wordpress.com/2011/12/11/una-mirada-sobre-el-libro-cultura-y-literatura-afro-uruguaya-de-graciela-leguizamon*.

———. *Red de escritores/as y creadores afro-descendientes*. n.d. Web. 12 Dec. 2011. *www.redescrea.blogspot.com*.

———. "Sin espejos." *Gracee Marty*. Blogspot, 30 Nov. 2011. Web. 12 Dec. 2011. *graceemartyblogspot.com*.

———. "Te daré mi humilde opinión." Message to Melva Perscio. 7 Dec. 2011. Email.

———. Personal interview. 28 May 2009.

Lewis, Marvin A. *Cultura y literatura afro-uruguaya: Perspectivas post-coloniales*. Montevideo, Uruguay: Casa de la Cultura Afro-Uruguaya, 2011.

———. *Afro-Uruguayan Literature: Post-Colonial Perspectives*. Lewisburg: Bucknell UP, 2003.

———. *Afro-Hispanic Poetry, 1940–1980: From Slavery to "Negritud" in South American Verse*. Columbia: U of Missouri P, 1983.

"Miguel Ángel Duarte López." *Portal Poeta Blogspot*. 2004. Web. 2 Apr. 2012.

"Miguel Ángel Duarte López." *Red Mundial de Escritores en Español*. n.d. Web. 2 Apr. 2012.

Mills Young, Carole. "Cristina Rodríguez Cabral." *Africa and the Americas: Culture, Politics, and History: A Multidisciplinary Encyclopedia*. Eds. Richard M. Juang and Noelle Morrissette. Santa Barbara: ABC-CLIO, 2008. 220.

Montaño, Oscar. Personal interview. 26 May 2009.

———. *Umkhonto: La lanza negra: Historia del aporte negro-africano en la formación del Uruguay*. Montevideo, Uruguay: Rosebud Ediciones, 1997.

"Montevideo Carnival." *Welcome Uruguay.com*. Interpatagonia S.A., n.d. Web. 12 Dec. 2011. *www.welcomeuruguay.com/carnavales/index_i.html*.

Paredes Pacheco, José Luis. "El spoken word, más cerca de la escenificación que de a simple lectura." *La jornada*. 5 Nov. 2005. Web. 10 Mar. 2012.

Pereda Valdés, Ildefonso. *Antología de la poesía negra americana*. 1936. Santiago, Chile: Ediciones Ercilla; Montevideo, Uruguay: B.U.D.A, 1953.

Persico, Melva. "Counterpublics and Aesthetics: Afro-Hispanic and Belizean Women Writers." Diss. Miami: U of Miami, 2011.

Premio Victoria. Web. 3 Jan. 2012. *premiovictoria.jimdo.com/premio-victoria*.

Rama, Ángel, Pablo Rocca, and Véronica Pérez. *Literatura, cultura, sociedad en América latina*. Montevideo, Uruguay: Ediciones Trilce, 2006.

Remedi, Gustavo. *Carnival Theater: Uruguay's Popular Performers and National Culture*. Minneapolis: U of Minnesota P, 2004.

"Resolución N°.11.197." Junta Departamental de Montevideo. 23 June 2011. Web. 20 Sept. 2012. *www.juntamvd.gub.uy/es/archivos/decretos/4375–11197.htm*.

"Resolución N⁰· 5397/11." Junta Departamental de Montevideo. 28 Nov. 2011. Web. 20 Sept. 2012. *www.montevideo.gub.uy/asl/sistemas/gestar/resoluci.nsf/0bfcab2a0d22bf 960325678d00746391/95485b16811fa76383257961004bea2d?OpenDocument.*

Rodríguez Cabral, Cristina. Personal interview. 13 May 2009.

———. *Memoria y resistencia.* República Dominicana: Editorial Manatí, 2004.

———. *Desde mi trinchera.* Montevideo, Uruguay: Ediciones Mundo Afro, 1993.

Santos Arrascaeta, Beatriz. Personal interview. 27 May 2009.

Somma, Lucía Scuro, coord. *Población afrodescendiente y desigualdades étnico-raciales en Uruguay.* Montevideo, Uruguay: PNUD, 2008.

Trigo, Abril. "Candombe and the Reterritorialization of Culture." *Callaloo.* 16.3 (Summer 1993): 716–28.

Trigona, Marie. "Uruguay: Spirit of Afro-Resistance Alive in Candombe." *Upside Down World.* 21 Feb. 2008. Web. 11 Mar. 2009.

Vianna, Hermano. *The Mystery of Samba: Popular Music and National Identity in Brazil.* Trans. and Ed. John Charles Chasteen. Chapel Hill: U of North Carolina P, 1999.

Yúdice, George. *The Expediency of Culture: Uses of Culture in the Global Era.* Durham: Duke UP, 2003.

Quilombismo and the Afro-Brazilian Quest for Citizenship

Niyi Afolabi

Brazilian citizenship is a recurrent subject of interest among Afro-Brazilian social movements' activists as well as the Brazilian government itself. Yet while these social activists seek inclusion and equality through cultural mobilization and political agitation, the Brazilian government continues to pay cosmetic service to the desire for true representative Brazilian identity beyond the fallacy of a racial paradise. The lack of a consensus dates back to the discourses of race-mixture that have perpetuated an institutional mythology for many centuries. In a sociological study, France W. Twine articulates her frustrations at the discovery that in reality genuine race-mixture hardly occurs; marriages in recent times tend to be among the same races in Brazil. This confirms the suggestion that the race-mixture phenomenon was a historical experimentation of enslavement and has since failed to be sustained at least as a national phenomenon. For Twine, "In contrast to what I expected there was a pattern of resistance to interracial marriage among Euro-Brazilians of all socioeconomic positions. Euro-Brazilians resisted *mestiçagem* by actively discouraging family members from establishing families with Vasalians of predominant or salient African ancestry."[1]

A positive resolution to the contradictions of race and racism in Brazil, though hypothetical, has been advanced by Abdias do Nascimento as *Quilombismo*. Nascimento sees in this inclusive way of life an Afro-Brazilian alternative that will not only unite all Brazilians but also give Afro-Brazilians their due in the articulation of Brazilian citizenship. In "Quilombismo: An Afro-Brazilian Political Alternative," Nascimento elaborates this concept as that which has the potential to empower Afro-Brazilians and well-meaning Brazilians who are supportive of Afro-Brazilian liberation from the fangs of racism and marginality. In addition to defining Quilombismo as such, Nascimento goes on to propose an Afro-Brazilian Memory Week as an event to recuperate Brazilian amnesia regarding African contribution to Brazilian society. By highlighting the horrendous conditions in which Africans were brought to the Americas, the exploitation that ensued in the process of enslavement, and the current squalid conditions in which most Afro-Brazilians live in the slums, Nascimento demands justice and equal rights before some of these historical dislocations could be redressed to the satisfaction of all members of the Brazilian society.[2] Nascimento is not alone in this call for *Quilombismo* and a critique of racial democracy that often contradicts the social reality. For Elisa Larkin Nascimento, the supremacy of whiteness in the Brazilian context translates as racism, and the efforts to counter this state of affairs continue to be marred by what she calls the "sorcery of color" in Brazil.[3] To redress these structural hindrances to true citizenship, Elisa Nascimento calls for an anti-racist posture through an elaborate documentation of the strategies of disempowerment deployed by the virtual white establishment that includes the media. Dislocations will continue to shift from the tortuous Atlantic journey to the inconsistencies of discourses that set out to mask the oppression of the very people (implicitly Afro-Brazilians) who are responsible for the building of the Brazilian nation.

Between the radicalism of black Brazilian movements of the 1980s, an aftermath of the negation and rejection of the myth of racial democracy that denies Brazilian subtle racism, the rise of re-Africanization sensibilities among Afro-carnival groups, and the current ambivalent co-optation that has been packaged as "affirmative action" in the new millennium, a missing link to the many quests for Afro-Brazilianness lies in the (dis)locations that permeate the issues of identity, consciousness, and Africa-rootedness. Recent studies have remained invested in the polarity between the rigidity of "race" (one drop rule) from the North American perspective and the fluidity of identity as professed by the South American miscegenation thesis.[4] Regardless of the given schools of thought, or discourses, that have not resolved the oppressive socio-political realities on the ground, one must face the many levels of (dis)locations that define Afro-Brazilian identities. This chapter draws upon the cultural productions of five Afro-Brazilian poets from various regions of Brazil, namely, Oliveira Silveira, Lepê Correia, Jamu Minka, Abelardo Rodrigues, and Carlos de Assumpção. Beyond introducing the marginalized poets to a wider readership in English, it also engages the current debate in the shift from "racial democracy" to "affirmative action" in Brazil and the implications for continued racial tensions and contradictions in the Brazilian state. A close examination of these poets reveals a commonality of quests: each defines a world of oppression in which transgressing that world must come in the form of rebelliousness and ideological consciousness through poetic fury.

In his book of essays, *Literatura, Política, Identidades* (2005), Eduardo de Assis Duarte accuses Western colonialism and enslavement of what he calls *purismo estético*, that is, arrogant "aesthetic purity," in which ethnic representations that are by nature characteristically different from the canonical or the mainstream are considered less than what hegemonic schools of thought see as "true art." If Duarte is concerned with canonical exclusion of creative and critical imaginations, Beatriz Góis Dantas in *Nagô Grandma and White Papa: Candomblé and the Creation of Afro-Brazilian Identity* (2009) argues for the validity of Afro-Brazilian religion as the crux of Afro-Brazilian identity. Yet she further posits that despite this seemingly unifying space in which black groups see Africa as a point of reference, they must also consider the reality of the immediate social, political, and economic structures in which they have to function as they negotiate between radicalism and co-optation. For Dantas, "In so far as African culture assigns great importance to explaining the present through a tradition that is always associated with the group's past and, specifically, with its African origins, this methodological position is a consequence of a generic orientation and the search for Africanisms that has deeply marked anthropological writing on Afro-Brazilian cults . . . the purity of the African tradition were [was] not somehow prized by certain sectors of society so as to use it to advantage in competing for the religious market's place in society" (30–31). From the foregoing perspective, the cultural division existing between "authenticity" and "adulteration" can only be reconciled through some form of negotiation, co-optation, and conscious or strategic (dis)location.

In engaging the elusive quest for Brazilian citizenship by Afro-Brazilian and indigenous populations, Abdias Nascimento has, in many seminal works, joined hands with Afro-Brazilian social movements to articulate alternatives to the present state of Brazilian racism and prejudice in a formulation he termed *Quilombismo*. The thrust of this conceptualization resides in the need to recognize African contributions and adopt a political organization that is steeped in the legacy of South American and Caribbean maroon communities, especially the Quilombo of the Palmares that was led by Zumbi. In "Quilombismo: An Afro-Brazilian Political Alternative," Nascimento cogently elaborates *Quilombismo* as a viable political alternative that empowers Afro-Brazilians while subjecting the fallacy of "racial democracy" to rigorous critique. He further proposes as mentioned the establishment of an Afro-Brazilian Memory Week in which Brazilian amnesia regarding the historical past is confronted with the horror of slavery and the consequent dispossession of Afro-Brazilians, which ultimately explains their current marginality in the society. After reviewing the antiquity of black African knowledge systems and the vital role of memory in the construction of the pre-Columbian Americas, Nascimento delves into the emergence of Quilombist sentiment and black consciousness in Brazil, making the case for blacks to be viewed not as strangers in Brazil but as the bonafide "body and soul" of Brazil (149). For Nascimento: "Quilombismo and its various equivalents throughout the Americas, expressed in the legacy of *cumbes*, *palenques*, *cimarrones*, and maroons, constitute an international alternative for popular Black political organization. Quilombismo articulates the diverse levels of collective life whose dialectic interaction proposes complete fulfillment and realization of the creative capacities of the human being" (151–52). Negating the hypocrisy in "racial democracy," Nascimento proposes a new approach to citizenship devoid of social segregation and economic inequality.

Echoing Nascimento's critical position, Elisa Nascimento in "Aspects of Afro-Brazilian Experience" suggests that *Quilombismo* seeks to establish a Brazilian nationalist Quilombist state that is not only based on the model of the Quilombos but which constitutes "Brazil's most authentic national tradition of liberation" (214). Elisa Nascimento argues that the marginality of Brazilian black and indigenous populations is predicated on the legacy of slavery and must be confronted with a Quilombist ideal that legitimizes Afro-indigenous claims to Brazilian citizenship. In associating Afro-Brazilian poverty and destitute living conditions with slavery and racism as a "shared experience" of the Americas, Elisa Nascimento traces the emergence of anti-racist movements and the quest for Afro-Brazilian identity back to the Black Experimental Theater (TEN) that was created by Abdias Nascimento in the 1950s. While Abdias and Elisa Nascimento agree about the centrality of *Quilombismo* as an alternative political model, twenty-five years later, Sérgio da Silva Martins et al. in "Paving Paradise: The Road From 'Racial Democracy' to Affirmative Action" caution about the optimism of the achievements of Affirmative Action in Brazil while alerting us to the reality of Brazil in the new millennium as a "land of paradise promised and privilege sustained" (812) when it comes to the allocation of resources and opportunities for blacks and whites. Affirmative Action has been challenged by white elites who argue that it is a form of reverse discrimination in the sense that it excludes whites from opportunities such as quota-sponsored university admissions that are now provided to blacks whether they are qualified or not, while the same privileged white group struggles to maintain its hegemonic hold on power, control, and resources.

While efforts to ensure racial equality in Brazil (especially since the Durban Conference of 2002) have yielded some dividends, one must proceed with caution since racism is far from being completely eradicated in Brazilian reality. For Elisa Nascimento, the open discussion of affirmative action policies actually provides some hope that more concrete policies will be enacted toward continued improvement of racial relations: "the debate on affirmative action signals the ultimate failure of the racial democracy myth, so effectively legitimized by the Brazilian ruling elite and by the State itself, which concocted an image of racial harmony that masked the existence of a huge racially segregated labor reserve and reduced the race issue to one of class conflict that would be solved by the building of socialism or the implementation of universal race-neutral income distribution policies" ("Kilombismo" 788). Arguably, having affirmative action policies on the books without actually enforcing them results in a vicious cycle of "cosmetic change" and continuity in which such policies become rather symbolic of intent and not of actualization or realization.

In aspiring to a society in which the discussion of race is preferably silenced to bring about a more "pragmatic" discussion of class, gender, and development in isolation, Brazilians continue to live in a fantasy world of harmonious racial paradise. Edward E. Telles in *Race in Another America* (2004) has cautioned that skin color continues to be determinantal and significant in Brazilian political reality. Telles argues that despite changing realities of Afro-Brazilian movements in terms of access to limited spaces within the Brazilian state, these activist organizations are still generally struggling to consolidate their slow incorporation of race-based affirmative action and democratic processes into a resistant Brazilian state. As long as citizenship is limited to cultural symbologies that disappear after annual ephemeral celebrations and festivities, Afro-Brazilian identities will continue to be defined by shifting processes of accommodation and negotiation which make the quest for Brazilian citizenship in terms of equal access to political power elusive and dislocated. The following cultural producers from across Brazil define their own identities from poetic ruminations of cultural resistance.

Singing to Palmares with Modern Tamtams

Through his militancy and consciousness of Afro-Gaúcho identity, and by extension, Afro-Brazilian identity, Oliveira Silveira embodies a steadfast position in the vanguard of Afro-Brazilian letters and culture of both the new and old generations. From a depressing state of mind to what Zilá Bernd calls the "constitution of *Quilombos*,"[5] the works of Silveira expose Afro-Brazilians in their best affirmative state of being, where imaginative expression is both therapy and unrestrained vindication of injustices. Just as Solano Trindade states in one of his poems, "I sing to Palmares without complex or jealousy," Silveira sings to Palmares using the modernist percussion of the pen and the written word. In addition to collaborating in many anthologies such as *Cadernos Negros: Os Melhores Poemas, Axé: Antologia Contemporânea da Poesia Negra Brasileira,* and *Poesia Negra Brasileira,* Silveira has published eight volumes of poetry, including *Roteiro dos Tantãs* (Manual of the Tantams) *Germinou* (Germinated), *Poemas Regionais* (Regional Poems), *Anotações à Margem* (Annotations on the Margin), *Banzo—Saudade Negra* (Dream: Black Nostalgia), *Décima do Negro Peão* (Decimal of a Foot Soldier), *Praça da Palavra* (Square of the Word), *Pêlo Escuro* (Black Skin), and *Orixás: Pinturas e Poesias* (Orixás: Paintings and Poetry), thus testifying to a diverse outlet for a consistently searching soul who is committed to the full liberation of his people. In age, experience, and cultural production, Silveira qualifies to be among those I have termed "pioneers of Afro-Brazilian Modernity," but due to his location in Rio Grande do Sul, he is often "excluded" in the canon defined by the Rio–São Paulo–Salvador critical axis.

Such an unjustified exclusion of Silveira is remedied by a few anthologies that represent his enviable contribution to Afro-Brazilian letters. One such anthology is Zilá Bernd's *Poesia Negra Brasileira: Antologia,* which samples Silveira's poems from about three volumes of poetry. Although an under-representative sampling, it all the same captures the "warrior"-posture and warrior-motif in Silveira's worldview. Another anthology, *Cadernos Negros: Os Melhores Poemas,* contains two selected poems Silveira contributed to the series over the twenty-one years of its existence. In "Ser e Não Ser" ("Being and Non-Being"), Silveira subjects Brazilian racial democracy to scrutiny, humorously playing with antitheses and contradictions (existent versus non-existent; yes versus no) as if to ridicule Brazil and its denial of racism:

O racismo que existe,   Existent racism,
o racismo que não existe.   Non-existent racism.
. . . .
É assim o Brasil (108:1–2, 5)   Such is Brazil

Beyond this subtle but effective indictment of racial hypocrisy in Brazil, Silveira, in the poem "Outra Nega Fulô" parodies Jorge de Lima's "Essa Nega Fulô" as if engaging in an intertextual exercise geared toward revisiting and critiquing the objectification and beastification of the slave figure called *Fulô.* Instead of the romantic and idealistic image of *Flor* (flower) that the black slave would love to be associated with in the hands of the perverse master, this corrupted slave *Fulô* (flow, or symbolic passage for sex) is defiled, violated, and deflowered. Contrastively, in the parodied version by Silveira, the black slave is no longer passive but revolutionary. Instead of passively performing the will of the master, she fools the master that she is actually going to sleep with him only to hit him in the scrotum at the earliest opportunity.

In two sociological and critical studies respectively, *O Negro: Consciência e Trabalho* and *Negritude e Literatura na América Latina,* Zilá Bernd illustrates and synthesizes the imaginative essence of Oliveira Silveira. In the first text, adopting a literary-historicity duality approach, Zilá Bernd and Margaret Bakos use literary texts such as those by Silveira and others to situate historical moments in Afro-Brazilian culture that have been marginalized, especially in Afro-Gaucho experience. In the second text, Bernd focuses on a number of creative works by Silveira—stressing the interconnectedness between being Afro-Gaucho and Afro-Brazilian in Silveira's imagination. From syncretism of traditions (African and Gaucho), to the epic as an appropriate genre to translate historic events and heroes, to the tragic consciousness of the African experience in consonance with the New World (such as in the Caribbean), Silveira's *oeuvre* is summed up by what Zilá Bernd enumerates as "an explicit presence of the poetic 'I,'" "revolt and protest as driving semantic forces," "search of origins," and the trope of "tamtams" (drums) as an oral call to solidarity—all operating within a modernist impulse which is simultaneously affirmative, resistant, and critical in order not to resign to the devouring tentacles of assimilation and racial democracy. In *Pêlo Escuro*, the poem "Sou" ("I Am") provides a cogent philosophical window into the mind of the poet-persona as if declaring his own *ars poetica*:

Meu canto é faca de charque	My song is the jerked knife
voltada contra o feitor,	pointed against the foreman,
. . . .	. . . .
não é de nenhum senhor. (14.1–2, 4)	belongs to no master.

With the same defiance and resistance, in "Requiem para Luther King" ("Requiem for Martin Luther King") (*Banzo Saudade Negra* 49), the persona pays homage to Dr. Martin Luther King Jr., the assassinated Civil Rights leader, pointing out the irony in the fact that he died violently although he preached non-violence. Here is Silveira providing comfort and solace to King even as the activist lives on in his heroic sleep:

Descansa em paz, irmão, porque	Rest in peace, brother, because
tuas pernas estão cansadas	your legs are tired
. . . .	. . . .
das grandes marchas negras (49.1–2, 4)	from long black marches

Such are the strong articulations of a militant voice that transcends the limits of regional Rio Grande do Sul, and even Brazil as a whole, but expresses a pan-African consciousness geared toward solidarity with humanity as symbolic divinity.

Since Southern Brazilian literature is less critically examined, it is useful to place the works of Oliveira Silveira within this specificity to uncover its regionalist import at least for the purpose of the local color. In "Negro do Sul" ("Southern Black") (*Pêlo Escuro* 4), Silveira delineates a tripartite function of the Southern Afro-Brazilian and his/her contribution to the overall socio-cultural and economic formation of Rio Grande do Sul: slave economy, music, and resistance tradition. Using the active voice and stripping the poem of adjectivizations and embellishments, the poem dramatizes the persona's historical formation and accomplishments in an enumerative fashion: "no sul o negro brigou / guerreou / se libertou" (4.1–3). [In the South, blacks fought / they battled / they freed themselves.] This cohesive rendering about Afro-Brazilian resistance in Rio Grande do Sul is perhaps the missing link between the South and other regions as they share a commonality of oppression and memory of their liberation.

Of Silveira's impressive cultural ensemble and overall imaginative corpus, two volumes, namely *Orixás: Pinturas e Poesias* (Orixá Divinities: Paintings and Poetry) (with Pedro Homero) and *Poema Sobre Palmares* (Poem on the Marroon Settlement) are particularly instructive of the author's commitment to Afro-Brazilian culture and his determination to document the sacred, the political, the cultural, and the human in the survival of African cultures in Brazil. While *Orixás* illustrates the many different African divinities now translocated to the syncretic New World, Silveira has synchronized poems which have been written in other volumes into a book of Orixáesque poems illustrated with Pedro Homero's paintings of those very *Orixás*. "Ogum no Mapa" ("Ogun on the Map") is one such poem as well as the *Orixá* that transcends continental borders. Originally included in *Roteiro dos Tantãs*, in "Ogum no Mapa" Silveira focuses on the multiple identitarian and culinarian properties of *Ogun* (Yoruba/African deity of iron and war) in different parts of Brazil. Known as *Nagô* from North to South of Brazil, *Xangô* in Recife, *Candomblé* in Bahia, and *Batuque* in Rio Grande do Sul, *Ogun* has put itself on the world map with minimal effort. Other divinities are equally illustrated, with their characteristic properties and poetry provided by Silveira.

The cumulative totality of Silveira's creative corpus is entrenched in *Poema Sobre Palmares*. Not only is the subject of historical significance, but it is also emancipatory in its modernist desire for new meanings for old truths within a conditioned state of being which almost makes dreaming and resisting quite a daunting proposition.[6] A long poem, written over the fifteen-year span between 1972 and 1987, as if targeting the centennial celebrations of abolition in 1988, *Poema Sobre Palmares* re-enacts, like Milton Nascimento's classic musical *Missa dos Quilombos* (Quilombos' Mass), a historical moment in the life-journeys of Afro-Brazilians. In this epic rendition of Palmares, Silveira adopts a paradoxical approach, contrasting the version of white oppression with Zumbi warriors and their symbolic resistance as well as Zumbi's heroism. As a blurb, Silveira uses a stanza to state that Palmares was constituted not only by its heroes such as Zumbi or Ganga Zumba, but also by the thousands of warriors who lost their lives, for "Palmares is not just one, they are in their thousands."[7] In using "poem" in the singular, *Poema Sobre Palmares* translates a sustained reflection on history and its implications in the present within the overall legacy and significance of the Palmares resistance. Perceptively capturing the transatlantic journey, the anguishing reality of flagellation in the historic *Pelourinho* in Bahia, and offering some consolation of resistance signified in the bravery of Zumbi as well as other entities and individuals who not only celebrate such bravery but equally engage its ramifications in their own works, *Poema Sobre Palmares* pays a double homage to heroes past and present in Afro-Brazilian culture:

em toda parte renascendo	all over being renewed
a semente do brio,	the seed of brightness
. . . .	. . . .
quilombo em pleno centenário (14.8–9, 15)	Quilombo in centennial celebration

Beyond the rebirth of the *quilombo* in the tradition kept alive by Afro-Brazilian cultural producers, the elevation of Palmares to the first instance of freedom in Brazilian history occupies an even more distinctive place in the significance of this long poem.

Palmares as a resistant community would not exist without the bravery of Zumbi. His martyrdom, heroism, and legendary standing are summed up in many instances of praise in the long poem. The sustained evocation sees Zumbi as strong, brave, fearless, and stoic in the face of considerable odds orchestrated by the adversary who is, by contrast, portrayed as weak and mercenary-styled:

Então Zumbi chegou	Then Zumbi arrived
—é o general das armas.	—He is the Army Chief.
. . . .	. . . .
de exemplo. (12.7–8, 14)	exemplary being.

Immortalized more in death than in life, Zumbi is the king, leader, commandant, and warrior that Afro-Brazilian history will continue to honor and celebrate as their personal hero, and one who provides courage and resolve of purpose in the midst of the modernist storm that constantly confronts Afro-Brazilians in their daily living.

Resolving the "Casa Grande e Senzala" Paradox

In Recife, the capital city of Pernambuco, the notion of racial democracy is not a public issue, as the dean of the concept, Gilberto Freyre, hails from Pernambuco, hence more celebrated that critiqued, at least publicly. With many statues, emblems, and institutes honoring his contribution, Gilberto Freyre's Master-Slave paradigm is very much alive. Indeed, during my visit to the Fundação Joaquim Nabuco in the company of Lepê Correia in the summer of 2001, I was intrigued by the sheer reverence for the preserved legacy of Gilberto Freyre, and I ended up with more questions than answers after visiting the anthropologist's house-library. The courteous female official tour-guide had only accolades and scripted eulogies for Freyre. Interestingly, and according to our tour-guide, all members in Freyre's family had a room of their own in addition to the living room and Freyre's iconoclastic study and library. To my question of why the so-called black "family friend" who "enjoyed" cleaning, cooking, and attending to the Freyres did not have his "own room," and my inquiry as to where he slept after the day's cheerful and willing chores, the tour-guide suddenly became nervous and evasive, stating that in compensation for his generosity, his photograph has been permanently placed on the wall as a gesture of recognition. It is remarkable that in the Institute located behind the Freyrean "Casa Grande e Senzela" type home, the tomb of the scholar is esoterically preserved for touristic purposes, while that of the "friendly black" was nowhere to be found. The contradictions confirm the absurdity of the Freyrean notion of a harmonious relationship between the Master and the Slave while discounting the violence of slavery. In fact, as a souvenir, Dr. Fátima Quintas presented each person in my party with a copy of a volume that she had recently edited: *A Obra em Tempos Vários*, dedicated to and commemorating ninety-five years of the birth of Gilberto Freyre. A hefty volume of over four hundred pages, it brings together many perspectives about the legacy and controversies surrounding Freyre in the humanities and social sciences. Of these divergent views, Raul Lody's "Ancestralidade e Memória em *Casa-Grande & Senzala*" ("Ancestrality and Memory in *The Masters and the Slaves*") argues for Freyre's attempt at the humanization of slavery. This is perhaps an acceptable explanation for those who want to "invent" Brazil as the "cosmic nation" and an embodiment of the "cosmic race," but I do not find anything "humanizing" about violence, violation, and subjugation. It is within this complexity of struggles that I situate the three Pernambucan cultural producers—Lepê Correia, Inaldete Pinheiro Andrade, and Rogério Andrade Barbosa. Their common artistic and ideologic grounding lies in the necessity to transcend the daily obstacles of being black that hinder the maximization of the fullness of life.

Lepê Correia is one of the cogent Afro-Pernambucan voices to have emerged in the post-dictatorial era. Being a psychologist, teacher, poet, leader, and an *Ogan* (initiate) of *Ilê Asé Ogun Toperinã* (a *Candomblé* temple) has provided an exposure that has formed his worldview as well as his works. He is an indefatigable orator and conversationalist with whom I spent almost a week navigating the streams and estuaries of Recife and learning about human rights abuses and the burdens of being black in Brazil. He is a total human being with many functions—as a psychologist, Correia has the task of "solving" others' problems, teaching them to overcome the visible and invisible odds against them, turning to his own five children as a source of support and encouragement for the future, and selflessly serving as the voice of the voiceless. In addition, Correia was instrumental in helping poor young Afro-Brazilians gain admission into the university despite their background. Providing opportunities and rendering a helping hand to the needy forms part of Correia's mission. He was formerly editor of the Afro-Brazilian review *Djambay*, and he was one of the founders of the *Núcleo de Identidade Negra* (Nucleus of Black Identity), which is affiliated with the *Instituto de Tradição e Cultura Afro-Brasileira* (Institute of Afro-Brazilian Tradition and Culture), an organ responsible for the defense and affirmation of Afro-Brazilian religiosity. In this "integrated" relationship that Correia has between his art, profession, and community involvement, it is no surprise then that *Caxinguelê* (Squirrel), his only published collection of poetry, bolsters this truism. In his own study on the sacred in Afro-Brazilian poetry, Steven F. White opines that "Lepê Correia and others have worked against the grain to publish books of poetry that attempt to reinvent a sacred past by means of direct references to Brazilianized religions of African origin, primarily in the Yoruban and Bantu traditions" (76). The "reinvention of the sacred," in this pragmatic sense, serves as an instrument of legitimization and politicization of Afro-Brazilian religion, an approach that is more aggressive and effective than the "passive" approach of oratory declamations appealing to an audience that does not want to be converted from their perpetual ignorance and biases. *Candomblé*, even in its most "diluted" and "inauthentic" form is not just performance nor garbled ritual of incantations, but a source of energy, indeed, a treasure of political resistance.[8]

Against this background, Correia's *Caxinguelê* embodies what Pedro Lourenço[9] calls *poetação quilombola* (*quilombo*-inspired poeticization), that is, the poetic imagination that is subject to the ideals and aspirations of the *Quilombo*, of the ultimate desire for freedom. The title itself calls attention to the politics of naming: *Caxinguelê* means "squirrel," a symbolic name in African mythology that refers to the "traitor" figure in the animal kingdom. The folktale has it that the squirrel had a covenant with *Ifá*, the oracle of divination, but the squirrel betrayed *Ifá*, an act considered an abomination in the sight of the gods since to betray *Ifá* is to betray the earth, and thus the necessity of retributive justice by paying the ultimate price of death, that is, a return by the transgressor to the earth that he/she has betrayed, and consequently, offended—there is no appeasement in betrayal. A powerful title for a powerful poet, yet it is not clear to me what it all means. *Caxinguelê* is ambivalent, for it can refer to the betrayal of Afro-Brazilians by the Brazilian polity or the betrayal of Afro-Brazilians by the "traitors" among themselves. The first possibility fits the politics of challenging the mythology of racial democracy while the second unravels the stumbling block toward unity among Afro-Brazilians—fragmentation, internal strife, and competition. Even if Correia has not succeeded in redressing this fragmentation or mythology, at least he has contributed the allegory of the squirrel figure to Afro-Brazilian modernism.

Caxinguelê translates what Correia, in the title poem, calls "the new without being modern," the conscious interface between tradition and modernity, and yet with a certain resistance to that modernity. When situated within this context, the squirrel, an alter ego of the poet himself, projects his character as that of a revolutionary squirrel. Not the one who betrays *Ifá*, but the one who deliberately goes "against the current" of unverified claims of social equality and justice, hence betraying not the truth, but the lie that racial democracy represents. The entire poem "Caxinguelê" serves as Correia's *ars poetica*, where the poet self-defines in terms of his poetic philosophy and ideology:

Eu sou o nó na tua linha	I am the knot of your thread
Sou aquele que caminha	I am the one who walks
. . . .	. . . .
O novo sem ser moderno. (65.1–2, 11)	The new without being modern.

This is perhaps the most accurate testament of the personality of Correia and one that is faithful to the point of being a self-portrait. Consciously or not, the poet has adopted the *oriki* tradition of self-praise in the enumeration of his own "qualities" and even idiosyncrasies, as in the phrase "I am," which translates identity.

Although other poems address other issues of Afro-Brazilian religiosity, family genealogy and occupations, Afro-Brazilian dance, survival strategies, racial discrimination, and other inequalities, Correia provides consolation in the form of resistance as articulated in the poem "Resistência" ("Resistance"), in which the poet-persona offers the African body and the African drum as alternative instruments of resistance if the voice is censored or silenced, a dimension found in the popular manifestation of the *Capoeira* dance:

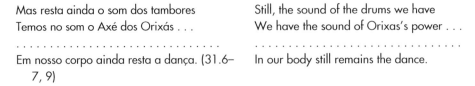

Mas resta ainda o som dos tambores	Still, the sound of the drums we have
Temos no som o Axé dos Orixás . . .	We have the sound of Orixas's power . . .
. . . .	. . . .
Em nosso corpo ainda resta a dança. (31.6–7, 9)	In our body still remains the dance.

The resolve to find ways to resist inequality captures the squirrel metaphor, for in finding alternatives, the Afro-Brazilian community is actually subverting the obstacles placed on their path to self-determination and empowerment.

Ancestrality, Populism, and Urbanity

Without any doubt, and with the sole exception of carnival festivity, that week-long celebration when "everyone" is able to display ephemeral freedom from many months of frustrations, marginality defines Afro-Brazilian cultural production in all its mani-festations. The de-marginalization comes through resistance and defiance, a risky ven-ture in a controlled society that appears free and "perverse" on the surface. Given the urban reality of slavery and post-enslavement settlements in locations such as Salvador, Belo Horizonte, and São Paulo, among others, Afro-Brazilian cultural manifestations have become reminiscent of an intricate nexus of ancestral memory, popular culture, and urbanization. Consequently, cultural production is stifled by the exigencies of modernity and economic expediency.

Jamu Minka belongs to the *Quilombohoje* generation, which founded *Cadernos Negros* even before opting for the name of the group two years after the first issue of the series in 1978.[10] A Neo-Negritudist in orientation, Minka is closer to Cuti, the group's leader, in temperament, and is equally nationalist and Pan-Africanist. Minka has enjoyed neither the national nor international critical attention he deserves. As noted by Márcio Damazio, who wrote the preface to Minka's *Teclas de Ébano* (Ebony's Harps), a number of influences inspired young, idealistic, and romantic Afro-Brazilians of the 1970s with a sense of awareness about black struggles all over the world, especially the North American Civil Rights Movement and the liberation struggles in Lusophone Africa—evoking leadership names such as Dr. Martin Luther King Jr., Malcolm X, Angela Davis, Agostinho Neto, Frantz Fanon, and Amilcar Cabral. Instead of limiting himself to the imaginative world of his poetic explorations, Minka translates his commitment into a political involvement within the community, where he participates in fora and conferences to help the cultivation of consciousness among the underprivileged. Before the publication of *Teclas de Ébano* and the advent of *Cadernos Negros*, Minka tried his creative hand in a number of journalistic and artistic endeavors with outlets such as *Árvore das Palavras*, *Versus-Afrolatinoamérica*, and *Jornegro*. In the special issue of *Cadernos Negros: Os Melhores Poemas*, Minka's five poems demonstrate a wide variety of cogent Afro-Brazilian issues: colonial exploitation, social and racial inequalities, inter-personal tensions, dashed hopes, and ancestral strength. In "Efeitos Colaterais" ("Collateral Effects") Minka takes a powerful jab at the mythology of racial democracy by calling it "deceitful propaganda" which validates and reinforces the "dictatorship of whiteness" as well as the resistance against all those who challenge the official position:

Negros de alma negra se inscrevem	Blacks with black soul self-inscribe
naquilo que escrevem	In what they write
. . . .	. . . .
negro que não se nega. (76.9–10, 12)	Blacks who do deny themselves.

"Efeitos Colaterais" testifies very early to Minka's consciousness and resolve to effect change in the country he loves so much and which treats him like a stranger. The "col-lateral" trope adequately translates the dilemma of conscious Afro-Brazilians face and the price of persecution they pay by speaking up against oppression and hypocrisy.

Teclas de Ébano, his only collection of poems, brings together poems Minka wrote over ten years, 1975–1985, and is hence representative of a wide variety of concerns without a sustained thematicization. From commentary on national politics defined by its crooked disposition ("O Tanq . . . Credo!"), to the critique of Brazilian world fame in soccer and the irony in the fact that there is no equality in Brazil and blacks are far from being happy at home ("Gol Contra (II)"; "Bate-Bola, Bate Vida"), to a disenchantment with multinational companies, foreign debt, and environmental pollution ("Sangue-Cola"; "Dívida External"), to provocative and sometimes sarcastic takes on racial issues ("Alma e Pele"; "Identidade II"; "Afro-América"; "Malhação II"), to an express solidarity with the suffering people of South Africa under Apartheid ("Apartheid"), Minka's imaginative world is multiple and committed. Ultimately, Minka's most profound protest lies in "Identidade II" ("Identity II") where, once again, he attacks race mixture with an autobiographical twist, affirming his blackness:

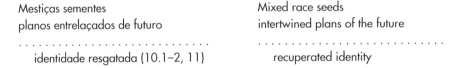

Mestiças sementes	Mixed race seeds
planos entrelaçados de futuro	intertwined plans of the future
. . . .	. . . .
identidade resgatada (10.1–2, 11)	recuperated identity

Here is a very mature, stylistically refined poet with an uncompromising attitude despite his subtle irony in his indictment of racial oppression. The sense of victory lies in knowing the self and affirming that self with pride and conviction without the shame that racial democracy seems to assert on the non-conscious individual.

In the constellation of Neo-Negritudist poets, Abelardo Rodrigues may be situated in the intersection between Africa and Afro-Brazil, not as the *Esu* (*Exu*) figure who plays in the crossroads of both continents but a synthetic voice that recuperates the memory of Africa in Brazil as translated by his *Memória da Noite*. As Hélio Pinto Ferreira points out in the foreword to the collection, Rodrigues is compared to Arlindo Barbeitos and Agostinho Neto, prominent Angolan poets, whose works seem to have influenced Rodrigues through "a texture of words in which the cry of the man of color is heard" (6). Instead of this express comparative praise, Oswaldo de Camargo, another poet and critic, is more critical, questioning why Rodrigues has chosen to be influenced by African poets and not by the Afro-Brazilian literary tradition of Lino Guedes (1920s), Solano Trindade (1930s), and a host of poets of the 1950s, such as Eduardo de Oliveira, Oswaldo Camargo, and Carlos de Assumpção. Camargo further notes a "dislocation of influences" in Aberlardo Rodrigues. According to him, Rodrigues's poetry is marked by "Africanness as opposed to Afro-Brazilianness" (9). Although very critical, Camargo at least admits that Rodrigues represents the "African poetic whisper among us" (10). While Rodrigues may have been influenced by a search for form in African poetry, I disagree with Camargo's generalization about the totality of Rodrigues's creative imagination. Both *Memória da Noite* and his poems included in *Cadernos Negros: Os Melhores Poemas* embody a profound Afro-Brazilian sensibility in the issues as well as the critical eye toward them. In "Garganta" ("Throat"), the poetic voice appeals directly to his interlocutor to ensure that her/his throat is properly cleansed in order to receive a pure blackness. Indeed, the throat or "voice" must be subversive like the carnivalesque ash-Wednesday[11]. Likewise in "Zumbi," in the tradition of the revolutionary-warrior to whom it is dedicated, the poetic voice calls for solidarity of voice, hands, and action in order to continue the legacy of Zumbi, because:

20 de novembro	November 20
é uma canção	is a warrior
guerreira. (25.1–3)	song.

Even if the style echoes "Africanness," that should not be a defect but a compliment to Pan-Africanism. The mention of the date alone should suffice for a conscious mind that innovates while paying homage to the ancestral African tradition.

Beyond the renewal of African tradition in Afro-Brazilian culture, Rodrigues in "Blues" captures a Pan-American sensibility as well when he contrasts slavery with Samba, Afro-Brazilian history, and Blues, suggesting that none captures the profound historical significance of this injustice to humanity but History itself:

Esta escravidão, amigo	This slavery, friend
não é como o samba	Is not like Samba
. . . .	. . . .
é História. (31.1–2, 8)	It's History.

In his overall poetic cosmovision, Rodrigues is perplexed by the suffering and agonies of Afro-Brazilians from slavery through the present and their perpetual existence in a condition best summed up by the trope of the "night." It takes the night to unleash unruly winds and tempests of evil spirits, wreaking so much havoc and pain to those quietly sleeping and unwary that they may wake up literally dead. Rodrigues is the "wake up" call not to death but to life as he calls attention to the memories of past "deaths" that need to be confronted so they do not repeat their atrocities. Pan-Africanist and Pan-American, Rodrigues is a conscious poet, a cultural producer who recuperates memory as a way of staying alive in the valley of death that the Afro-Brazilian condition symbolically represents.

According to Oswaldo de Camargo, Carlos de Assumpção is another representative of the Afro-Brazilian tradition that needs to be celebrated. Critically, sociologically, and culturally, Assumpção is a rebellious poet—attacking the injustices against blackness in general and exposing black identity as beautiful in the *Negritude* tradition of Léopold Senghor and Aimé Césaire. In the poems included in *Cadernos Negros: Os Melhores Poemas*, Assumpção addresses two interrelated issues of *Quilombo* and *Zumbi*. In "Batuque" ("African Percussion"), the poet-persona adopts African oral tradition by combining assonance and alliteration in four main words: *quilombo* (runaway settlement), *tambor* (tambourine), *batuque* (percussion) and *tenho* (I have). By repeating these words many times, the poem creates an auditive musical effect that is reminiscent of Mozambican José Craveirinha's "Quero ser tambor" ("I Want to Be a Drum"). Assumpção's entire poem is a song of protest and yet of praise and celebration, a clarion call to action and readiness, for whoever has a musical spirit will also be inspired to fight and protest when necessary:

Tenho um tambor	I have a drum
. . . .	. . . .
Dentro do peito	Within my heart
Tenho um tambor. (28.1–2, 6)	I have a drum.

The musicality is inescapable, and this is where Assumpção is unique among Afro-Brazilian poets with the exception of Solano Trindade and Oliveira Silveira, who adopt a similar approach in their poetry. Perhaps this musicality also explains why Cuti collaborated with Assumpção in a musical CD entitled *Quilombo de Palavras*—taken directly from one of Assumpção's poems in *Protesto*, "Meu Quilombo."

Protesto (Protest) embodies many liberation songs that provide strength to the poetic voice as he wanders through life, speaking up against social injustices and articulating or maintaining a stoic posture against a seemingly invincible and invisible enemy. For Assumpção, the entire world must know that the Afro-Brazilian has a heart like anyone else, and indeed not just any heart but a "heart made of granite" (20). Attacking the mythology of racial democracy and the expectation that the "good" citizen, black or white, must have a white soul, Assumpção sarcastically asks: "Quem já viu a alma algum dia / Pra saber se ela tem cor?" (Who has seen the soul someday / To know that it has a color?) (5.4–6). In addition to resistant echoes in many of the poems, including the praise of the Afro-Brazilian woman in "Mulher Negra," in which the gracefulness, laughter, beauty, voice, and walk are appreciated and celebrated as a total song in the mouth of a passionate lover, it is in "Protesto"—the title poem and a long composition which is part history, part declaration—that the poet-persona synthesizes his anguish and pleasure of protest at the same time. The tone of the poem is so reassuring and convincing that the poet defies death as a witness of conscience and a victim of injustices who refuses to be a victim even in death. The declarative voice of Assumpção embodies one of the allegories of Afro-modernity in the sense that the voice of the other is constantly being heard by the promoters of culture, thus relegating the "marginal" voice to the zone of forgetfulness and irrelevance.

In this panorama of Afro-Brazilian modernist voices, it is a sad note of conclusion that the Afro-Brazilian literary tradition continues to be conditioned by the exigencies of mainstream or canonical critical machinery that does not see any value in these cogent and viable cultural productions. The clarity of mind within the revolutionary impulses of most of these poets in their quests for social equality and cultural identity; the diverse manifestations of the *Quilombo* in the songs to Palmares that Oliveira Silveira composes; the trope of betrayal aptly demonstrated as the duality of oppression in the Brazil exposed in Lepê Correia's imaginative world; the love for the Afro-Brazilian women painted in the works of Jamu Minka, Abelardo Rodrigues, and Carlos de Assumpção; and other manifestations of protest and black pride by other cultural producers are significant contributions to Afro-Brazilian modernity, and by extension to the human condition when perceived as an indictment of hate and the proclamation of love beyond elusive quests for citizenship and legitimacy.

Notes

1. For a detailed discussion on the contradictions of racial democracy, see France Windance Twine 98.
2. I use "dislocation" in the sense used by Laclau and Mouffe, in which they identify three dimensions of dislocation: as a "form of temporality," a "form of possibility," and a "failure of hegemonization." See Pile and Keith, eds., *Hegemony and Socialist Strategy* and *Place and the Politics of Identity*.
3. See Elisa Larkin Nascimento, "Kilombismo, Virtual Whiteness, and the Sorcery of Color" and "Aspects of Afro-Brazilian Experience." See also Sérgio da Silva Martins et al., "Paving Paradise: The Road from 'Racial Democracy' to Affirmative Action in Brazil."
4. See, for example, Michael Hanchard's *Orpheus and Power*, Hendrik Kraay's *Afro-*

Brazilian Culture and Politics, Edward Telles's *Race in Another America*, David Covin's *The Unified Black Movement in Brazil*, Reginald Daniel's Race and *Multiraciality in Brazil and the United States*, and Agnes Mariano's *A Invençao da Baianidade*.

5. Zilá Bernd, ed. *Poesia Negra Brasileira: Antologia* 96.

6. *Palmares* (or *Quilombo dos Palmares*) refers to the largest community of escapees from slavery and others seeking freedom in colonial Brazil. It existed from 1605 until its destruction in 1694 in the present-day state of Alagos. The Palmares settlement was led by the famed Zumbi dos Palmares (1655–November 20, 1695) who resisted Portuguese colonial oppression during slavery and was captured and beheaded on November 20, 1695, a date now celebrated by African Brazilians as their national day of Afro-Brazilian consciousness, as Zumbi is seen as hero, freedom fighter, and symbol of freedom.

7. See blurb on the back of the volume *Poema sobre Palmares*; stanza taken from the same (45.6–7).

8. For a detailed discussion of the politics of race and Afro-Brazilian religion, see Rachel Harding, *A Refuge in Thunder: Candomblé and the Alternative Spaces of Blackness*.

9. Pedro Lourenço, "Prefácio," *Caxinguelê* 3.

10. Similar sections of this analysis on Jamu Minka have been previously published in my book *Afro Brazilians Cultural Production in a Racial Democracy*. Rochester, NY: U of Rochester P, 2009. 351–56.

11. Ash Wednesday refers to the first day of Lent in the Christian tradition. The Lenten (fasting) season lasts for forty days with the exception of Sundays and ends on the "Holy Saturday," that is, the day before Easter Sunday. Ash Wednesday thus references the day signaling the end of carnival (a public celebration and parade involving circus, masks, and public party) and the beginning of the Lenten season.

Works Cited

Afolabi, Niyi. *Afro-Brazilians: Cultural Production in a Racial Democracy*. New York: Rochester UP, 2009.

Assumpção, Carlos de. *Protesto*. São Paulo: Sociedade Impressora, 1982.

Bernd, Zilá. *Negritude e Literatura na América Latina*. Porto Alegre: Mercado Aberto, 1987.

———, ed. *Poesia Negra Brasileira: Antologia*. Porto Alegre: Editora AGE, 1992.

Bernd, Zilá, and Margaret Bakos. *O Negro: Consciência e Trabalho*. Porto Alegre: Editora da Universidade, 1991.

Cadernos Negros: Os Melhores Poemas. Eds. Esmeralda Ribeiro and Márcio Barbosa. São Paulo: Ministério da cultura, 1998.

Camargo, Oswald de. "Comentário." Abelardo Rodrigues, *Memória da Noite*. São José dos Campos: Self-Edition, 1978. 3–5.

Correia, Lepê. *Caxinguelê*. Recife: Sambaxé Consultoria, 1993.

Covin, David. *The Unified Black Movement in Brazil*. Jefferson, NC: McFarland, 2006.

Cuti and Carlos de Assumpção. *Quilombo de Palavras: Poemas*. Manaus: Microservice, 1997. CD.

Damazio, Márcio. Preface. *Teclas de Ébano*. By Jamu Minka. São Paulo: Ed. do Autor, 1986. 4–5.

Daniel, Reginald. *Race and Multiraciality in Brazil and the United States*. Pittsburgh: Penn State UP, 2006.

Dantas, Beatriz Góis. *Nagô Grandma & White Papa: Candomblé and the Creation of Afro-Brazilian Identity*. Chapel Hill, NC: U of North Carolina P, 2009.

Duarte, Eduardo de Assis. *Literatura, Política, Identidades (ensaios)*. Belo Horizonte: UFMG, 2005.

Ferreira, Hélio Pinto. "Prefácio." Abelardo Rodrigues, *Memória da Noite*. São José dos Campos: Self-Edition, 1978. 1–2.

Hanchard, Michael G. *Orpheus and Power: The Movimento Negro of Rio de Janeiro and São Paulo, Brazil, 1945–1988*. Princeton: Princeton UP, 1988.

Harding, Rachel. *A Refuge in Thunder: Candomblé and the Alternative Spaces of Blackness*. Bloomington: Indiana UP, 2000.

Kraay, Hendrik, ed. *Afro-Brazilian Culture and Politics: Bahia, 1790s to 1990s*. New York: M. E. Sahrpe, 1998.

Laclau, Ernesto, and Chantal Mouffe. *Hegemony and Socialist Strategy*. London: Verso, 1985.

Lima, Jorge de. "Essa Nega Fulô." *Poesia Completa*. Rio de Janeiro: Nova Aguiar, 1997, 15–17.

Lody, Raul. "Ancestralidade e Memória em *Casa-Grande & Senzala*." *A Obra em Temos Vários*. Ed. Fátima Quintas. Recife: Fundação Joaquim Nabuco—Editora Massangana, 1999. 145–51.

Lourenço, Pedro. "Prefácio." *Caxinguelê*. Recife: Sambaxé Consultoria, 1993. 3–5.

Mariano, Agnes. *A Invenção da Baianidade*. São Paulo: Quilombhoje, 1986.

Martins, Sérgio da Silva, et al. "Paving Paradise: The Road from 'Racial Democracy' to Affirmative Action in Brazil." *Journal of Black Studies* 34.6 (2004): 787–816.

Minka, Jamu. *Teclas de Ébano*. São Paulo: Ed. do Autor, 1986.

Nascimento, Abdias do. "Quilombismo: An Afro-Brazilian Political Alternative." *Journal of Black Studies* 11.2 (1980): 141–78.

Nascimento, Elisa Larkin. "Aspects of Afro-Brazilian Experience." *Journal of Black Studies* 11.2 (1980): 195–216.

———. "Kilombismo, Virtual Whiteness, and the Sorcery of Color." *Journal of Black Studies* 34.6 (2004): 861–80.

Pile, Steve, and Michael Keith, eds. *Place and the Politics of Identity*. New York: Routledge, 1993.

Quintas, Fátima, ed. *A Obra em Tempos Vários: Livro Comemorativo dos 95 Anos do Nascimento de Gilberto Freyre*. Recife: Fundação Joaquim Nabuco Editora Massangana, 1999.

Rodrigues, Abelardo. *Memória da Noite*. São José dos Campos: Self-Edition, 1978.

Silveira, Oliveira. *Germinou*. Porto Alegre: Self-Edition, 1962.

———. *Banzo Saudade Negra*. Porto Alegre: Self-Edition, 1970.

———. *Décima do Negro Peão*. Porto Alegre: Self-Edition, 1974.

———. *Praça da Palabra*. Porto Alegre: Self-Edition, 1976.

———. *Pêlo Escuro*. Porto Alegre: Self-Edition, 1977.

———. *Roteiro dos Tantãs*. Porto Alegre: Self-Edition, 1981.

———. *Poema sobre Palmares*. Porto Alegre: Self-Edition, 1987.

———. "Ser e Não Ser." Ribeiro and Barbosa, *Cadernos Negros* 108–10.

———. "Outra Nega Fulô." Ribeiro and Barbosa, *Cadernos Negros* 12–14.

———. *Orixás: Pinturas e Poesia*. Porto Alegre: Evangraf, 2000.

Telles, Edward. *Race in Another America*. New Jersey: Princeton, 2004.

Trindade, Solano. *Cantares ao meu Povo*. São Paulo: Brasiliense, 1981.

Twine, France Windance. *Racism in a Racial Democracy*. New Jersey: Rutgers UP, 1998.

White, Steven F. "Reinventing a Sacred Past in Contemporary Afro-Brazilian Poetry: An Introduction." *Callaloo* 20.1 (1997): 69–82.

12

(W)riting Collective Memory (De)spite State

Decolonial Practices of Existence in Ecuador

Catherine Walsh with Juan García Salazar

State in Latin America has never been an ally of African-descendant communities, nor has it been a key referent. Similarly, the written word has not been the medium or mechanism by which Afro communities typically position and pass on their stories, teachings, philosophies, knowledges, and thought. In essence, both writing and State have been considered as forces *casa afuera* (out-of-house). While State negates, orders and regulates, writing re-presents for a world that is not—or not only—the community's own. As such, the theme of this volume and project, *Black Writing, Culture, and the State in Latin America,* brings to the fore a number of interesting and crucial tensions and questions, including about the significance of State and writing today and about the intersections of both with collective memory and the ongoing struggles of and for existence.

Afro-existence has, without a doubt, been molded, signified, and constructed without, despite, and notwithstanding State; in essence, to spite State itself. That is, in its margins, blind spots, and "wastelands," and outside the very frames—of recognition, rights, and citizenship—that State assumes as constitutive and dear. Collective memory and oral tradition find their historical base here. They are grounded in the experiences, practices, and pedagogies of thinking and being that people of African origin have sown and cultivated on lands they were forced to make their own. What happens then when the present-day State offers its embrace? And in this context how is a new "riting" and writing of collective memory emerging today that recalls, spites, and transgresses State, while at the same time warning of newfound affections?

Such questions are particularly relevant in contemporary Ecuador. The making absent of African descendants is, in fact, a legacy and characteristic of the Ecuadorian State, one that can be traced back to the nineteenth-century decrees of abolition and

manumission, where there is no mention of the identity and subjectivity of the enslaved. The first official recognition of blacks only came with the Constitution of 1998,
189 years after "independence." Here and in the more radical 2008 Charter, Afro-
Ecuadorians are identified as "peoples" with collective rights.[1] The 2008 document
also recognizes ancestral territory and knowledge, makes nature the subject of rights,
and identifies racism and the need for reparation, compensation, and affirmative action. The state that historically denied existence and rights now confers. Yet as Abuelo
Zenon, the voice of Afro-Ecuadorian collective memory, makes clear, State is, and
always has been, part of the problem. With state recognition comes a new set of norms
and apparatuses of state control that work to negate, supersede, and disrupt ancestral
memory and being. The sad reality is that in the policy and practice of rights, recognition, and "progressive" government today, Afro-community and territory-based
existences have probably never been more challenged.

This chapter examines how collective memory as the philosophy and teachings
of the elders has been used in most recent years as a decolonial practice to recuperate,
strengthen, reposition, and reconstruct Afro existence as ancestral right. Such practice
is re-presented in the figure of *Abuelo Zenon*, who many years ago passed to the other
side, and is strategically put in voice and writing by his grandson Juan García Salazar,
who is considered by Afro-Ecuadorian communities as the "guardian of tradition"
and the "worker of the process." The chapter works to return the word, question the
present order from State, and act against the deterritorialization and social-cultural
dispersion of ancestral land, knowledge, and will that threaten existence and/as life.

The "riting" and the writing today of this memory and these struggles by García
and others allied to this process (in which Catherine Walsh includes herself) are socially, politically, culturally, and epistemically insurgent and strategic. This insurgency
and strategicality work both *casa adentro*, or "in-house," and *casa afuera,* or "out-of-
house." In house, the project is to build and strengthen a sense of belonging, understanding, and engagement among the newer generations distanced by modernity
and technology from oral tradition and the elders, and to leave a record supported
in the written word. Out-of-house, the work and project are meant to transgress,
disrupt, and interrupt the frames, visions, and perspectives within which and through
which African descendants are studied and written "about," as well as those within and
through which they are now "included" as State's subjects-objects.

The interest of this chapter is to bring all of these considerations, processes, and
projects to the fore. As such, the chapter does not speak in a single voice, nor does it present
findings "about" Afro-Ecuadorians gleaned through observation, study, and research.
Instead, it is conceived and constructed as a dialogue and thinking "from" and "with"
collective memory and the decolonial practices of existence in Afro-Ecuador as expressed
in the words, thoughts, writings, and personas of Juan García and Abuelo Zenon.

With this interest and proposition in mind, we have chosen a nonconventional writing style of italics and non-italics. The italicized represents the words of García spoken
in an ongoing dialogue and conversation with Walsh, and the non-italicized represent
the words of Walsh and the quoted citations of García and Zenon, along with other
related references.[2] This style, which we have used together before, attempts to break
the singularity and homogeneity of voice most often present in co-authored texts as

well as the authoritative-interpretative stance frequently assumed when one individual writes about the thoughts and writings of another.[3] In so doing, it raises important considerations about the logics, methodologies, pedagogies, and ethics of writing, and, of course, of collective work itself, considerations that are constant in our individual and shared work and in our efforts toward decolonial praxis.

In what follows, then, we will explore the significance of collective memory and its present-day (w)riting, consider the notion of existence and/as ancestral right, and engage the problematic of the present ordered from State, including its accompanying deterritorialization.

Collective Memory and its (W)riting

For us collective memory is the reaffirmation of that which tradition teaches us, of what the ancestors teach. And, precisely, it is collective memory because it is in the entire collective. While some may have more and others less knowledge about an act, fact, or event, about a way to do things, about a value or saying, about a person or being, all [in the community] generally have a shared comprehension of what it means to have a way 'casa adentro' to understand; everybody [in-house] knows what we are talking about here. Collective memory is collectivized knowledge; for us the guarantee and verification of the ancestral, then, is in its shared and collectivized nature. It is that which enables us to live on.

In Ecuador in general and most particularly in the Afro-Pacific territory-region of the north of Esmeraldas,[4] collective memory is not an ephemeral account of the past, but an enduring register and construct that signifies, nourishes, builds, and sustains belonging, existence, and continuance as present with past. In this the elders have always been key. As Abuelo Zenon says, "the elders are our witnesses and from their word we have much to learn" (qtd. in García, *Territorios* 15). Their oral re-creations and narrations pass lived knowledges from generation to generation, weaving through words what Lewis Gordon has referred to as "transcendental reality," that is: "the world by which and through which meaning is, in a word 'meaningful'" (164–65).

The problem, of course, arises when the meaningfulness of this world and its ontological-epistemological-spiritual-methodological-pedagogical base are transgressed and displaced; when the elders as ancestors lose their captive audiences, when those who have passed on are not replaced, when the shared and collectivized are broken, and when, as Zenon argues, those in the community begin to assume an other's truth (García, *Territorios*). Without a doubt, the dictates of schooling, of Western "universal" knowledge and progress, and of today's individual-based inclusion of Afro-descendants by State are central factors that contribute to, push, and enable the transgressions, ruptures, and displacements. Together, all are constitutive mechanisms of modernity and its underside that is the coloniality of power, mechanisms that have long worked to advance, denigrate, and negate what the elders name as collective memory, ancestral philosophies and teaching, and existence as ancestral right. "To learn from the past means to look for valid proposals in the community's collective memory, to recuperate our sense of belonging and rights in order to continue being ourselves as community, family, as Afro-Ecuadorian peoples" (García, *Territorios* 158), because "The simple life of those that came before us, their particular ways of understanding wellbeing and richness or wealth, are a mirror so that the new generations can measure that value of their interior being and the greatness of their ancestral philosophies" (Zenon qtd. in Garcia, *Territorios* 16). A resistance to and a working against the modern/colonial matrices and mechanisms of power define such a proposal as a project. Yet resistance is not the only descriptive force. Also and more critically involved are the pro-positive insurgent dynamisms of re-creation and re-existence that collective memory and its "riting" and writing work to engender and bring forth.[5]

With "riting" we refer to the acting and enacting of collective memory, to the practices—past and, especially, present—that not only give ancestral teachings a special place and space, but that also, through this acting and enacting, position tradition-based words as humanizing forces of collective re-creation and re-existence. Such riting brings to mind Gordon's call for incantations: "With incantation we evoke, call forth, and sometimes invoke—bring forth, summon or conjure—special forces. We sing—and often chant—magical words" (Gordon 164). The writing down of these words is indicative of a new practice of riting that, in Ecuador, responds to the exigencies of the present times.

Today's putting on paper of collective memory, of ancestral teachings, has two vertients. The first is what we call "el encargo generacional" (the generacional responsibility). Those of my generation listened to our elders narrating, telling, explaining; our hearts and our minds were ready to learn through oral transmission the knowledges and wisdom they imparted. Our generational encargo*, then, was to listen and to learn. But that has now changed precisely because of the second vertient, the "brecha generacional" (the generational gap), where the willingness to learn listening no longer continues, the fault, in part, of the schools that have come to replace the elders.*

The ancestral mandate to learn by oral tradition went as far as us—our generation. As such, we who still carry this "encargo" have decided to change the method, to put the ancestral mandates in written word so that they can get to this new generation that is not interested in learning by listening, or in giving audience to "los saberes" (the knowledges).

But we have also made a backup of the oral memory; the Fondo Documental, which we continue together to build and promote, keeps these memories in oral word as a parallel support so that one can return to the recorded voice of the ancestors; the voice is preserved.[6] This is a way, in a moment of crisis, to resort to or adopt another strategy or tool, another medium, which is writing, as a way to maintain this voice and enable a listening and learning from it. The oral backup verifies that what is written really does belong to the ancestor.[7]

These are the two vertients that come together to give reason to writing oral memory and oral traditions; it is a reason that works to challenge the history and coloniality of power: this subjugation that schooling signifies for our youth and children. We assume this decision with caution and with much in-house reflection, knowing that by putting it in writing means that it is no longer oral tradition per se, although this is where it comes from. All this—the word of memory and the written word—is something still new to the community. There are still not many of us writing this memory and, for this reason, it still needs much reflection casa adentro.

However, we are clear of writing's strategic use. If writing has been the principal medium to impart knowledge that is not our own, why not use it now to disseminate our own knowledge? Of course the bottom line here is to make clear the criterion that this is neither individual knowledge nor the words of a single author, but rather that of the collective reproduced in the memory of the elders.

In this way, the reproduction of the memory of the elders in written form is not a product or result of the reflections of the individual author that records them. The elders themselves are clear about this and, as such, demand that their words be written as they are said, as they are transmitted. If one respects the words of the elders, then one should not try and translate or rephrase them into standardized form. Nor should one attempt to give them meaning, interpret them, or change their focus, because in so doing one often loses or obscures all that is underneath. "Say it as I say it," the elders caution. "This is how I want people to hear what I am saying in ten years, which means that you are my voice, you are my generation." This does not just mean simply writing down what they say, transcribing; it means contemplating each word, each phrase, the order of words, listening to the silences and to what is done with sound. This is a labor that is not easy, particularly when one assumes its in-house significance as ancestral responsibility. One has to have lived and seen this in context in order to put it in written words. Oral tradition, then, understood casa adentro, *is complex and respectful; those of us who respect this are those of us committed to this tradition.*

The problem comes often when this material is used casa afuera *as quotations or citations that simply support the idea of an individual author and do not support or give presence to the collective thought that the citations themselves signify, construct, and recall. One thing is to do an interview of someone in the community for a research project, for example, and another is a conversation about a historical event, a foundational myth or story, an ancestral practice; with each come distinct intentionalities, logics, rationalities, and responsibilities. Moreover, there are some things that cannot or should not be written if one is aware and respectful of the ancestor and of ancestral knowledge, and there are others that lose their force and significance when put on paper. For these reasons, the work with oral tradition is complicated and, even more importantly, entails, from the ancestral vision, an obedience to tradition.*

In all of this process, the personage of Abuelo Zenon, both literal (as García's long-deceased grandfather) and figurative (as an ancestral referent born in the sowing of collective memory), has come in recent years to play a central role.[8] Zenon is generally and increasingly understood *casa adentro* as the ancestor that brings Afro-Ecuadorian existence-based thought into one single voice, a voice that is *sparing, simple, and "propia" (of our own), without additions.* It is a voice that *always dismantles words that are not our own, words that Zenon uses as counterwords. When Zenon speaks, the people speak. Tradition and memory are talking.*

The role of Zenon has much to do with collective memory, because when Zenon talks, I know what he is saying, I find meaning in it, and I find myself there but also my grandfather in the voice, the sayings, the proverbs. Collective memory is also this force with regard to which one says, "I know this; I know what he is talking about." Zenon is the voice I listened to, I don't know when or how many years ago, but I know I heard this voice before. This is important for what it says about the role of Zenon: folks can easily connect because it is their own voice; it is the voice of all of us. The role of Zenon is to bring together thought in a single collective voice.

Zenon is a way for groups to address collective memory. His assertion, for example, that schools were put in the communities not to teach us but to subjugate us serves as a charge for reflection, as food for thought, as a stimulus to think and rethink in a way that is our own. Folks can use Zenon and Zenon's phrases with total liberty, without the fear of reprisal, without the fear that someone will say they are copying or misquoting. It is a way to not cite what the academic intellectuals cite, and it is the pride in being able to say, "This is my personage, and I can talk from him." And, of course, there is another element as well: that no one can cite Zenon better than those from the community, because they can put in the tonality, the voice. Zenon works to bridge the differences within the communities, to lower the levels of confrontation among different ways of thinking and epistemic positionings. By attributing a thought or a saying to Zenon and not to one individual, collective memory and knowledge are repositioned and once again taken up.

Zenon thus plays a useful and important role that does not belong to any one person. It is a role that has been functioning in memory; Zenon is the black community's intellectual property. When Michael Handelsman is working with Zenon,[9] *or when community leaders work with Zenon and say, "Listen, Zenon is now speaking," they are evoking memory and tradition; they are giving space for memory and tradition to talk, whether that talking be in oral form or written down.*

The writing of Zenon, in this sense, interrupts while simultaneously contributing to what Richard Jackson described as black literature in Latin America. For Jackson, this literature can be defined within a humanist legacy and within the theoretical framework of *ethnopoetics*: "a term associated with oral tradition and with new forms of poetry created when oral and preliterate forms merge with new written or formal languages. . . . It is a human poetics . . . a poetics 'of the Other,' but it is also a poetics 'of our kind' and 'of who we are'" (Jackson xvi–xv). Latin American literature about blacks by blacks themselves is, as Jackson argues, clearly distinct from that written about blacks by non-black authors. Yet it is still typically understood and read within the Western academic frame that attributes authorship to an individual and that makes writing the medium and place from which literature is defined and from which authors speak.

For Handelsman, this is the difference and tension that Zenon marks with what has been constituted as Afro-literature in Ecuador and more generally in the Afro-Latin American diaspora. While authors like Nelson Estupiñan Bass speak from writing—from the privileged place of a literary artist that speaks for and about the necessities of the people, and from the individualism characteristic of the literary world—Zenon personifies orality and articulates community-based thought. "We that have planted in our hearts the sense of belonging to the community, do not just speak of the community, we suffer with the community, our pain is the pain of the community, we are the community," Zenon says (qtd. in García, *Territorios* 12). It is in this context that Handelsman asserts: "Far from considering [literary] artists as their principal representatives and advocates, the communities look within to assume the responsibility of their own construction as collective people" (111).

The fact that it is García who calls forth Zenon's thought and puts his teachings, evocations, and incantations to word is reflective and indicative of García's own ancestral role as guardian of the tradition. Through his community-based and oriented writings, community study-groups, workshops, and oral-tradition schools, and his more than half a century of dedication to listening to the elders and compiling their testimonies, narratives, stories, and life histories, García has worked to position and enable collective memory as an ancestral, sociopolitical, cultural, existential, and epistemic force. In these processes of articulation and (w)riting, the lines between Zenon and García are blurred; both appeal to, and are constitutive of, the many elders and guardians of tradition whose words, teachings, and thought continue on in anonymity.

The Present Ordered from State

What is the interplay of State with these issues of memory, ancestral tradition, and writing? And how does State in Ecuador today re-present and re-create the same tension previously described with regards to black literature? That is, how does the state's appointment of Afro individuals within high-up government institutions today position and enable a privileged space from which these state appointees, like the literary figures, speak for and about the necessities of the people from the individualism and intermediarism characteristic of State?

Here Zenon's words, written and interwoven with García's, once again articulate community-based thought as they make tense, unsettle, and call into question the past and present role of State and its contemporary practices of representative inclusion. Handelsman stresses, likewise, the communities' adherence to their own sense of community identity, over and above the representativity that might ensue from the appointees of the state (2011).

Zenon reminds us that African-origin peoples predate State, which is the imposed referent through which domination, subjugation, regulation, and exclusion have been proffered:

> We cannot forget that our right to live in these territories is born in the historic reparation of the damage/harm that meant the dispersion of our African blood through America, dispersion that through the will of others we had to live these hundreds of years before the configuring of the states which now order/regulate us.
>
> What we are today as people is what we never wanted to be, because what we are today does not depend solely on our will or desire to be. Today we are what the laws of the State direct and dictate that we will be. (qtd. in García, *Territorios* 67)

With the 2008 Constitution and its radical rethinking of society, law, and State, including the recognition of racism, reparation, affirmative action, collective rights, and aspects of indigenous and Afro life-visions (i.e. ancestral knowledges, collective well-being, and nature's rights), a new era of visibility and inclusionary politics was ushered in.[10] The interrogative that seems to naturally follow is: What happens when the historic concerns of African-origin people become part of—are assumed by and within—State?

The Afro-descendent political analyst and writer Jhon Antón Sánchez describes these new politics of visibility and inclusion positively as an opening of "cultural citizenship." Afro-Ecuadorians presently or formerly in government, including Oscar Chalá and Alexandra Ocles, recognize the advance as well as the complexities, difficulties, and contradictions of its present application.[11] Yet it is only García and Zenon who, through their thought, voices, and/in writing, make present the problematic inherent in the very idea and practice of State, preceding and current. For both, such problematic is grounded in, among other concerns, the "dis-memory" that inclusion as a kind of new beginning engenders.

This government of the Ecuadorian State, or any other government for that matter, does not want or know how to confront the historic debt it has with the Afro-Ecuadorian community. It does not know how because it does not know history or the perspective of the Afro community. It knows a national history where we Afros form a very small part, if at all, but supposedly we have done nothing, we have given nothing. And because they have not measured the debt as a contribution to a people that against its will had to give much work to this [state and national] construction, it is assumed that there is no debt, or need, for reparation. The state is not doing anything in this regard, and society and the community are not doing anything either. Only a few Afros agree on the necessity of reparation. The majority thinks they are being included and have an equality of opportunities. The Afro community as a whole is not thinking about reparation, and this seems to me to be a kind of historical dis-memory (desmemoria histórica) *on our side.*[12]

This dis-memory works to reverse collective memory and to position it as a bygone tradition with little present-day relevance or significance. State thus becomes both representative and constitutive of the new beginning. Certainly for peoples historically kept outside the frame and practice of the nation-state, recognition, equality, citizenship, and inclusion have weighted meaning. Hope and the light ahead can easily shadow and obscure the road back. Of course, the problem here is not only that the elders and ancestral knowledge lose their contemporary role, but also that individual representation and rights begin to supersede (or make less necessary) the community as collective. Furthermore, *the politics of inclusion itself work to leave behind, to undo, our black mind, our "negritud."*[13] Dis-memory, in this sense, is a strategy of power—a re-coloniality of sorts—that weakens the very elements upon which a collective black identity, memory, and existence were built. Recalled is Frantz Fanon's assertion (re-taken up in Gordon) that affirmation within the system depends on the system's denial of ever having illegitimately excluded.[14]

Inclusion is, without a doubt, functional to the new plurinational and intercultural Ecuadorian State in its progressive positioning and construction. However, it is not necessarily transformative of State's historical relation (or non-relation) with African descendants. The problem, of course, is not that there are now Afro-Ecuadorians in, and part of, State. Rather, the problem is the fact that *it is a representation that is always subject to the vision of the state. They are designates of the state, not put there by the community. It is an inclusion that does not touch power.*[15]

Besides the problematic of dis-memory and representative inclusion, García and Zenon bring to the fore another related concern of the present ordered from State: the denial, negation, and usurpation of ancestral rights, in which territory—as existence and life—remains fundamental. Territory in the Afro-Pacific is central to the equation of memory and living: "We understand that without territory culture cannot be born, and without culture identity cannot grow or flourish" (García, *Territorios* 15). Territory situates, grounds, evokes, and recalls memory, the ancestors, collective consciousness, and the struggles of and for life, freedom, and humanity. Moreover, it ties all together.

It is frequently that we hear the elders say that when the states were not, the ancestral philosophies and mandates of the people of African origin settled in these territories, ordered our way of living. This reflection has a historical root: we cannot forget that the first family trees of African origin arrived to live in this region between 1560 and 1760. As such, the ancestral mandates were first, well before the formation and laws of the states. The communities recuperated their ancestral right of their forms of life and ways of being in a time when the state did not exist. That is why the elders speak of a greater right that was born in-house, before the other rights were born. That is the ancestral right to territory.

As Zenon says:

> The configuration of a territory for life was for us always the *Gran Comarca Territorial del Pacífico* [Great Territorial *Comarca* of the Pacific], that is the land that the ambition of others brought us to. [It is] where we anchored the love for the land lost, that which remained on the other side of the sea. This, hundreds of years before . . . the States that now order us. (qtd. in García, *Territorios* 44)

> [As such] of all the ancestral rights . . . the right to collective territory is the one that is easiest to recognize. The former enslaved that won this right arrived to these lands against their will. To recognize the ancestral right over the territories that they occupy is the minimum that the States can do to repair this historic injustice. (qtd. in García and Walsh 352)

García's writing and thinking with Zenon about territory and territoriality as ancestral right and about the deterritorialization supported and proffered today by State (in complicity with extractivist interests) are fundamental in understanding not only the ancestral and the collective as present-day signifiers that walk with the past, but also the problem of State itself. In this sense, the writing and written words are pedagogically political and politically pedagogical in a decolonial way.[16]

This is made particularly evident in García's book *Territorios, Territorialidad y Desterritorialización*, subtitled as a pedagogical exercise for reflection about ancestral territories. This text brings together the narratives and testimonies of a long list of elders, community-based members, and youth from the north of Esmeraldas about the palm-oil industry and palm-oil cultivation and its devastating effects on Afro communities. Here, as in all of his texts, García does not name himself as author but as compiler, editor, and worker of the process. The "authorship" is in the collective, something that the Western world has a difficult time fathoming. Similarly, the proposition or objective goes beyond the individual reader. It is conceived in a praxical sense: to generate thought and reflection and push engagement and action across and among individuals out-of-house as well as in-house as a way to position the ancestral, build solidarities, and strengthen the collective.

Zenon and García make this clear in the Introduction, as represented in the following passages:

> Surely others can be seeing only from their shore that which is affecting and destroying us. But from the shore or riverbank of the communities of African origin, that which affects us has to be said as we feel it and narrated in the way that we see it. (Zenon, 16)

The narrations about the philosophies of the elders [made by the witnesses here] . . . recuperate the category of proposals, of suggestions for all the social actors that have something to do with the management of the environment in this region. The philosophies about the solidarity-based use of natural resources need to be seen as a teaching offered by the cultural particularity of the Afro-Ecuadorian communities of the territory-region of the north of Esmeraldas. All of this . . . is a clear questioning of the present. Above all the present that is ordered from State, where the appropriation of great extensions of the mother mountain are permitted for a few "without respecting the right of those who have less." (García, 16–17)

The deterritorialization and the social dispersion that we live in these . . . communities, in these territories of the north of Esmeraldas, are the product of a social and political injustice that all of us have the obligation to get back to, to re-think again, above all those who have the power to make decisions. (Zenon, 17)

The notion of "the ancestral" is central here. *The guardians of tradition share the opinion that what gives a determined collective territorial space the category of "ancestral" are the particular ways that its resources are used, taken advantage of, and managed. The elders are sure that we—the ancestral peoples of African origin and the indigenous peoples—are the very essence of these territories. These territories are spaces for life. We use the resources that they have to guarantee collective well-being.*

The ancestors teach that the ancestral territories are constructed for social, cultural, and spiritual control that includes the just distribution of [natural] resources as part of an economic ethic; for that reason they have to be collective and community spaces. The construction of an ancestral territory is born in the history of the people that reclaim ancestrality and has to be understood as ancestral collective memory about the cultural occupation of these physical surroundings. The occupation has to be proven by the collective memory of the people; without historical memory there is no ancestrality. And this goes beyond the laws of the state.

Today in the ancestral territories the biggest threat is what the elders call deterritorialization, understood as the loss of the ancestral right[17] and the negation by State of the legal recognition to live in these territorial spaces. The state deterritorializes our communities–that is to say it negates the recognition of our right to the territory where we have always lived. The loss of ancestral right to territory makes it impossible for the communities to connect with the new social proposals that are announced in the Constitution and collective rights.

Despite the Constitution, collective rights, and the representative inclusion of Afro-descendants, more than 27,000 hectares of land in the north of Esmeraldas had been sold or concessioned to palm-oil cultivators as of 2012; 15,000 of these are in the collectively titled ancestral territory of the Cayapas-Santiago Commune. During the present government of Rafael Correa, more credit has been given to palming companies for more hectares of Afro ancestral lands than ever before in history. Of course, the spread of palm cultivation and the loss of ancestral lands have to be understood in the broader scenario of the regionalization of the Colombian conflict. The active presence of Colombian paramilitaries, hit squads, and narcotraffickers and their growing control of both palming and mining produces a situation of violence, displacement, and deterritorialization that State has not stopped but rather enabled.[18]

When the state legitimizes the sale of ancestral territories, when it gives concessions for mining and land to palm-oil cultivators, the message that the Afro-Ecuadorian people are given is that these lands are wastelands, that they do not have owners, and for that reason they can be appropriated and used by external actors. In this sense the illegality is part of the state itself.

(In)Conclusion

In this context and reality, the struggles to rite and write collective memory are not simply about maintaining tradition; they are about the continuance of Afro existence itself, an existence that, as Zenon and García argue, is shaped and defined by the ancestral making of a territory for, and as, life. Territory grounds and situates memory and existence as life-based processes constructed and constituted by African-origin peoples. For this reason and taken together, territory, memory, and existence are decolonial practices that have not only gone against or resisted state ordering, but that, more importantly, have endeavored to build and create ways of being, knowing, and doing otherwise, despite State. The threat to such practices and creations comes, at least in part, again from State, one today made much more complicated with its progressive discourse, its representative inclusion, and its incorporation of laws and rights. The problem is the extent of this threat, which, as Zenon and García contend, puts the future of Afro-existence itself in more peril now than in any other time in history:

> When a community loses its ancestral territory, when the mountain stops being the "mother of God" for the families of African origin, when the water of the rivers stops being the fountain of life for tangible beings and the refuge of the intangible, then the spirit of the ancestors crosses the sea and looks for the land of the mother continent in which to rest. (qtd. in Walsh, *Interculturalidad, Estado, Sociedad* 223)

> The people of the north of Esmeraldas have always dreamed of leaving a territory for our descendants so that they can live in peace as we have done for so many years. Now that this right over this territory is taken away, we will have to leave as inheritance the testimonies of this injustice so that the motive for resistance does not die in the new generations. (Zenon qtd. in García, *Territorios* 172) [translation by Walsh]

> ('Los pueblos negros del norte de Esmeraldas, siempre soñábamos con dejar a nuestros herederos un territorio para que vivan en paz como nosotros mismos hemos vivido por tantos años, ahora que nos quita el derecho sobre este territorio, tendremos que dejarles como herencia los testimonios de esa injusticia, para que en las nuevas generaciones no muera el motivo para la Resistencia")

Unfortunately, this is the lived reality that is increasingly giving, in the north of Esmeraldas and in the Gran Comarca of the territory-region of the Afro-Pacific, the reason and motive to the riting and writing of collective memory today. *Zenon once said that all letters are not good, and writing is just that: letters.* As such and in closing, we both ask: Is this what collective memory will soon become—letters on a page emptied of ancestral and life-built significance? Or, rather, will letters and their (w)riting become another way to strengthen the bulwark against dis-memory, enabling what Jerome Branche has termed "a *malunga* ethics" that "creates and takes part in structures of memory and alterity in critical tension with the dominant narratives and official histories"(44)? An ethics and practice—of decolonial sorts—that does not (re)order collective memory to fit the structures of literature and writing, but that instead alters what we have known as literature and writing and their relation with oral tradition; a writing and riting that works, as Montaño argues, "to re-live intentional histories and ignite clarities with the force of 100 (and more) tomorrows" (7). Such is the challenge today, *casa adentro* and *casa afuera,* that we face in Ecuador, and possibly elsewhere in the Afro-Latin American diaspora.

Notes

1. The designation as "peoples" is significant in that it recognizes the historical-ancestral collective status of African descendants, a status initially afforded to indigenous peoples in Convention 169 of the International Labor Organization (1989).
2. The translations from Spanish to English of García and Zenon are by Walsh.
3. See for example Catherine Walsh and Juan García, "El pensar del emergente movimiento afroecuatoriano. Reflexiones (des)de un proceso" and Juan García and Catherine Walsh, "Derechos, territorialidad ancestral y el pueblo afroesmeraldeño."
4. This region forms part of what the communities refer to as the *Gran Comarca*, the ancestral Afro-Pacific territory-region that begins in the south of Panama and continues to the province of Esmeraldas in Ecuador, a territory-region that shares history, kinship, and familial relations. *The borders were born to fragment the totality of the community of African origin of this territory-region. But while the borderline has become a state mandate that the community must respect, in practice it is only a "raya" (line) that the people— literally and figuratively—cross over daily.*
5. I use *re-existence* here in the sense that Adolfo Albán has defined it, as the "mechanisms that human groups implement as a strategy of visibilizing and questioning the practices of racialization, exclusion and marginalization, procuring the redefining and resignifying of life in conditions of dignity and self-determination, while at the same time confronting the biopolitic that controls, dominates and mercantilizes subjects and nature" (85–86).
6. This reference is to the Fondo Documental Afro-Andino, the Afro-Andean Archive or Document Fund, a collaboration between *Procesos de Comunidades Negras* and the Universidad Andina Simón Bolívar in Quito, established in 2002 when García entrusted to the University an archive of over three-thousand hours of oral testimonies and narratives and more than ten-thousand photographs, collected by himself and other Afro-Ecuadorian intellectual-activists beginning in the 1970s. Since 2002, García and Walsh have worked together and collaboratively with a team that has included Edizon León, Sonia Viveros, Adolfo Albán, Freddy Cevallos, Enrique Abad, Diana Ávila, Lucy Santacruz, and others in preparing these materials for public use, disseminating the materials in communities through workshops, publications, and multimedia projects, and adding to the collection.
7. Concrete examples of this writing of oral tradition can be found in the texts published by the Fondo Documental Afro-Andino, including *Papá Roncón: Historia de vida* (Juan García Salazar, comp., second edition, 2011), *Cuentos de animales en la tradición oral del Valle del Chota* (Juan García Salazar, comp., 2003).
8. *This idea of sowing is something that always attracted my attention. Once I asked, "Is it true that*

black folk brought seeds in their head from Africa to here?" And they answered me: "Yes, yes, in the head, but inside not outside because maybe their hair was cut off due to the lice, inside in the craneum, these were the seeds that were planted, and many of these seeds were sown first in the heads and later on the earth." In a workshop, someone said that maybe Zenon is a modern sower, but what we do know is that he was witness to the first sowings and knows what was sown.

9. The reference here is to Michael Handelsman's text "Nelson Estupiñan Bass en contexto," in which he establishes what García refers to as a respectful dialogue and thinking with Zenon as collective memory.

10. See Catherine Walsh, "Afro and Indigenous Life-Visions in/and Politics: (De)colonial Perspectives in Bolivia and Ecuador" and Catherine Walsh, *Interculturalidad, Estado, Sociedad: Luchas (de)coloniales de nuestra época.*

11. See ALAI, "Entrevista a Oscar Chalá. Ecuador: Camino a la autodefinición" and Jean Muteba Rahier, "Interview with María Alexandra Ocles Padilla," respectively.

12. These words were also published in Catherine Walsh, "Afro In/Exclusion, Resistance, and the 'Progressive' State: (De)Colonial Struggles, Questions, and Reflections" 29.

13. Ibid.

14. See Frantz Fanon, *Black Skin, White Masks.*

15. Ibid., 30.

16. Recalled here is the slave pedagogy poignantly described by Stephan Nathan Haymes in "Pedagogy and the Philosophical Anthropology of African-American Slave Culture." For an elaboration of decolonial pedagogy, see Catherine Walsh, "Introducción, Lo pedagógico y lo decolonial: Entretejiendo caminos" and "Decolonial Pedagogies Walking and Asking. Notes to Paulo Freire from Abya Yala."

17. *Ancestral right, as we the black communities of this territory-region of the Pacific understand it, is above all rightness and reason: reason that has as its witness a history that many of us know and understand. For this reason our elders insist that "reason does not lose force," something that the younger generations redefine in saying, "Right and reason cause of force they are not." Seen from the philosophy of being of the African origins that live in this region, this old refrain shows us the level of trust that our ancestors had in the nature of justice justice that we the new generations are obliged to re-think, above all, after all the injustice we have lived.*

18. See Roa, "El desborde de la violencia."

Works Cited

ALAI. "Entrevista a Oscar Chalá. Ecuador: Camino a la autodefinición." *Afrodescendencia: Memoria, presente y porvenir.* Spec. issue of *América Latina en Movimiento* 467 (June 2011): 22–25.

Albán, Adolfo. "Interculturalidad sin decolonialidad? Colonialidades circulantes y prácticas de re-existencia."*Diversidad, interculturalidad y construcción de cuidad.* Eds. Wilmer Villa and Arturo Grueso. Bogotá: Universidad Pedagógica Nacional / Alcaldía Mayor, 2008. 64–96.

Branche, Jerome. "Malungaje: Hacia una poética de la diáspora africana," *Poligramas* 31 (2009): 23–48.

Fanon, Frantz. *Black Skin, White* Masks, NY: Grove, 1967.

García Salazar, Juan. *Territorios, territorialidad y desterritorialización. Un ejercicio pedagógico para reflexionar sobre los territorios ancestrales.* Quito: Fundación Altropico, 2010.

———, comp. *Cuentos de animales en la tradición oral del Valle del Chota.* Quito: Fondo Documental Afro-Andino/Universidad Andina Simón Bolívar, 2003.

————, comp. *Papá Roncón: Historia de vida*. 2nd ed. Quito: Fondo Documental Afro-Andino/Universidad Andina Simón Bolívar, 2011.

García Salazar, Juan, and Catherine Walsh. "Derechos, territorio ancestral y el pueblo afroesmeraldeño."*¿Estado constitucional de derechos? Informe sobre derechos humanos Ecuador 2009*. Programa andino de derechos humanos. Quito: Universidad Andina Simón Bolívar/Ediciones Abya-Yala, 2010. 345–60.

Gordon, Lewis. *Existentia Africana. Understanding Africana Existential Thought*. NY: Routledge, 2000.

Haymes, Stephan Nathan. "Pedagogy and the Philosophical Anthropology of African-American Slave Culture." *Not Only the Master's Tools: African-American Studies in Theory and Practice*. Eds. Lewis R. Gordon and Jane Anna Gordon. Boulder, CO: Paradigm, 173–203. 2006.

Handelsman, Michael. "Nelson Estupiñan Bass en contexto." *Género, raza y nación en la literatura ecuatoriana: Hacia una lectura decolonial. Guaraguao. Revista de Cultura Latinoamericana* [Barcelona: CECAL] 15:4 (2011): 110–32.

Jackson, Richard. *Black Literature and Humanism in Latin America*. Athens: U of Georgia P. 1988.

Montaño Escobar, Juan. "Esencias de guaguancó." *Letras del Ecuador. Literatura afroecuatoriana. Homenaje a Nelson Estupiñan Bass* [Casa de la Cultura Ecuatoriana] 185 (2002): 6–13.

Rahier, Jean Muteba. "Interview with María Alexandra Ocles Padilla, Former Minister, Secretaría de Pueblos, Movimientos Sociales y Participación Ciudadana, Ecuador." *Black Social Movements in Latin America: From Monocultural Mestizaje to Multiculturalism*. NY: Palgrave, 2012. 169–82.

Roa, Iván. "El desborde de la violencia: Raza, capital y grupos armados en la expansión transnacional de la palma aceitera en Nariño y Esmeraldas." MA thesis. Quito: FLACSO, 2011.

Sánchez, Jhon Antón. "Multiethnic Nations and Cultural Citizenship: Proposals from the Afro-Descendant Movement in Ecuador." *New Social Movements in the African Diaspora: Challenging Global Apartheid*. Ed. Leith Mullings. NY: Palgrave, 2009. 33–48.

Walsh, Catherine. "Afro and Indigenous Life-Visions in/and Politics: (De)colonial Perspectives in Bolivia and Ecuador." *Bolivian Studies Journal* [University of Pittsburgh] 18 (2011): 47–67.

————. "Afro In/Exclusion, Resistance, and the 'Progressive' State: (De)Colonial Struggles, Questions, and Reflections." *Black Social Movements in Latin America: From Monocultural Mestizaje to Multiculturalism*. Ed. Jean Muteba Rahier. NY: Palgrave, 2012. 17–47.

————. "Decolonial Pedagogies Walking and Asking. Notes to Paulo Freire from Abya Yala." *International Journal of Lifelong Education* 34:2 (2014). 1454–519. Web.

————. *Interculturalidad, Estado, Sociedad: Luchas (de)coloniales de nuestra época*. Quito, Ecuador: Universidad Andina Simón Bolívar / Abya Yala, 2009.

————. "Introducción, Lo pedagógico y lo decolonial: Entretejiendo caminos." *Pedagogías decoloniales. Prácticas insurgentes de resistir, (re)existir y (re)vivir*. Ed. Catherine Walsh. Quito: Ediciones Abya-Yala, 2013. 23–68.

Walsh, Catherine, and Juan García Salazar. "El pensar del emergente movimiento afroecuatoriano. Reflexiones (des)de un proceso." *Estudios y otras prácticas intelectuales latinoamericanos en cultura y poder*. Ed. Daniel Mato. Buenos Aires: CLACSO, 2002, 317–26.

Contributors

Niyi Afolabi teaches Luso-Brazilian Literature, Yoruba, and African diaspora studies at the University of Texas at Austin. He is the author of *The Golden Cage: Regeneration in Lusophone African Literature and Culture*; *Afro-Brazilians: Cultural Production in a Racial Democracy*; and editor of *The Afro-Brazilian Mind* and *Marvels of the African World*, among others.

Jerome Branche is the author of *Colonialism and Race in Luso-Hispanic Literature*, University of Missouri Press, 2006, and *The Poetics and Politics of Diaspora: Transatlantic Musings*, Routledge, 2015. He also has several edited books and essays on Latin American and Caribbean literature and on pedagogy. He teaches at the University of Pittsburgh.

Odette Casamayor-Cisneros is a Cuban-born scholar and writer, and an associate professor at the University of Connecticut-Storrs. She is the author of *Utopia, Dystopia and Ethical Weightlessness: Cosmological Reconfigurations in post-Soviet Cuban Fiction*, published by Iberoamericana/Vervuert, 2013. Her current book in progress will be titled *On Being Black: Racial Self-identification Processes in Post-Soviet Cuban Cultural Production.*

Lesley Feracho is the author of *Linking the Americas: Race, Hybrid Discourses, and the Reformulation of Feminine Identity*, SUNY 2006. She teaches at Georgia University, and her areas of interest are in Afro-Hispanic literature, feminist theory, race and popular culture in the Americas, with particular reference to Brazil and the United States.

María Mercedes Jaramillo is a professor at Fitchburg State University. She is also a past-president of the Colombianist Association, 2009–2013. She is the author of *El Nuevo teatro colombiano: Política y cultura*, 1992, and co-author of *¿Y las mujeres? Ensayos sobre literatura colombiana*, 1991. She has also edited several books on Latin American theater and women's writing.

Ifeoma Kiddoe Nwankwo is the author of *Black Cosmopolitanism: Racial Consciousness and Transnational Identity in the Nineteenth-Century Americas*, University of Pennsylvania Press, 2005, and articles on African American hemispherism; race and digital humanities; and Langston Hughes's international engagements, among other topics. An associate professor at Vanderbilt University, she is editor of four volumes on Caribbean and Afro-Atlantic studies, including *Rhythms of the Afro-Atlantic World* (with Mamadou Diouf; 2010) and *African Routes, Caribbean Roots, Latino Lives* (2010). Kiddoe Nwankwo is Founding Director of *Voices from Our America*, an international community-engaged research, curriculum development, and digital humanities program, and of the linked *Wisdom of the Elders: Life Lessons From and For African American Seniors* initiative.

Melva M. Persico teaches at Clemson University in South Carolina. She holds a PhD from the University of Miami. Her dissertation was entitled "Counterpolitics and Aesthetics: Afro-Hispanic and Belizean Women Writers." Her areas of interest are Afro-Hispanic and Caribbean Literature and Cultural Studies, with a new focus on the impact of social media on literary studies.

Matthew Pettway is an assistant professor at Bates College. He is currently engaged in a book project to be entitled "Afro-Cuban Literature in the Age of Conspiracy: Race, Religion, and Ritual in Juan Francisco Manzano and Gabriel de la Concepción Valdés." His articles on race, slavery, gender, and Afro-Caribbean religiosity have appeared in *PALARA*, the *Zora Neale Hurston Forum*, and the acclaimed Cuban journal, *Del Caribe*.

Paulette A. Ramsay has an interest in Language Pedagogy, Writing Theories, and Afro-Hispanic literature and culture. She is also a writer and poet whose work has been translated into German and Italian. Her scholarly articles have appeared in such major international journals as *The Afro-Hispanic Review*, *Bulletin of Latin American Review*, and others. She teaches at the University of the West Indies, Mona.

Elisa Rizo is an associate professor at Iowa State University. Her scholarly articles focus on the literatures and cultures of Equatorial Guinea and the African Diaspora in Latin America. She has three literary anthologies of Equatorial Guinean literature and a forthcoming, co-edited special issue on Equatorial Guinea in the *Revista Iberoamericana*.

Marveta Ryan is an associate professor of Spanish at Indiana University of Pennsylvania. She has published articles in such journals as *The Afro-Hispanic Review*, *Chasqui*, and the *College Language Association Journal*. She is currently preparing a book on less well-known writings by and about nineteenth-century Afro-Latin Americans.

Juan García Salazar is a historian, community-based researcher and educator, and founder of the Fondo Documental Afro-Andino (Afro-Andean Archive) housed at the Universidad Andina Simón Bolívar in Quito. He has written extensively on black oral tradition, ancestral rights, and on the territorial struggles facing Ecuador's Afro-descendant communities.

Catherine Walsh is senior professor and director of the doctoral program in Latin American Cultural Studies at the Universidad Andina Simón Bolivar-UASB in Quito, Ecuador, and a frequent teacher at Duke University. She is co-editor (with W. Mignolo) of the series *On Decoloniality* at Duke Press. Among her most recent books are *Pedagogías decoloniales. Prácticas insurgentes de resistir, (re)existir y (re)vivir* (2013), and *Interculturalidad crítica y (de)colonialidad. Ensayos desde Abya Yala* (2012).

Index

"A algunos de mis hermanos de raza" ("To Some of My Brothers by Race," Silveira Arjona), 44–47

Abakuá Society, 68, 71

"abolición de la esclavitud, La" ("The Abolition of Slavery," Alcalá Galiano), 52–57

academic institutions, 6, 66, 214, 217–19, 232, 240, 245

Acree, William, 216

Adire y el tiempo roto (Adire and Broken Time, Granados), 63, 65, 79nn5–6

affirmative action, 3, 238, 240, 254, 259

Afolabi, Niyi, 7, 267

Africa, 40, 94–95, 97–100, 140–42, 204, 209, 238–39, 247–49

African American Language (AAL), 175–76. *See also* language

African-derived religion and ritual
  Afro-Mexican, 209
  Caribbean, 158
  Cuban, 47, 64, 69–71, 78, 133–34
  death rituals, 119–23
  loyalty oaths, 9–18

African diaspora, 6, 83–86, 90, 129, 141, 209, 229–30, 254–55

Africanía y etnicidad en Cuba (Guanche), 22

Afro-American community, 85–86, 129, 164, 171–76, 181, 183–84

afroantillanismo movement, 151–53, 166

Afro-Blue (Bolden), 176

Afro-Brazilian community, 6–7, 237–40, 242–46

Afro-Brazilian literature and art, 213, 221, 223, 238, 240–51

Afro-Colombian community, 3–4, 6, 103–9, 112–13, 116–23

Afro-Colombian literature and art, 3, 5–6, 85, 103, 109–23

Afro-Costa Rican community, 6, 91, 196

Afro-Cuban community
  black press, 33–35, 41–42, 59
  education, 36–38, 41–42, 44, 48–49, 55–56, 68
  New Black concept, 64–65, 77
  political strategies and resistance, 14–18, 33, 48–49, 53, 57–59, 134–35
  racial improvement, 41–43
  religion, 11–13, 24–27, 47

Afro-Cuban literature and art
  cinema, 65–79
  music, 76, 80n28
  poetry, 33–59, 151

and racial identity, 63–65, 78, 142

and slavery, 4, 129–35

Afro-descendant communities, 1, 5–6, 141. *See also individual communities*

Afro-Ecuadorian community, 3, 6, 136–37, 253–61, 264n1

Afro-Ecuadorian literature and art, 6–7, 129, 136–38, 245, 253–64

Afro-Gaucho identity, 240–42. *See also* Brazil

Afro-Hispanic literary culture, 1, 5–6, 83–102, 100n1, 127–48

Afro-Hispanic Review (US), 5

Afro-Hispanic women writers, 127–48

Afro-Mexican community, 193, 196–97, 204–8

Afro-Mexican literature and art, 193–210, 215

Afro-modernity, 250. *See also* modernity

Afro-Puerto Rican community, 139, 151–52, 165

Afro-Puerto Rican literature and art, 6–7, 129, 146, 150

afrorealismo, 85–86. *See also* realism

Afro-Romance Institute (University of Missouri, Columbia), 5

Afro-Uruguayan community, 89, 100, 214–17, 220–21, 231–32, 233n20

Afro-Uruguayan Literature (Lewis), 216–17

Afro-Uruguayan literature and art, 87, 213–25, 228, 230–32, 232n15, 250

Agamben, Giorgio, 12

Ahoranián, Coriú, 220, 222

"A la raza de color (en la apertura del círculo de recreo Cervantes)" ("To the colored race [upon the opening of the Cervantes Recreational Center]," Rosales Morera), 35–42, 53

"A la raza negra" ("To the Black Race," Peña), 42–44

Albarado Zabaleta, Pedro Alfonso, 124n7

Alcalá Galiano, José, 52–56

Allen, Lillian, 172, 187

Alma cimarrona (Maroon Soul, Torres Díaz, and Reyes Larrea), 195–99, 204–6

Álvarez, Santiago, 66

Amerindians, 2

"Amo a mi amo" ("I Love my Master," Morejón), 142–43

Amores, José, 9–12, 18–27

"Amy Son" (Bennett), 172–73

"Ancestralidade e Memória em *Casa-Grande & Senzala*" ("Ancestrality and Memory in *The Masters and the Slaves*," Lody), 244–45

Anderson, Benedict, 34

Andrade Barbosa, Rogério, 245
Andrade Pinheiro, Inaldete, 245
Andrews, George Reid, 209, 216, 222
animal imagery, 2, 53–55, 161–62
Antología de la poesía negra americana (Pereda Valdés), 217
Antología de poetas negros uruguayos (Britos Serrat), 218
Antonio Varese, Juan, 220
Anzaldua, Gloria, 173
A Obra em Tempos Vários (Quintas), 244
Aparicio Prudente, Francisca, 195–97
apartheid, 2–3, 248
Aponte, José, 33
Aponte Rebellion (1812), 14
Arango, Gonzalo, 107–9
Arango y Parreño, Francisco, 64
Archaeology of Knowledge (Foucault), 28n6
Ardila Arrieta, Laura, 122, 123n6
Argentina, 2, 5
Arocha Rodríguez, Jaime, 120–21
Asociación de Cultura y Sociedad Uruguaya Negra (ACSUN), 223–24
"Aspects of Afro-Brazilian Experience" (Nascimento), 239–40
Assman, Jan, 138
Association of Uruguayan Writers, 216
Assumpção, Carlos de, 238, 248–50
Atrato River (Colombia), 103–5, 111–12, 117, 123n4
Austin, J. L., 12
authoring, space of, 194, 210
Autobiografía (Manzano), 4
Autonomist Party (Cuba), 43
Avila Laurel, Juan Tomás, 83, 95–100
Ayala, Cristina (María Cristina Fragas), 52, 56–59

"Baby If You Give It to Me" (Danger Man), 183–84
Badiou, Alain, 76
Bailey, Benjamin, 176
Bainoa (Cuba), 13, 15, 18–20, 23, 29n24
Baker, Houston A., 176
Bakhtin, Mikhail, 194
Bakos, Margaret, 242
Balibar, Etienne, 3
Ballagas, Emilio, 151
Bantu, 245–46
Barbeitos, Arlindo, 248
Barcia, Manuel, 18, 23, 30n31
Barnet, Miguel, 131–32
Barrios, Pilar, 217
Barrow, Alberto, 177
Basso Ortiz, Alessandra, 22–24
"Batuque" ("African Percussion," Assumpção), 249
Baugh, Eddie, 172
Beatles, The, 74–75
beauty, 29n17, 198–205, 208, 250
belabored body, 159–67
Bellavista (Colombia), 103, 105–6, 118–20
Bello, Andrés, 5
Beltrán, Aguirre, 193
Beltrán, José, 48–49
Benavides, Washington, 218
Benítez-Rojo, Antonio, 65, 159–61, 210
Bennett, Louise, 172–74
Benton, Lauren, 87–88
Bernd, Zilá, 241–42

Between the Lines (Callahan), 56
Bhabha, Homi, 128, 146
Biblioteca de Literatura Afrocolombiana (Blanco et al.), 3
bilingualism, 173, 175–76, 181–87. *See also* language
Biography of a Runaway Slave (Barnet), 131–32
black body, 21, 23, 25–27, 152–60, 164, 246. *See also* blackness; race
Black Experimental Theater (TEN, Brazil), 3, 240
"Black Idiom" (Smitherman), 175–76
black literary movements, 85–86, 151–53, 166
black nationalism, 14–15
blackness
    cultural and literary history, 29n12, 172
    and literary culture, 151–54, 195–96, 225, 248–50
    and national identity, 139, 198–201, 206–7, 210, 250
    and raceless nation, 75–77
    state manipulation, 59
black press, 34–35, 41–42, 44, 55–56, 216–17, 220–21
Blacks in Hispanic Literature (DeCosta Willis), 6
black societies (Cuba), 68
black speech, 175–76, 178–79. *See also* language
black women
    agency and resistance, 139–42
    and beauty, 29n17, 198–205, 208, 250
    language, 175–76
    objectification of, 139–42, 159–60
    racialized and gender roles, 132, 150
    and racial pride, 196–201
    sexual exploitation and abuse, 140, 142, 159
    and sexuality, 152–59
blanqueamiento (whitening), 2, 63, 110, 152, 221. *See also* race
Bloque Elmer Cárdenas (AUC), 103–5
"Blues" (Rodrigues), 249
Blues, Ideology, and African American Literature (Baker), 176
Boehmer, Elleke, 143–44
"Bojayá, la guerra sin límites" ("Bojayá, the War without Limits," National Commission on Reparations and Reconciliation), 109
Bojayá: Los cinco misterios de un genocidio (Bojayá: The Five Mysteries of a Genocide, Vargas), 110
Bojayá massacre, 103–4, 106–23, 123nn4–6, 124n7, 124nn13–14
Bolden, Tony, 176
Bolekia Boleka, Justo, 94
Bolívar, Simón, 30n36, 136
Borrero, García, 70
Borucki, Alex, 216
Boukman, Dutty, 14
Bourdieu, Pierre, 213–14
Boyce Davies, Carole, 128, 131–32, 135–36, 145–46
Branch, Gloria, 178, 180
Branche, Jerome, 5, 29n12, 84–86, 95, 264, 267
Brand, Dionne, 172, 187n1
Brathwaite, Edward Kamau, 173–77
Brazil, 2–3, 6–7, 239–43, 245, 251n6. *See also* Afro-Brazilian community; Afro-Brazilian literature and art
Brindis de Salas, Virginia, 217
British Caribbean, 2–3, 172–76, 178, 181–85, 187, 188n6, 189n11
Britos Serrat, Alberto, 218

Cabral, Amilcar, 247
Cabral, Cristina, 225
Cabral, Manuel Del, 151
Cabrera, Lydia, 30n33
Cadernos Negros (Ribiero et al.), 241, 247, 249
Café con leche (Coffee with Milk, 2003), 75
Callahan, Monique-Adelle, 40, 56–59
Cállate burrita prieta (Be Quiet Black Donkey, Aparicio
    Prudente et al.), 195–97
Camargo, Oswaldo de, 248–50
Candau, Joël, 118
Candombe
    history, 100, 220–21
    legitimation in Uruguay, 213, 222–24, 231
    music and performative tradition, 88–90,
        101n10, 222, 233n24, 233nn17–18
"Candombe and its Socio-Cultural Space, The"
    (UNESCO), 222
Candombes de los Reyes, Los (Olivera Chirimiri et al.),
    220
Candomblé, 245
Cantos populares de mi tierra (Obeso), 4
Carbonell Walterio, 64, 69
Cardoso, Jorge Emilio, 83, 87–90, 93–95, 100, 223–24
Cardozo Ferreira, Carlos, 217
carnival
    and Afro-Brazilian identity, 238, 246–47
    and Afro-Uruguayan Candombe, 213, 221–24,
        226, 233n17
    and black identity, 151–53
    and Christianity, 248, 251n11
    role in Cuba, 42, 76
Carpentier, Alejo, 63
Cartey, Wilfred, 5
Casa de la Cultura Afro-Uruguaya (Montevideo),
    224–25, 231
Casa del Lago (Mexico), 219
Casamayor-Cisneros, Odette, 4, 6, 267
Casas, Bartolomé de las, 2
Castillo Bueno, María de los Reyes (Reyita), 129,
    132–35, 138–42, 146
Castro, Fidel, 61–62, 66–67, 74–76, 78
Catholic Church
    and African-based religion, 9–12, 78, 209
    and Bojayá massacre, 13–17, 107
    funeral rites, 119–23, 150
    influence in Cuban society, 20, 27
    rituals and sacraments, 10, 18–23, 25–27, 248,
        251n11
Cato, Dionysius, 38
Caxinguelê (Squirrel, Correia), 245–46
Cecilia Valdés (Villaverde), 130–31
censorship, 4–5, 11–12, 26, 27n5, 28n8, 65, 74–75,
    78–79
Césaire, Aimé, 2, 249
Chagas, Jorge, 218, 231, 232n11
Chalá, Oscar, 259
children
    and Bojayá massacre, 107, 119–21, 123n5,
        124n13
    and education, 34, 39–41, 48–49, 52, 215, 256
    and slavery, 37, 164
Childs, Matt, 14
Chiriboga, Luz Argentina, 129, 135–42, 146
Chocó region (Colombia), 5–6, 103, 105–14, 123

Christianity, 2, 12, 26, 47, 58, 156–58, 164, 209. *See
    also* Catholic Church
Christophe, Henry, 158
Cienfuegos, Camilo, 75, 78
cinema, 65–79. *See also* film and film making
citizenship
    African, 94
    Afro-Brazilian, 237–51
    Afro-Cuban, 34, 47, 50, 61–64
    and Latin American Afro-descendant
        communities, 1, 253
    in Panama Canal Zone, 177
    and slavery, 129, 137
Civil Rights Movement (US), 74, 171, 189n12, 247
Cocco de Filippis, Daisy, 127
cocolos, 152, 163, 165
code-switching, 171, 173, 175, 185. *See also* language
Coffea Arabiga (1968), 72–74, 76
Cofiño, Miguel, 65
collective memory
    of Bojayá massacre, 111–19
    and identity, 85, 88–90, 217, 229–30, 239,
        247–49
    and language, 174–75, 183
    of slavery, 129–30
    writing and state recognition, 253–64
Colombia, 3–4, 6, 66, 103–12, 114–18, 123nn4–6,
    262. *See also* Afro-Colombian community; Afro-
    Colombian literature and art
colonialism
    and Afro-Caribbean identity, 172–73
    and black literary culture, 4–5, 127, 130, 203,
        227–28, 238, 247
    and Cuban slave uprisings, 9–22, 25–27
    decolonial practices, 254–56, 260–64
    decolonization, 130, 263, 265n16
    and independence struggles, 137–38
    and language, 172–75, 178
    objectification and exploitation of women, 140–
        44
    political ideology, 168n21
    postcolonial discourse, 127–28, 151–54, 156,
        160, 195, 204, 227–28
    racial policies and integration, 1–2, 27, 30n37,
        33–34, 59, 200, 203–5
Colonialism and Race in Luso-Hispanic Literature
    (Branche), 29n12
communism, 64–66. *See also* socialism
Como surgió la cultura nacional (How National Culture
    Emerged, Carbonell), 64
co-mothering (*comadrismo*), 162–63. *See also*
    motherhood
"comparsa, La" ("The carnival procession," Pichardo
    Moya), 151
Concepción Valdés, Gabriel de la (Plácido), 10, 13,
    17–18, 28n8, 28n11, 29n20, 30n27
Congo people, 30n33, 189n10
connective marginalities, 183, 189n13
consagración de la primavera, La (The Rite of Spring,
    Carpentier), 63
Conservación, La (Uruguay), 216
Conspiración de la Escalera, La (the Ladder Conspiracy,
    1843–1844), 18–19, 23, 25, 28n10, 29n20
Cooper, Carolyn, 172
Copeland, M. Shawn, 21, 27

Cordón de La Habana, 72
Correa, Rafael, 262
Correia, Lepê, 238, 244–56
Cortijo, Rafael, 154, 166
"Costa" (Zapata), 207–8
Costa Chica (Mexico), 7, 195, 202, 204–6, 210–11
Costa Rica, 6, 83, 91–93, 100. *See also* Afro-Costa
    Rican community
costumbrista literature, 65
counterpublic, 3
Craveirinha, José, 249
Creoles, 33, 187. *See also* race
Crespo, Elizabeth, 161
Critical Perspectives on Afro-Latin American Literature
    (Tillis), 5
Cuando la sangre se parece al fuego (When Blood
    Resembles Fire, Cofiño), 65
"Cuando las mujeres quieren a los hombres" ("When
    women love men," Ferré), 150, 154–58
Cuba
    agriculture, 70, 72–76
    black press, 34–35, 56
    colonialism, 2, 43–44, 48–49
    Cuban Revolution (1959), 61–64, 66–67, 72, 78,
        130–32, 138
    education, 36–38, 41–42, 44, 48–49, 55–56,
        66–68
    1844 Movement, 6, 9–32, 28n10
    independence movement, 14–15, 62, 133–34
    Massacre of 1912, 59, 132, 134, 151
    New Man and national identity, 6, 61–67, 72,
        75–78, 132–33, 135–36, 153
    race relations, 48–50, 57–59, 61–79, 131
    religion, 15, 20, 24
    slavery, 9–27, 41, 52–59
    and United States, 61, 73–74, 153, 159, 161
    women's roles, 73, 135
    See also Afro-Cuban community; Afro-Cuban
        literature and art
cuento uruguayo, El (Benavides et al.), 218
cultural capital, 4, 213–14, 218, 220–21, 231–32
cultural memory, 138–39, 143–46
Cultura y Literatura Afro-Uruguaya (Lewis), 224
Cuti, 249

Damazio, Márcio, 247
dance
    and African contemporary theater, 94
    Afro-Brazilian, 223, 246, 249
    Afro-Colombian, 85, 111
    Afro-Cuban, 39–40, 42, 70, 73–76
    Afro-Mexican, 201–2, 208–9
    Afro-Puerto Rican, 153–54, 161, 165–66,
        168n15
    Afro-Uruguayan, 88–90, 220
    and black counterpublic, 3
Danger Man (Alonso David Blackwood Drakes), 171,
    181–87
Dantas, Beatriz Góis, 238–39
"Dared to Live, The" (Russell), 180
Darío, Ruben, 5
Daughters of the Stone (Llanos-Figueroa), 129, 138–46
Davis, Angela, 247
Davis, Darien, 131
De cierta manera (One Way or Another, 1974), 70–71

Declaration of Autonomy (Colombia), 106
DeCosta-Willis, Miriam, 5–6, 56
De La Fuente, Alejandro, 62
del baile, Los (The Party People, 1965), 76–77
Deleuze, Gilles, 86–87
Del gatillo al pincel (From the Trigger to the Brush,
    Bogotá), 110
"Deliverance" (Harper), 56
Del Monte, Domingo, 4
desalojo en la calle de los negros, El (The Eviction on the
    Street of the Black People, Cardoso), 83, 87–90,
    93–95
"Desarraigo forzado" ("Forced Uprooting," Arocha
    Rodríguez), 120–21
Descartes, René, 40
Desde La Habana ¡1969! (From Havana, 1969!, 1969),
    74
Desde mi trinchera (Rodríguez Cabral), 226
DeShazer, Mary K., 128
Díaz, Javier, 223–24
Díaz Perez, María Cristina, 195–97
Diccionario de la literatura cubana, 35
Dirección General de Culturas Populares (Mexico), 193
Directorio Central de Sociedades de la Raza de Color
    (Cuba), 34, 41–42, 48–50
Discourse on Colonialism (Césaire), 2
dislocation, 238, 250n2. *See also* migration
dis-memory, 260, 263
Distichs of Cato (Cato), 38
Doctors Without Borders (Médecins Sans Frontières),
    97
Dodson, Jualynne, 23
Dominican Republic, 151, 153, 167n5, 176
Douglass, Frederick, 189n16
drug trafficking, 104–5, 123n4, 149, 158–59, 262
drumming
    in religious rituals, 24, 78
    and resistance, 74, 76, 198–99, 217, 242, 246,
        249
    in traditional music and dance, 90, 209, 220–23
    See also African-derived religion and ritual; music
Duarte, Eduardo de Assis, 238
Duarte López, Miguel Ángel, 219, 231, 232n14
Duncan, Quince, 83, 85–86, 91–95, 100
Duron-Almarza, Emilia Maria, 176
Dussel, Enrique, 98

Echavarría, Juan Manuel, 110
Echeverría, Esteban, 5
Ecuador, 3, 6–7, 253–64, 264n4, 265n17. *See also*
    Afro-Ecuadorian community; Afro-Ecuadorian
    literature and art
Editorial Manatí (Dominican Republic), 225–26
Edwards, Jonathan, 2
"Efeitos Colaterais" ("Collateral Effects," Minka), 247
1844 Movement (Cuba), 9–32, 28n10
Enciclopedia popular cubana (ICAIC), 66
England. *See* British Caribbean
En la otra isla (On the Other Island, 1968), 66–68
Enlightenment, 2
enslaved blacks. *See* slavery
entierro de Cortijo, El ("Cortijo's funeral," Rodríguez
    Juliá), 151
En un barrio viejo (In an Old Neighborhood, 1963),
    77–78

"Envidiosos, Los" (Danger Man), 184
Equatorial Guinea, 6, 22, 95–100
"esclavitud, La" ("Slavery"), 50–51
Ese Atrato que juega al teatro (Playing at Theatre in the Atrato Region, Kleutgens), 111
"Essa Nega Fulô" (Lima), 241
"Esta noche he pasado" ("Tonight I walked through," Cortijo), 166
Estupiñan Bass, Nelson, 258
ethnopoetics, 258
Eucharist, 10, 18, 20–21, 27. *See also* Catholic Church
Eurocentrism, 3, 35, 64, 165, 196

Fang ethnicity, 96–97
Fanon, Frantz, 247, 260
FARC (Revolutionary Armed Forces of Colombia), 103–5, 107, 123nn5–6
Feal, Rosemary, 136
Federation of Cuban Women, 134
feminism, 128, 131, 154–55, 217. *See also* women
Feracho, Lesley, 5, 267
Fernández, Nadine, 63–64, 72
Ferré, Rosario, 150, 154–58, 163–64
Ferreira, Hélio Pinto, 248
Ferrer, Ada, 34, 59, 62
Festival de Poesía en Voz Alta (Mexico), 219
figured world, 194–95, 198, 202–3, 209–10
film and film making, 1, 65–79, 131, 150, 214
Finch, Aisha, 10, 22
"500 años después" (Rodríguez Cabral), 227–28
Flórez López, Jesús Alfonso, 104
folklore, 3, 151, 195, 215–17, 232, 245–46
Fondo Documental Afro-Andino (Ecuador), 256, 264nn6–7
"Fool on the Hill, The" (McCartney), 74
Fornaris, Rafael Roberto, 164
Fornier, Ted, 138
Foucault, Michel, 11, 28n6, 84, 101n5
Fragas, María Cristina (Cristina Ayala), 52, 56–59
Fra-Molinero, Baltasar, 27n2
France, 14, 70, 73, 158
Franklin, Benjamin, 38, 40
Fraser, Nancy, 3
Fraternidad, La (Havana), 34, 42, 44–47
free blacks, 13, 15–17, 33. *See also* slavery
Freud, Sigmund, 156–57
Freyre, Gilberto, 244–45
Fundação Joaquim Nabuco, 244
funeral rituals, 110, 117, 119–23

Galileo Galilei, 38
gangá, 22–25, 30n31, 30n33
Gangá, Fermin, 19–27, 29n24
"gangá longobá, Los" (Basso Ortiz), 22–24
Ganga Zumba, 243
Garcia Casarrubias, Adela, 195–97
García Caturla, Alejandro, 153
García Salazar, Juan, 7, 253–64, 264n6
García Yero, Olga, 75
"Garganta" ("Throat," Rodriques), 248–49
Garvey, Marcus, 132–34
Gates, Henry Louis, 176
gender
    class and racial hierarchies, 150–55
    and hip hop, 184–85
    objectification of women, 139–42
    politics and racial stereotypes, 16–17, 20, 26, 62–64, 71–72, 132–35, 200
    and slave narratives, 132–41
    and women's writing, 6–7, 127–31, 225
    See also malungaje poetics; sexuality; women
General, El, 181
Génesis, 110
Ginés de Sepúlveda, Juan, 2
Glissant, Edouard, 173–74
Gloria y Tormento (Chagas), 218
"Glosa" ("Gloss," Ruiz), 48–50
Goldberg, Theo, 2–3
Gómez, Juan Gualberto, 42
Gómez, Sara, 65–72, 75–76, 78–79
Gómez de Avellaneda, Gertrudis, 130–31
Gómez Nadal, Paco, 104, 109–10, 120
González, Anita, 202, 209
González, José Luis, 165
González, Ramón, 17
González, Tomás, 66
González Mandri, Flora, 130–31
Gordon, Lewis, 255, 260
Gortázar, Alejandro, 216
Granados, Manuel, 63, 65, 79nn5–6
Gran Cervantes, 35
Gran Comarca Territorial del Pacífico (Great Territorial Comarca of the Pacific), 261, 263, 264n4
gran familia (Great Puerto Rican Family), 139, 150, 152, 155, 167, 167n2. *See also* nuclear family
Grenet, Eliseo, 74
Griffin, Farah Jasmine, 176
Grosfoguel, Ramón, 98
Grosjean, François, 175, 181–82
Grupo de Teatro Varasanta (Colombia), 111
guali, 119–21
Guanabacoa (1966), 68–69
Guanche, Jesús, 22
Guattari, Feliz, 86–87
Guedes, Lino, 248
Guerra, Lillian, 62
guerra que no hemos visto, La (The War That We Did Not See, Manuel Echavarría), 110
guerrilla warfare, 66, 104–7, 114. *See also* Colombia
Guevara, Ernesto, 61, 63–64, 66–67, 75, 77–78, 79n4
Guillén Batista, Nicolás, 80n21
Guillén Landrián, Nicolás, 62, 65, 72–79, 80n21, 151, 153
Guillory, John, 214
Gutiérrez, Mariela A., 142
Gutiérrez Alea, Tomás, 66, 74

Haiti, 11, 14–15, 70, 73, 151, 153, 158, 167n5
Haitian Revolution (1794–1804), 9, 14–15, 22, 33, 73, 151
Hanchard, Michael, 221
Handelsman, Michael, 5, 258–59
Handley, George, 129
Harding, Frances, 94
Harper, Frances, 56, 58–59
Hegel, Georg Wilhelm Friedrich, 2
Helg, Aline, 42–43, 48, 59, 134
Hemingway, Ernest, 68
Hernández, Salud, 107
Hernández Colón, Rafael, 167n7

Hevia Lanier, Oilda, 42
Hidalgo y Costilla, Miguel, 208
Hijas del Progreso (Cuba), 41–42
hip hop music, 6, 171, 181–86. *See also* music
Hispanic African literary realism, 95. *See also* realism
Historia de la piratería (The History of Piracy, 1963), 66
Historical Memory Group (National Commission on
       Reparations and Reconciliation, Colombia), 109
historiography, 14–15, 121–22, 130, 151
Hobbes, Thomas, 2
Holland, Dorothy, 193
Holloway, Karla, 130, 175
hombres domésticos, Los (Homeboys, Avila Laurel), 83,
       95–100
Homero, Pedro, 243
homosexuality, 157, 184–85, 207. *See also* sexuality
Houchins, Sue, 27n2
Houghton Library (Harvard University), 10–11
housing, 87–88, 91–93, 96–97, 118
Howard, Philip, 41–42
Hoy Domingo (Cuba), 66
Hume, David, 2
Hurston, Zora Neale, 176

ICAIC (Instituto Cubano del Arte e Industria
       Cinematográficos, Cuban Institute of
       Cinematographic Art and Industry), 66, 72–73
"Identidade II" ("Identity II," Minka), 248
identity
       African discourse on, 94–95
       and Afro-Brazilian citizenship, 6–7, 237–51
       and Afro-Caribbean colonialism, 172–73
       and Afro-Ecuadorian community, 6, 136–37, 254
       and Afro-Gaucho ethnicity, 240–42
       and Afro-Mexican community, 193–94, 204–10,
           215
       and Afro-Uruguayan legitimation, 87, 90, 220–
           21, 231–32, 233n20
       and blackness, 139, 195–96, 198–201, 206–7,
           210, 225, 248–49
       and collective memory, 85, 88–90, 217, 229–30,
           239, 247–49
       and Cuban politics, 49–50, 62–64, 132
       and language, 171–72, 183, 186–87, 230
       and migration, 172–73, 176–77, 180, 189n11,
           230
       and New Man, 6, 61–67, 72, 75–78, 132–33,
           135–36, 153
       and place, 193–94, 196–97, 202, 204–8, 210
       postcolonial, 195, 204
       and Puerto Rico, 139
       and race, 49–50, 87, 139, 237–40
       and regionalism, 256, 258, 260–61
Igualdad, La (Havana), 34, 42
Imagined Communities (Anderson), 34
imagined community, 34–35, 59
inclusion, 6, 127–28, 237, 255, 259–63
Inside Downtown (2001), 78
Institute of Anthropology and History (Colombia), 3
Instituto de Tradição e Cultura Afro-Brasileira (Institute
       of Afro-Brazilian Tradition and Culture), 245
Instituto Guerrerense de Cultura (Mexico), 193
Insularismo (Pedreira), 151
"Insurgency at the Crossroads (Finch), 10, 22
International Poetry Festival (Medellín), 219

interracial marriage, 63–64, 72, 237
Iré a Santiago (I Will Go to Santiago, 1964), 66, 69–70
Isabel II, (queen of Spain), 10, 13
Ivory Coast, 22
Izquierdo, Pedro (Pello el Afrokán), 76

Jackson, Richard, 5, 258
Jamaica, 172–74, 181–85
James, Conrad, 5
Jaramillo, María Mercedes, 5–6, 267
Jefferson, Thomas, 2
Jemmott, Glynn, 193
Jim Crow system, 3, 177
Johnson, Lemuel, 5
Jonatás y Manuela (Chiriboga), 129, 135–38
José María Córdoba front (FARC), 103–4. *See also*
       FARC (Revolutionary Armed Forces of Colombia)
Judaism, 2, 68
"Juramento, El" (The Oath, Plácido), 10, 18

Kant, Immanuel, 2
kilele, 103
Kilele: Una epopeya artesanal (Kilele: A Homemade
       Epic, Vergara), 5, 103, 111–23
King, Martin Luther, Jr., 171, 189n12, 242, 247
Kleutgens, Inge, 111, 124n11
Kollwitz, Uli, 107
Krause, Karl Christian Friedrich, 38
Ku Klux Klan, 74

labor, 1, 14, 43, 72–74, 139–43, 161–63, 172, 240
Ladder Conspiracy, The (*La Conspiración de la Escalera*,
       1843–1844), 18–19, 23, 25, 28n10, 29n20
Lam, Wilfredo, 153
land and territorial rights, 6, 16, 107, 113–19, 204,
       207–10, 228, 265n17
Landers, Jane, 10
language
       African American Language and black speech,
           171–72, 175–76, 178–79, 181, 183
       African influences, 189n10
       bilingualism, 173, 175–76, 181–87
       code-switching, 171, 173, 175, 185
       Creole and Afro-Caribbean, 172–74, 178, 187n2,
           189n10
       English, 171–72, 175, 180
       identity and migration, 173, 230
       Jamaican patois, 174, 181–85
       linguistic layering, 179–80, 184
       multilingualism and diglossia, 176–79, 187
       poetic, 40–41, 43, 50, 58, 88–89
       Spanish, 171–73, 181
       and transnationalism, 183–84, 186
       West Indian, 171–72, 178
"Language and African Americans" (Smitherman), 175
"Language and Liberation" (Smitherman), 175
Laviera, Tato (Jesús Abraham), 173, 175
Law 70 (Colombia, 1993), 3
Leandro de Andrade, José, 218
Leguizamón, Graciela (Gracee Marty), 213, 215, 218,
       222, 224–25, 228–31
León, Fulleda, 69
lettered city, 5, 34
Lévinas, Emmanuel, 77
Lewis, Marvin A., 5, 216–17, 224

Ley Escolar y Plan de Estudios (Cuba), 41
liberatory narratives, 129, 135–39, 145–46
Liberia, 22, 30n31
libertos, 16–17. *See also* slavery
Libros sin Tapas (Books without Covers), 229
Life, Justice, and Peace Commission (Colombia), 107
Life of Sin (1979), 150
Life With Two Languages (Grosjean), 181–82
Lima, Jorge de, 241
Literacy Campaign (Cuba), 134
literary aesthetics, 225
literary prizes, 214, 217–19, 231
Literatura, Política, Identidades (Duarte), 238
Little War (Cuba, 1879–1880), 33
Llanos-Figueroa, Dahlma, 129, 138–46
Locke, John, 2
Lody, Raul, 244–45
Logiques des Mondes (2006), 76
López Baralt, Mercedes, 153
López Neris, Efraín, 150
López y Galaimena, Luisa María, 69
Lourenço, Pedro, 245
Lowe de Goodin, Melva, 177, 180
loyalty oaths, 6, 9–13, 17–27
Luberza Oppenheimer, Isabel, 149–51, 154–67
Luis, William, 5, 131
Luso-Hispanic literature, 29n12
Luz y Caballero, José de la, 64

"Majestad negra" (Palés Matos), 152
Malaret, Augusto, 151
Malcolm X, 247
Malpensante, El, 110
Maluala (1979), 130–31
malunga, 163–65, 264
malungaje poetics, 84–86, 95, 163
"Mamá Inés" (Grenet), 74
mambises, 134
mambises, Los (The Revolutionaries) (Rosales Morera), 35
Mandingo people, 22
Manzano, Juan Francisco, 4–5
Marcha del Guerrillero (Guerilla March), 73
marginality, 63, 65, 71, 77–78, 132, 237, 239, 247
marginalization
    Afro-Brazilian literary tradition, 237–39, 241–42, 247, 250
    Afro-Cuban community, 37, 132–33
    Afro-Hispanic drama, 90, 94
    Afro-Uruguayan legitimation, 213, 221–24
    black writing and national culture, 6–7, 255
    and modernity in literature, 127–29, 132–35, 143
maroon communities, 200–201, 239. *See also* mixed-race peoples
marriage, 63–64, 72, 156–57, 163, 237. *See also* nuclear family
Martí, José, 62–63
Martínez, Daniel, 219
Martins, Sérgio da Silva, 240
Marty, Gracee (Graciela Leguizamón), 213, 215, 218, 222, 224–25, 228–31
Marxism, 64, 67, 75, 78–79. *See also* socialism
master-slave paradigm, 244–45. *See also* slavery
Medici, Lorenzo di Piero de, 59n2
Medin, Tzvi, 61–62
Medina, Catalina, 111

Memória da Noite (Rodriques), 248
Memorias del subdesarrollo (Memories of Underdevelopment, 1968), 74
Memoria y Resistencia (Memory and Resistance, Rodríguez Cabral), 216
Méndez Tello, Donají, 202–3
Mercedes Porras, María, 110
mestiçagem, 237
mestizo and mestizaje
    and Puerto Rican identity, 139, 158
    racial construct in Mexico, 201–2, 210
    racial labels and ideology, 2, 7, 63–65, 76, 85, 152
    See also mixed-race peoples
"Meu Quilombo" (Assumpção), 249
Mexico, 6–7, 173, 194–210, 219. *See also* Afro-Mexican community; Afro-Mexican literature and art
Middle Passage, 131, 144, 158. *See also* slavery
Mignolo, Walter, 98
migration, 127–31, 133, 135–38, 172–73, 176–77, 180, 189n11, 230
Milagro de Anaquillé, El (1929), 153
Military Commission (Spain), 15–17, 26, 28n10
Millar, Michael, 122
Mills Young, Carole, 225
Minerva: Revista quincenal dedicada a la mujer de color (Minerva: A Bimonthly Magazine for Women of Color, Cuba), 42, 51–52, 55–56
Ministry of Tourism and Sports (Uruguay), 222–23
Minka, Jamu, 238, 247, 250
Minority Rights Group (Mexico), 193
miscegenation, 16, 164, 238. *See also* marriage; race
Missa dos Quilombos (Quilombos' Mass, Nascimento), 243
"Miss Anna's Son" (Russell), 179
Mitchell, Angelyn, 129
mixed-race peoples, 15–17, 20, 87, 200–201, 239. *See also mestizo and mestizaje;* mulatto *(mulato/ mulata);* race
modernism, 5, 241–44, 246, 250
modernity, 7, 99, 128, 138, 145, 241, 246–50, 254–55
Mohanty, Santya P., 86
Montaño, Oscar, 224
Montaño Escobar, Juan, 264
Montejo, Esteban, 131–32
Montejo Arrechea, Carmen, 35
Montevideo, 87–89, 217, 219–21, 224, 226–28, 231, 232n14
"Montevideo" (Rodríguez Cabral), 226–27
Moore, Robin, 153
Moorings and Metaphors (Holloway), 175
Moors, 2
Morales, Sebastián Alfredo, 28n8
morality, 38–39, 42, 68, 93, 150
Morejón, Nancy, 5, 131–33, 135, 139–43
Moreno, Emilio Leopoldo, 49
Moret Law (Cuba, 1870), 37
Morúa Delgado, Martín, 42
motherhood, 135, 139, 141, 156–57, 162–64, 167, 168n24, 202–3. *See also* nuclear family
Motivos de son (Guillén), 153
Moynihan Report, The (*The Negro Family: The Case For National Action*), 164
mozambique, 76, 80n28. *See also* music
muerte de los Santos Inocentes, La (The Death of Blessed Innocents, Sánchez Caballero), 109–10

muertos no hablan, Los (The Dead Don't Speak, Gómez Nadal), 109
Muhammad, Jameelah, 196–97
"Mujer Negra/Black Woman" (Morejón), 131–32, 142–43
mulatto (*mulato/mulata*)
    and African migration, 4
    employment discrimination, 161
    and literary symbolism, 153, 156–57
    position in Cuba, 14, 20–22, 33, 62–65, 68–72, 131
    terminology, 2
    See also *mestizo and mestizaje;* mixed-race peoples; race
"Mulher Negra" (Assumpção), 250
multiculturalism, 223, 231, 233n21
Multiculturalismo en el Uruguay (Díaz), 223–24
music
    and African contemporary theater, 94
    Afro-Brazilian, 249
    Afro-Colombian, 110–11, 119–21
    Afro-Mexican, 195, 201–2, 208–9
    as black cultural production, 6
    and Candombe, 88–90, 220
    and carnival, 226, 249
    and *cocolos,* 165
    in Cuba, 42, 68, 76, 78, 80n28
    hip hop and reggae, 6, 171, 181–86
    and *negrismo* movement, 152–53
    plena, 153–54, 161, 165–66, 168n15
    state appropriation of, 213
    See also drumming
"my graduation speech" (Laviera), 173
mythology, 85, 117, 130–31, 164, 244–45

Nagô Grandma and White Papa (Dantas), 238–39
Naipaul, V. S., 187
Nando Boom, 181
"Ñáñigo al cielo" ("Ñáñigo in Heaven," Palés Matos), 158
narrative forms
    and Afro-descendant resistance, 10–11, 18, 20–21, 59
    and Afro-Ecuadorian collective memory, 258, 261–64
    and Afro-Hispanic drama, 94–100
    and Afro-Hispanic slave experience, 128–46
    and Afro-Mexican oral tradition, 193–210
    as black cultural production, 1, 6, 95, 130
    and black women's sexual identity, 150–66
    and Cuban film, 69–70
    religious, 13–26, 56
    See also poetry
Nascimento, Abdias do, 3, 237–40
Nascimento, Elisa Larkin, 238–40
Nascimento, Milton, 243
nation
    Afro-Brazilian contributions, 238
    Afro-Hispanic development, 137–38
    and Afro-Hispanic women writers, 127–30
    Ecuadorian, 136–38
    and imagined communities, 34, 59
    and language, 171–79, 183–84
    and liberatory narratives, 135–36, 146
    and race, 34, 58–59, 62–64, 75–77, 179–80

    and regionality in Mexico, 208, 210
    and resistance of black women, 139, 145, 153
    role of poetry, 34–35, 43–44, 50
National Art Schools (Cuba), 67
National Department of Statistics (Colombia), 3
national identity. *See* identity
national imaginary, 149, 165, 217
nationalism, 7, 132, 135, 195, 205–6, 247
National Library (Montevideo), 216
nation language concept, 173–75, 178. *See also* language
natural resources, 7, 95–96, 104, 115, 204–8, 261–63
Nazi Germany, 2–3
Negrismo movement, 151–53
Negritude e Literatura na América Latina (Bernd), 241–42
Negritude movement, 94, 217, 225, 228, 241–42, 247–49
"Negro do Sul" ("Southern Black," Silveira), 242
Negro Family: The Case For National Action, The (the Moynihan Report), 164
Negron-Muntaner, Frances, 173
Neto, Agostinho, 247
New Black, 64–65, 77
New Granada, 137
New Man, 6, 61–67, 72, 75–78
New World, 2, 173, 209, 242–43
NGOs (non-governmental organziations), 109, 112, 214, 219
No Me Pidas Una Foto (Barrow), 177
Nora, Pierre, 122
novela de la tierra (novel of the land), 5
"no-whereian," 165, 168n28
nuclear family
    gran familia (Great Puerto Rican Family), 139, 150, 152, 155, 167, 167n2
    marriage, 63–64, 72, 156–57, 163, 237
    motherhood, 135, 139, 141, 156–57, 162–64, 167, 168n24, 202–3
    role of black women, 152, 156, 160
Núcleo de Identidad Negra (Nucleus of Black Identity), 245
Nuestra Raza, 216
Nuestra Señora de la noche (Santos Febres), 160–67
"Nueva Aurora, La" (The New Dawn), 52
Nwankwo, Ifeoma Kiddoe, 7, 13, 20, 267

OAS (Organization of American States), 107
Obeso, Candelario, 4
Obiang, Teodoro, 95
Ocles, Alexandra, 259
O'Donnell, Leopolda, 10
Oedipus, 156–57
Office of the Inspector General (Colombia), 109
"Ogum no Mapa" ("Ogun on the Map," Silveira), 243
Ogun deity, 243
oil boom, 95–96
Oliveira, Eduardo de, 248
Olivera Chirimiri, Tomás, 220
Ombudsman's Office (Colombia), 109
O Negro (Bernd), 241–42
Oppenheimer, Joselino (Bumbum), 165–66, 168n26
oppositional consciousness, 6–7, 130–32, 134, 137, 145
oral tradition

Afro-Colombian, 85, 119
and Afro-Ecuadorian literature, 253–58, 264
Afro-Uruguayan, 215, 219, 224
and black writing, 1
and censorship, 26
in Latin American Afro-descendant communities,
    83, 94, 249, 253–58
and *Negrismo* movement, 152–53
performance and race in Cuba, 131, 146
in Puerto Rican literature, 146
and racial consciousness in Mexico, 193–95,
    198–201, 204–10, 215
and storytelling, 122
orisha, 24, 69, 119, 144
Orixás (Orixá Divinities, Silveira et al.), 243
Orpheus and Power (Hanchard), 221
Ortiz, Fernando, 151–53
Oshun, 139, 143–44, 146
Osofisan, Femi, 94
Otero, Ramoso, 159
Otheguy, Ricardo, 175
otherness, 1–2, 76–77, 132, 158, 160
otro Francisco, El (1974), 130–31
"Outra Nega Fuló" (Silveira), 241

Padilla, José, 30n36
Páginas literarias (Literary Pages, Rosales Morera), 35
"'Pain of History Words Contain, The'" (Baugh), 172
"país de cuatro pisos, El" ("The four-storied house,"
    González), 165
Palés Matos, Luis, 151–54, 158–62, 166
Palmares, 239–44, 250, 251n6. See also *Quilombo dos
    Palmares*
palm-oil cultivation, 104, 115, 261–63
pan-Africanism, 242, 247, 249
Panama, 6–7, 171–92, 188n3, 189nn10–11, 264n4
Panamanian West Indians, 171, 176–87
Paquette, Robert, 10, 18, 25, 28n10
pardo, 20. See also mixed-race peoples
Parsley Massacre (Dominican Republic, 1937), 151
Partido Independiente de Color (Independent Party of
    Color, Cuba), 59, 132, 134, 151
Pascal, Blaise, 38
pastoral power, 101n5
patriarchy, 127–28, 131–32, 135, 150, 152, 157, 165
patronato, 37, 41
"Paving Paradise" (Martins et al.), 240
"Paz y Amor" (Danger Man), 181–82
Pedreira, Antonio, 151, 153
Pêlo Escuro (Silveira), 242
Peña, H. V., 42–44, 47, 58
Pereda Valdés, Ildefonso, 217
Persico, Melva M., 6, 268
Peru, 5, 137
Pettway, Matthew, 6, 268
Philip, Marlene Nourbese, 174–75
Pichardo Moya, Felipe, 151
Piel Oscura Panama (Barrow and Priestley), 177
place, 193–94, 204–10, 256, 258, 260–61
Plácido (Gabriel de la Concepcíon Valdés), 10, 13,
    17–18, 28n8, 28n11, 29n20, 30n27
Plácido: El poeta (Morales), 28n8
Plaza vieja (The Old Plaza, 1962), 66
plena, 153–54, 161, 165–66, 168n15. See also music
"Plena del menéalo" (Palés Matos), 153, 166

*Población afrodescendiente y desigualdades étnico-raciales
    en Uruguay* (Scuro Somma, ed.), 214
Poema Sobre Palmares (Poem on the Maroon Settlement,
    Silveira), 243
Poesia Negra Brasileira (Bernd), 241
poetry
    and Afro-Brazilian cultural resistance, 238–51
    Afro-Cuban, 34–59, 131–32, 142–43
    and Afro-Mexican racial identity, 193–210, 215
    Afro-Uruguayan legitimation of, 213–20, 224–32
    and black literary movements, 151–61, 166–67
    and discourse on race and nation, 4–7, 34–35, 73,
        94–95, 213
    language and identity, 172–75, 179–87
    literary techniques, 47, 158, 174, 198, 205, 242,
        249
    merging of oral and literate, 258
    in United States, 219
    See also narrative forms; oral tradition
Ponce (Puerto Rico), 149, 155–56, 161, 165
"Popular Theatre and the Guatemalan Peace Process"
    (Millar), 122
popular theatre for identification, 84–86
Portugal, 219, 247, 251n6
Porvenir, El (The Future), 68
positional identity, 94, 194–99, 207, 210
postcolonial discourse, 127–28, 151–54, 156, 160, 195,
    204, 227–28. See also colonialism
poverty, 68, 88–90, 96, 159, 183, 214–15, 221,
    239–40
Pratt, Mary L., 23
Premio Victoria prize (Uruguay), 219, 229
Prescott, Laurence, 5
Priestley, George, 177
Progresista, El (Uruguay), 216
Progreso, El (Cuba), 68
"Pronto Voy" (Danger Man), 186
Propoganda, La (Uruguay), 216
prostitution. See sex work
Protestantism, 158. See also Christianity
Protesto (Protest, Assumpção), 250
*Publication of the Afro/Latin American Research
    Association,* 5
publishing
    Cuban black press, 34–35, 51–52, 55
    and language in Afro-Caribbean literature, 171,
        186
    legitimation of Afro-Uruguayan literature, 3–4,
        214, 216–19, 224–26, 229, 231
Puerto Rico, 138–46, 150–53, 165, 167, 167n7,
    168n29. See also Afro-Puerto Rican community;
    Afro-Puerto Rican literature and art

"Quero ser tambor" ("I Want to Be a Drum,"
    Craveirinha), 249
Quibdó (Colombia), 104, 108–9, 111, 123n4
Quijano, Aníbal, 98
Quilombismo, 237–40
"Quilombismo: An Afro-Brazilian Political Alternative"
    (Nascimento), 237–40
Quilombo de Palavras (1997), 249
Quilombo dos Palmares, 239–50, 251n6
Quiñones, Manuel, 18
Quiñones Rivera, Maritza, 139
Quintas, Fátima, 244

race
    and Afro-Uruguayan legitimation, 87, 90, 214–
        15, 221–25, 227
    black body, 21, 23, 25–27, 152–60, 164, 246
    blood purity, 2
    Brazil politics of, 237–50
    colonial policies and integration, 1–2, 27, 30n37,
        33–34, 59, 200, 203–5
    and Cuban politics, 13–18, 41, 49–50, 62–65,
        67–70, 72, 130–31, 134
    and identity, 49–50, 87, 132, 139, 237–40
    improvement, 36–40, 46
    interracial marriage and miscegenation, 16,
        63–64, 72, 164, 237–38
    and language choice, 171, 176–84
    Mexico discourse and colonialism, 193–97,
        200–210
    mixed-race labels, 2, 7, 15–17, 20, 87, 200–201,
        239
    and nation, 34, 58–59, 62–64, 75–77, 179–80
    otherness, 1–2, 76–77, 132, 158, 160
    poetic discourse on, 34–35, 73, 94–95, 213
    poetic imagery and resistance, 7, 35–40, 45–47,
        50, 198–201, 203, 246–47
    racial consciousness, 7, 68, 193–210
    racial democracy, 133–34, 238–50
    racial state, 1–3
    reparations, 109, 123–24n6, 124, 254, 259–60
    and self-censorship, 4–5
    stereotypes, 15–16, 20, 22, 64–65, 70–71, 224
    See also blackness; black women; *blanqueamiento*
        (whitening); *mestizo and mestizaje;* mixed-
        race peoples; mulatto *(mulato/mulata);*
        whiteness
Race in Another America (Telles), 240
race relations
    in Brazil, 238–40, 248
    in Costa Rica, 91
    in Cuba, 33–34, 44–50, 57–59, 61–79, 131
    in Puerto Rico, 139, 145–46, 150–52, 163–66
    in Uruguay, 87–88, 214–15, 227–28
race war, 11, 15, 30n36, 57, 59, 134, 151
racist state, 3
Rada, Rubén, 222
Rafael (Cuban tenor), 67–68
Rama, Ángel, 5, 215–17
Ramos, Antún, 106–7, 112, 123n5
Ramos, José María, 17
Ramos, Julio, 75
Ramos Otero, Manuel, 150, 158, 161
Ramsay, Paulette A., 7, 268
Rancheador (1976), 130–31
rape, 26, 133, 140, 144, 164. *See also* slavery; women
Real Academia de la Lengua Española (Spain), 4
Real Cédula de Gracias, La (Royal Decree of Graces,
    1815), 151
realism, 5, 83–100
Rebambaramba, La (1928), 153
Recife (Brazil), 243–45
Red de Escritores/as y Creadoress Afro-Uruguayos
    (Redescrea/Redafu) (Network of Afro-Uruguayan
    Writers and Creators, blog), 229
"Redención" ("Redemption," Ayala), 52, 56–59
Reed, Ishmael, 176
re-existence, 256, 264n5

reggae and reggae en español, 171, 181–83. *See also*
    music
regionalism
    and oral tradition in Mexico, 204–8, 210
    place and cultural identity, 242, 260–62
    and Puerto Rican poetry, 151
Regla de Orisha, 69
Regla de Osha, 78
relational identities/positionality, 94, 194–99, 207, 210
religion, 2, 11, 18, 56, 68, 158. *See also* Catholic
    Church; Christianity
(re)membrance, 130, 145–46
Renato, 181
Rendón Herrera, Daniel ("Don Mario"), 123n4
Rendón Herrera, Freddy ("El Alemán"), 103, 106,
    123nn4–6
reparations, 109, 123–24n6, 124, 254, 259–60
Repeating Island, The (Benítez-Rojo), 159–60
"Requiem para Luther King" ("Requiem for Luther
    King," Silveira), 242
resistance
    and Afro-Brazilian poetry, 242–47, 249–50
    and Afro-Cuban anti-colonial activity, 33–34,
        40–41, 53–59
    and Afro-Mexican poetry, 198–201, 208
    and Afro-Uruguayan writers, 232
    and black women, 128–29, 132, 135–41
    and Bojayá, 106–19, 122–23
    and Candombe, 100
    and Cuban Revolution, 61–64
    1844 Movement (Cuba), 9–32, 28n10
    and memory, 122
    and slavery, 23–27, 136–37, 139–44, 161
    and uprising textualities, 128–46
resistance vernaculars, 183, 189n13
"Resistência" ("Resistance," Correia), 246
Revista Mella (Cuba), 66
Revista Uruguaya, 216
revolutionary novel, 63
Reyes, Dean Luis, 76–77, 80n29
Reyes Larrea, Israel, 195–96, 198–201
Reyita (Castillo Bueno), 129, 132–35
Ribera Chevremont, Evaristo, 161
Richards, Nelly, 140
Rio Grande do Sul (Brazil), 241–43
"riting," 253–56, 259, 263–64
ritual initiation, 9, 21, 23, 27
ritual poetics, 9, 11–12, 25, 28n9
Rizo, Elisa, 6, 268
Rodrigues, Abelardo, 238, 248, 250
Rodríguez, Jeannette, 138
Rodríguez Cabral, Cristina, 213, 216, 223–28, 231
Rodríguez Juliá, Edgardo, 151, 154, 166, 168n29
Roldán, Amadeo, 153
Romanticism, 5
Romero, César, 105
Rosales Morera, Antonio, 35–42, 44, 46–47, 53, 57
RoseGreen-Williams, C., 142–43
Rousseau, Jean Jacques, 2
Rubiera Castillo, Daisy, 132, 135
Ruiz, Marcos, 18
Ruiz, Santiago, 47–50
Rumbo Cierto (Uruguay), 216
Russell, Carlos, 171, 179–87, 189n12
Ryan, Marveta, 4, 6, 268

Sab (Gomez de Avellaneda), 130–31
Saco, José A., 64
Sacrament of Language, The (Agamben), 12
Saenz, Manuela, 136
Saint-Domingue, 14, 29n14
Salazar, Juan García, 268
"Saludos Pa Los Boy Del Town" (Danger Man), 185
Samba de Roda, 223. *See also* dance
Sánchez, Jhon Antón, 259
Sánchez Arroyave, Jhonover ("El Manteco"), 103
Sánchez Caballero, Freddy, 109–10
Sandoval, Chela, 130
Sanmartín, Paula, 132, 135
Santería, 69, 71, 78. *See also* African-derived religion
    and ritual
Santiago-Valles, Kelvin, 152
Santos Arrascaeta, Beatriz, 215, 223–24
Santos-Febres, Mayra, 5, 7, 139–41, 150–52, 160–67
scenarios of becoming, 86–87, 90–91, 93–95, 99–100,
    101n9
Scott, Rebecca, 37
Senghor, Léopold, 249
*Sentencia pronunciada por la Seccion de la Comisión
    militar establecida en la ciudad de Matanzas para
    conocer la causa de la conspiración de la gente de
    color* (Sentence pronounced by the Section of the
    Military Commission established in the city of
    Matanzas to uncover the motives of the conspiracy
    of the colored people), 10–11, 13–21, 25–27,
    29n23, 30n27
"Ser e Não Ser" ("Being and Non-Being," Silveira), 241
Sergio Giral, 130–31
Serra, Ana, 64
Serrano Soto, Juan Sebastián, 106
sexuality
    cultural stereotypes, 71, 150, 163–64, 186
    and dance, 202
    imagery of, 161–62, 164
    and *negrismo* movement, 152–53
    and objectification of women, 139–44, 150
    portrayal in literature, 91, 139–44, 152, 156–57,
        202
    racial stereotypes, 16, 20, 196–97
    sexual orientation, 67, 157, 184–85, 206–7
sex work, 135, 149–50, 156–57, 163–64, 168n15, 197
Sierra Leone, 22, 30n31
Signifying Monkey (Gates), 176
Silveira, Oliveira, 238, 240–44, 249–50
Silveira Arjona, Vicente, 44–47, 51, 57–58
"Sin espejos" (Marty), 229
slavery
    abolition, 40, 50, 138, 243, 253–54
    and African American literary tradition, 129
    and Afro-Hispanic women writers, 129–30
    agency of women in, 139–44, 161
    and black poetry, 50, 52–59, 203, 249
    in Brazil, 237, 239, 244, 251n6
    and children, 37, 164
    in Cuba, 9, 13–17, 33, 41, 62, 131
    cultural traditions, 209, 220
    and education and intellect, 36–38, 53, 55
    and language imposition, 174–75
    in Latin America literature, 1, 4–5
    rebellion and resistance, 9–32, 28n10, 30n37, 33,
        136–37, 139–44, 161

sexual abuse of women, 133, 139–40, 144, 241
    terminology, 30n26
Slemon, Stephen, 195
Smart, Ian, 5
Smitherman, Geneva, 175–76, 188n8
socialism, 63–67, 75, 77–79, 240
"Socialism and Man in Cuba" (Guevara), 61, 66–67,
    79n4
Societies of Color (Cuba), 68
Solar habanero (Havana Tenement, 1962), 66
song
    and Afro-Brazilian poetry, 250
    and Afro-Colombian cultural identity, 103, 110,
        115, 119
    and Cuban arts, 74, 76
    and Panamanian-West Indian culture, 181–88,
        188n3
"Sou" ("I Am," Silveira), 242
South Africa, 2–3, 238, 248
Spain, 2, 10, 13, 95
Spanish Caribbean, 2–3, 9, 11–18, 26, 97, 137, 173,
    176, 188n6. *See also specific countries*
"Spanish/English Speech Practices" (Toribio), 173
Spanish Government Cooperation Agency (AECID), 97
Spillers, Hortense, 164
Spinoza, Baruch de, 38
state
    Afro-Cuban rights and identity, 41, 48, 50,
        58–59, 66
    Afro-Ecuadorian exclusion, 253–54, 259–63
    and Afro-Uruguayan culture, 213–14, 223–25,
        228, 232
    and armed struggle in Colombia, 104, 107–12
    and collective memory, 138–39, 259
    and colonial power, 11, 17, 21, 34
    and international aid, 97–98
    and language marginalization, 175–77, 183–84
    and race relations in Brazil, 238–40
    racialized rule of, and black writing, 1–6
    and realist drama, 83–84, 87–91, 100, 101n5
Sterling, Demetrio, 165
Suárez Findlay, Eileen, 160
Sugar is Made with Blood (Paquette), 18

Tacón, Miguel, 11, 27n5
Taller Claudio A. Camejo Línea y 18 (Claudio A.
    Camejo, Línea and 18th Sts., 1971), 75
"Taxi, Taxi" (Danger Man), 181–82, 185
Taylor, Diana, 86
Teclas de Ébano (Ebony's Harps, Minka), 247–48
Telles, Edward E., 240
Ten Years' War (Cuba, 1868–1878), 33, 35, 37, 41, 59
Territorios, Territorialidad y Desterritorialización (García
    Salazar), 261
theatre
    Black Experimental Theater (TEN, Brazil), 3, 240
    and identity politics, 94
    popular, 1, 6, 84–86, 122
    theatricality, 101n11
"tierra y el cielo, La" ("The Earth and the Sky," Benítez
    Rojo), 65
Tillis, Antonio, 5, 127
Toribio, Almeida Jacqueline, 173, 175
Torres Díaz, Augustia, 195–96
torture, 13, 25

transculturation, 11–12, 23, 25, 127
trepasolo, El (The Lone Climber, Duncan), 83, 85, 91–95
Trigona, Marie, 220–22
Trindade, Solano, 241, 248–49
Trujillo, Leonidas, 151
Trullen, Gustavo, 219
tumba francesa, 70, 73–75. *See also* dance
"Tu No Eres Mi Friend" (Danger Man), 185

"Última plena que bailó Luberza, La" ("The last plena that Luberza danced," Ramos Otero), 150, 154
Una isla para Miguel (An Island for Miguel, 1968), 66
UNESCO Representative List of the Intangible Cultural Heritage of Humanity, 101n10, 222–23
UN High Commissioner for Human Rights, 109, 123–24n6
United Nations (UN), 107, 109
United Nations Committee on the Elimination of Racial Discrimination, 214–15, 220
United Self-Defense Forces of Colombia (AUC), 104–5
United States
    Civil Rights Movement, 74, 171, 189n12, 247
    and Cuba, 61, 73–74, 153, 159, 161
    language, 171–77, 179–81, 183–84, 187
    and Puerto Rico, 150–53, 161
University of the Republic (Uruguay), 218
uprising textualities, 128–46
Uruguay
    legitimation of Afro-Uruguayan culture, 6, 213, 216–18, 221–25, 231
    military dictatorship and state policies, 87–89, 228–29, 231
    race relations, 214–15, 227–28
    See also Afro-Uruguayan community; Afro-Uruguayan literature and art
Uruguayan Academy, 218

Valladolid debate (1550–1551), 2
Varda, Agnès, 66
Vargas, Roberti, 110
Ventura de Molina, Jacinto, 213, 216, 222
Verdi, Giuseppe, 68
Vergara, Felipe, 111–19, 124n12
Vietnam War, 74
Villaverde, Cirilo, 130–31
Vizcarrondo, Fortunato, 151, 167

Walcott, Derek, 174–75
Walsh, Catherine, 3, 7, 264n6, 268
war taxes, 104, 123n3
Wa Thiong'o, Ngũgĩ, 94–95
West Indies, 165, 171–84, 187–89, 187n2, 188n3. *See also* Panamanian West Indians

White, Elizabeth, 194
White, Steven F., 245
whiteness, 2, 13, 20–21, 110, 151, 238, 247. *See also* race
whitening *(blanqueamiento),* 2, 63, 110, 152, 221
Who Set You Flowin' (Griffin), 176
Williams, Lorna V., 131–32
witchcraft, 21
women
    and beauty, 29n17, 198–205, 208, 250
    black political agency and resistance, 130–36, 139–44, 158
    feminism, 128, 131, 154–55, 217
    and language, 175–76
    and marriage, 63–64, 72, 156–57, 163, 237
    motherhood, 135, 139, 141, 156–57, 162–64, 167, 168n24, 202–3
    and nuclear family, 139, 150, 152, 155–56, 160, 167, 167n2
    objectification of, 139–42, 159–60, 185, 196–97
    poetic imagery of, 39, 41–42, 150–66, 189n14, 202–3, 225
    race and gender identity, 132, 152–59, 161, 196–201
    sexual abuse and exploitation, 26, 133, 140, 142–44, 159, 161–62, 164
    and sex work, 156–57, 163
    and slavery, 129–30, 133, 139–42, 161
    writers, 6–7, 51–52, 56–59, 127–31, 136–38, 142, 225
Women Do This Every Day (Allen), 172
World Conference against Racism (Durban, 2001), 240
Writing the Afro-Hispanic (James), 5–6

Yancy, George, 160
Yoruba religion, 24, 30n33, 69, 78, 243, 245–46
Yúdice, George, 222

Zafira (Manzano), 4
Zanjón Pact (Cuba), 33, 133–34
Zapata, Efrain Villegas, 207–8
Zapata Olivella, Delia, 3
Zapata Olivella, Manuel, 3, 84–86, 94
Zárate Arango, Francisco, 204
Zayas, Manuel, 75
Zenón, Abuelo, 254–64
Zenón Cruz, Isabelo, 152
Zona de carga y descarga (Cuba), 153–54
"Zumbi" (Rodrigues), 248–49
Zumbi dos Palmares, 239, 243–44, 248–49, 251n6